Sources Of
American Spirituality

Henry Alline
SELECTED WRITINGS

Edited by George A. Rawlyk

PAULIST PRESS
New York ◇ Mahwah

Library of Congress Cataloging-in-Publication Data

Alline, Henry, 1748–1784.
    Henry Alline, selected writings.

    Bibliography: p.
    Includes index.
    1. Theology—Collected works—18th century.
2. Evangelicalism—Nova Scotia.   I. Rawlyk, George A.
II. Title.   III. Title: Selected writings.
BR85.A542   1987   230   87-8866
ISBN 0-8091-0396-6

Published by Paulist Press
997 Macarthur Boulevard
Mahwah, N.J. 07430

Printed and bound in the United States of America

CONTENTS

GENERAL INTRODUCTION

In this the eighth volume of the Sources of American Spirituality series we are presented with the works of Henry Alline, "the Nova Scotia Awakener." This is the first book in the series to deal with the writings of an individual from present day Canada and as such demonstrates the intention of the series to include texts from all of North and Central America. Alline (1748-1784) ministered to the Maritime Provinces during the era of the American Revolutionary War. He, like itinerant preachers George Whitfield and Gilbert Tennent a generation earlier in the American colonies, was a major catalyst in the development of a sense of national community and self-identity among the Maritimers in an age when their loyalties to New England and to Old England were both thrown into confusion by the Revolution. His charismatic preaching gave his hearers a sense of their own unique place in history. They were to carry on the work of shining as a beacon of Christ's light to the nations in an age when the two Protestant countries that had mothered them had abandoned reason and rushed headlong into a foolish and destructive war. His message of free grace and free will fit the mood of the times, as did his emphasis on New Birth as an immediate experience of Christ and his kingdom.

That Alline is not better known among residents of the United States is not entirely surprising given the subsequent histories of New England and the Maritime Provinces. Yet he deserves our attention as more than just a quaint piece of the local history of Nova Scotia. As William James recognized, his style of relentless, sometimes morbid, introspection made him a master of the dynamics of the type of religious experience James described as that of the sin-sick soul. Alline's acute sensitivity to the state of his soul, to its agonies and its ecstasies, was shaped to some extent by a familiarity with the mystical dimension as it appeared in the writings of Jacob Boehme and especially William Law. Yet what is perhaps more intriguing is not his embodiment of the teachings of an earlier master but his originality—an originality that bursts through the rough, sometimes crude phrases of a farmer-tanner whose main source of knowledge about God was his own rich experience. The epitaph on his gravestone calls him ''a burning and shining light.'' That he burned is obvious, and the intensity of his flame is evident even in the stodgy style of the day. Dead at thirty-five from his relentless labors and driving asceticism he like so many other flames who have been kindled by a taste of the divine fire offered his experience as a paradigm to his countrymen and in so doing provided them with new creative energies and a boldness in self-determination.

Professor Rawlyk in a major introduction delves into these and other aspects of Alline's legacy. His sensitivity to the interaction of spirituality and culture is manifest throughout, as is his extensive knowledge of both the history of the Maritime Provinces and the intricacies of Alline's theological thought. I am especially pleased that so able a scholar has produced a volume, the placement of which in our series carries on a task, begun by Robert T. Handy over a decade ago, of examining the religious histories of the two great North American nations together.

John Farina

PREFACE

I was both genuinely surprised and delighted when, a few years ago, Dr. John Farina asked me to prepare a volume about Henry Alline for the Sources of American Spirituality series. I was surprised that another scholar, especially an American historian, shared my conviction that the late eighteenth century Nova Scotian charismatic preacher-theologian and hymn-writer was indeed significant and noteworthy not only within the narrow confines of Canadian Evangelicalism but also within the larger context of North American spirituality. Moreover, as might have been expected from a Canadian who has, for almost twenty-five years, been dealing with aspects of Alline's career and legacy often on the periphery of even Canadian historiography, I was delighted that the Paulist Press would make Henry Alline available to an American audience.

Since 1962, when, as a graduate student, I wrote a research paper on Henry Alline and Nova Scotia's response to the American Revolution, I have been intrigued and indeed haunted by Alline. I have been eager to try to understand what made the Nova Scotian farmer-tanner tick in order to come to grips with the essential nature of the Evangelical tradition and ethos in the evolution of Maritime Canada. In my Hayward Lectures, given at Acadia University in October 1983 and published the following year under the title *Ravished by the Spirit,* I was particularly interested in tracing how Alline profoundly shaped the religious contours of Nova Scotia and New Brunswick not only in the late eighteenth century but throughout the nineteenth and twentieth centuries. In these Hayward Lectures, for

1

a variety of reasons, I underplayed the importance of Alline's actual preaching and writing during the apex of his career, which coincided with the American Revolution.

In this book, I want Alline to speak for himself from his particular vantage point in late eighteenth century Nova Scotia. The charismatic preacher would have perceived the reprinting of his journal, sermons, hymns, and theological writing in what he often referred to and underscored as the "ONE ETERNAL NOW."[1] As far as Alline was concerned, there was no "Time and Space and successive Periods." "With God," he argued, "there is neither Succession nor Progress; but that with Him the Moment He said let us make Man, and the Sound of the last Trumpet, is the very same instant, and your Death as much first as your Birth . . . with God all things are NOW . . . as the Center of a Ring which is as near the one side as the other."[2] Thus, according to Alline, the "ONE ETERNAL NOW" telescopes the late eighteenth century into the late twentieth; in other words, Alline's works are now being written by Alline; his sermons are "NOW" being preached. If the imagination could permit, even for a moment, such a collapsing of time, the jagged edges of memory and immediacy that were felt by Alline's contemporaries could perhaps be experienced by readers today. We too could try to walk the tightrope between extreme immanence and radical transcendence.

Many people helped in the preparation of this volume. I am particularly indebted to Pat Townsend, the archivist at the Acadia University Archives, who has done everything in her power to facilitate my research. Much encouragement for this project has been provided by David Bell, of the University of New Brunswick Law School; Marlene Schoofs, now in Doar Hazorea, Israel; Stephen Marini, Wellesley College; Carman Miller, McGill University; Sam Shortt, Kingston, Ontario; Elizabeth Mancke, Johns Hopkins University; and John Farina. In addition, I am indebted to Susan Young, at the Consortium for Research on North America, Harvard University, who was able to transform my difficult hieroglyphics into clear type.

---

1. H. Alline, *The Anti-Traditionist* (Halifax, 1783), pp. 62–63.
2. H. Alline, *Two Mites on Some of the Most Important and Much Disputed Points of Divinity* (Halifax, 1781), pp. 20–21.

The Consortium provided me, moreover, with an excellent environment in which to work during my sabbatical at Harvard University. My colleagues there, Elliott Feldman and Harry Hiller, both gave me their own special brand of encouragement. For this I will always be grateful.

INTRODUCTION

Henry Alline was a remarkable eighteenth-century preacher, hymn-writer, and Protestant pietist, intensely spiritual, morbidly introspective, and endowed with unusual charismatic powers. His influence on the religious development of the Nova Scotia–New Brunswick–New England region would not, however, be limited to the American Revolutionary period. His so-called Radical Evangelicalism would also significantly affect the popular religious ethos of this entire area, but particularly Maritime Canada, until the present day.

Many of Alline's contemporaries regarded him as Nova Scotia's George Whitefield—as a powerful instrument of the Almighty, charismatic and uniquely spiritual. Scholars writing in the nineteenth and twentieth centuries have been, almost to a person, genuinely impressed by Alline's imaginative theology, his amazing creative powers, and his unusual ability to communicate to others his profound sense of Christian ecstasy. Some writers have been content to describe him as the "Prophet" of Nova Scotia's First Awakening and a "Flaming evangelist" who channelled successfully the intense religious enthusiasm he had helped to create during the American Revolution into a form of "neutrality."[1] Others see him as an "intellectual and literary giant" who significantly shaped the "Ca-

---

1. See for example, Maurice W. Armstrong, *The Great Awakening in Nova Scotia 1776–1809* (Hartford, American Society of Church History, 1948).

nadian pietistic''[2] tradition or else as a charismatic preacher who provided confused, disoriented Nova Scotians with a special sense of collective identity and a powerful ''Sense of Mission'' at a critical time in their historical development.[3] Moreover, there are some younger Canadian historians who, in recent years, have gone much further than this. According to David Bell, for example, Alline, the Falmouth farmer-tanner, ''stands unrivalled as the greatest 'Canadian' of the eighteenth century, the greatest Maritimer of any age and the most significant religious figure this country [Canada] has yet produced.''[4]

ALLINE: ''WRAPPED UP IN GOD''

Henry Alline was born in Newport, Rhode Island, in 1748. In 1760 he moved with his parents and hundreds of other Yankees to the Minas Basin region of Nova Scotia. The Alline family settled in Falmouth, where the young Alline worked on his father's farm and then in his twenties developed certain skills in tanning and currying. There was little in Alline's Nova Scotia upbringing to suggest that he would develop into one of the region's most influential religious leaders.

In the early months of 1775, the twenty-seven-year-old Alline experienced an intense spiritual and psychological crisis—a crisis that when resolved would provide the turning point in his life. His conversion—the traumatic ''New Birth''—was significantly shaped by his finely developed morbid introspection, his fear of imminent death, and the considerable pressure he felt to commit himself one way or another during the early months of the American Revolutionary struggle. Alline's conversion, it should be stressed, was the

---

2. Jack M. Bumsted, *Henry Alline* (Toronto, University of Toronto Press, 1971).

3. Gordon Stewart and George Rawlyk, *A People Highly Favoured of God* (Toronto, MacMillan, 1972).

4. David G. Bell, ed., *New Light Baptist Journals of James Manning and James Innis* (Hantsport, Lancelot Press, 1985), p. xiii. See also idem, ''All Things New: The Transformation of Maritime Baptist Historiography,'' *Nova Scotia Historical Review* 4 (Spring 1984): 69–81.

central event of his life and he felt compelled to persuade others to share in his newfound spiritual ecstasy. One perceptive nineteenth-century observer noted that Alline was "converted in a rapture; and everafter he sought to live in a rapture"; he judged the validity of all other religious experiences through the prism of "his enjoyments and raptures."[5]

It is noteworthy that Alline's graphic description of his conversion experience captured the attention of William James, who, in his *Varieties of Religious Experience,* first published in 1902, used it as a "classic example" of the "curing of a sick soul."[6] Alline noted in his *Journal:*

> FEBRUARY 13th, 1775, when about midnight I waked out of sleep, I was surprised by a most alarming call as with a small voice, as it were through my whole soul; as if it spoke these words, How many days and weeks, and months and years has God been striving with you, and you have not yet accepted, but remain as far from redemption as at first; and as God has declared, that his spirit shall not always strive with man, what if he would call you no more, and this might be the last call, as possibly it might be; what would your unhappy doom be? O how it pierced my whole soul, and caused me to tremble in my bed, and cry out for a longer time. O Lord God do not take away thy spirit! O leave me not, leave me not; give me not over to hardness of heart, and blindness of mind.[7]

For over a month Alline struggled to find peace of mind, or, as he put it, "to be stripped of self-righteousness." And then, just when it seemed that he had reached the mental breaking point, he experienced what seemed to him to be the profound delights of spiritual

5. John Davis, *Life and Times of the Late Rev. Harris Harding, Yarmouth, N.S.* (Charlottetown, [Privately Printed] 1866), 178.

6. William James, *Varieties of Religious Experience* (New York, Longmans, Green and Co. 1902) pp. 159, 217.

7. Henry Alline, *Life and Journal of the Rev. Mr. Henry Alline* (Boston, Gilbert and Dean, 1806), pp. 26, 27.

regeneration. He described the beginnings of his conversion experience in this way.

> O help me, help me, cried I, thou Redeemer of souls, and save me or I am gone forever; and the last word I ever mentioned in my distress (for the change was instantaneous) was, O Lord Jesus Christ, thou canst this night, if thou pleasest, with one drop of thy blood atone for my sins, and appease the wrath of an angry God. At that instant of time when I gave up all to him, to do with me, as he pleased, and was willing that God should reign in me and rule over me at his pleasure: redeeming love broke into my soul with repeated scriptures with such power, that my whole soul seemed to be melted down with love; the burden of guilt and condemnation was gone, darkness was expelled, my heart humbled and filled with gratitude, and my will turned of choice after the infinite God. Attracted by the love and beauty I saw in his divine perfections, my whole soul was inexpressibly ravished with the blessed Redeemer . . . my whole soul seemed filled with the divine being.[8]

As far as Alline was concerned, the black gloomy despair of his acute depression and morbid introspection had been miraculously removed. "My whole soul," he proclaimed,

> that was a few minutes ago groaning under mountains of death, wading through storms of sorrow, racked with distressing fears, and crying to an unknown God for help, was now filled with immortal love, soaring on the wings of faith, freed from the chains of death and darkness, and crying out my Lord and my God; thou art my rock and my fortress, my shield and my high tower, my life, my joy, my present and my everlasting portion.[9]

The sudden, transforming power of what he was certain was the Holy Spirit compelled the young Falmouth farmer to declare: "O the

---

8. Ibid., p. 34.
9. Ibid., p. 34–35.

infinite condescension of God to a worm of the dust! for though my whole soul was filled with love, and ravished with a divine ecstasy beyond any doubts or fears, or thoughts of being then deceived, for I enjoyed a heaven on earth, and it seemed as if I were wrapped up in God."[10]

These emotionally charged words would provide the cutting edge of his Christian message until his death in 1784. Over and over again in his *Journal* and published sermons and pamphlets and in his hymns and spiritual songs Alline referred to his having been "ravished" by the "Divine ecstasy," and also to his having been "married" to his Savior by the redeeming power of the Holy Spirit. Divine love had overwhelmed him to such an extent that he viewed his own experience as being the pattern set for all others. It is not surprising, therefore, that Alline expected his followers to share his own unique brand of spiritual rapture—the central New Light experience—which he himself had so recently experienced and which he regarded as being the only satisfactory means of regeneration.[11]

Alline's traumatic conversion was obviously the critically important event of his life and this point merits repetition. His description of it in his *Journal,* available and distributed in manuscript form in the region as early as 1789[12] and in print in 1806, and in his *Two Mites on Some of the Most Important and much disputed Points of Divinity,* first published in Halifax in 1781, provided the pattern for his disciples to appropriate, and to emulate. Alline was eager to generalize from the experience of his particular conversion and to make it the universally accepted evangelical norm. His audacity—some would call it spiritual arrogance—appealed to many Nova Scotians, who were certainly confused and disoriented by the divisive forces unleashed by the American Revolution.

Alline's "Radical Evangelical" and New Light message, it is

---

10. Ibid., p. 35.

11. The crucial importance of the "New Birth" in the New Light tradition in New England's First Great Awakening is discussed in Alan Heimert, *Religion and the American Mind* (Cambridge, Harvard University Press, 1966).

12. See my discussion of this point in Rawlyk, *Ravished by the Spirit: Religious Revivals, Baptists, and Henry Alline* (Montreal, McGill-Queen's University Press, 1984), p. 13. See also James Beverley and Barry Moody, eds. *The Journal of Henry Alline* (Hantsport, Lancelot Press, 1982), pp. 23–26.

clear, in its essentials at least, reflected what Stephen Marini has sensitively referred to as "the distinctive elements of the Evangelical tradition . . . intense conversion experience, fervid piety, ecstatic worship forms, Biblical literalism, the pure church ideal, and charismatic leadership." Marini correctly locates Alline at the heart of this so-called Whitefieldian New Light framework.[13] There was also, of course, an important heterodox element in the volatile mixture making up Alline's theology. Many of his contemporaries were aware of the potentially explosive nature of his highly "spiritual theology," consisting of experiential religion and a belief in the perseverance of the Saints. In a particularly discerning critique of Alline's theology, the Reverend Matthew Richey, a Nova Scotia Methodist, pointed out that the Falmouth preacher's "tenets were a singular combination of heterogeneous materials derived from opposite sources." According to Richey:

> They were fragments of different systems—without coherence, and without any mutual relation or dependence. With the strong assertion of man's freedom as a moral agent, he connected the doctrine of the final perseverance of the saints. He allegorized to such excess the plainest narratives and announcements of Scriptures, that the obvious and unsophisticated import of the words of inspiration was often entirely lost amidst the reveries of mysticism.[14]

Henry Alline, it is clear, was not only a late eighteenth century transmitter of what was often referred to as the Evangelical "Whitefieldian sound," but he was also a person who was able to perceive a special purpose for his fellow Nova Scotians in the midst of the disorienting American Revolutionary situation. He became the charismatic leader of a widespread and intense religious revival that swept

---

13. Stephen A. Marini, "New England Folk Religions 1770–1815: The Sectarian Impulse in Revolutionary Society" (Ph.D. diss., Harvard University, 1978), 20. See also his important book, based on the dissertation, *Radical Sects of Revolutionary New England* (Cambridge, Harvard University Press, 1982).

14. Matthew Richey, *A Memoir of the Late Rev. William Black* (Halifax, William Cunnabell, 1839), p. 45.

the colony during the war years. "The Great Awakening of Nova Scotia" was, without question, one of the most significant social movements in the long history of the colony. It was, among other things, the means by which a large number of Nova Scotians—especially the so-called Yankees—extricated themselves from the domination of neighboring New England, which they had left a decade and more earlier. By creating a compelling ideology that was specifically geared to conditions in the isolated northern colony, Alline enabled many Nova Scotians to regard themselves as what Gordon Stewart and I once called "A People Highly Favored of God."[15] These people were provided by Alline with a unique history, a distinct identity, and a special destiny. A new sense of Nova Scotia identity had clicked into fragile place—to replace the disintegrating loyalty to New England and the largely undermined loyalty to Old England.

At the time of the American Revolution, it should be kept in mind, Nova Scotia was inhabited by approximately 20,000 people, 60 percent of whom were recently arrived New Englanders. These Yankees would be particularly affected by Alline's evangelical message. Halifax and Lunenburg were the major centers of the colony unaffected by the revival Alline helped to articulate into existence. The Lunenburg area was peopled by "Foreign Protestants" who understood neither Alline's brand of Christianity nor the American Patriot ideology of independence. Their loyalty to Britain was a mixture of self-interest, indifference, and splendid isolation. In Halifax, economic and military ties with Great Britain, together with the heterogeneous nature of the population and the influence of the Anglophile-elite, created a consensus violently opposed both to the Revolution and to evangelical religion.

The Nova Scotia Yankees, in particular, were disoriented and confused both by the events leading up to the American Revolution and by the Revolutionary War itself. By emigrating to Nova Scotia in the early 1760s, they had missed a critical decade in the ideological development of the New England colonies.[16] Consequently, they

---

15. For a critical discussion of this thesis see Beverley and Moody, eds., *The Journal of Henry Alline,* pp. 11–13 and David Bell, "All Things New: The Transformation of Maritime Baptist Historiography," 72–73.

16. This is a key argument in Stewart and Rawlyk, *A People Highly Favoured of God.*

found themselves locked into a pre-1765 colonial framework that they had left behind. Their entire world, at the beginning of the Revolution, had suddenly and dramatically assumed an unfamiliar shape; men with familiar Yankee names, from familiar New England places, were using old words and phrases in a radically new and foreign manner. Bitter civil strife pitting New Englanders against New Englanders and against Britain had engulfed their former homeland. American privateers and British press gangs introduced further elements of instability into an already chaotic situation. There were frequent references made in the Yankee outsettlements to "the utmost confusion and disorder . . . prevailing thro' the whole country"[17] and the widespread "fears and confusions"[18] and the fact that "the whole province is in Confusion, Trouble & Anguish."[19]

Alline was one Nova Scotian who was able to make sense out of the seeming "Confusion, Trouble & Anguish" that had engulfed Yankee Nova Scotia in the late 1770s and early 1780s. He was sensitive to the fact that what he referred to as this "most inhuman war"[20] had precipitated an acute disorientation in the traditional loyalties and value systems of the Yankees in Nova Scotia. They felt themselves increasingly cut off from New England, but they were not particularly attracted to Old England. They sensed a profound need for a new sense of collective identity—one that was neither Yankee nor British but something uniquely their own.

Almost single-handedly Alline was able, by his frequent visits to the settlements, to draw the isolated communities together and to impose on them a feeling of oneness. They were sharing a common experience and Alline was providing them with answers to disconcerting and puzzling contemporary questions. For Alline, the Nova

---

17. J. Wingate Weeks to S.P.G., September 1783, Public Archives of Nova Scotia. S.P.G. Papers, No. 247.

18. Peter de la Roche to S.P.G., December 1778, P.A.N.S., S.P.G. Papers, No. 208.

19. See "Extract of a Letter from John Allan," September 22, 1777, in Frederick Kidder, ed., *Military Operations in Eastern Maine and Nova Scotia During the Revolution* (Albany, J. Munsell, 1867), p. 228.

20. Alline's attitude toward the "most inhuman war" which was "spreading Desolation through the world" is developed at much greater length in Stewart and Rawlyk, *A People Highly Favoured of God,* 160–162.

Scotia revival was, among other things, an event of world significance. The social, economic, and political backwater that was Nova Scotia had been transformed into the new center of the Christian world. Alline thus was attempting to lift the Yankees from their parochial surroundings and to thrust them into the middle of the world stage. In the process, he was helping to transform them into Nova Scotians.

In sermons preached as he crisscrossed the colony, Alline developed the theme that the Nova Scotia Yankees, in particular, had a special predestined role to play in God's plan for the world. It must have required a special effort for Alline to convince Nova Scotians of their special world role. However, striking deep into the Puritan New England tradition that viewed self-sacrifice and frugality as virtues, Alline contended that the relative backwardness and isolation of the colony had removed the inhabitants from the prevailing corrupting influences of New England and Britain. As a result, Nova Scotia was in an ideal position to lead the world back to God. As far as Alline was concerned the revival was convincing proof that the Nova Scotians were "a people on whom God had set His everlasting Love" and that their colony was "as the Apple of His Eye."[21]

The implication of the conjunction of events—of civil war in New England and an outpouring of the Holy Spirit in Nova Scotia— must have been obvious to Alline and to the thousands who flocked to hear him. God was obviously passing New England's historical mantle of Christian leadership to Nova Scotia. With New England gone madly off course, there was apparently no longer any solid basis there from which true Christianity could spread throughout the world. With two powerful Protestant nations furiously battling one another, the whole course of events since the Reformation seemed to be ending in a meaningless tangle. In the world view of those New Englanders fighting for the Revolutionary cause, Old England was corrupt and the Americans were engaged in a righteous and noble cause. There was therefore some meaning to the hostilities. For Alline, however, the totally evil civil war had no such meaning. Rather, along with all the other signs of the times, it could indicate only one

------

21. Henry Alline, *Two Mites on Some of the Most Important and Much Disputed Points of Divinity* (Halifax, A. Henry, 1781), p. 234.

thing: that the entire Christian world, apart from Nova Scotia, was abandoning the true and narrow way of God. Moreover, Alline was convinced that the end of the world was imminent and that he and his fellow Nova Scotians could actually telescope human time into Christ's apocalyptic "Moment."[22] This reality fueled Alline's "Sense of Mission" concern.

What was regarded by Alline and his followers as the tragic backsliding of New England had presented Nova Scotia with an opportunity to put things right. The Falmouth preacher was determined that the new "City upon a Hill" would lead the world back to the pristine purity of the Christian faith. By permeating his Evangelical preaching with this mission-oriented rhetoric, Alline provided his audience with what he termed "an omniscient eye" to read the "map of the disordered world."[23] He was helping them find a new collective identity—an awareness of being regenerate Nova Scotians. Alline was also, it should be stressed, pointing the way to a new kind of lasting and meaningful relationship at a time when he began the process of extricating the Yankees from their cultural dependence on New England that had, among other factors, placed them in such a confusing predicament during the Revolutionary War. Instead of being a mere outpost of New England on the remote fringes of the continent, Alline argued, Nova Scotia could now be regarded as a distinct society. The ideology that emerged during the period of Alline's leadership made the revival a movement with somewhat broader implications than has hitherto been acknowledged. By generating a religious ideology that was specifically relevant to the situation and problems of the northern colony, the revival began the process of turning Yankees into Nova Scotians. They were, as he cogently expressed it, because of the grace of God, "a people highly favoured of God, indeed."[24]

At the core of his Sense of Mission ideology was to be found not a Nova Scotia Evangelical version of Patriot neo-Whig rhetoric but rather Alline's growing obsession with the central importance of

---

22. Ibid., pp. 20–21.
23. Henry Alline, *A Sermon Preached at Liverpool, 21 November 1782* (Halifax, A. Henry, 1782), p. 23.
24. Ibid.

the New Birth. All of his preaching was permeated by a single-minded preoccupation with disintegrating, disintegrated, and renewed relationships. This helps to explain how Alline was able to use his pietistic gospel to help resolve the Yankees' collective identity crisis. Generalizing from his own religious experience—the ravishing ecstasy of his own regeneration—Alline emphasized that every Nova Scotian could emulate him—if only they reached out, in faith, to Christ. In a world where all traditional relationships were falling apart, a personal "interest in Christ," as Alline put it, created by the "New Birth," was the means whereby all these threatened relationships would be strengthened.[25] Conversion was, therefore, perceived by Alline and his followers as "the short-circuiting of a complex process—a short-circuiting which produced instant and immediate satisfaction, solace, and intense relief."[26] The First Great Awakening was, in one sense, a collection of these positive individual experiences and helped to give shape and substance to a new and distinct Nova Scotia sense of identity. It was Alline's powerfully charismatic and evangelical preaching and not his published work that significantly shaped the contours of the First Great Awakening.

Alline's preaching may also be perceived as a special ritual whereby, as Victor Turner has brilliantly argued, "well-bonded" human beings created "by structural means—spaces and times in the calendar or, in the cultural cycles of their most cherished groups which cannot be captured" in what he calls the "classificatory nets of their routinized spheres of action." "By verbal and non-verbal means," Alline's charismatic preaching was the means whereby many Nova Scotians were able to break away from their "innumerable constraints and boundaries" and capture what has been called the "floating world" of creativity and self-discovery. People, according to Turner, alternate between "fixed" and "floating" worlds; they oscillate between, on the one hand, preoccupation with order and constraints and, on the other, a search for novelty and freedom. Alline's revival was the occasion for thousands of Nova Scotians to experience what has been called an "anti-structural liminality." The revival became a symbol of the social and religious

---

25. See my *Ravished By The Spirit*, 9.
26. Ibid.

mood in which all sorts of hitherto internalized and sublimated desires, dreams, hopes, and aspirations became legitimized. Women, for example, broke through the hard shell of deference to express deeply felt feelings and to criticize their husbands; children often demanded obedience from their parents. Traditional behaviour and values were challenged; the ''anti-structural liminality'' of the revival meetings helped to give shape and form, however transitory, to a profoundly satisfying ''tender, silent, cognizant mutuality.'' In a sense, this aberrant behaviour may be regarded as ''rituals of status reversal.'' ''Cognitively,'' as Turner has pointed out, ''nothing underlines regularity as well as absurdity or paradox'' and ''emotionally nothing satisfies as much as extravagant or temporarily permitted illicit behaviour.'' The rituals of status reversal, moreover, as seen in the revival, not only challenged community values but also subconsciously reaffirmed the hierarchical principles still undergirding society.[27]

There was, it should also be stressed, an intensely satisfying and pleasurable feeling of Christian fellowship as the ''ecstasy of spontaneous communitas'' virtually overwhelmed Alline's followers. In October 1782, Alline recorded the following evocative description of what he called ''the glorious work of God'' in Argyle ''where the people were so engaged, that almost all in the place both old and young attended night and day; and the Spirit of the Lord wrought with such power, that many were constrained to cry out in the meeting; some with joy, and others in the deepest distress of soul.'' A few months later in Liverpool, Alline noted that a revival he had triggered months before was still ''flourishing.'' When he went

> to preach at the meeting-house, at the hour appointed, the people were crowding to hear; and when the sermon was over, I was obliged to stop many hours in the broad-alley, to discourse with the people; for it seemed as if they could not go away. While I was there this last time, the Chris-

27. The quotations in this paragraph are from Victor Turner, *The Ritual Process: Structure and Anti-Structure* (Ithaca, Cornell University Press 1979), pp. 94–140.

tians gathered together in fellowship, by telling their experiences and getting fellowship one for another.[28]

The "spontaneous communitas" produced by Alline's preaching had something almost magical about it. People, despite themselves, shared a "feeling of endless power," and this feeling was both exhilarating and frightening. They were drawn by the "mystery of intimacy" toward one another—as Christian love challenged what seemed to be a selfish, limited, almost worldly, fidelity. They saw Christ in their friends and their neighbors and they wanted desperately to love their friends as they loved Christ. Some did—for a moment—and their joy must have been glorious. They also realized that "spontaneous communitas" was only "a phase, a moment, not a permanent condition" as "the mystery of distancing and of 'tradition' " regained firm control of their hearts and minds.[29] But it was a return to the status quo with a difference. For things had changed despite the power of the forces of continuity; life in Nova Scotia for the Yankees would be very different after the Revolution.

ALLINE'S PUBLISHED WRITINGS

Alline's charismatic preaching, it should be stressed, was of primary importance in bringing about and influencing Nova Scotia's First Great Awakening. His two published books were not. His *Two Mites on Some of the Most Important and much disputed Points of Divinity* (Halifax, 1781) and *The Anti-Traditionist* (Halifax, 1783) were not widely read in the colony. If anything, his *Two Mites*—a convoluted anti-Calvinist work, permeated by what Maurice Armstrong once referred to as "Alline's peculiar doctrines"[30]—probably helped to dampen the revival fire. These two books tell us a great deal about Alline's theology, which according to one contemporary was a strange mixture of "Calvinism, Antinomianism and Enthusi-

---

28. Beverley and Moody, eds., *The Journal of Henry Alline*, pp. 206–208.
29. Turner, *The Ritual Process*, pp. 139–140.
30. Armstrong, *The Great Awakening in Nova Scotia*, p. 92.

asm.''[31] But *Two Mites* and *The Anti-Traditionist,* especially the latter, taking into account its ''rhetorical and extravagant'' views and when it was actually published, throw little real light on the Awakening and Alline's charismatic powers. Alline's *Journal* does, but it was not published until 1806, although a manuscript version was in circulation, among Alline's followers, soon after his death in February 1784. The *Journal* provides a superb introspective and illuminating account of the spiritual travails of an unusually gifted eighteenth-century North American Christian and preacher. It also describes, often in graphic detail, how Alline actually made an impact on the Nova Scotia communities. When his accounts of his preaching exploits are checked against existing contemporary records, they are found to be amazingly accurate. If anything, Alline tended to underrate the kind of influence—direct and indirect, short-term and long-term—he had on the myriad of communities he frequently visited.

During his lifetime, Alline published a tiny volume of 22 hymns, *Hymns and Spiritual Songs on a Variety of Pleasing and Important Subjects* (Halifax, 1781). Two years after his death, his 381-page *Hymns and Spiritual Songs*—containing 488 original hymns and spiritual songs—was published in Boston. Eventually at least four editions of this volume were published in the United States. The extraordinary popularity of Alline's *Hymns and Spiritual Songs* in both the United States and in New Brunswick and Nova Scotia provides convincing proof that Alline had brilliantly succeeded in making his hymns and spiritual songs communicate deep religious truths to ordinary believers.

In 1782 and 1783 Alline had published in Halifax three of his sermons: *A Sermon preached to and at the Request of a religious Society of young Men . . . in Liverpool, on the 19th of November, 1782; A Sermon on a Day of Thanksgiving . . . on the 21st of November, 1782;* and *A Sermon Preached on the 19th of February at Fort-Midway.* This last sermon was reprinted twice in New England, in 1795 and 1797, under a different title—*A Gospel Call to Sinners.*

---

31. Patterson, *Memoir of the Rev. James McGregor* (Philadelphia, J.M. Wilson, 1859), p. 351.

What Alline actually said in his sermons and what he wrote in his two published treatises and in his *Journal* and *Hymns and Spiritual Songs* was most significantly influenced, it is clear, by his conversion experience. He went, however, beyond the New Light paradigm because of his reading of such British writers as William Law, Joseph William Fletcher, and William Young, and also because of his fertile imagination.

Despite the fact that Alline may have lived in an isolated Nova Scotia rural backwater, his theology owed a great deal, it has been argued, to "that stream of mystical teaching which had come down through William Law, John Milton and the seventeenth century English sectaries, from Jacob Boehme."[32] Alline himself made a number of explicit references to William Law in both *Two Mites* and *The Anti-Traditionist*. In fact, when Law's *Spirit of Prayer* is carefully compared with the *The Anti-Traditionist,* it is clear that even some of the language used by Alline is carefully lifted from the work of the older author.

Alline closely followed Law in the latter's emphasis on the Out-birth and the fact that the world was in fact created out of nothing. For both men the creation of the entire natural world, including Adam and Eve, was in essence an emanation from God. Although Alline did not emphasize in his theology the actual word "emanation," his Out-birth meant precisely the same thing. As Maurice Armstrong has argued, for Alline, the Out-birth was "something which emanates or is exhaled from God." It was "closely akin to the mysterious Jewish doctrine of the *Shekinah,* and the *Kabbala* and to the external forms and ideas of Neo-Platonism."[33] Though perhaps closely akin, Alline's Out-birth idea in fact owed nothing to these exotic ideas.

Alline was especially impressed with the way in which Law, in particular, accounted for the presence of sin and evil in a universe created by a benevolent and loving Creator. Almost paraphrasing Law's argument, Alline declared:

---

32. Armstrong, *The Great Awakening in Nova Scotia,* p. 94. See also Bumsted, *Henry Alline,* pp. 79–89; and Stewart and Rawlyk, *A People Highly Favoured of God,* pp. 79–80, 82–85.

33. Armstrong, *The Great Awakening in Nova Scotia,* p. 96.

you must observe that thro' the whole chain of Revelation
you hear of God's being in Heaven, and the Kingdom of
Heaven; which is the Kingdom of God, sometimes called
his Pavilion, and some times the everlasting Hills; all holding forth his Residence or everlasting Outbirth, but let not
my Reader imagine these created, or corporeal Heavens or
any Place made for his Residence, but what he was from
Eternity possessed of sin and of himself: therefore from the
eternal Kingdom, Pavilion or Out-Birth, Adam and all angelic Beings derive their Clothing or Out-birth, or paradisical Kingdom.[34]

Being made in the image of God, and being neither male nor
female, all humanity shared the Almighty's "immortal Power of
thought" as well as God's "immortal Cloathing or Outbirth." In
other words, not only Adam but all human beings were spiritual en-
tities existing in this paradisical and pre-material state. According to
Alline:

And now you have a more clear Discovery of the Glory of
this angellic System and innumerable Crowd of Adorers,
standing as one in divine Union and Glory, a paridisical
system to bask in the boundless Ocean of their Father's
Love and Perfections . . . Ah! think, think, my dear
Reader, what a glorious Display of Love, and Manifestation of infinite Goodness is here broke forth from the overflowing uncontainable Fountain! Countless Millions of
empty Vessels forever to drink large Draughts of the celestial Stream.[35]

But the empty Vessels were not satisfied with drinking from the
celestial stream, and sin entered the universe of pristine purity. The
fall of man and woman occurred simply because they were made in
the image of God and "shared in the freedom of choice and of will
which is part of the divine nature."[36] Viewing "the Beauty and

---

34. Henry Alline, *The Anti-Traditionist*, (Halifax, 1783) p. 24.
35. Ibid., pp. 24–25.
36. Armstrong, *The Great Awakening in Nova Scotia*, p. 97.

Grandeur'' of their ''outward Creature'' they fell ''in love'' with their ''paradisical Clothing'' so that ''of Consequence the inward Creature or Power of Choice turned from the only Spring of Life into his own Clothing.''[37]

With this individual yet universal decision, the entire human race, according to Law, ''broke off from his true center, his proper place in God'' and plunged ''into a life of self, into an animal life of self-love, self-esteem and self-seeking in the poor perishing enjoyment of this world.''[38] In the material world, Law continued, all mankind was in ''a state of contrariety to the order and end of our creation.'' Yet, and this point is of critical importance in dealing with Calvinism, there existed in each being ''a spark of the Divine nature'' as the ''external word of God.'' The divine spark was the one remnant left in humankind from ''paradise'' and it provided ''a natural strong and almost infinite tendency, or reaching after that eternal Light and Spirit of God.'' Since the soul had, in fact, ''come from God'' and ''came out of God,'' it partook ''of the divine nature, and therefore it is always in a state of tendency and return to God.'' Alline enthusiastically endorsed Law's argument and almost word for word made it his own justification for his Free Will gospel of hope. Like Law, Alline maintained that everything about humankind was alien to the Almighty except for the divine spark, which ''held him in possibility of redemption.'' Alline, echoing Law, declared that the conversion experience was simply a ''turning of the inmost soul after God.'' The initiative was ''man's'' and not God's and salvation was freely and lovingly given, not imparted by a vengeful and arbitrary God.[39]

Alline's God, like the God of so many Roman Catholic and Protestant mystics, as well as William Law, was ''divine immanence.'' The evolving physical world as well as the Incarnation was a manifestation of the Almighty's ''Interposition.'' Everything in the physical world thus proclaimed God's ''indwelling presence.'' ''Let it be observed,'' Alline wrote:

---

37. Alline, *Two Mites,* p. 30.

38. William Law, *An Extract from a Treatise by William Law* (Philadelphia, Henry Miller 1766), p. 16.

39. Ibid. pp. 29, 36; Alline, *Two Mites,* pp. 18, 121 and his *A Gospel Call to Sinners,* p. 16.

that the Creature tho' fallen was not passive, but still an active being, and now acting and raging in Contrariety to God: . . . and therefore, of Consequence nothing could hold or do him good, but what stopped and redeemed from that acting in Contrariety to God; so that if God undertakes for his Redemption he must stop him from acting the Curse, and therefore, this was God's Incarnation, so to enter in the fallen Creature, as to hold his active and raging Powers from Action, and as God was not a passive but active Spirit, therefore of Course, they were acting in Opposition to one another; and when God thus holds this contrary Spirit under such Suppression as to be kept from action, it must consequently stand forth corporeal; so that neither God nor the Creature are in themselves corporeal: but made or become so by the meeting Contrarieties of their two Natures. And thus my Dear reader may see that wherever there is any thing corporeal, there is fallen Nature interposed, so that Sun, Moon and Stars; Rocks, Hills and Stones; Fire, Air, Earth and Water, and every Thing that you see or feel corporeal, proclaims God incarnate, and that you are stopped a Moment from the Course of fallen Nature to be redeem'd, O my Soul, and what could God do more! . . . For there is nothing but this interposing Hand or suppressing and restraining Spirit that keeps the Race of Adam from the same Pain and Misery that the fallen Angels endure, yea, and that Moment that this restraint is broke thro', the Creature awakes in keen Despair; but God being thus in them by his Incarnation they are held in a Possibility of Redemption.[40]

Without question, Alline was greatly dependent on Law for his basic ideas concerning the nature of God, creation, sin, and free salvation. The Falmouth preacher was also influenced by John William Fletcher, the so-called Shropshire Saint whose *A Rational Demonstration of Man's Corrupt and Lost Estate* provided him with arguments about an androgynous God and "freedom of the will" and

---

40. Alline, *The Anti-Traditionist,* p. 35.

"ideas concerning the state of man before the fall."[41] Alline also owed a great deal to Edward Young's (1683–1765) *The Complaint or Night-Thoughts on Life, Death and Immorality* (London, 1743). Young's vivid imagination and morbid sentimentality colored Alline's spirituality as well as his concern about the imminent "Day of Judgement."[42] In his approach to the triggering of conversion, the importance of a converted ministry, and living the good Christian life, however, Alline was dependent not on Law, Young, and Fletcher but on his Yankee New Light legacy.

It has been argued that "it is the weakness of Boehme and Law that the Gospel message of the loving Fatherhood of God is driven almost out of sight, and that the name of the Father appears to stand almost predominantly for the awful essence of fire, darkness, and chaos which underlies all existing things."[43] Yet as Maurice Armstrong has persuasively argued, "certainly no one reading Alline's books and sermons would accuse him of this fault."[44] Rather, at the core of Alline's theological system is to be found the essential love and goodness of his "interposing God" who "since the Foundation of the World" has been "striving Night and Day to redeem immortal Souls from eternal Sorrow."[45]

As far as Alline was concerned the resurrection was a spiritual rather than a physical phenomenon. Neither heaven nor hell, for him, was a place but rather both were eternal conditions of the soul. In a profound sense, therefore, every day was judgment day since "all things must be both spiritual and NOW." All time was thus telescoped into the "Eternal Now," for "there is no such thing as before or after."[46] Nevertheless, Alline believed in and preached the imminent return of Christ.

---

41. Armstrong, *The Great Awakening in Nova Scotia*, p. 95.
42. Ibid.
43. Stephen Hobhouse, *Selected Mystical Writings of William Law* (London, The C.W. Daniel Co., Ltd., 1938), p. 315.
44. Armstrong, *The Great Awakening in Nova Scotia*, p. 103.
45. Alline, *Two Mites*, p. 74.
46. Alline, *The Anti-Traditionist*, pp. 62–63.

ALLINE'S THEOLOGY:
"THE GOLD AND DROSS SHUFFLED TOGETHER."

It should be kept in mind that Henry Alline, though a member of a Congregational Church, adhered to no one particular church. He had no formal education; his family owned a marginal farm and possessed little social status. He therefore cannot be identified as a leader who derived his authority from traditional institutions or from traditional ideas. He and his followers insisted that his authority stemmed from his close personal relationship with the Almighty and his special charismatic powers. His ascendancy in the out-settlements of Nova Scotia and later in northern New England was unprecedented and was not soon to be emulated.

Alline's reading of the Scriptures as well as his own conversion experience, it should be stressed, had convincingly shown him that Calvinism as preached in Nova Scotia was a pernicious heresy. "The lesson, why those, that are lost, are not redeemed," he argued, "is not because that God delighted in their Misery, or by any Neglect in God, God forbid." Rather, it resulted "by the Will of the Creature; which, instead of consenting to Redeeming Love, rejects it, and therefore cannot possibly be redeemed." "Men and Devils," he asserted—and this would be the bedrock theological position buttressing all of his written work, "that are miserable are not only the Author of their own Misery," but they also act "against the Will of God, the Nature of God, and the most endearing Expression of his Love."[47]

According to the Falmouth preacher, there was no spiritual basis for the doctrine of predestination. God did not predestine the salvation or the damnation of anyone. Nor was there any such thing as "Original Sin" imputed to all mankind by Adam. "You have no more Reason to say," Alline once observed, "that Adam's Sin was imputed to you, than he has to complain and say, that your Sin was imputed to him."[48] Relentless in his attack on the underpinnings of predestination, and determined to persuade his hearers of the efficacy of what he referred to over and over again as "free grace, free

---

47. Alline, *Two Mites*, pp. 150–51.
48. Alline, *The Anti-Traditionist*, p. 25.

grace,"[49] Alline stressed the importance of each individual's choosing freely to return to his or her "paradisical state." This could be done only if the "spiritual and immortal . . . mind," found "in everyone," was presented to the "Son of God" leaving behind "the fallen immortal Body in its fallen State still."[50] For, according to Alline, the New Birth was "that Moment" when "the Will and Choice was turned after God" and the regenerate "acted with God, and therefore partake of God; and thus again brought to enjoy the Tree of Life, which they had lost; and are reinstated in that Paradise that they fell out of."[51]

Since, for Alline, each individual was both free to and capable of "consenting to Redeeming Love," he felt it necessary to trace in as simple terms as possible the actual pattern of the New Birth process. Conviction, "bringing the Sinner to a Sense of its fallen, helpless and deplorable condition"—of falling into a state of eternal separation from "The True God"—was, he had to admit, sometimes a gradual process. Nevertheless, he asserted that "the Work of conversion is instantaneous."[52] The convicted sinner felt both drawn to and repelled by the Almighty. The now completely disoriented individual

> sees that to fly from his Guilt and Misery is impracticable: and to reform or make Satisfaction, as much as possible; and therefore like the four Lepers at the Gates of Samaria (2 Kgs 7:3,4) he is determined to try the last Remedy; for to stay where he is, is certain Death, and to return back unto his former State of Security, will be Death, and therefore, altho' he cannot see, that Christ has any love for him, or Pity towards him; neither doth he see, whether He intends to have Mercy on him or not; yet he is determined to cast himself at his Feet, and trust wholly to his Mercy, and

---

49. Beverley and Moody, eds., *The Journal of Henry Alline*, p. 63.
50. Alline, *Two Mites*, p. 94.
51. Alline, *The Anti-Traditionist*, p. 40.
52. Alline, *Two Mites*, pp. 121–35, for a detailed description of the "morphology of conversion."

Free Grace for Salvation; and cries out with the trembling Leper. *Lord if thou wilt.* (Mk 1:40)[53]

The merciful, loving God always answers yes not because of some obsession with substitutionary atonement but because Christ "dies to lift a Dying World While Love Doth graft them on the tree of Life."[54] By having his perfect life squeezed from him because of the weight of human sin—not as a sacrifice to his Father—Christ enables everyone to return to their original home in "the Mansions of Delight."[55]

At that precise moment when the convicted individual "is willing to be redeemed out of his fallen state on the Gospel Terms," then "the Redeeming Love enters into his soul" as Christ "the hope of Glory takes possession of the inner man." The ravished souls find "the Burden of Their Sin gone, with their Affections taken off this World, and set on things above." Moreover, "their Hearts" were "drawn out after Christ, under a feeling sense of the Worth of his Redeeming Love; at the same Time with a sense of their own Vileness, and the Vanity of all things here below, together with the worth and Sweetness of heavenly Things, and the Amiableness of the Divine Being."[56]

Despite his anti-Calvinism, and possibly because of it, Alline declared that there was indeed a "final Perseverance of the Saints." Of course, as long as one lived on earth, there would be, as the Nova Scotia New Light himself had painfully experienced, an often bitter struggle between the sanctified "inmost Soul" and the "fallen immortal Body." Yet because of his dualism and his emphasis on the centrality of the "ravishing of the soul by Christ" he found himself asserting that "which is born of God cannot sin."[57]

Realizing the threat posed to his theological system by Antinomianism, Alline carefully balanced his emphasis on perseverance with what has been accurately referred to as a powerful "asceticism

---

53. Ibid., p. 126.
54. Alline, *The Anti-Traditionist*, p. 34.
55. Ibid., p. 54.
56. Alline, *Two Mites*, pp. 128–29.
57. Ibid., p. 95.

and bodily mortification worthy of the most austere monasticism.''[58] In *Two Mites,* for example, and also in his sermons, he would maintain that ''true redemption is raising the desires and life to the inner man out of this miserable, sinful, and bestial world, and turning it to Christ, from when it is fallen.''[59] Simply put, to be a Christian was to be like Christ—radically different from ''the world.'' In *The Anti-Traditionist,* it would be stressed that it was incumbent on the truly redeemed to ''Turn from all, Deny all: Leave all.'' He went on:

> I do not mean the outward and criminal Acts of Idolatry and Debauchery only: but any and every Thing in the Creature that in the least Degree amuses the Mind or leads the Choice from God. For even the most simple Enjoyments and Pleasures of Life will keep the Choice in Action, and therefore the Creatures amused from God, and consequently sinking deeper and deeper in its fallen and irrevocable State. Nor will you ever return to be redeemed until every Idol, Joy, Hope or Amusement so fails you that you are wholly starved out, and there is not only a Famine in all created Good.[60]

Carefully blended, his ''perseverance of the spiritually ravished saints'' and his introspective asceticism produced what he once called ''true zeal.''[61] Perseverance without asceticism, he knew all too well, would lead directly to the evils of Calvinist Antinomianism he had so vehemently denounced. The latter without the former was mere hypocrisy. Alline would carefully weave these two themes through his sermons, producing in the process the impression that he was not only a special instrument of the Almighty—Nova Scotia's John the Baptist preparing the way for the Lord—but also the articulator of the Radical Evangelicalism of George Whitefield and Jonathan Edwards. There was in Alline's message, despite his many unorthodox views, what has been called an Orthodox ''Whitefield

58. Armstrong, *The Great Awakening in Nova Scotia,* p. 101.
59. Alline, *Two Mites,* p. 93.
60. Alline, *The Anti-Traditionist,* p. 42.
61. Beverley and Moody, eds., *The Journal of Henry Alline,* p. 216.

sound.''[62] In other words, Alline *sounded* like a New England New
Light from the 1740s; his dynamic and charismatic preaching produced many of the same results. Moreover, and this point needs to
be emphasized, the Falmouth evangelist intuitively realized that his
New Light movement, without his careful nurturing, would fragment
into warring Antinomian and anti-Antinomian factions.

There is certainly a ring of truth in both John Wesley's conten-
tion that in Alline's message ''the gold and dross'' were ''shuffled
together,''[63] and in the view of the Reverend Matthew Richey that
''he allegorized to such excess the plainest narratives and announce-
ments of Scriptures, that the obvious and unsophisticated import of
the words of inspiration was often entirely lost amidst the reveries of
mysticism.''[64]

The Falmouth itinerant had always made it quite clear that the
''scriptures are not to be understood in their literal sense, but have a
spiritual meaning.''[65] He tried to make each verse in the Bible speak
directly and profoundly to each of his listeners—as throbbing thrusts
of spirituality. He shattered the hard outer case of Calvinist ortho-
doxy in order to enable divine ecstasy to ''ravish'' the collective soul
of Nova Scotia and New England. In the process, he abandoned certain ideological constructs of Orthodox Christianity—such as the
Creation, the Atonement, the Resurrection of the Body, the Sacra-
ments, and the centrality of the Bible. Instead, he was driven by the
inner compelling logic of his own intense conversion and his conviction that he was in direct communication with the Almighty to
push the parameters of experiential religion to, and some would say
beyond, even radical Evangelical norms. Certainly in the 1790s and
the first decade of the nineteenth century some of his followers

---

62. For a further discussion of this point see Marini, *Radical Sects of Rev-
olutionary New England,* and Rawlyk, *Ravished By The Spirit.* See also John B.
Bowles, *The Great Revival 1787–1805: The Origins of the Southern Evangelical
Mind* (Lexington, University Press of Kentucky, 1972).

63. John Wesley to William Black, July 13, 1783, in J. Telford, ed., *The
Letters of the Rev. John Wesley,* VII (London, The Epworth Press, 1931), pp. 182–
83.

64. Richey, *A Memoir of the Late William Black,* p. 45.

65. Hannah Adams, *Alphabetical Compendium of Various Sects which have
Appeared in the World* (Boston, B. Edes and Sons, 1784), p. lxv.

pushed his views into a Nova Scotia and New Brunswick variant of Antinomianism.[66] Alline, if he had been alive, would have been both humiliated and incensed by what he once called this anti-Christian "vanity and sin."[67] Yet he should have realized that it would be extremely difficult, if not impossible, for many of his followers to walk his knife-edge of "true zeal."

ALLINE: THE PREACHER

On experiencing the New Birth, Alline felt called to preach the gospel to his fellow Nova Scotians, but his Congregational background and parental influence, which stressed the importance of an educated ministry, discouraged him from doing so. First he felt compelled "to proceed to New England . . . to get learning there."[68] But wartime conditions together with family responsibilities made this impossible. Finally, after months of procrastination, he resolved to preach the Gospel.

News that "Henry Alline was turned New-Light preacher" drew scores of visitors to Falmouth. "Some came to hear what the babler had to say," Alline noted, "some came with the gladness of heart that God had raised up one to speak in his name; and some came to make a scoff, but it did not seem to trouble me much; for I trust God was with me and supported and enabled me to face a frowning world."[69] By early November 1776, it was observed in the Falmouth-Horton area that "the Lord was reviving a work of grace."[70] Throughout December 1776 and the early months of 1777 the Falmouth preacher itinerated in the Cornwallis-Horton-Newport area—the region in the colony he knew best. When opposition to his preaching created unanticipated problems in the Cornwallis area in May, he decided to visit Annapolis—almost eighty miles to the

---

66. See George Rawlyk ed., *New Light Letters and Songs* (Hantsport, Lancelot Press, 1983), pp. 37–66, and David Bell, ed., *Newlight Baptist Journals*, pp. 14–19, 337–54.

67. Beverley and Moody, eds., *The Journal of Henry Alline*, p. 216.

68. Alline, *Life and Journal*, p. 42.

69. Ibid., p. 47.

70. Ibid., p. 48.

southwest—where he saw little evidence of "the power of religion."[71]

In February 1778, Alline experienced his first long dark night of despair and doubt. The "horrors of darkness" engulfed him and "the strong bulls of Bashan have beset me around." He movingly described the "darkness and distress" of his mind and conscience:

> This was the first distress, darkness or doubt of my standing that ever I had known since my conversion: for now I gave way to the enemy (it being new to me) so that I wholly doubted my standing, that I tried to invalidate all the evidences I had since my conversion of having enjoyed the presence of God, and to throw it all away: yet I found something like an anchor of hope within the veil, which I could not get rid of; though I tried much, and prayed to God to take it away. O the unspeakable distress I was under! I could neither eat, drink nor sleep with any satisfaction; for it was wholly new to me, so that I knew not what to do, what to say, where I had been, where I now was, nor where I was going. O my soul cried out to some unknown God. Help, help, O my God: if thou art mine; if not, O my God undeceive me.

For "three days and three nights (as Jonah was)" Alline found himself "in the belly of hell." He had tumbled from the mountain peak of "ravishing ecstasy" to the "bottom of the mountains, and the earth with her bars" surrounded him. Just when he seemed to be devoid of redeeming faith, the Almighty "remembered me, and brought me again to rejoice in the wonders of his love, and to triumph over the powers of darkness." When the New Light leader was delivered from the hell of his intense doubt, he experienced "unspeakable happiness" and was "convinced it was all in great love, yea, of unspeakable benefit to fit me for the work I had before me, which God knew, though I did not."[72]

---

71. Ibid., p. 54.

72. All the quotations from Alline in these two paragraphs are to be found in ibid., pp. 61–62.

Alline's was an amazing and honest admission of agonizing doubt; he was not afraid to scrape into the inner recesses of his faith and declare to posterity both his vulnerability and his integrity. This basic and almost transparent honesty and openness helps to explain his tremendous appeal. Nova Scotians, obviously, could empathize with him and resonate with the wild oscillations of his feelings. In his sinfulness, he was one of them; and in his ongoing redemption, he was one of them. He did not try to edit out of his *Journal* his obvious flaws and weaknesses.

Throughout the summer and autumn months of 1778, as he itinerated up and down the Annapolis Valley, he sadly noted that the spiritual awakenings he had helped spark into existence were often quickly followed by periods of spiritual declension and sectarian conflict. He found the activities of the Baptists in the Horton area particularly annoying, with their ''disputes about such non-essentials, as water Baptism.'' When in January 1779 the Cornwallis Congregational Church offered to ordain him, his response was to stress that he could never ''be settled in any one place; for I would rather stand wholly alone in the world, than go contrary to the gospel.''[73] And, for him, going contrary to the gospel meant refusing to itinerate as the Spirit directed him. On April 6, Alline was ordained ''in a large barn'' in Cornwallis as an ''itinerant minister.'' ''After prayer and singing, and a sermon preached,'' he ''received the imposition of hands by nine delegates, three chosen out of each church,'' from Cornwallis, Horton, and Falmouth-Newport.[74]

In late April 1779, he sailed from Cornwallis to the Saint John River where in the Maugerville area the ''work of the blessed God increased'' and Alline was able to breathe new life into a disintegrating church. On his return to the mouth of the river, to present-day Saint John, he was depressed with the ''darkness of the place.'' ''The greatest part of the people,'' he noted ''as if they were to die like beasts.'' ''I suppose,'' he went on, ''there were upwards of 200 people there come to the years of maturity, and I saw no signs of any christian excepting one soldier.''[75]

---

73. Ibid., p. 68.
74. Ibid., p. 70.
75. Ibid., pp. 71–73.

Sometime in June, Alline sailed to Annapolis, where he "found the work of God in some degree reviving: some in distress and in some sense of their danger." But he also discovered that one of his early converts was spreading malicious rumors about Alline's sexual life. The Falmouth preacher, it was asserted, had been seen "in bed with a young woman" and Alline was "looked on . . . with cold-ness." Eventually, Alline's accuser confessed that "he had told a lie" and had "been imposed upon by the devil and his malicious nature." Though he had never before endured such bitter calumny, the New Light preacher "learned to pay no regard to false reports" and used the occasion to trigger a revival of religion. There was much "travailing in the pangs of the new birth" and many nights he "sat up until twelve, one, two and three o'clock, labouring with dis-tressed souls."[76]

When he returned to his home base in July, Alline once again discovered the old distress produced by "the enemy getting among the christians in warm debate, and sowing discord about non-essen-tial matters" especially "water baptism." The "vain disputes" were such that he resolved in August to escape by riding down to Annap-olis. In the Annapolis-Granville region, Alline found "the society still engaged in the cause of God: but many scoffing, making their bands strong." Seeing little evidence of the Spirit's work, he re-solved in late August to sail once again to the Saint John River, where he was certain there would be a far more positive response to his message. He rejected on October 29 a "call to stay" as minister to the Maugerville Church, explaining, in some detail, that he had "no expectation of being called to settle over any particular church or flock." Nevertheless, he promised to visit them regularly, thus "making you the people of my particular care while present."[77]

On November 13, 1779, the Falmouth preacher was back in An-napolis, where he "enjoyed great liberty in the gospel" despite growing and often vociferous opposition. He spent December, Jan-uary, and February in the Cornwallis-Falmouth region, where, he noted, "the Lord seemed to be reviving his work again." After many of his sermons, some of his audience "would arise, exhort and wit-

---

76. Ibid., pp. 73–74.
77. Ibid., pp. 75–78.

ness for God.'' Exhorting became an integral part of the New Light worship service. Men and women were encouraged to witness to their faith, but they were encouraged to do more than merely witness. They were urged to personalize Alline's evangelistic message—to dissect it into meaningful segments—and then bombard their friends with these verbal projections, projections that in a sense took on themselves an aura of divine inspiration. His message was thus powerfully reinforced and in the prisms of the exhorters' enthusiasm redirected in a myriad of directions.[78]

In early March 1780, Alline set out for Annapolis on snowshoes accompanied by a young man—probably Thomas Handley Chipman—who carried his saddle-bags. Alline was planning to spend six months in the Annapolis region and the Saint John River Valley. He found up the Saint John River that ''the work of God was not so powerful as it had been'' and that around Annapolis there were stultifying and divisive ''disputes about water-baptism''—bitter disputes that had affected the entire Annapolis Valley.[79]

It was realized that in the white heat of revival, nonessentials were seldom talked about; but when the revival fires went out, peripheral issues became central ones, small differences became matters of principle, and a profound sense of Christian oneness was replaced by what Alline called ''sectarian zeal.'' He detested, it is clear, sectarian bickering about nonessentials and longed for the ''love of the meek and lowly Jesus'' to ''burn up and expel'' the all too pervasive ''stuff and darkness'' that he saw was putting a brake on the revival movement.[80]

In the summer of 1780, he was delighted to spark yet another revival in Falmouth and Newport but found ''not much moving of the Spirit'' in Horton or Cornwallis. Alline was depressed because, despite all of his entreaties, ''the fallen world is sleeping, musing, rejecting, fighting and opposing all the endearing charms, cutting, chaining, tormenting and plunging themselves down deeper and deeper into the bottomless gulf of irrevocable despair.''[81] Dispirited

---

78. Ibid., pp. 78–82.
79. Ibid., pp. 82–89.
80. Ibid., p. 85.
81. Ibid., p. 93.

by the indifference and apathy he found in Horton and Cornwallis, he once again rode off, early in September, for Annapolis, where he was soon involved in a major revival and the "great blessings" attending his preaching followed him to the Saint John River in October and the first three weeks of November.

On November 25, 1780, Alline was back in Cornwallis, where most of his time and energy were spent "in order to settle some matters in dispute, to heal breaches, and make up divisions." In early December he visited "the darkness and death" of Halifax for the first time "to commit a small piece of my writings to the press." The small piece was his *Hymns and Spiritual Songs on a Variety of Pleasing and Important Subjects*—a collection of twenty-two of his recently composed "hymns and spiritual songs."[82] The remainder of December was spent in Horton and Cornwallis, where once again Alline found himself embroiled in heated debates about what he regarded as nonessentials. On the last day of 1780, a morbidly introspective Alline noted in his *Journal:*

> Another year is drawn to a period, and O, what have I done, what advance have I made in the only thing for which I have my being? How many thousands have landed in the eternal world since this year commenced, whose die is cast and doom unalterably fixed, and I am spared? But O if I look back on the year past and review my walk, how dark and how crooked is it, and how little have I advanced my Redeemer's name and how little useful have I been to my fellowmen.[83]

Throughout the first seven months of 1781, Alline oscillated wildly between the "sweetness of that peace beyond what tongue can tell" and the "great darkness" produced by the "absence of my Lord and Master." Despite his spiritual turmoil, Alline continued to preach, hoping thereby to recapture the pristine purity of his faith.[84] He was also writing his major treatise *Two Mites,*

---

82. Ibid., pp. 97–99.
83. Ibid., p. 103.
84. Ibid., pp. 105–36.

which, in late March, he delivered to his Halifax printer, Anthony Henry.

Alline's acute morbid introspection of 1781 was probably shaped by four important factors. First, he was writing a major theological work and literary creativity of this kind often produces introspection and self-doubt. Second, he was feeling the early effects of tuberculosis—a disease that led to his early death three years later. It is well known that "alternating states of euphoria and depression" have always characterized those suffering from "consumption," as has what has been called a "self-driving behavior."[85] Third, he desperately wanted to be married—to have a female friend "to lean upon," but he also felt it necessary to surrender "all up to God, let what would come."[86] Fourth, for the first time in his ministry he was confronted by "ruffians" and "military officers" who threatened him with physical abuse and who "with drawn swords . . . cursed and blasphemed him." There was much "mocking and hooting" as the British soldiers from neighboring Windsor intimidated the famous "Yankee Neutral preacher." It is not surprising, therefore, that Alline would plaintively observe on July 6: "Yea, I found by what trials and persecutions I went through, that it was hard to have the mind in such a frame, as to suffer wholly for Christ."[87]

On July 7, perhaps in order to escape from an environment that seemed to produce too much morbid introspection, he sailed for the Chignecto Isthmus region of Nova Scotia. Here, among the Yorkshire and Cumberland Methodists and Yankees he was "blessed" . . . with a longing desire to spend and be spent in his blessed cause."[88] Some of his former enthusiasm was returning, as was his unquestioning faith in his own redemption; there were a number of instantaneous conversions as women and younger peo-

---

85. Peter Shaw, *American Patriots and the Rituals of Revolution* (Cambridge, Harvard University Press, 1981), p. 165. See also E. D. Witthower, "Psychological Aspects of Pulmonary Tuberculosis: A General Survey," in P. J. Sparer ed., *Personality Stress and Tuberculosis* (New York, International Universities Press 1956), pp. 157–58.

86. Alline, *Life and Journal*, p. 131.

87. Ibid., pp. 131–33.

88. Ibid., p. 136.

ple, in particular, were affected by the New Light message. On
Sunday August 12 he preached three sermons on this not untypical
"Sabbath."

> and God brought some souls to Christ, and many christians
> to rejoice in great liberty. The hearers were so numerous,
> that I was obliged to preach in the fields. O how my soul
> travailed, while speaking, when I beheld many groaning
> under almost unsupportable burdens, and crying out for
> mercy. This day the church met to receive members, and
> according as I had advised them, no mention was made, of
> what think ye of Paul, Appolos, or Cephas; but what think
> ye of Christ. O the power of the Holy Ghost that was
> among the people this day. A number joined the church,
> and some sinners were brought to rejoice in Jesus Christ
> their friend.[89]

When he left the Chignecto two weeks later, he was delighted
to be able to report "Methinks I could say, I conversed with God as
with a friend."[90]

On July 25, 1781, the indefatigable intinerant was back at Horton after escaping, en route, from a Patriot privateer. "Let them that
wish well to their souls flee from privateers as they would from the
jaws of hell," he stressed, "for methinks a privateer may be called
a floating hell."[91] He found, much to his relief, that Christ was once
again "all my joy."

> Jesus, my Lord, I call thee mine.
> I feel thy word that makes me thine
> Now on me gird the gospel sword,
> With the whole armour of thy word,
> To spread the wonders of thy grace abroad.[92]

---

89. Ibid., p. 140.
90. Ibid., p. 143.
91. Ibid.
92. Ibid., p. 144.

Alline was disappointed, however, with the "dead people" who came out to hear him, and he felt that his message "seems to slip by them without any more impression then, than water upon glass."[93] What a contrast with Cumberland, and Alline looked longingly at the Yarmouth-Liverpool corner of the colony "where I never have been." Perhaps, here, there would be a "sweetness of labouring in Christ's kingdom."[94]

On October 18, 1781, he arrived, via a small boat, at Cape Orsue—present-day Yarmouth. Here he faced a furious Reverend Jonathan Scott, the Congregational minister, who "raged very high" against him, regarding the Falmouth itinerant as a dangerous interloper. After visiting Argyle briefly, Alline made his way to Barrington, whose inhabitants he found "very dark," and then sailed to Liverpool, where he finally arrived, after being captured by an American privateer, on December 11. At Liverpool he "found a kind people, but in midnight darkness, and vastly given to frolicking, rioting and all manner of levity." Soon after, a revival began. On January 1, 1782, he observed:

> I preached twice every day, and the houses were crowded. Many were very much awakened; which was such a new thing (neither known or heard of among them) that many did not know what ailed them; but still thirsted to hear me speak in the name of Christ. Many would hover around me after sermon, who seemed as if they longed to speak to me and unfold their case, but dared not open their mouths, for it was new and strange to them and to the whole town; for there never had been such a talk as a guilty conscience, a burdened mind, a hard heart or a stubborn will, or about any convictions or conversions; nor of the love of God, or declaring what he had done for their souls.[95]

---

93. Ibid.
94. Ibid., p. 145.
95. Ibid., pp. 146–49. See also Gordon Stewart, ed., *The Great Awakening in Nova Scotia* (Toronto, The Champlain Society, 1982), pp. xxxv–xxxvi, 119–41. The point should be emphatically made that when Alline's accounts of his visits to various parts of Nova Scotia are checked with other contemporary accounts, that is, Scott's, Perkins's, and so forth, Alline is seen to have been an accurate, fair and

On January 7, 1782, he left Liverpool; the previous night he had found that his "soul was full, and the truths of God seemed to pour into my mind faster than I could deliver them." He had "everything to say to the people, that I desired to, and the hearers were greatly taken hold of, and it seemed they could not go away." He then returned on foot to Chebogue, where the Reverend Scott called him "an impudent fellow" and Alline had replied by telling him that "he showed what kingdom he belonged to by his rage and malice." On February 20, Alline "set out to go on foot with two men in company" making his way to Annapolis, where he arrived on March 1. One of his early converts, Thomas Handley Chipman, was preaching in the area and there was much spiritual vitality being manifested. On April 25, Chipman was ordained amidst "a vast concourse of people." Alline's brother-in-law, John Payzant, now an effective New Light preacher, opened proceedings at seven in the morning. Later in the day, Alline "preached a sermon, and then delivered the charge." It was, according to Alline, "almost like the day of Pentecost" with "some of the christians . . . so carried away, that they were almost past speaking."[96]

The following day, after preaching a sermon, he hurried off to Windsor, from which port he sailed on April 29 for the Saint John River. He spent most of May preaching twice a day, in and around Maugerville, during which time he "had happy days and much of the spirit of God moving . . . among the people." On his way down to the mouth of the river on May 28, he had "an evening much to be remembered." He

> preached about Elijah's translation, and I had such a sense of his flight, that I thought . . . I should almost leave the body. O the sweet and transporting attraction that my soul felt, which carried away the old prophet that, stole in upon my heart with unspeakable joy and delight. And methinks in a degree I know and have experienced the nature and manner of his translation. Yea, never was my soul before so bore away to the realms of eternal felicity.

---

perceptive observer. If anything, perhaps because of his sensitivity to the sin of *hubris,* he seems to have underestimated his influence.

    96. Alline, *Life and Journal,* pp. 149–53.

Early June 1782 was spent in the Chignecto region and early July in Cumberland to the east. On July 9, he sailed to present-day Prince Edward Island, where he found only three Christians among a "very dark people" who were "openly profane." Two weeks later he was back on Nova Scotia soil, this time at Pictou, on Northumberland Straight.[97]

On September 30, the so-called Whitefield of Nova Scotia rode off to Annapolis, where he "preached often and saw blessed days." Then, accompanied by T. H. Chipman, his most trusted disciple, Alline traveled in the direction of Liverpool. It was decided that Chipman should sail to "the river St. John's" while his mentor continued on to his original destination. After brief stops at Yarmouth, Barrington, Ragged Islands, and Sable River, Alline finally arrived at Liverpool on November 20.

> Almost all the town assembled together, and some that were lively christians prayed and exhorted, and God was there with a truth. I preached every day, and sometimes twice a day; and the houses where I went were crowded almost all the time. Many were brought out of darkness and rejoiced, and exhorted in public. And O how affecting it was to see some young people not only exhort their companions, but also take their parents by the hand, and entreat them for their soul's sake to rest no longer in their sins, but fly to Jesus Christ while there was hope. One young lad . . . I saw, after sermon, take his father by the hand, and cry out, O father, you have been a great sinner, and now are an old man: an old sinner, with grey hairs upon your head, going right down to destruction. O turn, turn, dear father, return and fly to Jesus Christ: with many other such like expressions and entreaties, enough to melt a strong heart.

"The work of God," it was observed, "continued with uncommon power through almost all the place." There was some "raging and scoffing, and some blaspheming" and at least one critic shouted

---

97. Ibid., pp. 153–64.

out, during one of Alline's sermons, "that is damned foolishness." An aroused Alline turned on his critic, demanded silence, and urged him "to remember what his doom would be, that dares to blaspheme the gospel of the Lord Jesus Christ."[98] It was not he but Jesus Christ, that was being interrupted or blasphemed.

On January 1, 1783, he sailed to Halifax, where he stayed for ten days; he still found that Haligonians "in general are almost as dark and as vile as in Sodom." He returned to Liverpool for a brief sojourn, where he saw "the waters troubled, and souls stepping in." He spent the first two weeks of March in Halifax and then made his way overland to Falmouth. On March 26, at Windsor, he was "taken so ill, that my life was despaired of." During most of April, May, June, and July, he remained gravely ill "and it was thought by almost every one, that I should soon quit this mortal stage." During his prolonged sickness Alline "was in divine rapture," expecting imminently to return to Paradise.[99]

He slowly regained his strength and as he recovered he became increasingly convinced that God was calling him to New England. It is impossible to be certain about his motivation for visiting New England. He felt a powerful attraction, as he put it, to "go and proclaim my Master's name, where I never had preached," especially since he had already "preached almost all over this country."[100] Expecting to die at any minute, the Falmouth preacher felt compelled to return to his homeland in the hope of persuading the Yankees to return to the evangelical faith of their parents.

Moreover, Alline knew, in the summer of 1783, that he was dying, and he evidently wanted to die in New England. Before he died he first wanted "to blow . . . the gospel trump." His parents encouraged him to go, expecting to meet him again only in heaven; his friends knew that nothing they said or did could dissuade him from doing what he was convinced was the will of God. On August 27, he sailed from Windsor and after an unplanned stop at the mouth of the Saint John River reached northern Maine early in September. He would never return to Nova Scotia—to what he now regarded as

---

98. Ibid., pp. 165–67.
99. Ibid., pp. 168–70.
100. Ibid., p. 171.

his "native province."[101] He left behind him scores of disciples, hundreds of followers, and a spiritual legacy reflected in both the oral and written tradition of the religious culture of Nova Scotia and New Brunswick.

IMPACT ON NEW ENGLAND

Alline's influence on the Nova Scotia–New Brunswick evangelical tradition was indeed significant—both in the short and long run. What is sometimes forgotten, however, is that the Falmouth preacher—perhaps indirectly—provided spiritual shape and substance to what has recently been called the "New Light Stir"[102]—a religious revival that swept through much of northern New England between 1779 and 1781. Moreover, Alline, at a critical moment, gave to the Yankee Free Will Baptist movement in general, and to its founder Benjamin Randel in particular, a ready-made theological system.

It was a remarkable coincidence—to say the least—that in the early autumn of 1783 both Benjamin Randel and Henry Alline were preaching their respective versions of the "Free Grace Gospel" to the inhabitants of southern Maine. As he rode southward in early October, an exhausted and sick Alline noted in his *Journal:*

> I endured vast pains and anguish of body almost every day, and was many times scarcely able to preach; but I endured it without much complaining, for I enjoyed health of soul, and was very happy at times in the Lord Jesus Christ. But as I had just got into that part of the vineyard, and saw the fields as it were white unto the harvest, I had intended (if Providence permitted) to blow the gospel trumpet through the vast country, and I could not bear the thoughts of leaving the world; although I was happy and had not the least doubt of my salvation: for I longed more than tongues can

---

101. Ibid., pp. 172–73.
102. See Marini, *Radical Sects of Revolutionary New England,* which takes into account Canadian studies dealing with Alline.

express, to be the means of bringing some of those poor souls to the Lord Jesus Christ.[103]

Just before he had arrived at Brunswick, Maine, on October 17, he encountered some zealous but "counterfeit" revivalists who were deceiving "young christians." He chastized the immature believers for being "so fond of every thing that appears like the power of God, that they receive almost any thing that has a zeal." He then concluded with an observation permeated with fear, anxiety, and perhaps prophetic insight:

> I love to see preachers zealous, yea, and I believe, if they have the spirit of God, which brings meekness, love and humility with the zeal, and solemnizes the person speaking, it will not be all over as soon as they have done speaking in public, but will go with them: when those who have nothing but a spirit of self, and a false zeal . . . it will be soon over, and have no solemnizing sense abiding.[104]

After spending almost four weeks preaching in southern Maine, visiting local Congregational ministers of New Light and Old Light persuasions, Alline entered New Hampshire, probably on November 13. Within five days he was in such pain—"scarcely an hour free from pain, excepting when asleep"—that he stopped writing his journal. Eventually, he made his way (January 22, 1784), "very feeble," to the house of the Reverend David McClure, the Congregational minister at North Hampton, New Hampshire, where, eleven days later, he died. McClure described the Nova Scotia preacher's last few hours on earth in the following evocative manner:

> By reason of his great bodily pains and longing to be with Christ, he would sometimes check himself, fearing he was too impatient to be gone. I desire, says he, to wait God's time. He said, he had begged of God, that he might not outlive his usefulness. O I long, said he, that poor sinners

---

103. Alline, *Life and Journal*, p. 173.
104. Ibid., p. 174.

should have such views of the Lord Jesus, as I have . . .
In the evening I observed to him that Christ was now his
only help, he said, I need not be told of that, he is now my
only desire. His distress increased, and he longed to depart. I observed to him, that I trusted he would soon obtain
the gracious fulfillment of the promises. I have no doubt,
said he, not one, no more than if I was now there. He lay
in great distress, groaning and reaching for breath . . . It
was evident soon after, that his reason was going, and his
broken sentences were the breathings of a soul swallowed
up in God.
In this state he lay about two hours in great distress for
breath, and the last intelligible sentence he spoke was . . .
"Now I rejoice in the Lord Jesus."[105]

The Falmouth itinerant would have appreciated McClure's description of his being "swallowed up in God" since, when he had
been converted in early 1775, he had "enjoyed a heaven on earth,
and it seemed as if I were wrapped up in God." "Ravished with a
divine ecstasy beyond any doubts and fears," death merely and finally confirmed what Alline had once referred to as "the infinite condescension of God to a worm of the dust."[106]

The itinerant preacher left with the Reverend Mr. McClure "a
number of hymns, which it was his desire," according to McClure,
should be published, "for the benefit more especially of his friends
in Nova Scotia."[107] This manuscript was sent by McClure to Alline's
namesake and cousin then residing in Boston. Two years later, in
1786, Alline's *Hymns and Spiritual Songs* was published. Alline
also gave McClure a manuscript copy of his journal. The *Journal*
would not be published, however, until 1806.

According to McClure, Alline was "a burning and shining light
in Nova Scotia and elsewhere . . . his christian virtues, zeal fortitude, faith, hope, patience and resignation shone bright as the lamp
of life burnt down into the socket." McClure added that during the

---

105. Ibid., pp. 178–79.
106. Ibid., pp. 30, 39.
107. Ibid., p. 180.

months the Nova Scotian had spent in New England before being "united with seraphs and saints in their pure ardours of holy and everlasting joy," he had preached "with power to the consciences of sinners."[108] Many residents of North Hampton, though not ardent New Lights, were forever marked by Alline's remarkable influence. As late as 1839, for example, it was noted by the Reverend Jonathan French, one of McClure's successors, that several persons were still alive

> who saw Revd Mr. Alline while at Mr. McClure's. They represent every thing in his appearance and conversation as have been very spiritual and as become one just on the verge of heaven. He seemed scarcely to belong on earth. He passed the last week of his life at Mr. McClure's, & preached on the Sabbath from "Zacheus come down etc." Many visited his sick and dying chamber, he had something spiritual to say to everyone. Widow Hepzibah Marston, now 95, the oldest person in the town and sister of the church, was one of his watchers the last night of his life and speaks of the prayerfulness and heavenly frame of mind with which he anticipated his departure.[109]

Fifty-five years after his death, the deeply etched image of the remarkable Nova Scotian visitor could not be removed from the memory of an American like ninety-five-year-old Hepzibah Marston, who had spent only a few days with him. For every Hepzibah Marston in New Hampshire, there were thousands of Nova Scotians who, as late as the 1850s, believed that Alline was indeed the "Whitefield of Nova Scotia."[110]

Though he never met Alline, Benjamin Randel, too, was significantly affected by the man from Nova Scotia and his Free Will message. Randel was born in 1749 in New Castle, New Hampshire.

---

108. Ibid.

109. North Hampton Congregational Church Book, New Hampshire Historical Society, Concord, New Hampshire.

110. See, for example, the critical account of Alline's influence on the Maritimes in the *Christian Instructor and Missionary Register of the Presbyterian Church of Nova Scotia* (Pictou, NS. March 1859).

Soon after hearing one of George Whitefield's last sermons, preached in September 1770, Randel was converted. Years later he left the Congregational Church and became a Baptist, and in 1776 was ordained a Baptist minister. Because of his anti-Calvinist views, however, Randel was "disfellowshipped" by his local Baptist Church and became an ardent advocate of the Free Will position. Throughout northern New England, during the latter years of the Revolutionary War, Randel discovered that the New Light Stir, as well as the work of hosts of itinerating ministers and a widespread acceptance of emotionalism at the popular level, had "prepared the ground" for his "message of free salvation." As might have been expected, Congregationalists and Regular Baptists regarded the Free Willers as "wolves in sheep's clothing." Randel and his disciples took creative advantage of situational pressures in a variety of communities and directed them along Free Will Baptist lines.[111]

There was, despite its universalism and Free Will emphasis, what contemporaries referred to as the "old Whitefield sound" in Randel's preaching. The same point was frequently made as well about Alline's message. Randel and his associates also resembled Whitefield in that they loved to itinerate—crisscrossing Maine, New Hampshire, and northern Massachusetts frequently and regularly. Yet despite their concern about isolated and leaderless congregations, little could be done during the formative years of the Free Will Baptist movement to consolidate in any effective organizational manner the fruits of revival. It was realized that despite the heroic work of Randel and others, endemic discord would intensify until there was "a coherent social design that facilitated theological agreement, financial coordination, and disciplinary cooperation." Randel was particularly sensitive, as early as 1782, to the threat posed to his movement by "the Shaker delusion."[112]

Randel felt threatened by competing sectarian groups like the Shakers in the realm of theological discourse. It is noteworthy that until his death in 1808, neither Randel nor any of his lieutenants produced a "published work devoted to an exposition of theology."[113]

---

111. See my *Ravished by the Spirit*, pp. 42–45.

112. Marini, "New England Folk Religions," p. 109.

113. I. D. Stewart, *History of the Freewill Baptists,* (Dover, Freewill Baptist Print Establishment, N.H., 1862), p. 55.

This "paucity is startling," observes Norman Allen Baxter in *History of the Freewill Baptists,* "when we recall that Randel separated from the Calvinistic Baptists for theological reasons."[114] In a sense, Baxter is right; the paucity is startling when one takes into account the scores of theological treatises published during these years by men with a lot less to say and also by men who lacked Randel's creativity, sense of urgency, and native intelligence. But in another sense Baxter is wrong, for the Free Will Baptists had their own theologian: Henry Alline. There was consequently no need for them, in the formative period of their movement, to find one of their own number to formulate both a positive assertion of Free Grace and a powerful critique of Calvinism. Alline had already accomplished this in his published work.

During the early months of 1783 Randel was experiencing what his biographer described as a "very trying season." He was "violently seized by a fever, which ran so high, that his life was despaired of." Once recovered, he had to work day and night at his tailoring and his farming "to maintain my little family" and to "redeem time to travel and preach Jesus to poor sinners." On September 26, he set out for Maine. Nineteen days earlier, Henry Alline had left Nova Scotia for the same northern frontier region of Massachusetts. Randel, "deeply impressed to go further east," made his way to the Damariscotta River, and then along to Bristol. "After labouring a short season" in this locality "he returned homeward," stopping along the way in Brunswick and Harpswell. The Free Will Baptist preacher was not reunited with his family in New Hampshire until November 22.[115]

Despite the fact that they visited Maine at the same time in 1783 and despite the fact that they preached to some of the same congregations and traversed the same roads, there is no available and explicit evidence that Randel and Alline ever met. That Randel was aware of Alline and his theological work there is absolutely no doubt; that Alline was totally ignorant of Randel there is little doubt. The

---

114. (Rochester, American Baptist Historical Society 1957), p. 55.

115. John Buzzell, *The Life of Elder Benjamin Randel, Principally Taken from Documents Written By Himself* (Limerick, Hobbs, Woodman and Co., 1827), pp. 115–16.

Nova Scotian always noted in his *Journal* the names of ministers he had met and, moreover, he frequently discussed the theological views of such men. In his *Journal,* Alline neither referred to Randel nor to his Free Will Baptist movement—despite the fact that their basic theological views had so much in common. When Alline was buried on February 3, Randel played no role whatsoever in the funeral service.

Yet sometime during the early months of 1784, Randel became directly acquainted with Alline's writing. There is some evidence to suggest, moreover, that Randel's own journal accounts of his spiritual travails and the actual language he used were based on Alline's *Journal.* The Reverend I. D. Stewart, in his official *History of the Freewill Baptists,* published in 1862, noted that at the September quarterly meeting "convened at Edgecomb, Me.," there was a determined "first effort to bring the power of the press into the service of the church." He explicitly referred to "Henry Allen, a New Light preacher from Nova Scotia," who had come "into Maine, bringing with him a work of 250 pages, written by himself, and called Two Mites, in which he discussed several theological questions, such as the Fall of Man—His Recovery by Christ—Embassadors of Christ— The Power of Ordination—The Church—and the Day of Judgement." Stewart then enigmatically commented that "both the man and the book were favourably received, as it was voted to try and have brother Henry Allen's Two Mites' reprinted."[116] How Alline the man had been favourably received by the Free Will Baptists was never discussed by Stewart. Some might argue that Stewart merely telescoped events; in referring to the September 1784 quarterly meeting he really meant to refer to an earlier meeting. There was a quarterly meeting, it is true, on December 6, 7, and 8, 1783, in Hollis, Maine, but at this time Alline was totally incapacitated in the Falmouth area "by his sickness and pains" and he was expecting to die at any moment. There was another quarterly meeting held during the first week of March 1784, by which time Alline had been dead for over a month.

We know that Alline proudly carried with him to New England printed copies of his *Two Mites,* his *Anti-Traditionist,* his three pub-

---

116. Stewart, *History of the Freewill Baptists,* p. 81.

lished sermons, and also, in manuscript form, "a number of hymns, which he had prepared to be published." In addition, there was his journal, part of it still written in a form of shorthand.

In 1786, the Free Will Baptists published Alline's 381-page *Hymns and Spiritual Songs*. This extraordinarily popular volume would be reprinted no fewer than three times—in 1795, 1797, and 1802. Alline's "Fort-Midway" sermon was reprinted in 1795 in Massachusetts under the new title *A Gospel Call to Sinners* and again in 1797 in New Hampshire. In 1797, as well, the Yankee Free Will Baptists had reprinted Alline's controversial pamphlet *The Anti-Traditionist*. Seven years later, in 1804, *Two Mites* was finally reprinted and in 1806 Alline's *Life and Journal* was published in Boston.

Though it may still be unclear why there was a twenty-year delay in the reprinting of *Two Mites,* it is clear that Randel was greatly influenced by its contents and also by the ideas in Alline's other writings and his hymns. In late 1783 and early 1784, Randel was desperately looking for something like Alline's theological writing in order to deal with the increasingly virulent counterattacks of his Calvinist critics and also to provide his Free Will Baptist movement with some kind of articulated ideological framework. On a more personal level, Randel needed some kind of intellectual justification for his Free Will commitment. But Randel and his followers needed more than this. They found in Alline a dynamic New Light message that linked their movement to a Whitefieldian past and also a nineteenth-century evangelical outlook with its special emphasis on individualism, optimism, and sense of mission. Alline was therefore a key link in the chain connecting orthodox eighteenth-century Evangelical thought and action with an important component of what has been termed "New England Folk Religion."

Alline's theological writing significantly affected all of Randel's religious thinking and provided him with the words and concepts that in turn profoundly influenced the Free Will Baptist movement. Moreover, Alline's *Hymns and Spiritual Songs* directly influenced ordinary rank-and-file Free Will Baptists. It is of some consequence, I think, that Alline's *Hymns and Spiritual Songs* was divided into five equal sections that blended together to produce a musical and popular "history of redemption." The first section was entitled "Chiefly consisting of man's fallen state"; the second, "Gospel invitations and a free salvation"; the third, "the New Birth and the knowledge and joys of that glorious work''; the fourth, ''The joys and trials of the soul''; and the fifth, ''Consisting chiefly of infinite wonders, transporting views, and Christian triumphs.'' There was, Marini argues, a ''hymnic proclivity'' not only in the early Free Will Baptist movement but also among the Shakers, the Universalists, and almost every evangelical group. ''A flourishing Evangelical style in both lyrics and music'' permeated popular religion during the so-called golden age of New England hymnody from 1775 to 1815.[117]

It has been noted that the Free Will Baptists were the last sect to publish their own hymnal—John Buzzell's *Psalms, Hymns and Sacred Songs,* in 1823. ''It is likely,'' it has been argued, ''that Alline's hymnal in these several editions (1786, 1795, 1797, 1802) served as the main song-book for Free-will Baptists before Buzzell's.''[118] The popularity of Alline is further confirmed in Buzzell's collection; more of his hymns were included than those of any other author except Isaac Watts. Alline obviously set the tone and shape of the content of Free Will hymnody until well into the nineteenth century.

In a superb overview of the importance of hymnody for various New England Folk Religions, Marini contends that the popular music ''preserved the major stylistic characteristics of Evangelical sacred song yet employed that style toward distinctly sectarian purposes:''

> the sects used the sensuous imagery, subjectivism, and Biblical paraphrase of Evangelical hymnody to create songs for virtually every event and activity of their religious lifestyles. The Evangelical hymn became an indispensable medium for sectarian self-expression and self-reflection. Through hymns, sectarian congregations shared collective experiences and individuals articulated their faith. Hymn-writing in the sects had begun as a spontaneous mode of ordering the disarray of intense, even ec-

---

117. Marini, ''New England Folk Religions,'' pp. 450–51. See also, idem, *Radical Sects of Revolutionary New England,* pp. 158–62.
118. ''New England Folk Religions,'' p. 452.

static, worship. But by 1815 the composition of sacred poetry had become a mental habit of sectarians lay and ordained, and in the publication of formal hymnals the folk religions promulgated detailed symbolization of all aspects of their identity and experience.[119]

For Marini, "Hymnody gave each sect a medium through which to render its distinctive beliefs, practices, and institutions into objective symbolic form." The actual medium "was part of the Evangelical heritage shared by all the sects, and the folk religions did not stray far from the poetic style of the Evangelical hymnists."

> Sectarian hymns were for the most part derivative and imitative; the sects did not contribute anything to poetic art by their hymns. Their creativity lay in giving the hymn new content, based on the distinctive religiousness. As that religiousness developed clear-cut social forms and theological claims, the sects came to possess unique vocabularies and characteristic modes of reflection. It was these vocabularies and intellectual styles, expressive of sectarian spirituality, social design and theology, that filled the Evangelical lyric with enough new content to create a distinctly sectarian hymnody.[120]

By 1815, the distinctive Free Baptist hymnody and theology, together with a certain preaching style—all greatly influenced by Alline, it may be argued—had evolved. His new-Whitefieldian "subjectivity and emotionalism"[121] seemed to infuse all Free Will sacred language—as did his emphasis on the Edenic experience, Free Will, the Incarnation, the New Birth, the fusing of divine love into human action, Christian community, and the imminent return of Christ and the return to Paradise.

---

119. Marini, *Radical Sects of Revolutionary New England,* pp. 170–71.
120. Marini, "New England Folk Religions," pp. 480–81.
121. Ibid., p. 481.

IMPACT ON NOVA SCOTIA AND NEW BRUNSWICK

As the nineteenth century unfolded, the Free Will Baptists of northern New England found themselves torn apart by bitter sectarian centrifugal differences and by the powerful forces of alienation sweeping through the region. By mid-century Randel's movement had been pushed to the extreme periphery of the region's religious culture. In neighboring New Brunswick and Nova Scotia, however, the Free Baptist situation was somewhat different.

It should not be forgotten that in 1871 out of a total New Brunswick population of 285,594 (33.6 percent of which was Roman Catholic), there were 42,729 Calvinist Baptist—15 percent of the population and 25,861 Free Christians Baptists—9.8 percent of the population. Four years after Confederation, therefore, one out of every four New Brunswickers was a Baptist adherent. In Nova Scotia in 1871, out of a total population of 387,000 (26.5 percent was Roman Catholic), there were only 19,032 Free Christians Baptists (4.9 percent of the total population) and 54,263 Calvinist Baptists (14.0 percent of the total population). Thus, one in five Nova Scotians was a Baptist.[122]

Both groups of Baptists were transmitters of the Allinite tradition in the Maritime Provinces of Canada. Most of Alline's early Nova Scotia disciples, men like Harris Harding, T. H. Chipman, James and Edward Manning, Joseph Dimock, and Theodore Seth Harding, became leaders of the Calvinist Baptists in the region. These Baptists became the mainstream of the denomination. Although these so-called Baptist Patriarchs may have rejected Alline's anti-Calvinism and his belief that adult baptism was a nonessential, they continued to enthusiastically endorse his neo-Whitefieldian evangelical paradigm. The Free Baptists, throughout the nineteenth century, stressed that they were the true "Allinites," and in a sense they were. They were not as concerned as were their Calvinist brothers and sisters with order and respectability. Moreover, they were not afraid to be associated publicly with the legacy of Henry Alline. Most of the Calvinist Baptists, however, were.

---

122. See the religion and population tables in my *Ravished By The Spirit,* pp. 170–72.

Though not a Baptist, Henry Alline probably exerted more influence than any other single individual on the Baptist movement in New Brunswick and Nova Scotia in the nineteenth and twentieth centuries. Moreover, he significantly affected the Free Will Baptists of Northern New England at the zenith of their influence. But Alline accomplished even more than this. He injected into the religious culture of the Maritime Provinces, in particular, a special brand of spiritual individualism. His was a religion, or more accurately a way of life, that was concerned with the individual's special and continuing personal relationship with Christ and with eternal verities rather than with here-and-now ephemeral societal problems. Clearly seeing himself as being very much involved in a bitter cosmic struggle between the forces of evil, as represented by Satan and Calvinism, and the forces of righteousness, as personified by Christ and articulated in the Free Will message, Alline and his thousands of followers had little real interest in achieving impossible dreams on earth. Their New Jerusalem, in other words, was to be located in Paradise and not in Nova Scotia, New Brunswick, or even the United States. Alline and his followers had no desire to develop a mature and sophisticated social and political ethic that could either influence or challenge institutions and power relationships. They were far more eager to prepare themselves for the imminent "return of their Lord."

There is therefore, it may be argued, a strong link between Alline's religious message and its reverberation throughout the Maritimes in the nineteenth and twentieth centuries and the strong conservative political culture of the region. The political culture of the Maritimes had congealed by the 1850s into something "fundamentally conservative"[123] and traditional and this process of congealment owed a great deal to the power of Evangelical religion in the region. This so-called pragmatic conservatism of the Maritimes was strengthened, as the nineteenth century blurred into the twentieth, by the fact that the region was largely bypassed by the flood of immigrants into Canada after 1896 and also by the fact that the disenchanted and disaffected felt compelled to leave the Maritimes in order to realize their full potential elsewhere in North America. In

---

123. Sydney F. Wise, "Conservatism and Political Development: The Canadian Case," *South Atlantic Quarterly* LXIX (1970): 234–41.

the twentieth century, these factors, together with the economic underdevelopment of the region and the continuing influence of Evangelical religion, have further strengthened the fundamentally conservative political culture of the Maritimers.[124]

There is a simple gravestone on Alline's grave in the cemetery near the Congregational Church in North Hampton, New Hampshire. It is difficult to read the inscription and few people now try to do so. The original inscription reads:

> The Reverend Henry Alline
> of Falmouth, Nova Scotia,
> in the midst of his zealous
> travels in the cause of Christ,
> languished on the way, and
> cheerfully resigned his life
> at North Hampton, 2 Feb. 1784,
> in the 35 year of his age,
> whose remains are here interred.

Sometime after 1784, one of Alline's relatives added the following sentence to the gravestone:

> He was a burning and a shining light
> and justly esteemed the Apostle
> of Nova Scotia.[125]

---

124. See George Rawlyk and Doug Brown, "The Historical Framework of the Maritimes and Confederation," in George Rawlyk, ed., *The Atlantic Provinces and the Problems of Confederation* (St. John's, Breakwater Press 1979), pp. 4–7. For a radically different view see Gary C. Burrill, "Maritime Nationalism and the Decline of Maritime Political Culture: An Alternative View" (M.A. thesis, Queen's University, 1978).

125. Armstrong, *The Great Awakening in Nova Scotia*, p. 86.

ALLINE'S JOURNAL

Just before he died, Alline gave to the Reverend David Mc-
Clure, the Congregational Church minister at North Hampton, New
Hampshire, his manuscript journal, some of which was still written
in a form of shorthand. Alline "had begun to draw off the journal of
his life in a legible hand," McClure informed Alline's father, William, on August 3, 1784, "but had proceeded but a little way in it."
Before his death Alline had "expressed a desire to have the remarkable providences of God towards him made public for the good of
souls." And McClure had urged William Alline to find "some ju-
dicious person who is acquainted with the characters in which he
wrote" to undertake the vitally important project. Alline's father was
assured that his son had been "a burning and shining light in Nova
Scotia and elsewhere" and that "his christian virtues, zeal, fortitude, faith, hope, patience and resignation shone bright as the lamp
of life burnt down into the socket."[1]

Alline's *Journal* was not actually published until 1806, but it is
clear that manuscript versions of the journal were circulating in Nova
Scotia as early as 1789. These manuscript journals were laboriously
copied as they were passed from community to community and from
New Light family to New Light family. In this process Alline's *Journal* became a source of inspiration to his followers and also a guide-
book for spiritual and evangelical behavior. Alline's experiences
were therefore as important as, if not more important than, his some-

---

1. Henry Alline, *Life and Journal*, p. 180.

55

times confused, disjointed, and heterodox theology. Nova Scotians and later New Englanders could relate to Alline as a person very much like themselves. He was one of them and each line of his *Journal* emphatically underscored this fact. If he could experience spiritual ecstasy, then they could. If he could recover from his intense morbid introspection, then they could. And if an uneducated tanner and farmer, in his late twenties and early thirties, could help to bring into existence a widespread religious awakening, then they could as well. Alline, in a very real sense, became a symbol and a popular hero; his life was convincing proof that with God all things were indeed possible.

Alline's *Journal,* in my view, is a remarkable document—one of the two or three most illuminating, honest, and sensitive accounts I have read concerning the spiritual travails of any late eighteenth-century North American evangelical. The *Journal,* in other words, is not only a significant historical document within the somewhat limited context of Nova Scotia development but also within the much larger matrix of American religious life and society. The *Journal,* as Jack Bumsted has recently pointed out, may merely represent ''advertisements for myself in terms of self-mythology rather than self-publicity.''[2] On the other hand, it may be argued that the *Journal* in fact combines ''self-mythology'' and ''self-publicity'' and this combination helps to give the document its exciting and evocative style.[3]

The *Journal* is not really a journal at all and this point needs to be emphasized. In fact, only four pages of the printed *Journal* (pp. 215–18) are ''almost certainly drawn unedited from Alline's contemporary 'journal.' ''[4] Everything else in the printed text is either ''straight autobiography written years after the events described''or else Alline's often carefully edited version of this original journal kept in his unique shorthand.

What follows from the *Journal* is Alline's autobiography up to

2. See Bumsted's review of *Ravished by the Spirit* in the *Canadian Historical Review* LXVI (Dec., 1985):617.

3. For a ''literary'' approach to the *Journal,* see Jamie S. Scott, '' 'Travels of my Soul': Henry Alline's Autobiography,'' *Journal of Canadian Studies* XVII (1983): 70–90.

4. David Bell, ''All Things New,'' *Nova Scotia Historical Review* 4, No. 2 (1984): 78.

July 1776 written years after the events he actually describes. It is not surprising that this section captured the attention of William James, who in *Varieties of Religious Experience* (first published in 1902) made excellent use of it as he endeavored to come to grips with the experience of regeneration.

HENRY ALLINE, THE LIFE AND JOURNAL OF THE
REV. MR. HENRY ALLINE (BOSTON, GILBERT AND DEAN 1806),
3–47

CHRIST is the fountain of life, the source of happiness, the glory of angelic realms, and the triumph of Saints, and I trust is the life of my soul, the joy of my life, my present and everlasting portion. I therefore desire, and intend by his grace that his name should be my theme, until the last period of my days. And O, may his blessed Spirit be breathed into all my endeavours, may his love sweeten all my trials, invigorate all my labours; may his name fill up every period of my life, when in private, and every sentence, when in public: and hoping that he will cause me to write and leave amongst the rest of my writings this short account of my life. And as that is my design, I shall not overburden the reader with a relation of many passages that would be of no benefit, but shall only relate that, which may be worth the reader's perusal.

I WAS born in Newport, in the government of Rhode Island, in North America, on the 14th day of June, 1748, of William and Rebecca Alline, who were born and brought up in Boston, who gave me an early instruction in the principles of the christian religion. I was early sent to school, and was something forward in learning; was very early moved upon by the spirit of God, though I knew not then what ailed me.

THE first moving I remember was, when about eight years of age, by some discourse between my father and my eldest sister, in a thunder-storm, when I heard her say, that she had reason to be so distressed, that if she should be killed with the lightning, as many had been, she should go right to hell. I heard the words, and they struck me to the heart, thinking within myself, what that could mean, and saying to myself, what is that hell, I began to recollect what I had been taught about hell; which before I had thought no more of, than to repeat the words, as they were taught me: and as I thus pondered (though so young) I began to have horrible conceptions of that place, and often said to myself, what, is my sister Rebecca going there? what, is she going to hell? This distressed my soul to that degree, that I went to bed, and began to cry, and to pray to some great God, which I began to conceive of; for I had before thought no more of prayer, though I was taught (and my father prayed in his family every night and morning) to repeat a number of words, as I did my lesson at school; but I now began to think there was a heaven and hell; that there was a God, who was such a hard hearted and cruel being, that there was need of praying a great deal, to get him pleased, and get his favour, and did not wonder, that my father prayed so much; I thought if he had not prayed so much, we should all be sent to hell.

I NOW used to pray at every opportunity, even while I was walking along, when going to school, or elsewhere, that this angry God would not send me to hell. I used likewise to pray for my relations, that they might be all saved. I would sometimes give way to play and vanity with my playmates, and then I would think that God was more angry than ever, and so I would pray and confess, and promise to make it up.

I NOW began to examine and study what I read, and what I was taught in my catechism, that Adam had rebelled, and that all the world must be sent to hell and be punished with all that could be inflicted on them for that sin, excepting here and there one, that God had picked out, and the rest, though they were invited to come to Christ, and a sort of sham-offer of salvation made them, yet there was none of them, neither did God intend to save them, when he made them the offer, and yet would punish them to all eternity for rejecting Christ, when there was no Christ for them.

SUCH blasphemous, but natural consequences arose from what I had been taught; which caused me to conceive God to be an ill-natured, cruel being, pleasing himself with seeing and keeping poor creatures in everlasting torments, and then I would tremble, sometimes expecting he would sent me immediately to hell, for charging him with it in my mind, and yet I could not help it, for I was still obliged to think so. Thus I was led to think of God as bad as of the devil by that blasphemous doctrine, that God decreed or fore-ordained whatsoever comes to pass, and consequently the death and damnation of the greatest part of the world, and yet made them an offer of salvation, when there is none for them; and thus they make him a dissembler, and charge him with hypocrisy; offering to a poor soul, that which he doth not design he should have.

WHY will they dress up a loving, good (yea all good) and glorious Being, in such a black and ridiculous habit? Why will they drive poor bewildered souls to hell with not only such shocking blasphemous thoughts of God, but likewise despairing of any mercy from him? Why do they not let God speak for himself, when he swears by himself, that he has no pleasure in the death of the wicked? Why do they not let sinners know, that he has said, that it is not his will that any should perish, but all should come to the knowledge of the truth, and trust that whosoever will, may come? And instead of telling sinners that God will damn them and send them to hell, if they live in their sins, why do they not tell them that they are already under the curse of a hellish nature by their own sin, which they acted in Adam, and those that reject salvation and love darkness rather than light, they make their own hell, and go to their own place, and that their own nature will torment them and be at such an enmity and rage against God, as will exclude them from all possibility of ever receiving help by the love and mercy of God, for there is nothing they so much hate and will so much rage against, as the love, goodness and purity of God.

I STILL remained distressed in mind a great part of my time, and though my plays often led me away for hours, yet I was not happy in them; for I thought myself in great danger, and often, when writing at school, would so ponder on my miserable condition, that I could scarcely keep my distress concealed. O the unhappy hours I waded through, and knew not what to do, neither did I reveal my mind to any one. I would often go up in the garret, where I could see the burying place, and many younger children than I was, carried there, and thought I would give all the world, if I knew where they were gone; and would cry as if my heart would break, and pray to this unknown Being, that he would not send me to hell, and that I might not die, until I knew how to prepare for death; for I thought there was something to be done, which I could do, when I was grown up. I still felt a continual fear, that I might die; and if I should, Oh, the thoughts where I should awake. I often in my heart felt angry with old Adam, and thought he was very foolish, and ought to have punishment for ruining himself and all his posterity only for the sake of a few apples, or some other sort of fruit, as I thought, yea and many, many professed christians do think still, that trees of that paradise were corporeal.

WHEN I was about nine years of age, I began to read much in the books that I could understand, and studied much to find out how to get in favour with the great invisible God. I went to meeting almost every Sabbath and some would tell me about the stars, and great things that God had made, and others the necessity of externals, and being moral, &c. but I do not remember, that ever I heard any one of them adapt their discourse to the capacity of children, and tell them in plain words, that they must be born again by the spirit of God, and that they must feel and know this new birth each one for himself. Indeed, I suppose, that if the minister in many churches and societies was to leave his old town [tome], or old paper that he is reading, and begin with the young people and children, asking them what they knew of conversion and impress the immediate necessity of the knowledge of the spirit of God in their souls, it would be so new, that the people would start and stare, as if the man was running wild. O what a curse are such poor formal blind leaders! Lord have mercy on them, and open their eyes, and save the poor souls, that they are leading to perdition, before they are gone beyond recovery.

WHEN I was about ten, I had got something of a theory of religion, but it did not satisfy me; I was much afraid of being called away by death, and O the distressing thoughts I had of dying and going I knew not where; yea I was afraid of death, that whenever I felt any pains in my body, I would tremble, thinking was some disorder, that would carry me off; and whenever I went a swimming with my mates, I would pray, that I might not be drowned; and almost every night I went to my bed, I was afraid I should die, because I could not die praying.

IN the year 1760, my parents (after a long consultation) concluded to move to Nova-Scotia; this filled me with hope and fear: I had great desires to live in the country; I thought there were many things in the country to amuse me, and make me happy, that there were not in a town; and I thought myself wearied with everything that the town afforded me: but still I had two things that I greatly feared in going; the one was the danger of the sea, the other was the fear of the Indians in that country. However upon the whole I rather chose to go than stay, and though we had a long passage, we were carried safe into Nova-Scotia, my parents with seven children. I was now for a short time pleased with the country; I thought I should enjoy happy days, but alas my joys and hopes were soon eclipsed, when it was frequently reported, that the Indians were about rising to destroy us; and many came out among us with their faces painted, and declared that the English should not settle this country. And now I was more uneasy than ever. I did not think myself fit to die, and expected to be killed. I was so distressed, that I have laid awake many and many an hour, sometimes almost all night listening, and often thought, when I heard the dog bark, or the cattle walking round the house, that they were really coming or come; and what would be the consequence? why they would kill us, and I was not fit to die: and O then the racking thoughts, perhaps in a few hours or minutes I should be in hell. O no tongue can tell what I endured. I still continued praying and watching over all my outward conduct, and guarding against every public vice, still hoping that I might yet obtain the favour of God, and be saved from everlasting misery. The days I spent (when I was not about some worldly employ) much in walking in the fields and in meditation, and the more I contemplated my own state and the certainty of death at some uncertain moment, the more distressed I was, and found that the scenes and pleasures of a country life would not satisfy me, and I began to wish myself back again with my mates and the amusements of the town.

THUS the poor awakened soul in his distress is seeking and roving here and there, and every scheme he can contrive to find peace, rest and happiness fails him, and can find nothing beneficial to his poor, starving wandering soul, until he finds the Lord Jesus Christ. And as for him, they have no knowledge of him any further than a historical account, which will not satisfy a soul under deep conviction. Thus I was wandering night and day in this distressed state, loaded with guilt and darkness, and a stranger to one moment's solid rest or true happiness. All the glories and joys of creation appeared empty, and yet my mind like a drowning man, who will catch at a straw, would catch at this and that prospect of some enjoyments here on earth, or better days by and by: but oh they all failed me. Many were the temptations I was led into by my dark mind: once for a considerable time I was led to believe that God had neither love nor regard for any of his creatures, but would leave them all in misery, and only give them all existence without taking any care of them: I would say within myself, I know not who or where he is, and I see all mankind in some degree of misery, want and disappointment, and I see almost all that I see, with their knowledge and attention in this world, without discovering any knowledge of or relation with that God they pretended to know. And when I saw the darkness, ignorance, stupidity and misery of this miserable race rushing to the eternal world without any visible manifestations of God's care over them, or concern for them, I could but conclude, that the fall of man was true enough; for I felt and saw the misery, but that their recovery or mercy from God through Christ towards them, was all uncertain: for how could we know there was any more truth in that history, than in the alcoran of Mahomet?

OH the distressing days and unhappy nights, that I have waded through! nothing but darkness, nothing but distress and slavish fear. Sometimes when I was wandering in the fields, I would throw myself down on the grass, and lament as if I should go into despair: and it is a wonder of wonders that I did not embrue my hands in my own blood. I still continued praying to this unknown God, for although I had not much hope there, yet it was my last resource. I thought if sickness was to come upon me, I should go into despair; but it was not so: for when I was about fourteen years of age, I was taken down, and my bodily disorder so stupified my mind, that I had no more sense or concern for my soul, than a beast, or than if I had no soul; and although I heard the doctor tell my mother, when asked what he thought of me, say, that he believed I never should recover, yet it did not even cause one thought, as I remember, what would become of my soul, or when I should awake: I felt a desire for ease from my pains, but was so stupid, as to have no concern at all about those eternal things, which before had so employed and racked my attention.

I NOW began more earnestly than ever to seek this unknown God, praying every opportunity; did read and study much, by which I soon attained to a great theory of religion for one of my age, and got a considerable Babel built up; but oh the temptations and trials that I now began to fall in, which almost drove me to despair. I first began to be puffed up with a conceit that I was endowed with uncommon gifts and powers of mind, which if improved, I should be able to find out and fathom that long hidden mystery, Eternity. I began to embrace the temptation, and to pursue the hidden mystery and dive for the bottomless ocean.

> Soon did the devil with all his whiles control
> the active pow'rs of my deluded soul;
> Presumed to unfold the depth unknown
> To all, but the eternal God alone.

O ETERNITY, eternity, unfathomable eternity! The joy of the righteous, but the dread of the wicked. I now spent hours and hours poring on this unknown mystery; not expecting to find any period to this never ending duration; but that I might find the consistency of an endless duration and the nature of it; for I did not believe that eternity ever had any beginning or should ever have any end, but expected to get so far into the mystery as to see clearly how it was that eternity was in itself a duration without beginning or end: yea I thought I never could be happy, until I had thus far comprehended the mystery: neither had I any thought all this time, that I was under a temptation, or guilty of any sin in attempting it, but rather imagined that it was my duty; that I might likewise be able to communicate the mystery to others, although I had already found by woeful experience the unhappy consequences of my folly: for I had been so intense and engaged in the pursuit of this mystery, that sometimes I thought my soul and body would have parted asunder, and my mind was in such a confusion as to border on despair. Often times I would sit down in my private hours, or at my work, with a determination neither to leave the place or subject until I had some insight in this infinite mystery. Then I would begin to extend and stretch every faculty of my soul through a long succession of future ages, and would sometimes imagine, that I had almost fathomed the mystery. Thus being encouraged and hurried on by the grand Adversary, would still stretch my conceptions, grasp a repeated multiplicity of years, and millions of ages in futurity, I being still so impatient to conceive of duration, soaring into the infinite ocean, until I was almost racked to despair: for all the conception I attained to at last was, that I found myself a mystery of unhappy existences between two inconceivable eternities, or as an unextinguishable spark of life hanging over or fluctuating in an infinite, unbounded abyss or bottomless ocean. When I was in this almost despairing moment by these distressing views, the devil would tell me, that in a continued duration and perpetual round of existence, it was not in the power of God himself to make any of his creatures happy; for the greatest pleasures and happiness, that could possibly be enjoyed by a continual succession or repetition, would become a torment. Oh what racks of horror and despairing views I would then be in, beyond what tongue can tell. Being in such a distress I would rise up, and leap, and step, and then stop and turn and stalk about like a mad man, or a frightened ghost, when I have been in the field, or my private walks; at the time being filled with blasphemous reflections against God, because he had given me an unhappy existence, that could never be extinguished, and yet could not bear the thoughts of annihilation. And thus I may say I have been times without number, both night and day, on my bed and in my solitary walks, by this temptation plunged into inexpressible horrors and racking views of despair; yea I thought never a poor soul could be in more horror on this side of hell; so that I was many times constrained to cry out with an audible voice and horrid groans. And although the devil had almost made me believe that it was not in the power of God to make me happy, yet I remember, that the first words that I would generally express, when I was in such scenes of horror and distress, would be, O Lord God, O Lord God, have mercy on me, have mercy on me, have mercy on me! O Lord God have mercy on me, have mercy on me, have mercy on me, &c. with a great many more such repetitions, until that God, who was more merciful to me than I was to myself, would in some measure retrieve me from the verge of despair, give me a gleam of hope, that there was a who can tell, but that God is able to make me happy, if I was in heaven with him. Thus I was hurried and driven by the devil and my own heart almost to despair, and nothing but the mighty power of God kept me from laying violent hands on myself; and although I began sometimes to be convinced, that it was a mystery that never was, nor never could be known or unfolded by men or angels, yet when the devil would come again with his infernal snares, and tell me that I had almost found out the mystery, and that if I would try once more, I might unfold the whole, I would again summon up every faculty of my soul to follow the suggestion.

> So like a fool, swift for destruction bent,
> Then re-inforc'd, and to the battle went:

Nor would retreat, until a venom'd dart
Turning with fury to my bleeding heart;
Then would my tortur'd soul despairing cry
Forgive me Lord, and save me, lest I die.

O MY soul, never forget the hand, the blessed and invisible hand that kept me from embruing my hands in my own blood. Ten thousand praises belong to the Lamb, that kept me from the jaws of the roaring lion, and interposed between me and eternal ruin.

THUS for three years I was racked in diving into that infinite unfathomable mystery. O eternity! eternity! incomprehensible eternity! known by none but God, and yet the existence of every soul, both of the wicked and of the righteous: and unhappy only are they who are prepared for a blessed eternity. And O will the wicked endure everlasting night? and O blessed, forever blessed be the Lamb: he not only warned me from that eternity of unspeakable misery, but likewise convinced me of the danger I was in, while out of Christ being wholly exposed to take up my miserable abode in that bottomless gulf, and shewed me that unless I had an interest in his love I must certainly exist in keen despair, in that endless duration, which I had seen but a small glimpse of. I now began to see more of my lost, undone condition, than ever I had seen before. I saw that I was in the gall of bitterness and bonds of iniquity, and had no lot nor portion among the righteous, and therefore was exposed every breath to be cut off and drop into that bottomless gulf; and was now so sensible of my lost undone condition, that I thought I should never rest any more till I had found rest for my soul: and although I was again often taken in the former temptation, yet I continued seeking and begging for mercy from the unknown God. I was now very moral in my life, but found no rest of conscience. I now began to be esteemed in young company, who knew nothing of my mind all this while, and their esteem began to be a snare to my soul, for I soon began to be fond of carnal mirth, though I still flattered myself that if I did not get drunk, nor curse, nor swear, there would be no sin in frolicking and carnal mirth, and I thought God would indulge young people with some (what I called simple or civil) recreation. I still kept a round of duties, and would not suffer myself to run into any open vices and so go along very well in time of health and prosperity, but when I was distressed or threatened by sickness, death or heavy storms of thunder, my religion would not do, and I found there was something wanting, and would begin to repent my going so much to frolicks, and I promised to break off from bad company; but when the distress was over, the devil and my own wicked heart, with the solicitations of my associates, and my fondness for young company, were such strong allurements I would again give way, and thus I got to be very wild and rude, at the same time kept up my rounds of secret prayer and reading; but God not willing I should destroy myself still followed me with his calls, and moved with such power upon my conscience, that I could not satisfy my self with my diversions, nor attend them without some reluctance, and in the midst of my mirth sometimes would have such a sense of my lost and undone condition, that I would wish myself from the company; and after it was over, when I went home, would make many promises that I would attend no more on these frolicks, and would beg for forgiveness for hours and hours; but when I came to have the temptation again, I would give way, and promise that I would keep up a better watch, and not give way to be so rude and vain as I was before; and then thought, when I came away I should not be distressed, nor find any guilt on my mind: but when I went, the devil and my own heart, and the amusements of the time would soon make me be as wild as before: so sooner would I hear the music and drink a glass of wine, but I would find my mind elevated and soon proceed to any sort of merriment or diversion, that I thought was not debauched or openly vicious, or that I thought would be a blot in my character; but when I returned from my carnal mirth I felt as guilty as ever, and could sometimes not close my eyes for some hours after I had got home to my bed, on account of the guilt I had contracted the evening before. O what snares where these frolicks and young company to my soul, and had not God been more merciful to me than I was to myself, they would have proved my fatal and irrevocable ruin. O let all those that love their own soul flee, flee from carnal pleasures, and young carnal company, as they would from the gates of eternal misery; for it is poison to the soul, as ratsbane is to the body: such ways are the ways of death, and such steps take hold of hell; which sins I began to follow, when about seventeen years of age and continued in following them until I was twenty three, and part of my twenty fourth. O what a wonder that ever I was snatched from that alluring snare. The Lord still followed me, and would not give me up; I began to be more and more afraid of the condemning power of sin, and my lost and undone condition. I then engaged more closely into morality and followed my duties; but all did not take away the fear of death and hell: yea, I was so burdened at times, that I could not rest in my bed; when I had been to any frolick or into carnal company I was often afraid to close my eyes for fear that I should awake in hell before morning. I was one of the most unhappy creatures that was on earth. When I felt the least disorder in my body, I would be in such distress that I could hardly contain myself, expecting that God was about to call me away, and I unprepared; for although I was so strict in my morals, yet my religion would not stand by me in a time of distress or when death stared me in the face. Not that I thought being willing to die is sufficient to be fit to die; for the wicked have no hands in their death, but when a man's eyes are open, death is very distressing, without an evidence of being prepared.

GOD in his infinite goodness did not leave me to rest on a form of religion, but still gave me a sense of my lost and undone condition in a great degree: fearing almost everything that I saw, that it was against me, commissioned from God to call me away, and I unprepared: I was even afraid of trees falling on me, when I was in the woods, and in a time of thunder would expect that the next flash of lightning would be commissioned to cut me off. Thus I was one of the unhappiest creatures that lived on earth; and would promise and vow, in time of danger, that I would leave all my carnal mirth and vain company, and that I would never rest, until I had found rest to my soul: but when the danger appeared to be over I would soon return to my folly, though not without great reluctance; for the spirit of God wrought with such power that it followed me night and day, when I was in company or when I was retired; but I was so attached to young company and frolicking, that it seemed like parting with my life to leave them. Although many will say, they must wait God's time, and wait for God's irresistible power to put them in his way, and they wish God's time was come; yet for my part I have nothing of that to say, for I knew that God would not mock me; I knew that he followed me night and day intreating me to forsake all and accept him: and I knew that going to such carnal mirth, and hugging my idols was against his spirit and against my everlasting happiness; and yet I would go and hug my pleasures, still hoping and praying that God would not seize the forfeiture at my hands, nor leave me to myself.

I plead that God would let me enjoy my pleasures a little longer, and call me by and by. So I would of choice put off the Lord when going to my carnal mirth and company, would pray to God not to cut me off, when I got there, nor suffer me to give way to any sin; and thus I have not only stopped to pray as I was going, but sometimes prayed all the way, that God would keep me from sinning when I was determined to go, and rush on the devil's ground. I knew I could not refrain myself from sinning; yea I knew it was sin for me even to go in such company, if I remained wholly passive, when I got there; as I promised I would. O the subtlety of the devil and the deceitfulness of man's heart! If the Lord had not been infinite in mercy, I should have been lost for ever; for I still continued my evil ways, and hugged my idols. Sometimes when I knew that a great frolick was intended, which I wanted to attend, I would begin for sometime beforehand and keep up an uncommon watch and pray more often and more earnestly; so that I thought if I was left to be something rude and sinful, when I got there, for the sake of keeping up my name among the polite company I should not feel so guilty when I was there, or when I came away; and although I was thus chained to the covenant of works, yet I would not allow myself to think I had any self-righteousness, but intended to be saved by free grace. Thus one may see that the greatest pharisee and most strict moralist are ignorant of it, and will say, that he expect salvation by free grace. I believe thousands and thousands perish there forever, and go down to their graves depending on their own performances, for want of knowing what it is to depend on, and receive free grace; and imagine they do it, and do not know that they are deceived, until lost to all eternity. But O the goodness of God to me a wretch! his spirit still followed me and would not suffer me to settle down; for even in the height of my carnal mirth, I was often, while on the floor in my dance, so alarmed to a sense of my condition, that I could hardly contain myself, seeing that I was rushing against the bosses of God's buckler, with such dreadful views of the gulph of perdition beneath my feet, and the danger of my being cut off, and dropping into an irrevocable state, that I have often, while in the dance, cried out with mental cries, O Lord God, have mercy on me, have mercy on me, have mercy on me! and do not cut me off in my sins. Sometimes I would leave the company, (often speaking to the fiddler to cease from playing, as if I was tired) and go out and walk about crying and praying, as if my very heart would break, and beseeching God, that he would not cut me off, nor give me up to hardness of heart, but spare me, until I was brought to repentance: yea I had now such a sense of my lost and undone condition, and the emptiness of all those pleasures and earthly enjoyments, that I did not attend nor carry on the frolicks, because I found any happiness or sweetness in them, but only that I might keep up my credit among the young people; and not be cast out of their esteem, and despised by them; and I would make an excuse of that before God, alledging that I did not want to follow them, and took no pleasure in them, but that I must and thought it to be my duty to keep good fellowship with my neighbors, and keep up civil society, &c. and thus, wretched mortal as I was, I continued hugging my sins, and making excuses for them, and prayed to God to forgive them; still being burdened with a continual load of guilt, which I tried every way to cover or expiate, and at the same time pretended that I was depending on Christ. I was now more and more weaned from taking any delight in my carnal company, and instead of contriving to meet them or continue any frolicks, would labour hard to obstruct them by many excuses I made, but did not tell them the cause of it; and when I was constrained or overpersuaded to meet them, and drawn out to dance with them, I would often speak to the fiddler in French, to desist playing, who would make some excuse to them (to oblige me) that he was tired, although he knew nothing of the cause I had of so doing, and would break up the diversion as soon as I could; but O! when I got home to my bed chamber I had no more peace or rest than I had before, so that I could not sleep nor hardly lay in my bed, reflecting on my folly, for going at all, knowing certainly if I was to die, I should immediately drop into hell: rolling on my bed, I would call for mercy and pardon. Spare me, spare me, O Lord God, and cut not me off; forgive me, forgive me, O forgive me, or I am gone forever. Oh, what unhappy hours and nights I thus wore away, and my wicked heart would not bow, and though I was one of the most unhappy men on earth, yet I was so wicked that I was determined no mortal should know my state, lest I should be cast out as a poor, deluded, melancholy wretch! The distress of my mind was so great, that it was sometimes almost impossible to keep it concealed, and I often feared that the distress of my soul would break through all my fortitude; but I endeavoured as much as possible to dissemble in my countenance. When I met sometimes with merry companions, and my heart was ready to sink, I would labor to put on as cheerful a countenance as possible, that they might not distrust anything was the matter, and sometimes would begin some discourse with young men or young women on purpose, or propose a merry song, lest the distress of my soul would be discovered, or mistrusted, when at the same time it was a grief to my very heart to hear of any vain or carnal mirth, and would then rather have been in a wilderness in exile, than with them or any for their pleasures or enjoyments. Thus for many months when I was in company, I would act the hypocrite and feign a merry heart, but at the same time would endeavour as much as I could, without giving them reason to suspect me, shun their company. O wretched and unhappy mortal that I was! Everything I did, and wherever I went, I was still in a storm, and yet was taken to be one of the most careless, merry, and light hearted youths in the whole town. And indeed I continued to be the chief contriver and ringleader of the frolicks for many months after; though it was a toil and torment to attend them; but the devil and my own wicked heart drove me about like a slave, telling me that I must do this and do that, and bear this and bear that, and turn here and turn there, to keep my credit up, and retain the esteem of my associates: and all this while I continued as strict as possible in my duties, and left no stone unturned to pacify my conscience, watched even against my thoughts, and praying continually wherever I went: for I did not think there was any sin in my conduct, when I was among carnal company, because I did not take any satisfaction there, but only followed it, I thought, for sufficient reasons.

BUT still all that I did or could do, conscience would roar night and day. About this time, after repeated counsels and admonitions of my faithful parents, I went home one morning about two or three o'clock, when all was in bed, and I hoped asleep, because I feared an admonition: however my parents, although awake, acted the prudent part, not to speak to me then; fearing, I suppose, that I was then warm with my carnal passions, and omitted their reproof till the morning. When the morning came, I was in hopes it would pass by, but no; for although I had endeavoured to shun giving them an opportunity, as much as I could, yet when I came to the table at breakfast, they were wise enough to improve the opportunity, and begin in a tender but emphatical manner to reprove me for my conduct. After I had endeavoured to vindicate my conduct as much as possible, telling them, that I was not guilty of anything criminal or openly vicious; and that it was only a simple recreation, that was allowable, my mother replied, that although I might not be guilty of anything openly vicious or criminal; yet it was opening a door, that would soon lead me to it; and that she expected nothing less, but that if I continued, I should soon be guilty of almost every vice; and eternally ruined both in soul and body: and speaking in behalf of herself and my father, who was then at the table and engaged in the discourse with her, she said, Well, if you are determined to take no advice, but will have your own way, remember that it will not affect our happiness. We can but advise you, and warn you of your danger, but if you will go to hell and be forever miserable, remember you go for yourself; and further signified, that they should be as witnesses against me, at that great and dreadful day. Oh, those words were like pointed arrows, to my inmost soul, and struck the greatest blow than ever I had struck, to cut off my frolicking (although I did not wholly break off). What, said I to myself, shall I one day see my parents, (whom I do love as my own life) in heaven saying to my condemnation while I am in hell? O how can I bear the thoughts of that! I then immediately went out of the house, walked about in the field, crying and praying, as if my heart would break. What, said I repeatedly, shall my parents go to heaven and I to hell, and they rejoicing to see me miserable! O shocking thought indeed!

I NOW renewed my engagement for a reformation and watchfulness, and was almost ready to promise, that I would never go to any more of these carnal frolics. I now kept more close to my duties than ever I did, praying six or seven times a day. I have reason to bless God, that I was not left to split on that rock; a rock on which I believe thousands and thousands perish to all eternity. I remained yet in inexpressible distress, finding no rest to my troubled mind. The devil now set in with the cutting temptation, that I was not elected, and was the only cause, why I was not converted, or had not been converted long ago. God had chosen a certain number, which would certainly be saved to eternal life, and the rest were left and could not possibly be saved, do what they would; yea, he persuaded me to believe, that God by some unalterable decree had put it out of his power to redeem me, and therefore I must certainly perish to all eternity. A doctrine too much preached up by those that are the ambassadors of Christ as well as by the devil. There is no tongue can express, but of those that have experienced it, the unspeakable distress I was under. O, to think that my eternal state was already fixed in misery beyond any alteration or recovery! O, the thoughts of being a vessel of wrath to all eternity! This brought me to reflect on the divine Being; for as I thought it cruelty, I could hardly contain myself from blaspheming and cursing the God that made me; and did really wish many a time from my very soul, that I had never been born; yea, I envied every beast, stick or stone I cast my eyes upon. I thought O if God had been so kind to me as to them, how happy I should have been; but no, he has given me a soul to exist forever, and put me beyond a possibility of redemption. Thus I was filled with blasphemous thoughts and reflections against God. O how strong is the Power of Darkness in the fallen soul of man! And if there is so much guilt and darkness appearing now while in this imprisoned state, what will be the rage of the ungodly, when they are beyond all restraint, and awake like themselves in their own hellish darkness and rage. O the deplorable state of the fallen race!

AFTER a while I began to have a hope, that there was a possibility of God's saving me, and therefore I would try: but O it was but a little hope or expectation; and thus I continued the most unhappy wretch that walked upon the earth; knowing that God, who I thought acted altogether as an arbitrary sovereign, was to summon me away by death, I was gone to all eternity; and although I was thus exposed, every breath I drew, to keen and everlasting depair, yet I was not willing to be saved on the terms of the gospel; that is, cast myself wholly on free grace, and thought all this time, that God was not willing to save me. Thus I continued begging for mercy and fighting against it at the same time.

BY this time I had read, studied and disputed so much, that I had acquired a great theory of religion, and spent much time disputing on the controverted points, such as election, reprobation, resurrection, baptism, &c. although I never let any one know, that I was any way concerned about them; and I thought, I was capable to hold an argument with any one that I could find: but instead of getting my rest, I only increased my distress, for I thought I could deceive the very elect. Oftentimes when I went to bed after I had been disputing with my parents, I felt so much guilt and distress on my mind, that it seemed I could not continue in the body, thinking how I had deceived them; but found I was not willing they should know my state.

I now promised that if ever I discoursed again with my parents, I would discover to them any state; but O my wicked heart kept back; and what made it more hard for me to speak and manifest my condition was the darkness of the time; it was a time of Egyptian darkness. I have reason to believe there were no more than five or six christians in the whole town, and they sunk into death and formality: there was nothing of the power of religion, the travail of the soul; and conviction and conversion were scarcely mentioned; only externals, and duties, and commands, and different principles, &c. I read of many experiences and accounts of work of grace in the souls of others, and therefore knew that I had no portion in the kingdom of heaven: and when I read of many that were converted in the former reformation, and that in a short time; some being but a few days under conviction and brought out rejoicing; I would then murmur against God, because he did not convert me; and thought, if I was a sinner, I was not worse, nor what I was harbouring: the evil of my own heart was yet undiscovered: I little knew that I was a hell and damnation to myself in my own nature: I little knew that God was more willing to save me, than I was to be saved. Oh, the blindness and ignorance in the ways and nature of God I was in: I knew I must believe; yea it is held by many, that if I could once get God to be willing, I should be sure of salvation: and it is the thoughts of thousands, who profess to be christians, that they must labour hard to prevail with God to have mercy on his creatures, as if he was scant in his blessings, and sparing in his mercy, and therefore he was to be prevailed with by effective arguments, to give consent, that the blessing should be given as if his mind was thereby changed, when it is wholly the reverse; for his nature is such that he cannot be but merciful, and willing to do good to all his creatures; and there is nothing keeps it from awakened sinners, but their own stubborn will, which debars them from his love, and it would be proper to plead with God to remove our opposition.

ONE evening as I was taking a walk of about two or three miles to spend the evening with some of my companions (as I had promised) being alone and pondering on my lost and undone condition, as I was at this time almost night and day, the evening was very dark, but all of a sudden I thought I was surrounded with an uncommon light; it seemed like a blaze of fire; I thought it out shone the sun at noon day: I was immediately plunged almost in keen despair. The first conception I had was that the great day of judgment was come, and time at a period. O what unspeakable horrors broke forth immediately upon my soul: every power of my mind strained with terror and surprise. I thought the day of grace was over, mercy abused, goodness rejected, time at a period, eternity commenced, the infinite judge approaching, conscience awake, and my soul burdened with almost an unsupportable load of guilt, darkness and tormenting fear, and a bottomless gulf beneath me. All this appeared as real as if it were actually so. I thought I saw thousands of devils and damned spirits, by whom I expected to be tormented. No friend, no Saviour, no Mediator! He that made me would have no mercy on me, and he that formed me would shew me no favour; and yet I clearly saw that his throne was just and wholly clear of my blood. I had nothing to lay to his charge, for I saw how I had wilfully refused his grace, and rejected his mercy: all times and opportunities of repentance were now at a period, and nothing but loss, incessant loss, like a dagger shot through my poor distressed and almost despairing soul. Thus God shewed me in some degree for about three quarters of a minute, what it would be to meet that dreadful day in the condition I was then in, without a Saviour; and therefore informed me how exposed I was at every breath I drew, and what an awful day I must soon see if I am found out of Christ; yea, methinks I saw more in that short time than I could express in one week. I stood all this time with my face towards the ground, trembling in body, and sinking in my mind, not having power to look, nor desire to ask for mercy, because I thought the case was really settled with me, and therefore it would be needless to ask for mercy, especially when I saw myself so justly condemned; and O too late I was convinced of my folly. My distress was so great that I believe it continued half an hour, as it would have separated my soul from my body, for my very flesh seemed to consume off of my bones with the weight; everything conspiring to load me with unspeakable distress.

> O what a day! how will the wicked stand,
> When scenes immortal open to their view?
> All time deserted, mortal changes past,
> And they awake before the awful Bar,
> Where Grace and Hope to them are known no more.

THE first thought I remember, exclusive of reviewing the shocking scene, was to look behind me and see how far the burning flood and sweeping deluge, which I imagined to be coming after me, was from me, that I might know how long I should be out of hell, or how long it would be before my doom should be finally settled. When I lifted up my eyes, I saw, to my unspeakable satisfaction, that it was not as I expected: the day was not really come, therefore I had an opportunity of repentance, and a possibility of escaping from that awful and eternal gulf. O how my heart seemed to leap for joy, and at the same time began to groan for mercy. I found the day of judgment was not come, nor the world in flames as I expected. There appeared, as I thought, a large blaze of light in the shape of a circle, with that side next to me open as though it yawned after me, and as it drew very nigh me, it closed up in a small compass, then broke out in small sparkles, and vanished away. It is no matter whether the light, which I saw with my bodily eyes, was one of the common phenomena of nature, such as exhaled vapours or nitre, that had gathered in the air; it was not the less alarming to me; for I believe it was really designed by God as an alarming means, as much as if it was a miracle sent to me in particular. We are very apt to evade the force of many alarming calls from God by such things as are not uncommon in nature.

WHEN the light seemed to vanish, and the scene to withdraw, my whole soul seemed to be engaged to implore mercy and grace. O mercy, mercy, mercy, was every groan of my soul, and I began to make many promises, that I would never hear [bear] to sin as I had done, nor rest another day, unless I had found a Saviour for my poor soul. I thought very much of the goodness of God to me in giving me one moment more for repentance, and that there appeared yet a possibility of my being saved.

> In that distressing moment how I stood
> On the tremendous verge of endless death!
> While rending horrors from approaching ruin,
> And hellish fancies, poison'd with despair,
> And rappid torrents pierc'd my bleeding soul.
> O far beyond what mortal tongue can say!
> Till the Almighty, with a breeze of hope,
> Calm'd all the storm, and bid, tho'dire, be still.
> To whose great name, ten thousand thanks are due.

I THINK I was determined to spend my remaining moments at the door of mercy, begging for redeeming love, and if I never found mercy, to go down to the grave mourning, and die a beggar. I went to the house I intended, but did not join in any diversion: I told what I had seen, but not what effect it had on me. I did not stay long there, for my distress was so great, that I returned and went home to my father's. When I came there, they were all in bed. I went to my bedroom, and crying for mercy like a person in agony. I had still a clear view of what I had seen and what it was sent for; neither did I think, that I could ever close my eyes, until I found some relief; but O the subtilty of the devil and deceitfulness of my own heart! I had not been long in the room, before there was represented to my view a beautiful woman (one whom I had seen before, but had not great acquaintance with) and the happiness that I thought I might enjoy with her stole away my affections from thinking much of God or my state. The devil told me that I need not commit any sin for to enjoy her; that I might marry her, which was lawful: yea, I so acquiesced in the temptation, that my affections were after her, and she appeared the most beautiful object that ever I beheld. My passions were so inflamed with the prospect, that I thought I would not omit the first opportunity to go to see her and propose marriage to her. I thought I would be the happiest man on earth, if I might but have her for a companion for life. O the subtilty of that grand adversary, who might by this temptation have proved my eternal ruin, if God had not interposed. And I believe many souls are ruined so for ever, who in time of distress, and under some convictions, will turn away after the enjoyments of the creature, under a pretension of going in the way of duty. I had almost forgot my distress and unspeakable danger, but blessed be God, after I had been about half an hour captivated with the delusive prospect, he stepped in for my help, and by this blessed spirit struck my heart with conviction of my state and the dangerous snare I was plunging myself in; he shewed me that I was on the devil's ground, and far from performing the vows I had so lately made; and at the same time convinced me that if I remained in the state I was in, I must soon meet reality, what I had a faint representation of, and that if I give way to this snare I might grieve the holy spirit, and that it might prove the means of my eternal ruin; and blessed be his name, I was not only made to see the temptation, but likewise to detest it from my very heart, and enabled to withstand it. I almost spoke out with an audible voice, saying, get thee behind me Satan, for I see the snare; at the same time also saying, I will not go, I will not go, neither will I think of marrying or enjoying any thing in this world, until (if God gives me grace) I find a Saviour for my soul; for what will all these enjoyments avail me in a dying hour.

I WAS now more distressed than ever; for I saw more and more my danger, and the necessity of an Almighty Friend to stand by me for time and eternity. I spent not only almost all that night, but also the next day and many days and nights, being bowed down with guilt and darkness, crying for mercy. O mercy, mercy for my precious and immortal soul.

I NOW began to be tried with another very heavy temptation, which was that I had committed the unpardonable sin, and therefore was certainly gone, gone for ever. I remembered, that at a certain time some years ago, when I was in company with some young women, who were making a derision at people's waiting for the moving of the Spirit, I joined with them in the laughter and mockery, and although it was the spirit of God that convinced me of this sin and gave me a great sense of the evil of it, yet the devil now set in and told me it was the unpardonable sin; for when I was convinced that I had made mock of religion, and made light of speaking reproachfully of the moving of the spirit: he said it was the Spirit of God I had made a mock of, and therefore was lost forever; for all blasphemy against the Father and Son may be forgiven, but the blasphemy against the Holy Ghost can never be forgiven, neither in this world, nor the world to come. O the distress I was now in! The thoughts of being lost beyond recovery would rack almost my soul and body asunder, and I thought I would give ten thousand worlds, if I had them, to recall what I had done. O, how it would rack me night and day; but it was done, and I could not recall it; yea, and the devil was telling me that I had sinned against light and with malice, and therefore it could not be forgiven me: but though I did not know then, that there was any thing in my favour, yet my being so distressed for fear that I had committed that sin, and that I was so desirous to recall it, was a sufficient evidence, that I had not committed it, as I have been taught since. At length it pleased God to relieve me from this temptation, by shewing me that I had not committed it out of malice or spite, neither had I much light at that time.

MY distress continued still night and day; and O what days and hours of grief and trial I waded through, being locked up in darkness, and a stranger to all joy and happiness. Every thing I saw seemed to be a burden to me; the earth seemed accursed for my sake: all trees, plants, rocks, hills and vales seemed to be drest in mourning, and groaning, under the weight of the curse, and every thing around me seemed to be conspiring my ruin. My sins seemed to be laid open; so that I thought that every one I saw knew them, and sometimes I was almost ready to acknowledge many things, which I thought they knew: yea sometimes it seemed to me as if every one was pointing me out as the most guilty wretch on earth. I had now so great a sense of the vanity and emptiness of all things here below, that I knew the whole world could not possibly make me happy, no, nor the whole system of creation. Thus seeing that there was not a possibility of happiness in all the creation, and none to be enjoyed in God or his ways (as that appeared to me the only shelter from misery) I thought it was a cruel thing in God to make me or any other immortal spirit of such a capacity, as I found I had; for I thought he had made hungry souls but nothing to feed them; for I could not see any thing to feed me or make me happy, and therefore must be miserable forever. Indeed it is so great a truth, that all mankind have hungry souls, which nothing can satisfy or feed but God himself, that I would to God, those who profess to be the Ministers of Christ, would labour to convince their hearers of the disordered, distressed, hungry and self-tormenting nature of their own immortal souls; instead of telling them, that God is revengeful and vindictive, and that they must go to this and that duty, and forsake this and that sin to please God, or to get him reconciled to them: for although it was contrary to what our ministers preached in those days, yet the spirit that convinced me shewed me, if I could command ten thousand worlds, it would be all in vain, for it could not give my soul one hour's peace.

WHEREVER I went, or whatever I did, night or day, I was groaning under a load of guilt and darkness, praying and crying continually for mercy; yea I would often be so intent in prayer, until I spoke to him, and as soon as I left him, would immediately begin again to cry within myself for mercy, mercy, mercy, Lord God, have mercy on me; and while I was in company, was so distressed and sunk in spirit, that I could scarcely keep the anguish of my soul concealed; and would often, as much as I possibly could, counterfeit a cheerful countenance, lest I should be discovered; and thus for hours, being in company I have exercised all the fortitude I was master of, to keep the storm within under a suppression. When I waked in the morning, the first thought would be, O my wretched soul, what shall I do, where shall I go? and when I laid down, would say, I shall be perhaps in hell before morning. I would many times look on the beasts with envy, wishing with all my heart I was in their place, that I might have no soul to lose; and when I have seen birds flying over my head, have often thought within myself, O that I could fly away from my danger and distress! O how happy should I be, if I were in their place. O how hard it is for the stubborn will to bow, and the wicked to come down and give up all. They often imagine that they are willing to receive God's grace and God is not willing, but it is quite the reverse. He standeth, saith the prophet, behind our walls. We have reason, both saints and sinners, to cry to God continually to take away the opposition of our will, our own stubborn will, and the corruption of our nature, that God's grace and love might enter in; as it certainly would, as soon as all is given up: and this necessity of praying, watching and wrestling, is wrought in the soul by the spirit of God, to subdue and destroy the rejecting nature and stubborn will in the creature, that the meek and lovely Jesus might enter in. But I knew nothing of all this at that time, but thought that God could bring me in by an arbitrary power when he pleased, but would not.

FEBRUARY 13th, 1775, when about midnight I waked out of sleep, I was surprised by a most alarming call as with a small still voice, as it were through my whole soul; as if it spoke these words, How many days and weeks, and months and years has God been striving with you, and you have not yet accepted, but remain as far from redemption as at first; and as God has declared, that his spirit shall not always strive with man, what if he would call you no more, and this might be the last call, as possibly it might be; what would your unhappy doom be? O how it pierced my whole soul, and caused me to tremble in my bed, and cry out for a longer time. O Lord God do not take away thy spirit! O leave me not, leave me not; give me not over to hardness of heart, and blindness of mind. Sleep was for some time driven from my eyes, and I thought I would rather never close my eyes again than to run such a risk, and that I rather would spend every breath I had to draw in begging for mercy, and go mourning all my days, than to get away in a careless state. O the thought of being given up and sealed over to ruin, was like a mountain on my soul. From this time I continued, almost every breath I drew in prayer, excepting when I was asleep; but O how hard is it to be stripped of self-righteousness! I had begged, reformed, read, studied, and attained so much head-knowledge, and got such a theory of religion, that it was almost impossible for me to be stripped and become a fool.

ONE night awaking suddenly out of sleep, the thought came into my mind, that I might live seeking all my days, until I began to think myself to be a christian, and perhaps fall short at last. O how the thought distressed me! O how the thought of being deceived would tear my soul and body as it were asunder: yea I thought I would rather spend all my days in distress and begging for mercy, if I might but be converted at last: but then not to get a hope, without a living evidence of being on the rock of ages, even if I was a christian: for the matter appears to me so important, that I think I could rest without a living evidence of my everlasting welfare.

WHILE I was thus querying in my mind, and ready almost to despair under a sense of my danger, I thought I saw a small body of light as plain as possible before me; at the same time, being surprised, and not knowing what this meant, a small still voice spoke through my very soul, telling me, that I need not fear knowing my conversion, if I ever was converted; for although I was not certain that I ever should be converted, yet if ever I was, it would be as clearly manifest to me, as that light. Which light, let it be what it would, I know I saw it so clearly, as to be indisputable that I saw it; for God, who, I doubt not, discovered that to me, could likewise discover his love to me as much beyond dispute. At the same time I seemed in some degree to be affected under a sense of God's condescension, and wondered that he should stoop so low; but could not get hold of any thing that would support my sinking spirit, nor remove my burden of fear and distress; for I still harboured some self-dependence, that kept me from bowing to the Redeemer. O the pride and stubbornness of man's will and nature, that will rather catch and hang upon any thing, than to give all up to Jesus; and there is no way for him to be redeemed, but by yielding all up, flinching from himself and being willing God should be all in all.

Just as a man, rack'd on the wat'ry grave,
Grasps weeds and straws his drowning life to save,
And fears to leave what will not grant relief,
So my poor soul, when trembling on the brink
Of endless death, expos'd each breath to sink,
Yet hugs himself and harbours unbelief.

ALTHOUGH I never yet had any thing sent home to my heart or any thing that I could get hold on as a foundation, nor would allow myself to think that I was born again, yet I still retained a secret dependence on something of my own, and would not give up all to the Saviour: And although my happiness was all taken away and I saw more and more the emptiness of all things here below, for all pleasures and amusements failed me, yet I would not go hungry to Christ alone. Yea, though all friends stood aloof from my sore, and millions of worlds appeared insufficient to make me happy, and the Saviour standing at my door to undertake for me, and be a complete Saviour and my portion, yet O my proud heart and stubborn will stood it out, and would not wholly give up to his will. O the contrariety of man's nature to the nature of God. Thus I still remained nights and days, weeks and weeks, wandering up and down the world, under the curse of sin and death, without one moment of peace or settled rest; seeing nothing in Christ neither, that was worth aspiring after any further, than to keep me from misery; for as yet I saw no beauty in Him, nor happiness in his ways: but still hoping that God would convert me, and bring me to enjoy something I could not tell what, and would still plead with God to undertake for me: and although I would not have suffered to expect salvation any way by my own works either in the whole or in part, yet all this time I was endeavoring to do a part, and would sometimes think that my prayers and fears would prevail with God, and sometimes that my being so engaged, so affected, and so humble, would affect God, and cause him to pity me, and be willing to convert me. And thus it is that children often imbibe such conceptions of God, by hearing of vindictive wrath and incensed justice in him; therefore, when awakened, will labour a thousand ways to pacify or reconcile God. I think it would be far better to teach them, as it really is, that God is nothing but love and goodness, waiting for sinners to be reconciled to him; and that all the wrath and darkness, anger and punishment that there is, is in themselves, which could be more likely to convince them of the necessity of a change of nature, and excite a more speedy escape to the great Redeemer.

I HAD got so much light that I knew almost as much as a christian in my head, but had nothing saving in my heart; but I had such a doctrinal knowledge of the necessity of conversion, that I thought it would be the most shocking judgment that could befall me, to be left unmindful or careless of the one thing needful: yea, I retained a fear, that I might sit down short of Christ, or forget my exposed state, that I now was in, and must be in, until converted. There was nothing I more feared, than getting back into my former state of security, so as wholly to forget my lost and undone condition. About this time I endeavoured to find out some way to prevent my falling into an insensible condition, or forget what I now saw of my miserable condition; for which end I concluded in my mind to engrave upon some large rock, in some private place in the woods, a few very striking sentences, that would express the distress I had once been in, or what I had once seen, and that I was still in the same lost and undone condition, and as much exposed unless I was born again: and thus I should be alarmed, whenever I passed by that rock, which might prove the means of the salvation of my precious and immortal soul. But my distress increasing and for want of some instrument and an opportunity I kept putting it off, and so never completed it. O the inconsistency of my conduct! for had I got so away and returned to my former carnal state, as to have no sense of, or desire to seek for salvation, I should have had no desire to have seen that rock. Thus it is that man will contrive thousands of ways to bring some power of his own and to carry on the work of salvation himself: but if they will not hear Moses and the Prophets, neither will they be persuaded though one arose from the dead. My desire for salvation was now so great, that I thought I would willingly do or suffer any thing, that could be laid on me which would effect the work: yea, had it been possible, I would have been willing to have suffered the pangs of death a thousand times, to have purchased salvation, or obtain redemption and everlasting life. But O it was all in vain: conversion yet was unknown to me; yea at a greater distance than ever.

ONE evening I was at a house, where there were some people, who made a game of what they had seen of the New-Lights in New-England, where some of them had been and had seen them; and in derision cried out, they were converted, they were converted, and a young woman fell down on the floor and frothed out of her mouth, and cried, &c. which I knew she did by way of mockery: neither did I believe to be true, what they said of the indecencies they committed; although I doubted not, but that through an extreme distress of mind they might do some things that seemed rather indecent to the world: but I still believed, though I had not seen any such work, that it was the work of God; it grieved me therefore to hear them making such a game of it; yet I had not the power to speak in behalf of it, and thought if I did it, they would laugh at me; and so, though I did not join with them I held my tongue, which I ought not to have done. I now believe, that had I come out and spoke, God would have given me strength, and it might have been a blessing to my soul. One of the young women in the company said in these words (by way of laughter) Lord have mercy; I wish I was there to see how the creatures act; her mother (who professed to be a christian) replied, O Abigail, I would not have you go there for all the world, for you know that we are not our own keepers, and how do you know you might not be taken so too. O how this cut me to the heart; be taken so too, said I to myself, why I would crawl on my hands and knees, if it were possible, all my days, if I might be taken hold of, as I think they are, or feel, as I think they feel for all what you may laugh at, and deride them; and you, thought I, who profess to be a christian, to be afraid that your daughter should be there, for fear of being taken hold of: but she was not alone, for I have seen in my travels great numbers since, poor blind souls, that professed to be christians, yea ministers and members of churches, as much afraid of the power of religion as she was. O that God would shake not only the earth but the heavens also.

    I STILL found no relief for my poor distressed mind; my perishing soul was yet in darkness and in the prison of unbelief. Sometimes I thought I depended on my prayers and tears, and then would begin to labour to strip myself of them, and when I thought I had no dependence on them, I would depend on my not depending; and then I thought I might expect mercy, because I had cast all away. I knew that I must be humbled, and therefore would labour, as many poor benighted men do preach, to humble myself, to prepare the way for Christ, and strive to be holy and to hate sin before I got Christ.

How great the pride of all the fallen race:
How hard to bow to the Redeemer's grace:
How much to help their guilty souls they'll try,
Before they wholly on the Lord rely:
Reflect on God and oftentimes complain,
While offer'd grace is offer'd still in pain.

THUS I continued until the 26th of March, 1775, and there being no preaching in the town, that day I spent, yea all the day, in reading, praying and meditating, sometimes in the house, and sometimes walking in the fields, but found no relief from any quarter. As I was about sunset wandering about in the fields lamenting my miserable, lost and undone condition, and almost ready to sink under my burden, I thought I was in such a miserable case, as never any than was before; and did not see any prospect of ever obtaining any relief. O the thought of continuing in such a dark vault and distressing storm as I was in, how could I bear it, or what must I do! Oh, why did God make me to be thus miserable, and leave me, (as I thought he had) to perish in this condition, being a stranger to myself, to God and to all happiness. I returned to the house under as much distress as I could hardly bear, and when I got to the door, just as I was stepping off the threshold, the following impressions came into my mind like a powerful, but small still voice. You have been seeking, praying, reforming, labouring, reading, hearing and meditating, and what have you done by it towards your salvation? Are you any nearer to conversion now than when you first began? Are you any more prepared for heaven, or fitter to appear before the impartial bar of God, than when you first began to seek?

IT brought such conviction on me, and that immediately to my mind, that I was obliged to say, that I did not think I was one step nearer than at first, nor any more happy, or prepared than years ago; but as much condemned, as much exposed, and as miserable as before. Then were again in an instant impressed on my mind these words, Should you live as much longer as you have, and seek as much, pray as much, do as much and reform as much; as you have done nothing now, you will have done nothing then, and then what will you be the better? My soul cried out within me, no, no, I shall never be better, if I live ten or twenty years longer. Oh, what shall I do, what shall I say, or where shall I flee? I am undone; and if there be not some way found out, that I am a stranger to, and never stepped one step in, I am gone forever. O mercy, mercy, Lord have mercy on me, or I am undone to all eternity. And now I began to be stripped, and saw that I had done nothing, and never could do any thing. I had often thought that this was not right, and that was not right; I went wrong this way and that way; did not keep my watch this time or that time; which was the reason that I had not been converted; but if I had done so and so, and had not gone astray here and there, I should have found mercy before now, and I intend to keep a better watch, seek more earnestly, and seek more humbly, love, &c. and then I shall find mercy. But O these hopes and the ways I had so often and so long practised all failed me, and I saw that I could neither extricate myself out of my lost, undone condition, nor recommend myself to God by any thing I had done, or ever could do if I were to live a thousand years. And I appeared further from conversion than ever: for under some agreeable frames, when I felt my passions moved, I would hope, that I was nearer conversion; but now even all those agreeable frames were gone, and I found that I could neither love, pray, praise nor repent; but my heart felt hard, my will stubborn, my soul dry and barren, starving for want of one crumb of bread, all my wisdom and human prudence seemed to be gone, and I was as ignorant as a beast; and my original sin and fountain of corruption appeared ten thousand times greater and worse than all my actual sins. I cried out within myself, O Lord God, I am lost, and if thou O Lord dost not find out some new way, I know nothing of, I shall never be saved, for the ways and methods I have prescribed to myself have all failed me, and I am willing they should fail. O Lord, have mercy, O Lord, have mercy.

THESE discoveries continued until I went into the house and sat down, which was but a short time. After I sat down, being all in confusion, like a drowning man, that was just giving up to sink, I had nothing now to depend on, but on some invisible and unknown God, to whom I was continually groaning with groans unutterable. I have nothing now to support me, or help me, what must I do? or where shall I go? Will God have mercy on me, or must I sink forever? Being almost in an agony, I turned very suddenly round in my chair, and seeing part of an old bible laying in one of the chairs, I caught hold of it in great haste; and opening it without any premeditation, cast my eyes on the 38th Psalm, which was the first time I ever saw the word of God: it took hold of me with such power, that it seemed to go through my whole soul, and read therein every thought of my heart, and raised my whole soul with groans and earnest cries to God, so that it seemed as if God was praying in, with, and for me. This so affected me, that I could not refrain from tears, and was obliged to close the book, but still continued praying in the same words; for it seemed, as if I could repeat them almost as well without the book as with it. After I had sat thus for some time, repeating over and praying in that Psalm, I again opened the bible without any design to turn to any particular place; I cast my eyes on the 45th Psalm, the three first verses being different from the rest, came with power and energy to my heart; but did not still take hold of it as any evidence of my being converted, but things appeared new, and I could not tell what to make of it. About this time my father called the family to attend prayers; I attended, but paid no regard to what he said in his prayer, but continued praying in those words of the Psalm. As soon as my father had finished his prayer I immediately went to my bed-room without speaking a word to any one, and shut myself up in the room; neither can I say that I had any desire ever to come out or see a human face again, unless I found the Lord of Glory to appear for my soul with his love and grace, that I might know my Redeemer; for I thought I did not want to live any longer for any thing or every thing that this world with all that my nearest and dearest friends could do for me; therefore my cry was, why should I live in vain? If there is any mercy for me, O Lord let me know it to my soul's satisfaction. At the same time I could not bear the thoughts of falling short, but hungred, thirsted and longed after God and his love. O help me, help me, cried I, thou Redeemer of souls, and save me or I am gone for ever; and the last word I ever mentioned in my distress (for the change was instantaneous) was, O Lord Jesus Christ, thou canst this night, if thou pleasest, with one drop of thy blood atone for my sins, and appease the wrath of an angry God; as from what I had been taught, he appeared angry with me: although the anger, wrath and vengeance which I saw, was wholly in myself, by the hellish nature that I was possessed of. At that instant of time when I gave up all to him, to do with me, as he pleased, and was willing that God should reign in me and rule over me at his pleasure: redeeming love broke into my soul with repeated scriptures with such power, that my whole soul seemed to be melted down with love; the burden of guilt and condemnation was gone, darkness was expelled, my heart humbled and filled with gratitude, and my will turned of choice after the infinite God, whom I saw I had rebelled against, and been deserting from all my days. Attracted by the love and beauty I saw in his divine perfections, my whole soul was inexpressibly ravished with the blessed Redeemer; not with what I expected to enjoy after death or in heaven, but with what I now enjoyed in my soul: for my whole soul seemed filled with the divine being. My whole soul, that was a few minutes ago groaning under mountains of death, wading through storms of sorrow, racked with distressing fears, and crying to an unknown God for help, was now filled with immortal love, soaring on the wings of faith, freed from the chains of death and darkness, and crying out my Lord and my God; thou art my rock and my fortress, my shield and my high tower, my life, my joy, my present and my everlasting portion.

O THE astonishing wonders of his grace, and the boundless ocean of redeeming love! millions and millions of praises belongs to his name. O how shall I make the least return! O what a wretch have I been to stand it out against such love. I have long and often wondered, that God did not have mercy on me and convert me; but now I saw it was my own fault, and wondered why he waited so long upon such miserable rejectors of his grace. O how black appeared all my righteousness, which I saw I had hugged so long. And O the unspeakable wisdom and beauty of the glorious plan of life and salvation. I have often wanted some things in the world, and some plans to be altered, and wished this thing and that thing was not so, because it seemed hard, and not agreeable to my carnal mind and human reasonings; but I would not now have any alterations for ten thousand worlds. Every thing that God did was right and nothing wanting: I did not want then that God should alter any thing for me, but I was willing, yea chose (for it was the food and joy of my soul) to bow to him, to be ruled by him, to submit to him and to depend wholly upon him both for time and eternity; and it was the joy of my soul that he would be God alone forever. I wondered that ever an infinite God should turn a thought of mercy toward the fallen world, and be employed for the welfare of such a wretch as I saw I was. But O free grace, free grace! O how infinitely condescending was the Ancient of Days to become an infant of a span long to redeem perishing and immortal souls! He deserves their praises for ever; and my soul longs to praise him, for he is my prophet, my priest and my king: and this is my beloved, and this is my friend, O daughters of Jerusalem. O the infinite condescension of God to a worm of the dust! for though my whole soul was filled with love, and ravished with a divine ecstacy beyond any doubts or fears, or thoughts of being then deceived, for I enjoyed a heaven on earth, and it seemed as if I were wrapped up in God, and that he had done ten thousand times more for me than ever I could expect, or had ever thought of: yet he still stooped to the weakness of my desires and requests, made as before observed on the 13th of February; though I had no thoughts of it then, until it was given me. Looking up, I thought I saw that same light, though it appeared different, and as soon as I saw it, the design was opened to me, according to his promise, and I was obliged to cry out: enough, enough, O blessed God; the work of conversion, the change and the manifestations of it are no more disputable, than the light which I see, or any thing that ever I saw. I will not say I saw either of those lights with my bodily eyes, though I thought then I did, but that is no odds to me, for it was as evident to me, as any thing I ever saw with my bodily eyes; and answered the end it was sent for. O how the condescension melted me, and thought I could hardly bear, that God should stoop so low to such an unworthy wretch, crying out still, enough, enough, O my God, I believe, I believe; at the same time I was ravished with his love, and saying, go on, go on blessed God in love and mercy to me, and although I do not deserve thee, yet I cannot live without thee, and I long to drink deeper and deeper in thy love. O what secret pleasure I enjoyed! happiness and food that the world knows of: substantial food and settled joy. O I would rather be a door-keeper in the house of my God than to dwell in the tents of wickedness, crowned with all the dignities of this lower world, surrounded with all the enjoyments of time, and the most exalted pleasures of sense.

IN the midst of all my joys, in less than half an hour after my soul was set at liberty, the Lord discovered to me my labour in the ministry and call to preach the gospel. I cried out amen, Lord I'll go, I'll go, send me, send me. And although many (to support the ministry of antichrist) will pretend, there is no such thing, as a man's knowing in these days he is called to preach any other way, than his going to the seats of learning to be prepared for the ministry, and then authorized by men: yet blessed be God, there is a knowledge of these things, which an unconverted man knows nothing of. For my own part it was so clear to me, that I had not the least doubt, but I should preach the gospel; although to all appearance in the sight of man, there was none appeared more unlikely: for my capacity in the world was low, being obliged to labour daily with my hands to get a living; my father's estate was not very large, and my parents being almost past labour, I had the whole care of these temporal concerns. As for learning, it was true I had read and studied more than was common for one in my station, but my education was but small: what I had of human literature, I had acquired of my self without school-ing, excepting what I obtained before I was eleven years of age, for I never went to school, after I came to Nova-Scotia; so that if learning only would make ministers of Christ, as the world vainly imagine, I had it not: but, blessed by God, I trust I had that to go with me which was better than all the wisdom and learning; neither had I the least doubt, when I was near to God, of being not qualified, though after that, when I got in the dark, I had: but said with all my soul, I'll go, I'll go; send me, send me with the glad tidings of salvation and mes-sages of peace to my fellow-men: yea, my whole soul thirsted to go; and at that time found nothing of the fear of man or the storms and trials of a frowning world, in the way: although before I had any liberty for my soul from the 40th Psalm, those words, as before ob-served, were spoken to me: "Many shall see it, and fear, and shall trust in the Lord." O that ever God should make me instrumental in bringing one soul to the knowledge of a Saviour! O Lord, send me with meekness and humility.

I SPENT the greatest part of the night in ecstacies of joy, praising and adoring the Ancient of Days, for his free and unbounded grace, and rejoicing that God was about to send me with messages of peace, and the glad tidings of salvation to my fellow men; and thought, if I had a thousand tongues, I could employ them all to spread the Re-deemer's name, and to make manifest the wonders of his love to the children of men. O that they may taste and see the wonders of re-deeming love!

AFTER I had been so long in this transport and heavenly frame, that my nature seemed to require rest and sleep, I thought to close my eyes for a few moments; then the devil stepped in, and told me, that if I went to sleep, I should lose it all, and when I should awake in the morning I would find it all to be nothing but a fancy and delusion. I immediately cried out, O Lord God, can this be a delusion? O Lord, if I am deceived, undeceive me. My soul was immediately carried again beyond all fear of deception; for I could rest all my concerns on the Rock of Ages, and found myself in the arms of redeeming love. I then closed my eyes for a few minutes, and seemed to be refreshed with sleep; and when I awoke, the first inquiry was, Where is my God? and in an instant of time, my soul seemed awake in and with God, and surrounded by the arms of everlasting love.

ABOUT sun-rise I arose with joy, to relate to my parents what God had done for my soul. When I came from my room, my parents were just arising. I immediately broke out, and declared to them the miracle of God's unbounded grace to me, which so affected them with joy, that it almost overcame them, and what made it more astonishing to them, was, because I had never made known to them the distress I was in for weeks and months and years; though they after this told me, they had often seen me tremble, when discoursing about religion; and that though I did not discourse about my own standing, yet that my expressions and conduct often manifested, that I had an inward storm. When we had for some time discoursed on what I had passed through, I took a bible to shew them the words, that were impressed by God on my soul the evening before; but when I came to open the bible, it appeared all new to me, and I could not help mentioning many glorious promises I saw, and asked them many questions about them, as if they had never seen them before: for it seemed to me, they never had; or else, I thought, they would have told me of them; for how could they pass so carelessly by such expressions of love and condescension of an infinite God, as they now appeared to me. I then went to prayer in the family, returned public thanks to God for his infinite goodness to me, and unworthy worm of the dust, I believe, as I have thought since, that it must have been surprising to them, to have seen me thus bold to pray in public, when I had never been heard to speak even one word of my own standing, nor ever known to pray either in public or in private. O what happy hours we now had conversing about the Redeemer's Kingdom! I did not tell them any thing about my being called to preach, keeping that in my own mind; although I have since thought it was the work of the devil, to keep it concealed, for it kept me back from public improvement, longer than perhaps otherwise I might have done, and caused me to pass many a sorrowful hour, not knowing what to do; I having no one to tell my mind to, or ask advice from, who perhaps might have been instumental in God's hand of helping me out, and shewing me the way of duty. O how I now desired to be for God and for him only, and to live to his glory and the good of souls.

> O let my days and all my hours be thine,
> And lead my hungry soul to truths divine:
> Set me from ev'ry earthly lover free,
> And let me spend my mortal days with thee;
> To bring poor sinners round thy glorious throne
> And give the praise, O God, to thee alone.
> O let me never leave my Saviour more
> Till I shall reach that blest immortal shore,
> Bound up in thee, thy goodness to adore.

MARCH, 1775. Some account of my travels and the dealings of God with me from the 26th of said March to May, the year following.

LITTLE did I think now that I should ever have any doubts about my own state; for, I thought I should have nothing to do, but rejoice and walk in the light of God's countenance. I must acknowledge, that I lived a considerable time without any distressing doubts. I used now to walk out in private for hours and hours, and conversed with God oftentimes as with an intimate friend, and feasted on his love. The vanity, the pleasures, the grandeur, the esteem and the riches of the world appeared but empty sounds and shadows to me, and my soul rejoiced in riches and pleasures unknown to the world. O the happy days and nights I often enjoyed. I was enabled to forsake all my vain companions and pleasures, and was determined to bid them an everlasting adieu: and although I had before for nights and nights rolled and turned on my bed for fear of death, judgment and eternity, but now my heart would oftentimes leap for joy at the prospect of death; for I doubted not but I should go to my Father's House, and rejoice in his love forever. Oftentimes when walking out in the evening I would look up in the air, and think how my soul would rejoice to see the Judge of all the earth appear, who I doubted not but was my everlasting friend.

THE great trials that I now passed through, and burdens that I laboured under, was respecting my call to the ministry: the prospect of which, and how I should ever come out, would engross almost all my serious meditation; for I was convinced that I must preach, but knew not how, where or when. I was often afraid to come out, and often longed to come out: yea, wherever I went or whatever I did, I thought of little or nothing else: I would go to the Lord with it in all my prayers, pleading with him to shew me which way to begin.

IT was now published abroad that Henry Alline was turned a New-Light; for I talked much with young people about their evil ways, and what a wretch I had been in going with them in the way that led to death. Being one day at work with a young man, that had married my sister, he asked me, whether a man might not be born again, and not know it? I answered very positively; No, by no means, for although, said I, they may not know the very day or hour, yet the change is so great, that they will soon know it. This struck him with a great sense of his danger, as he had a hope before, though I did not know it then; and it never left him, until he came out rejoicing in redeeming love; which was but about one day after. Thus the glorious work of God began to spread in that dark land. It was astonishing to see how the conduct and behaviour of the young people was changed: frolicking ceased, and many began to be something thoughtful. I had been a leader of almost all the frolicks in the place, and therefore, although some of the youth were not awakened, yet they seemed to be deprived of opportunities to carry them on; and some became much engaged for the knowledge of a Saviour. O the reason that I should have to bless God all my days, if I could labour in the Redeemer's cause: yea, I think if God would give me my request, I would rather go in his name to my fellow men with the messages of peace, than to be a ruler of the whole world: and sometimes I so longed to be useful in the cause of Christ, in preaching the gospel, that it seemed as if I could not rest any longer, but go I must and tell the wonders of redeeming love. I lost all taste for carnal pleasures, and carnal company, and was enabled to forsake them. I still remained under great weight respecting my call to the gospel ministry; not knowing what to do, what to say, or where to go. Sometimes, when I got something cold, I would think, that it was all in vain for me ever to try; for it was impossible for me to come out, and attempt to speak in public: but when I got near to God, and my soul filled with his love, I saw I must go, and I longed to go, for it would have been very easy for me, believing that God would go with me:

but still the prejudices of education and the strong ties of tradition so chained me down, that I could not think myself qualified for it, without having a great deal of human learning; and although I sometimes had not the least doubt, but God had called me to the ministry, yet I could not believe, that it was his will, that I should preach, until he had found out some way to get me qualified by human assistance, for I thought I must go, but could not go without learning, neither could I believe that God expected that I should go without it. O the strong chains of tradition, and the great prejudices of education! how many trials and heavy hours might I have escaped, if I could have believed that God would or ever could call any one to the work of the ministry, with no more human learning, than what I had; or could I have believed that I was then called to go as I was. Oh, there was nothing but what I could have gone through or suffered, if I might thereby have been qualified to go. Sometimes I thought the prime of my days would be over, before I had found out any way for me to come out; and that I could not bear. O, my days were fleeting away and nothing done. I longed to be at work before the day was over and the night come when no man can work; and then, I must quit the world, and never be useful to souls. O how impatient was I for liberty, that I might be employed in the cause of Christ.

ABOUT April or May, 1775. I made known my mind to a man that married one of my sisters, who had been a christian some years. It seemed to rejoice his heart to hear that God was calling me to the work of the ministry; and told me, that he was convinced by what I had told him; and said he would spare no pains for my encouragement. He asked me what kept me from coming out immediately. I told him the whole reason was, because I had not a sufficient degree of human learning. O the prejudices of education and strong ties of tradition. He was under the chains as well as myself respecting human learning, in some degree. He advised me to apply myself immediately to reading and studying, until some door opened to me to attain to more learning. I still continued restless in my mind, not knowing what to do, nor which way to turn: for I knew that I must preach, but could not think it possible without college learning; and at the same time many trials and strong temptations began to beset me about preaching. The devil left no stone unturned to discourage me; but still the Lord was kind, and did not leave me long without a demonstration of his love and intention to bring me out, to go with me and to support me, so that I was often carried beyond all fear; but still I retained a strong persuasion, that I could not preach until I had acquired learning, and therefore must proceed to New-England, and endeavour some way or other to get learning there. Being now about the month of October, 1775, and hoping that God would open some door for me, I gathered what money I could, and although I got but a trifle for such an undertaking, yet I felt no way concerned about it, for I thought I should be provided for by some means or other. I then made known to my parents that I was going to New-England, but did not tell them for what; yet it was not hard to obtain their consent, as they were always very indulgent to me, and they had a great desire that I should go and see my friends, as I had many relations in Boston; and likewise as there was danger of young men being pressed to go to war; for it was about the time that the war broke out between Old and New-England. When I did set out my brother went part of the way with me towards Horton, for I was going to sail from Cornwallis. This brother was the only one I had, excepting brothers in law, and he has been a christian some years. When we were about to part, I told him my mind; he immediately gave me good advice, though I did not see it then; for he advised me to return immediately back, for if God had called me to preach, I was taking the wrong step; for I ought to come immediately out where I was called, and just as I was called. He could not persuade me to it, though I saw afterwards that this advice was good. He wished me the blessing of heaven, and we parted in great love.

I THEN went to Cornwallis, but found that the vessel was not to sail for some days, which was a great trial to me. I was impatient to be going, knowing that time passed away, and I longed to be preaching: thus it was with me. O the blindness of my mind respecting it! happy would it perhaps have been, if I had come out immediately, as God might have led me. I remained a few days, and heard that the vessel was seized, and would not get clear until the Spring. O the trial that I was now under; the devil setting in at the same time, telling me, I might now be convinced, that God had not called me to preach, because, if he had, he would have found out ways for me to have gone, and get learning, as he knew I could not preach without it. At the same time I heard from my relations, that they had all taken the small pox, and they advised me by all means to return, which I finally did (although with a heavy heart) and received with them the distemper by inoculation; as it was spreading through the whole town. Neither was the taking of it the tenth part of the trial to my mind as my disappointment was, I not knowing what to do, being still under great impressions about my call, which I could not throw off. We were all, by the great goodness of God, carried safe through the distemper. My father's family, and those that were married to my sister, and their families, excepting one infant. Indeed there was but one more, I think in the whole town, that died of the distemper. So uncommonly blessed was the use of inoculation.

I STILL retained a continual drawing to the work of the ministry, and was impatient to proclaim the everlasting gospel: although I sometimes feared, it was only my proud heart that aspired after a public station in the world, to make a great shew, and court the applause of men: but had I known how much it would have turned to the reverse, I might have had a weapon against the enemy; for although those that go without the power of the gospel under a form of religion, may have but few trials, and but little opposition; yet whoever goes in the name of Jesus with the power of the gospel must never expect the applause of the world, but on the contrary many frowns: but when I was brought near to God, and enjoyed his presence, I could say with all my heart (as I often told the Lord) that I would rather be called immediately out of time into eternity, than to be left to go in the name of God without his call, and without his spirit to lead and bless me, (it was now about November) and though I had been greatly attached to the world, courting its esteem and enjoyments; yet I think I could say with all my soul, that I rather would go with a dispensation of the gospel to my fellowmen (although the trials may be ever so great) if God would go with me, than to be the sole monarch of the universe.

ABOUT this time I was solicited by some of the officers to put in for a commission in the militia; I utterly refused to take one step in pursuit of it; yet after this, when I got a little in the dark, I began to wish that I had taken it; for that grandeur and the esteem of the world, which the devil and my own corrupt nature suggested, I might obtain by success in a few years, began to look pleasant to me, like Eve's apples, pleasant to the eyes, and a fruit to be desired: but while I was meditating on this, the Lord broke into my soul with the revivals of his grace, the sweetness of his love; and shewed me the vanity of all things here below, and the worth of souls, which gave me such a

longing desire to go forth with the gospel, and proclaim the Redeemer's name, that my soul cried out, Send me send me, O Lord God,
in thy blessed name, and take away all honour, but the glory of the
cross, and all commissions but a commission from heaven to go
forth, and enlist my fellow-mortals to fight under the banners of King
Jesus: and my soul rejoices to take it for my whole portion, while on
this mortal stage. Sometimes I feared that I was only imposed upon
by the devil and my proud heart, and tried myself, whether I did not
covet to have a great name in the world, and to become popular.

ONE day, being under great trials of mind, one of my brothers
in law spoke to me, and asked me if I was fully satisfied, that I was
called to preach the gospel? I told him yes. He asked me then, what
I was waiting for? If God had called me, I ought immediately to go,
and not wait for any more learning; God was able to give me all the
assistance that I needed. I answered, that although I was convinced
that God had called me, yet I could not think that it was his will for
me to proceed, until that he had given me more human wisdom.
Why, said he, has not Christ learning enough? Is he not able to teach
you in half an hour in his school, more than you'll be able to obtain
in the seats of human learning all your life? This I told him, was very
true; yet I thought I needed more of man's wisdom and learning than
what I had. He told me that my success in the gospel did not consist
in knowing so much myself, as in the spirit of God's going with me,
which certainly would go with me, if God had called me. I told him
if the Lord designed that I should preach with no more learning than
I had, he would certainly have made it manifest some way or other.
He answered, he thought it was already evidently manifest, when a
small number of people did meet in the town every sabbath day, and
I with them, and no minister, nor any one to give a word of exhortation; and I believe it would be very acceptable to the christians of
that society, if you was to improve. This bore much on my mind,
and led me to examine more closely, whether the Lord had really
called me; and what he would call me for, if he did not intend that I
should preach: but still I thought he was confined to human learning,
and that he would not send me without it; but would find out some
way to give it to me. O the prejudices of education! I had heard so
much of ministers coming through the orders of men, that is seemed
to be an infallible rule. But, blessed be the Lord, he still followed
me with divine impressions on my mind to that degree, that I could

hardly engage in any worldly employment; for it seemed as if it was not my work, and that I was out of my duty all this time. Oh, what a privilege it appeared to me, and what a happy prospect, when I thought I should one day speak in the name of the Lord God. The gospel appeared glorious, and my soul longed to be engaged in proclaiming the wonders of redeeming love. O, I could say many days and weeks, that I would have chosen it for my portion as long as life should remain, and prefer it above any blessing or enjoyment God could give me. Yea, sometimes my heart would leap for joy, when I thought of going in the name of the Lord, and would not regard any trials in the way, if God would only go with me, and give me strength equal to my day. Sometimes I did not doubt, but I should soon see the happy moment, that God would find out some way for me to go forth; and O when I got near to God, it would be the first request I had to make, that God would take me in his hand, and use me in his vineyard until my dying day.

ABOUT the 13th or 14th day of April, 1776, I began to see that I had all this time been led astray by labouring so much after human learning and wisdom, and had held back from the call of God. One day in my meditation I had such a discovery of Christ's having every thing I needed, and that it was all mine, that I saw needed nothing to qualify me but Christ; and that if I had all the wisdom that could ever be obtained by mortals, without having the spirit of Christ with me, I should never have any success in preaching; and if Christ went with me I should have all in all. And O what a willingness I felt in my soul to go in his name and strength, depending on him alone. I found I had nothing more to inquire into, but whether God had called me: for he knew what learning I had, and could have in the course of his providence brought me through all the seats of learning, that every man went through, together with all the orders of men but he had not; therefore I had nothing else to observe, but the call of God: and when I got near to him and enjoyed a sense of divine things, I was fully convinced (though in the dark I would often doubt) and was now determined to come forward the first opportunity I could get. The 18th April, being a day set apart for fasting and prayer, I came out and spoke by way of exhortation, had some liberty, but was under great trials the night following, when I was watching with a young man, that appeared to be near his end. The devil was all night against me, telling me that I had gone astray, and had no business to speak, and that I had wounded the cause of Christ in so doing: and so powerful and great was the temptation, that I was about to make a promise, that I never would speak again in public while I lived; for I had certainly gone astray; for if I had not, I should not be under such trials. But when I was about to make a vow, never to speak again in public, a thought came into my mind, that it was now not a proper time, for if I intended to make such a promise, I ought to take when I had nothing to encumber my mind, and when I should get near to God, with nothing to interrupt me: I then put off the vow until morning, intending to seek a convenient opportunity for it. Accordingly I went early in the morning in the woods, and endeavoured to lay my case before God, and the Lord gave me a nearness to him: and O what a change of mind I found; for I was willing then to make ten vows that I would speak, and that the first opportunity, which accordingly I did the next sabbath. I spoke a few words the Saturday before to my parents to know their minds, and although they did not dissuade me, yet I saw it was not agreeable to them. This was a great trial to me; and the devil made a great use of it for my discouragement, telling me, that I held them to be christians, and I saw they were against it, which was an evidence, that it was not the will of God. But the Lord carried me through it all; and I found I must go and speak before them; although I saw at the same time that it was disagreeable to them. They discoursed as if they were jealous that I was under a delusion; but two or three of my christian friends were exceeding solicitous for me to proceed: which by the Grace of God I did, and it immediately spread abroad over the whole place, and caused many to come out of curiosity; but the Lord gave me boldness to speak. I spoke from the following words: If thou are wise, thou art wise for thyself, but if thou scornest, thou alone shalt bear it. There seemed to be a great attention paid by some; although others made a scoff but some seemed to be taken hold of, and some christians took me by the hand, and bid me God speed: but all the trials I met from without were not equal to those within. I still continued improving every Sabbath-day, being sometimes in the dark and sometimes in the light; and when I was in darkness, and did not find the spirit of God with me, when speaking, I would be ready to sink, and thought I would preach no more; and when I got life and liberty again, my strength and my resolutions were renewed, and thus God dealt with me, and carried me through various scenes.

IT being reported at this time that Henry Alline was turned New-Light preacher, many would come from other towns, even whole boat-loads. Some came to hear what the babler had to say; some came with gladness of heart that God had raised up one to speak in his name; and some come to make a scoff, but it did not seem to trouble me much; for I trust God was with me and supported and enabled me to face a frowning world. The greatest trials I met with were from my parents, who were so much against my improving, as sometimes to leave the house as I was speaking. Oh, how it would cut me sometimes: but, blessed be God, he not only carried me through these trials but likewise so opened their eyes, that they were as much engaged for me to preach the Gospel, as I was, and would have plucked out even their eyes for my encouragement. Thus God was kind to me in every respect, and even worked for my good. He blessed my soul, supported my body, blessed my labours in some degree, increased my charges and my resolutions, lifted me above the fears and trials of the world, weaned me in a great degree from the flattering charms of this world of sense, and increased my faith.

IN July 1776, I was invited by one JOSEPH BAILEY to preach at his house at Newport. I accordingly went over, and found a great number of people attending: God gave me great boldness and freedom of speech in declaring the wonders of redeeming love: and although many came to watch for my halting, yet they seemed to be struck with awe, and some of the christians after meeting gave me the hand of fellowship.

ALLINE'S SERMONS

It was Alline's charismatic preaching that shaped the contours of Nova Scotia's First Great Awakening. He was widely perceived as a prophet "sent from God" who promoted a remarkable "Work of God."[1] Amos Hilton, one of Alline's most influential Nova Scotia converts, expressed in 1782 what he must have realized was a common opinion regarding Alline's so-called heretical views. When pressed hard by the Reverend Jonathan Scott, the Falmouth preacher's most bitter critic, on why he so eagerly accepted a message in which "all the Revelation of God's Word is over thrown," Hilton simply replied, "It was no matter of any great Consequence to him what a Man's Principles were if he was but earnest in promoting a good Work."[2] In other words, Hilton was arguing that in the midst of a revival it really was not important what a preacher's theology actually was. What was important, however, was whether he was truly an instrument of the Holy Spirit and his preaching precipitated conversions. This was the ultimate test of effective Christian preaching. Even Scott had to admit that most Nova Scotia Yankees regarded Alline as a supernaturally endowed leader. The people, he once sadly observed,

> throng his Meetings Night and Day—vindicate his Authority as one sent of God, and evidently approved of by

---

1. "Records of the Church of Jebogue in Yarmouth," P.A.N.S.
2. Ibid.

God—they are attentive to his Counsels, and punctual in
executing them without Delay—they become warm Advocates for a Number of his Doctrines, and quietly put up
with them all—they rely upon his Judgement in pronounc-
ing his Adherents converted—they approve of his examples, Walk and Behaviour, as coming nearer to that of the
Apostles than any they had seen before.[3]

During his preaching career in Nova Scotia and New England,
Alline preached hundreds of sermons. Only three of these sermons,
however, were ever published; the two Liverpool sermons preached
on November 19 and 21, 1782, were published by Anthony Henry,
the Halifax printer, in 1782 and the *Fort-Midway Sermon* of February 15, 1783, was printed by Henry soon after it was given. This
last sermon was reprinted twice in New England by the Free Will
Baptists, first in 1795 and then in 1797.

Alline, a typical New Light, was an extemporaneous preacher,
and despite the fact that his three printed sermons clearly highlighted
his unorthodox and highly personal preaching style, they were
preached without the wild and extravagant gestures of many of his
New Light contemporaries. The well-respected Liverpool merchant
and civic leader Simeon Perkins, for example, never criticized Alline's preaching style, regarding it as "very Good," "very ingen-
ious," and merely part of the New England Evangelical heritage.[4]
Perkins, however, denounced the "Wild and Extravagant Gestur-
ing" and the "over Straining his Voice"[5] of Allinite preachers such
as Harris Harding and the young Joseph Dimock. Alline, it should
be pointed out, did not preach with a high-pitched "Yankee New
Light whine" but rather made excellent use of his melodious, pen-
etrating tenor voice.

Little is known about how Alline's contemporaries actually
responded to the three sermons he eventually published. What is
known is that Simeon Perkins described the November 21, 1782,

---

3. Ibid.

4. D. C. Harvey and C. Bruce Fergusson, eds., *The Diary of Simeon Perkins, 1780–1789*, vol. 2 (Toronto, The Champlain Society, 1958), pp. 168–69.

5. Ibid., pp. 354–55.

Thanksgiving sermon as "a very Good Discourse."[6] A few months later, on February 16, 1783, the Liverpool merchant sensitively summed up his community's reaction to the Falmouth preacher:

> Mr. Alline Preached both parts of the day & Evening. A Number of People made a Relation of their Experiences after the Meeting was concluded and Expressed Great Joy and Comfort in what God had done for them. Mr. Alline made a long speech, very Sensible, Advising all Sorts of People to a Religious Life, & gave many directions for their outward walk. This is a wonderfull day and Evening. Never did I behold Such an Appearance of the Spirit of God moving upon the people Since the time of the Great Religious Stir in New England many years ago.[7]

For Perkins, Alline's revival had the same "Appearance" as New England's First Great Awakening. And it is clear that for Perkins and for most of his Nova Scotia Yankee contemporaries, Alline was carefully fitted in the Whitefieldian-Edwardsian evangelical framework. Alline's heterodox views were never mentioned by Perkins—only the "wonderfull . . . Spirit of God moving upon the people."[8] Hundreds of other Nova Scotians would have made precisely the same point and precisely the same connection.

Alline's sermons must be viewed within the context of his times, his theology, and his own personality. They must also be examined as sermons—as three extant sermons from the more than one thousand sermons Alline extemporaneously preached during his lifetime. He undoubtedly used many of the same points raised in these three sermons and much of the actual language in many of the other sermons that he preached as he crisscrossed Nova Scotia from 1777 to 1783. Alline did not have the time to prepare sermons; he preached as the Spirit inspired him and he soon learned

---

6. Ibid., p. 169.
7. Ibid., p. 177.
8. Ibid.

how to affect his listeners positively. He used language they could understand—earthy, sexual, simple, evocative, and often powerful. He instinctively knew how to link words together to create literary images that drilled into the human mind, first transforming doubt into agony and then agony into intense spiritual relief. For Alline, as for Augustine centuries earlier, effective preaching was the "ministry of the tongue" whereby the preacher succeeded in putting Christ in the worshiper's ears. Sometimes his preaching, "charged with emotionalism," delivered in a "fervent and eloquent manner"[9] in a resonating tenor voice, became superb poetry. Sometimes, the poetry was sung as a spiritual song, which was then immediately followed by an almost frenzied outburst of words directed at specific people in his audience. This too was an important characteristic of Alline's preaching. He loved to direct certain themes in his sermons at certain people—at the young, at the old, at the fishermen, at the community leaders, at the soldiers. People who heard Alline must have felt that he was preaching especially to them and hundreds positively responded to this form of directed intimacy.

It is not surprising that Jonathan Scott complained that Alline's books and sermons were "interspersed with Poetry calculated to excite and raise the Passions of the Reader, especially the young, ignorant and inconsistent, who are influenced more by the Sound and Gingle of the words, than by solid Sentences and rational and scriptural Ideas of divine and eternal Things."[10] Scott's observation tells us why Alline was such a success in Nova Scotia and Scott such a failure. Alline appealed to the "Passions"—especially of the young; Scott to the head—to the "rational." Alline articulated the novel, the experiential while Scott mouthed orthodox shibboleths. Alline's preaching triggered a widespread revival; Scott's "solid" and "rational" preaching resulted in indifference and spiritual apathy. Scott seemed to point back to an increasingly irrelevant Calvinist past; Alline, on the other hand, appeared to thrust his listeners into the future—a future promising "individual liberty" and eternal hope.

---

9. Maurice Armstrong, *The Great Awakening in Nova Scotia,* p. 82.
10. Jonathan Scott, *A Brief View,* p. 227.

SERMON
PREACHED TO, AND AT THE REQUEST OF
A RELIGIOUS SOCIETY OF
YOUNG MEN
UNITED AND ENGAGED FOR THE MAINTAINING AND
ENJOYING OF
RELIGIOUS WORSHIP
IN LIVERPOOL

[On the 19th of November, 1782.]

Dear Brethren.

ALTHOUGH it may be accounted arrogancy in me, yet I must omit that too common apology that preface most Books: *It was not my will, nor design, but the strong sollicitations of others introduced those lines to the publick.* For God forbid, that I should either preach or write any thing but what I would with joy and the greatest Delight spread (if possible) over the four quarters of the globe; and therefore with much satisfaction I answer your request not only rejoicing to find you possessed of such a godly zeal for the truths of the ever-lasting gospel: But likewise under a hope that God may make them of further benefit to your own souls (when I am far absent from you or cold in death) and likewise spread their usefullness where perhaps my voice may never be heard. And O should the spirit of God by these few lines hand one immortal soul to Jesus far more to you and me than all the applause of men, and dust of Peru; I have made some small (but usefull) additions to you (who heard the discourse deliv-ered) may observe, and now for your spiritual use and welfare I com-mit them to you as the service of your worthy servant in the gospel.

H. A.

A SHORT PREFACE

If aiming for the vain applause of men
From truths like these I must withhold my penn,
O if the frowning world I had to fear
These lines in publick never would appear:
But when my soul inspired with truths so grand,

(Tasting the clusters of the promis'd land)
And duty calls, I yield to the command.
And O that God may point them to your heart,
That you might feel, and with me share a part!
But if you wish to share the glorious prize
Let not tradition or your will arise,
To vail the scene, and darken both your eyes.
Be bigotry and superstition slain,
Then read with earnest cries a pearl to gain;
Like a wise bee search ev'ry field around
Extract where e'er there's sweetness to be found;
For if you would expell the shades of night,
Long as you live stand candidate for light.

*   *   *

SERMON

From Mark the 16, 5, And entering into the sepulchre they saw a young man sitting on the right side, clothed in a long white garment.

CHRIST! O that worthy and transporting name! well might the Apostle (and let me likewise) say, I am determined not to know any t[h]ing among you, save Jesus Christ and him crucified: For his name is not only a strong Tower, but likewise as ointment poured forth; therefore he is loved, and adored by virgin souls; yea he is God over all blessed forever more; he is the theme of angels, and joy of seraphs; he not only replenishes all heaven with his beauty, but with his smile hath brought many a mourning soul from the border of despair to Sion's chambers with songs of joy; yea countless millions from the Jaws of hell to the realms of everlasting light, with all tears wiped from their eyes, and their heavy groans turned to shouts of triumph. O! it was that name (let me say it with reverence and wonder!) that first taught my wandering soul the long lost paths of peace, and made me to drink of the long sought for streams of happiness, and rivers of pleasure, and ah! It is this Christ that I expect (when I am lingering

on the confines of the grave) will support and lead me, thro' the
dark caverns of death to the bright abodes of everlasting day, and
cause me to sing when terrestrial worlds are known no more, and
O that he might be my continual theme while mortal life endures,
and wholly engage my heart and tongue; especially at this time
when called to address this orditary! And ah! I can tell you my hearers it is with joy of soul, and gladness of heart, that I shall lift both
hand and voice to invite your attention to the glorious theme, and
intreat you to review (with me a few moments) the incarnation, life,
labours, sufferings, death, resurrection, conquest, and glory of the
world's restorer.

> Attend O mortals, ravished with that name
> Which angels lift on everlasting fame,
> While I with joy will lend my stamm'ring tongue
> To raise a note of that immortal song,
> Till we in heav'n unite the countless throng!

But O methinks my disorders of mind by my fall are so many,
my ignorance so great, my darkness so almost impenetrable, and my
distance from God so vast, that I am ready to say that (by being so
uncapable of doing his name justice), I shall but marr the glorious
theme; yet feeling an emulation even with angels, I must attempt the
subject, tho' I am but a worm; and O that he who inspired the heart
of Jesse's son to speak of his name in the great congregation would
release my imprisoned soul and loose my tongue (long clogged with
sin) to tell the world that Jesus reigns, and proclaim this day as the
disciples when they saw Jehovah riding the rude and unintelligent
beast blessed is he that cometh in the name of the Lord! Hosiana in
the highest! *(a)* and expecially while at this time I have the happiness
of taking a number of young men by the hand, to lead and incourage
them on their way to the promised land, instructing them by divine
help, for the heavenly war; which will call me to adapt my addresses
to those in the bloom of life which altho' may be of benefit to all the
young people present, yet designed principle to answer to the request
of a number of young men who have collected in this place for the
enjoyment and service of God. And O how can I express my unspeakable satisfaction in finding at my return so many in the bloom

of life rising up out of the sleep of sin and death, to follow the despised Nazaune [Nazarene], face a frowning world, and wittness for God before the tents of the ungodly! O may immortal blessing crown your endeavours, and eternal praises thereby be raised to the redeemer's name! ah may you as ornaments of the gospel cheerfully dedicate and wear out the flower of your days in the redeemer's cause, and then share in the bloom of immortal youth at Christ's right hand, where reproaches, storms, death, and sin, is known no more! But will Jehovah stoop so low as to seat a youth, a worm, a rebell at his right hand? Yet saith our text they saw a young man sitting on his right side; signifying at his right hand which is the grand subject that I am to entertain you with at this time: And which God grant may be applied to your hearts; And as I speak for the Lord of hosts, and the welfare of your souls at stake I dare not spend much time entertaining you with a dry historical account (as letter preachers is) but shall indeavour to discover the spiritual sense of our text (together with some usefull digressions, under four general observations).

First follow the Son of God to the sepulchre, and examine the nature and spiritual sense thereof.

Secondly the spiritual meaning of this young man being in the sepulchre.

Thirdly what we are to understand by this young man being at the right hand of Christ while in the sepulchre.

Fourthly and lastly, what we are to learn of his being clothed in a long white garment and something of the privileges of being thus with Christ in the sepulchre. And now as Christ came down from heaven to our earth and went from the womb to the sepulchre, according to our first observation, I must take my hearers by the hand and review the unspeakable sorrows, hard labours, grand design, agonies, death, and conquest of this great Messiah while we follow him from the manger to the sepulchre: And O what surprising and heart-melting scenes shall we discover, (omiting his travels and labours during the four thousand years before he assumed a particular body of clay) only in the short period of his mortal life! And O has the grand Visitant appeared; Has the foot of his incarnate love reached our guilty world, to wade thro' the unspeakable miseries of our fallen state! Ah! He who thought it no robbery to be equal with God, took on him the form of a servant. *(b)* and for what? Why to be come a servant to sinners, and wear out his life in the service of a miserable rebellious family; yea to wash their feet, not in water only, but in his own blood.

> O What a wonder of unbounded grace
> Jehovah stoops to save a treacherous race,
> Bears all their Pains, and spills his vital blood
> To reinstate them in the arms of God.

And how, O how will the sinking world receive him? will they not be ravished with immotral [immortal] raptures to acclamate his bless'd arrival to their (if I may say) starving perishing, and abandoned world? O no (but must I tell it in Gath or publish it in the streets of Askelon?) for God declares there was no room for him in the inn *(c)* and is it so still? Ah there never was nor ever will be any room for him in that heart where the amusing charms, ensnaring joys, and anxious concerns of this world's trading and trafficking have yet the possession; nor yet in the inn of self-righteousness: Witness ye beasts of Bethlehem whose filthy stable, and empty manger first found him room, was not you his first companions? And is it not still with those who not only see and feel themselves as vile as the beasts: but likewise an empty manger, that is whose earthly enjoyments fail them, see the emptiness of all created good like the starving prodigal finds a mighty famine *(d)* I say is it not with such that he takes up his abode? And rejoice O my soul that with such he deigns to dwell! But to return to his spotless, and yet miserable life, soon we find him, altho' so early in his father's business *(e)* driven to the wilderness exposed to the inclemency of estimental convultions, the fury of the rude monsters of the wood, the stratagems and wars of the infernal regions without a morsal of bread for the support of his starving and wasting body *(f)* and then from sorrow to sorrow his trials increasing as he advances in the service, labours and fatigues of the Messiah's office, and soon he has become, (apparently) the off-scouring of all things; the song of the drunkards, a spectacle to God, angels, and men; and naked to all that loss and misery can prey; so that we have already seen him in the sepulchre, a sepulchre indeed, in a spiritual sense, not only abasement, misery and death, but burried, as it were, from all the pleasures, and enjoyments of heaven and earth. O what an object of pity! And yet as a helpless victim to all the spite, and mallice of earth and hell.

Think, Think, O my hearers! was this for you and me? and yet how often when pinched in some small degree with losses, crosses and disappointments, do you murmer, and think you have a hard lot in the world? When he who gave life and being to all created systems, and with a smile makes arch-angels rejoice in sinking in the depths of misery; a man of continual sorrows, & acquainted with almost insupportable grief. Why if you have not the second garment to your back, or a second meal of victuals for your body, with ever so mean a cottage, to screen you from the storms of this disordered world your earthly entertainments are still far better than his, who was the father of the universe: For foxes have holes, and the birds of the air have nests, but he had not where to lay his head, *(g)* O then murmer no more at the loss, or want of every thing that this world affords: If you can but live to, walk with, and enjoy the meek and lovely Jesus; for why was his wants and distresses so great, and his abasement so low? Not because he could not have engrossed all the joy, and grandeur of the globe with a turn of his thought: But because his kingdom was not of this world; and consequently its pleasures, and enjoyments were in opposition to his glorious cause; and therefore he partook no more of the enjoyments of this world than was absolutely necessary; and that by no means for the enjoyment of it, or any good, or sweetness he found in it: but wholly for to support him in his state of abasement, (while he was clothed with an elimental body) to endure the hardships of prosecuting his grand design: And yet how many who profess his name, (who have indeed, but the name,) will plead for the indulgence of their earthly joys, pleasures, and recreations: Saying we ought to enjoy this, and may enjoy that for they are given to us for the comforts of life; and there is no harm in wearing this, drinking that, and indulging the other; while others will plead for some, what they call, simple recreations for a relaxation from the burden of an intent mind, but they need not lye. I fear they are not so studious, and will likewise say that we shall bring religion into contempt by being so strict, (tho' little they fear the wounding religion) and fear they shall be guilty of superstition: but O let me tell them not only that such pleas for indulgence is repugnant to the spirit of a true christian, and therefore they are as great strangers to Christ's kingdom as Simon the Sorcerer, but likewise that all such pleas arise from the love of some lust or idol, which if huged a little longer may prove their everlasting ruin; for he that will save his life shall loose it *(h)* and he that soweth to his flesh shall of the flesh reap corruption: *(i)* for the flesh lusteth against the spirit *(k)* and whatsoever is not of faith is sin, and therefore if there be any such here as I have been pointing out let me intreat you not to decieve your own souls, and like Esau for a morsal of meat sell your birthright, for ye know how that afterward when he would have inherited the blessing he was rejected, and found no place for repentance, altho' he sought it carefully with tears; *(m)* but O for your soul-sake put on self-denial and be willing to loose your life that you may save it, & if you would name the name of Christ make him your pattern, and see not only the self-denial but likewise the unspeakable trials that he went thro'; yea and his disciples likewise; they had as many enemies within as we, and ten thousands more without; they suffered the loss of all their earthly friends, and the esteem of the world, they suffered hunger, thirst, nakedness, and buffeting, in the face (and against the rage) of their innumerable enemies; they were stoned, were sawn asunder, were tempted, were slain with the sword, they wandered about in sheep skins, and goats skins, being destitute, afflicted, tormented, in deserts, mountains, dens, and caves of the earth, *(n)* yea even women were tortered [tortured], suffering cruel mockings, and scourgings, yea more over of bonds and imprisonment not excepting deliverance, when offered, that they might obtain a better, yea and eternal resurrection: *(o)* but I fear you will be wise enough to keep clear of such trials; yea and foollish enough likewise to keep as far from their crown and everlasting reward: unless you make a speedy return. But from my long degression I now return, to follow the lamb of God to the sepulchre; and O then how small are, or were, all the trials and sorrows of the people of God when compared with the sufferings of their mighty Captain! For if we follow him a little further in his agonizing conflicts we shall find him wading thro' sorrows so unspeakable, and loadened with a weight so innormous as hath diped his vester in blood.

Witness O Gethsemane the cutting pangs, accute tortures and bloody sweat of an almost expiring Jesus? *(p)* and from thence draged, by a band of ruffians, to the cruel bar of injustice, to be sentenced to, and endure all the cruelty that can be invented by all the intestine courts of earth and hell; and O! He dies under far greater miseries and tortures than could ever be inflicted in corporeal punishment by men and devils; neither was their cruelty to his body the cause of his death: But as this will be something new from the common opinion and traditions of men, I must a little enlarge.

And O! Let me intreat my hearers to shake of[f] some of the prejudices of their education, and receive a jewel that may not only be a blessing to your own souls, especially you who are in the prime of life, just coming out to espouse the Redeemer's cause: But likewise arm you against the Arian and Socinian invasions: For their hands have been much strengthened against the truths of the gospel by many preachers and writers, who were labouring to vindicate the gospel, by holding forth that Christ, who was the very God, suffered and died to satisfy God: which the Arians and Socinians say, and well they may from that hypothesis, was God punishing himself to satisfy himself, and fulfil some outward law which man had broken; and thus they say, (using their own comparisons) he takes out of one pocket and puts in the other; which indeed would be evidently inconsistent, as they observe, and yet it is held forth by every one that pretends that Jesus Christ died to satisfy and appease something in God, which they call insensed justice, and vindictive wrath. O! My dear hearers banish, yea forever banish, all such groundless, inconsistent, unscriptural, and God-dishonouring principles, or conceptions, from your mind! For if God hath made some such outward law, the breach of which will so insense him, that he must suffer to appease the wrath and repair the injury done to himself, then he hath not only made a law to discover an austere and ostentatious humour, but that exposes himself to an everlasting loss and injury: For, first, if sin could break any such law, as would insense the Deity, then his characture is forever impeached, for the wicked in hell will be forever perpetrating the same crime, and consequently increasing the same injury; to the law and dishonour to his name. Well, but saith one, which I know is the reply of them, that hold forth such an arbitrary insensed God and rigorous law, he will forever punish the wicked in hell for the breach of that law; to which I answer, if I admit your reply, yet you are still as deep in the mire as ever; for you thereby not only dress up a glorious being in rediculous habit, but likewise have fettered yourself with as many inconsistencies as ever; for you have thus not only declared that God is forever punishing the wicked in hell to be revenged, or to receive the penalty, as you say, of that law which they have broken: but likewise that the law must forever remain broken; for every sin deserves as I know you will say, everlasting punishment, and as they are continually prepetrating [perpetrating] their crimes to an infinite extreme; so that instead of God being even with them the penalty paid, or the law fullfilled, the breach is infinitely enlarged, the injury increased, and therefore God and his law forever sustaining an increasing loss: for they are forever increasing their rage, sin, and rebellion against him. Besides if God's justice was insensed, as you say, and his wrath stirred up by so insignificant a being, (in comparison with God) as an angel or man, who may not only stir up his wrath, and insense him: But keep him so forever, then what sort of a God, do you worship? For methinks you must be so well acquainted with the nature of any being insensed or stired up in wrath, as to know that a God insensed, or with wrath stired up in him is not only a God injured and wounded: But a God enraged; and a God thus vexed, injured and enraged, is a God in passion, misery and torment; and a God in torment is a God in hell; O how shocking is the natural constructions of such a principle! And yet I shall be branded by many as an enemy to the gospel, and set as a mark for the arrows of the tradi[ti]onists, because I oppose such principles as holds forth the great Jehovah to be possessed of such a nature, as is the nature of devils. Well saith one, if Christ did not suffer and die to satisfy that Insensed justice, or appease any wrath stired up in God, then what was the cause of all his sufferings? Well my dear hearer, I have been obliged to make a long digression to discover and extract the poison out of your wretched principle: but if you begin now to enquire after light, I shall weary your patience no longer: but with joy pass on to inform you the cause of his sufferings and death, which was what I first proposed; for this his suffering and death, is the sepulchre that he entered in, in a spi[r]itual sense. And first remember that he was not forced to enter this sepulchre: For he declares himself that no man took his life from him; but he laid it down himself freely, *(q)* and therefore they did not force him to any sufferings that was necessary to carry on the redemption; nay God forbid that I should ever attribute any part of my redemption to the cruelty of those blood-thirsty wretches, or imagine that my salvation was in the lest degree depending thereon or carried on thereby; or that it could not be carried on without: for blessed be his

name he came down freely for my redemption, and would have completed it if the hands of the ungodly had never touched him; for as
for the broken law which he came to fullfill; true it was broken indeed, and he came to fulfill it: But what was that law but the natural
reflection of his divine nature; and therefore when man broke off
from that God, or turned from the race of life, the law was broke in
himself to his own ruin; and now by reason of the contrariety of his
nature the reflections of the divine nature (law of the tree of life)
became to him as a flaming sword; and therefore the whole work of
Christ is to heal the wound, remove the contrariety; thereby fullfill
the law for and in the creature, and thereby bring him back, again to
a union with and enjoyment of that tree of life in the paradise of God
(r) and for this end he was obliged to enter in to all the disorders and
misery, yea I may say hell, of fallen nature; that is in this fallen and
disordered creature to bear (and bring back from) all the contrariety
of their hellish nature; labouring with his own incarnate spirit in the
fallen creature untill their contrariety is subdued and will reclaimed
and brought back from its state of contrariety to God again; and this
labour in the hell of the creature's contrariety was the cause of his
suffering, when he saith that his soul was exceeding sorrowful even
unto death; *(r)* and this is the way that God was in Christ reconciling
the world unto himself; *(s)* and declares himself that he suffered that
contradiction from the nature of sinners, against himself; *(t)* and that
even to the sheding of blood, which weight of contrariety was the
cause of his death, for when he entered in the fallen system at the
first instant of man's revolt he became incarnate, for he was then in
the flesh *(u)* and that incarnate spirit was labouring in and under all
this contrariety, a sepulchre indeed, untill the period of time that he
assumed a particular body of flesh and blood, and then this agony of
soul, which before was not visible began to appear, yea so great was
his agony of soul, or incarnate spirit in the whole fallen system that
when there was no corporeal punishment inflicted on his body, his
body, or elemental frame was crushed even to the sheding of blood,
under the infinite weight of that contrariety which he was so related
to; for you must not imagine that his incarnation was only in that
particular body but in, all the fallen system (sentering to that body)
the agonies of which forced the blood thro' every pore of his wasting
frame *(w)* and therefore, it is very easy, for you to see that the Jews
were so far from being the case of his death, altho' guilty of murder

in the strongest terms, that if they had never touched, or laid hands on his body he would, under the infinite weight of that hellish contrariety, labouring in agonies of soul to carry on his grand design, and reclaiming this fallen nature have soon expired and given up the Ghost; that is the agonies of his soul for it was his soul made an offering for sin, being so much greater than his body could bear would have so crushed his body as to overcome and put an end to his mortal life; but at that very instant that he was to expire, for he declares they could not before *(v)* they had got him nailed to the cross with his arms extended between heaven and earth; which position of body and manner of dying did import, and discover many important and glorious truths, some of which I will mention.

First, It was between heaven and earth; which was and is still his office as a days man or mediator bringing back from earth (yea from hell) to heaven.

Second, With his Arms extended, good Lord and is thy grace so free that thou not only lived but died with thine Arms extended, stretched to the farthest extend to receive returning Prodigals! Pause a while O my soul! And enter O my hearers, enter the wide leaved gates of eternal felicity display'd by the arms of a bleeding Saviour! or will some of you at last miss the boundless ocean of everlasting love; surely you are not straitened in Christ but in yourselves *(x)* fly fly and live forever!

Third, And it was there he give up the Ghost, this proves again my grand assertion that he expired in the agonies of his hard labour, viz. under the weight of fallen nature bringing back the fallen Creature to God.

Fourthly, as Moses lifted up the serpent in the wilderness to heal the poisoned Hebrews, so the Son of Man is lifted up to heal the sin stung souls *(y)* which likewise discovers to us that salvation is held forth in sight of all the world, as God declares, *(z)* and thus God holds forth his grace impartially to every one that will except [accept] and be saved thereby. But to return we find from the cross he is taken down, and laid in the sepulchre in the letteral sense, which cannot be denied, but as it was the spiritual sense of our text that I was to discover, I dwelt chiefly on that which I trust you now clearly understand; so that I hope you will never more imagine that he punished himself (for he was God) to satisfy himself, or be at a loss about the cause of his death and suffering, for he suffered even the miseries of hell, (but not as some vainly imagine that after he left the body he went into some other world among the damned, for if he had, he did not tell the thief the truth, for he told him that he should be with him that day in Paradise *(g)* Yea the greatest part of his life, I may say, he was enduring the anguish and misery of hell, for the absence of God and the weight of sin he endured even unto death, *(a)* which is greatly the miseries of hell. And now if any of my hearers should be at a loss about God's wrath, vengeance, anger, &c (which the scripture so often speaks of) let me inform them two things.

First, That where there is sin and guilt the nature of God is to them as wrath and vengeance indeed; by reason of the contrariety which, as before observed, was the cause of Christ's sufferings and agonies, when he had taken so much sin, guilt and contrariety upon himself; and therefore wherever this contrariety remains the nature of God will be as a rock to grind them to powder *(b)*.

Secondly, God in infinitive mercy condescends to speak to the fallen creature as things appear to them in their fallen state: but when you are wholly restored back to God you will find he will speak to you plainly without parables *(c)* and likewise find that there is nothing insensed in him: but you had been the wounded insensed and disordered miserable being yourself; and that it was in all these disorders, death and misery that Christ suffered, and all to extricate you therefrom. And Now, let me pause a while or rather, while pointing to the unparellel scene which I have discovered, call on my hearers to exclude the world with every amusing charm of time and sense, and chain the attention of every power of your souls to those grand, those heart-melting, heaven surprising, soul-saving and transporting wonders, and ask, WAS THIS FOR ME? AND O MY SOUL, WHERE. OF WHAT, AM I! WHAT HAVE I DONE! WHAT AM I ABOUT! WHAT MUST I DO! WHERE OUGHT I TO BE! AND WHERE SHALL I BE FOREVER?

> O love unbounded! love of antient date!
> That brought Jehovah to the dismal ken,
> To drink the dregs of our infernal cup
> Nail'd extramundane to the wood and death!
> O angels gaze to see your maker there!
> And sinners shout, your friend has won the field,
> And in his gore hands you the glorious prize,
> And bids you wear the everlasting Palm!

And O ye sorded souls that are so chained down to the carnal
amusements of this wretched world that you cannot give your
attention to the glorious scene, nor follow Christ to the sepulchre
nor find place in your heart for the suffering God! Are you
determined still to pass by slite, and reject all the privileges of
his dying groans, and rising glory? can you still wag your heads
with disdain as you pass by the bleeding Jesus? Will you this day
swear for that infernal band that shall commence an eternal war
against him and his peacefull kingdom, and utterly abandon yourselves from all the joys of his eternal favour? And after all that
has been done choose your portion in that bottomless gulf of fallen
nature? . . .

Say O YOUNG MAN does not your heart, begin to burn with love
to this lovely name this desire of nations at whose right hand I hope
many of you have already sat? Yea, methinks while I am speaking
some of you are saying with the antient Bard in his poetry, SURELY
THE LORD IS IN THIS PLACE, AND THIS IS NONE OTHER BUT THE HOUSE
OF GOD, AND THIS IS THE GATE OF HEAVEN! *(b)* O therefore be incouraged, O YOUNG MAN to go on bearing the reproach of the despised Nazarene without the camp, remembering that he has not only
bore the reproaches but infinite sorrows for you; ah! He who is the
root and offspring of David, the bright morning star, is your Captain,
leader, portion & everlasting joy.

>   Jesus your Lord will lend you his right hand
>   To lead and guard you thro' this desert land;
>   In ev'ry trial stand your bosom friend,
>   And bear your burdens till your sorrows
>   end.

But I must now lead you to our fourth and last general observation,

Which was to discover the spiritual meaning of this young man
being clothed with a long white garment; & O that you may be seen
to be thus clothed all your days, and then may your moments glide
away with joy.

First, They are internally made partakers of the righteousness
of Christ; not imputed as many imagine just, to cover up their sins;

or any thing done for them in some distant region, to answer the penalty of some outward law; and thereby stand their intercessor at a distance; but the pure spirit of Jesus Christ in them: for the pure in heart, and they only, shall see God, *(d)* and without holiness no man shall see the Lord: *(e)* and therefore whoever depends on any righteous of Christ imputed without being, to them, imparted, will e'er long have cause to take up that bitter lamentation of the foolish virgins, give us of your oil for our lamps have gone out. *(f)* For they who are prepared for eternal glory must really be made to partake of the divine nature here in this life *(g)* and if any should say that I am denying the imputation of Christ's righteousness, I answer that I not, only hold it in the strongest sense: but can easily prove that they are denying it who hold it in a strict sense any other way: for how can any thing be imputed to a man and he not made partaker? Surely if it is imputed it must of consequence be imparted; and therefore you may take it for a truth of no less importance than the everlasting concern of your immortal souls, that you will never be saved by any other imputation of Christ's rightiousness than the impartation to your miserable sinking and perishing souls; and thus it is by this impartation of Christ's righteousness that the young man is cloth in the sight of God. And thus far as he is made partaker of this divine nature he is restored to God.

Secondly this divine spirit, and righteousness of Christ in the heart does naturally produce a cleansing, from sin in the inward man, and thereby consequently made to forsake and detest sin in the outward man and therefore brought to a cheerfull conformity to the ways of God externally, so that others will thereby behold them clothed in a white garment; as saith our text, they saw a young man clothed in a white garment; yea it cannot be otherwise: for where there is fire there will be light; and therefore, as you have often heard me declare, a man will no more make me believe that he is a christian or at Christ's right hand unless I see the white garment, than he would make me believe that there was a candle burning in my room at midnight when the room is still in midnight darkness: for as certain as God's word is true where there is that immortal principle of light and love in the heart it will give light to the world; *(h)* and therefore saith God if any man be in Christ he is a new creature, old things are done, away and behold all things are become a new; *(i)* and therefore as Joseph, when he made himself known to his brethren changed their raiment, *(k)* so those that have Christ made known savingly to their souls have their garment changed; for they are made partakers of that which does detest every evil, thirst for holiness, and long to be redeemed out of all sin, and to be made pure even as God is pure; *(1)* yea there is no other redemption but to be redeemed out of sin and made like unto God.

And Thirdly this garment of the young man, was not only white but long; and so this divine spirit will finally clean them throughout, and so transform them that there shall be no spot nor blemish left in them, for saith the Lord it shall be in them as a well of living water springing up unto everlasting life; *(m)* & saith John when he shall appear we shall be like him *(n)* and O let me now enforce this truth on all the proffessors of christianity, especially to you O young men, in the strongest terms remembering that example is far more successful than a bare recept: but by no means would I send you under the thunders of mount Sinai to excite you to the hard task of dressing yourself with the garment of dry obedience without love; but to the flame or immortal love that bled on mount Calvary: one sight of which will constrain you chearfully to put on an external deportment sweetened with the spirit of love to the meek and lovely Jesus, and then the world seeing you clothed with a long white garment will take notice that you have been with Jesus *(o)* and this divine love will not only cast out all fear of death and hell, but cause you to turn a deaf ear to all the flattering charms of this ensnaring world; and likewise set your face as a flint against all its frowns, yea and cause you to take cold death by the hand without reluctance, and defy the terrors of an approaching grave; and this will lay the welfare of your poor fellow men so near your heart as to cause you at every opportunity to warn them with tears to fly from the wrath to come, point the wounded to the bleeding wounds of your all-conquering Captain, and court them to the unspeakable joys of his kingdom: that they might enlist under the same banner, fight in the same heavenly war, and share with you in the glorious spoil, when your master shall have won the field, attained the victory and given you the glorious prize to enjoy; at thought of which methinks your hearts begin to burn; O the thoughts of availing, (if I may say) to that vast angelic continent, where wars never wage, foes never come, crowns and kingdoms never revolve, nor laws never change; O the glory of such immortal scenes! How doth the divine attraction call up every power of you

transported souls while I speak and cause you to thirst, long, resolve, and re-resolve for CHRIST AND HIM ONLY! Yea methinks,
some carnal youth that has long set at nought the friendly warnings
of heaven, and turned a deaf ear to the voice of the lovely charmer,
that has charmed so wisely, begins to feel some consultations in
their breasts and say with Agrippa *thou almost perswadest me to
be a christian* and if so, O for your soul sake do not like him put
it of[f] for an uncertain hereafter, for I can assure you, you will
never have a more convenient season than the present moment besides if you was sure like the expiring thief as I suppose you often
promise yourself, to find mercy in the last moment! you would not
only loose all the prime of life but likewise wade thro' one continual scene of sorrow and uneasiness: for I can tell you by woefull
experience the danger, inconsistancy and misery of seeking happiness in this vain world! Upward of twenty years I rejected the
waiting Saviour and sought happiness in created good, where it
never was nor never will be found and had the nature [name] of a
christian too, but when thro' boundless grace I adhered to the voice
of the heavenly lover and cast my naked and perishing soul at his
feet, O! I found that that kingdoms nor worlds could not parallel!
Peace, and joys divine; yea joys unspeakable & full of glory; Ah,
it was then I drank with ravishing delight from those rivers of everlasting consolation that makes glad the City of God; Ah, that
wine that cheers the heart of God and man! yea and since the first
moment that I knew the joyfull sound I can say Lord ever more
give me this joy and living water for I can say with the poet, to
set one day beneath thine eye.

> And hear thy gracious voice
> Exceeds a whole eternity
> Employ'd in carnal joys.

Ah did you but know, my dear young friends, the happy moments we often enjoy when sitting, altho' here in the sepulchre, at
the right hand of king Jesus, you would not only envy us: but break
thro' all opposition and say with Ruth intreat me not to leave thee or
to return from following after thee for whether thou goest I will go,
and where thou lodgest I will lodge, thy people shall be my people,

and thy God my God; where thou diest will I die, and there will I be burried: the Lord do so to me and more also' if ought but death part thee and me *(q)* there are many of us here I trust bound by the grace of God to see the promised land and can say the same; and O let me tell you that we should rejoice in your company, take you by the hand, to run the christian race; O give your hearts to Jesus, join the sacred bond, and go arm in arm with us to the glorious mansions prepared by your Captain for all his dispised followers. Methinks I hear some saying again if all this be true, *which* ALLINE *declares, why should I not be prevailed with? why should I loose such unspeakable joys & destroy my soul forever for the empty sound of a few hours amusement? Methinks I will resolve a speedy escape, but O will God assist me, and have mercy on one so vile?*

Yea my dear friends so ready is God to help, that all heaven will be engaged on your behalf to espouse your everlasting welfare, Saints pray for you, mercy calls you, heaven invites you, and angels wait to raise a note of joy at your return; and O above all! God himself stands with extended arms inviting you to the bosom of eternal joy.

Ah methinks I hear the waiting Father saying, with joy, "MY LONG DESERTING SON BEGINS TO BE IN WANT, AND IS RESOLVING A RETURN FOR BREAD, AND GLADLY WILL I MEET HIM; YEA, LEST HE BE DISCHARGED, I WILL RUN TO MEET HIM, TO HASTEN AND INCOURAGE HIS LINGERING RETURN." *(r)* O sinner, and what would you more? The fatted calf is killed, the best robe is prepared, and a ring for your finger, yea all things is ready come, O come to the marriage.

> Forsake the world dispise the empty
> 　 joy,
> Act like a hero, life and soul employ
> To gain the field, and win immortal joy.

But time hurries me I must turn to the young man in the sepulchre, and conclude my message for to you O men I call, and my voice is to the sons of men, and especially to you that late profess Jehovah's name; and O I trust have known his love! and if so go on ye heavenly warriors cheerfully to spend and be spent for your masters cause, and the honour of his great name I speak unto you, as saith John, YOUNG MEN because ye are strong, and the word of God abideth in you and ye have over come the wicked one *(s)* Ah happy YOUNG MEN thus to get the victory over the powers of darkness in your bloom of life before so married to your fallen state that you cannot come and chained down to final impenitance! And O remember that Jesus who has wore out his life for you in a field of blood is still at hand with an immediate & full supply for all your wants as long as you tread this mortal stage! And soon, Ah! soon will call you from your mortal watch to the mansions of eternal glory!

And therefore O let me again and again intreat you to turn every stone, and concert every method for the advancing of his glorious kingdom in your own souls and others during the short period of your mortal stay.

Remember that immortal souls are invaluably precious, and O should you be the means of reclaiming one from eternal misery to the knowledge, of Christ, it would be ten thousand times more to you than the gaining of both Indias.

But O instead of that if some of you by growing cold and dead, should get involved in the carnal pleasures and amusing charms of this vain world how would you thereby bring up an evil report against the good land, and perhaps unhappily prove the means of some soul's eternal ruin!

But God forbid, that one of you should be of them that draw back to perdition! And let me now use the freedom to drop one word of advice respecting your manner of publick worship; and here altho' I doubt not but you meant for the glory of God in having your meetings something private, because you I imagined that the scoffing world would make a mock at your small gifts and graces, & broken improvements, yet I can but intreat you to come out boldly for Christ, and not only improve all the gifts of prayer and exhortation that is among you, which by improving will increase, but likewise open the door for (yea invite) the attendance of both saints and sinners; for allowing that many around you are the greatest scoffers and nay even come with a design to make a mock at religion: yet if they would mock there they would else where; and further I must tell you, I know of no way so likely to reclaim them from their mockery as to hold up the light before them, and draw them with the cords of love; and further I would observe (not by way of reflection) that some of

you who are now rejoicing in the God of your salvation, I have reason to suppose was once in the same darkness with them, but the
gospel being openly proclaimed, and hearing so much of Christ and
the privileges of his kingdom, you was thereby constrained to embrace the Christ and espouse the cause you once despised and rejected; besides you cannot be bound too strong to be wholly for
Christ, and therefore, your coming out publickly to witness for his
name may be a bulwark around you against strong temptations, and
for my part I would not desire any back door open to the world for
me to step out and commit sin, saying *I never professed to be a Christian.* But I think it a privilege to profess, and that publicly, therefore
be not afraid any of you, of being under too great obligations, or
being too much watched by both saints and sinners. I should not have
said so much, but fearing that some of you may too much indulge
the fear of man, and thereby fall into a cold dead state: and O if I
should, in the course of providence, once more tread this part of the
vineyard, how much more would the melancholy news of your desertion (even one of you) from the cause of Christ pierce my soul and
wound my heart than the solemn toll of your passage thro' the grave!

O therefore let me again and again reinforce my earnest intreaties for your perseverence in a close walk with God; and then when
I am treading the different parts of the globe, wading thro' the storms
and reproaches of an ungodly world and the trials of an unsanctified
heart to blow the jubilee trump; the Hebrews release; and with the
glad news of our maker's name to the gentile world, hear O hear me
and my labours continually on your mind in your wrestling cries to
the throne of grace; and O I trust when distant mountains with their
towering summits, or the wrestless ocean with her bellowing waves
far part our distant Bodies that our minds shall be one cemented in
that indissolvable band of everlasting love; and often meeting in our
joint cries to heaven; and O, if not before, when a few more hours
of grief and labour have run their speedy rounds I trust thro' the
boundless grace of him that has loved us we shall quit the ten thousand disorders of our fallen state, awake, and meet out of the sepulchre, but still at Christ's right hand with the countless band of
adorers to sollace in his immortal love; where foes never invade,
storms never beat, parting hours, sin, death and interposing clouds
are known no more; and O shall I say there to be one with this our
lovely Jesus, and join thro' all the realms of eternal felicity in one

harmonious strain of praise to his worthy name: which God of his infinite mercy grant, AMEN. [pp. 3–18, 25–33]

Notes

    (a) Mt 21:9.
    (b) Phil 2:6.
    (c) Lk 2:7.
    (d) Lk 15:14.
    (e) Lk 2:49.
    (f) Mt 4:1, 2.
    (g) Mt 8:20.
    (h) Mt 16:25.
    (i) Gal 6:8.
    (k) Gal 5:17.
    (m) Heb 12:17.
    (n) Heb 11:37.
    (o) Heb 14:35.
    (p) Lk 22:44.
    (q) Jn 10:18.
    (r) Rv 2:7.
    (r) Mk 14:34
    (s) 2 Cor 5:19.
    (t) Heb 12:3.
    (u) Rv 18:8; 1 Pt 1:11.
    (w) Lk 22:14.
    (v) Jn 8:20.
    (x) 2 Cor 6:12.
    (y) Jn 3:14.
    (z) 1 Jn 2:2. Jn 1:9. Heb. 2, 9.
    (g) Lk 23:43.
    (a) Mk 14:34.
    (b) Mt 21:44.
    (c) Jn 16:44.
    (b) Rom 8:28.
    (d) Mt 5:8.
    (e) Heb 12:14.
    (f) Mt 25:8.
    (g) 2 Pt 1:4.
    (h) Mt 5:14. 2 Cor 6:17.
    (k) Gn 45:22.
    (l) 1 Jn 3:3.

(m) Jb 4:14.
(n) Jb 3:2.
(o) Acts 4:13.
(p) Jgs 9:13.
(q) Ru 1:16, 17.
(r) Lk 15:20.

A

SERMON

ON A DAY OF THANKSGIVING

PREACHED AT LIVERPOOL

[On the 21st of November 1782.]

Halifax.

. . . Oh! think how much God has done, and endured for your redemption; yea and the very rocks, hills, and stones, sun, moon and
stars, are all engaged for you, groaning under you, and travailing in
pain for your redemption; and must it all be in vain?

Must God stoop, suffer, bleed and die; grace travail, woo and
plead; mercy labour, bear and forbear; wisdom propose; love court;
and goodness, infinite and everlasting goodness, open the bosom of
ravishing delight, and all in vain, and you at last go down into eternal
ruin? Yea not only in vain, but worse, all as mountains sinking you
down deeper in despair under the keen reflections, while wallowing
in the bottomless gulf. Why, why O sinners, why will you abuse
such love, and destroy yourselves? O! let me prevail with you to be
happy, yea forever happy in this goodness, and join in one eternal
thanksgiving, with songs of everlasting praise to Jehovah, for his
goodness and his wonderful works to the children of men!

And now the fifth and last general observation I proceed; which
was to point out some of the singular instances of the goodness of
God to us in particular; but O they are so innumerable I know not
where to begin!

If I speak of the gospel privileges, surely I may say that our lines
are fallen in pleasant places, and we have a goodly heritage; for we

came forth from the loins of our predecessors to have our trial for salvation in a day when the gospel is in its meridian brightness.

Ah! what millions have appeared for their trial in the antedeluvian darkness? millions more under but the glimmering light of the Mosaic dispensations; when Oh! methinks even the poor lovers of Jesus waded in obscurity, looking through those dark types and shadows to a promised Messiah, impatiently waiting for the long expected morning, when the Messiah should visibly appear; and thousands more since he has appeared, have gone to heaven in a storm against the cruel rage of persecution, wading after their Captain in seas of their own blood; while we, with all those evidences of the truths of the gospel, are sitting under our own vine and fig-tree and none to make us afraid.

Think O my hearers, how infinitely we are indulged, invironed with the arms of omnipotence, wrapped in the mantle of love, and cultivated with the word and spirit under the balmy wing of everlasting kindness. O how largely have we been made to partake of the goodness of God, and share in the favours of his hand! and O how little returns! yea and if I come a step nearer still omiting our being excluded from heathenish darkness and from the cruelty of oppression and tyranny, how are we screened from the trials of our (once happy) Nation in the convulsions of the present day? how have we sat in peace while this inhuman war hath spread devastation thro' our Neighbouring Towns, and Colonies like a flood! not my dear hearers because of the cleaness of our hands, or past righteousness: for surely we have not only had our hands equally engaged in the sins that have incurred the lamentable disorder; but have likewise perpetrated the same crimes, and remained unfruitful and incorrigible under such distinguishing advantages.

Yea and when we have daily expected the impending cloud, and to share in the bitter cup, heaven's indulgent hand has interposed and averted the blow.

Yea, and more to be admired still we have not only been excluded from the destructive scene, but while they were involved in the dreadful calamity, we have been blest with that unparallel blessing the moving work of the Spirit of God; a work of grace, and the advancing of the Redeemer's kingdom in almost every corner of the Province; which blessed by God, (although many may and do despise it) I have been an eye witness to, and a happy partaker of; yea, and many hundreds will likewise forever adore God for the blessed Work. Neither has your little corner of the vineyard been excluded from a share in the unspeakable prize; witness some of my hearers now present who had long been involved in Egyptian darkness; has not some of your souls not only been brought out of your unhappy bondage and unspeakable danger, but likewise made to partake of God's free and boundless grace, and taste of the sweets of redeeming love? has not Jesus come into some of your families, and caused some of your souls to drink of those rivers of pleasure that makes glad the city of our God? have you not forgot your sorrows and sung for joy? O praise him then, praise him ye happy souls for his infinite goodness; or I may say in the words or our context, Let the redeemed of the Lord say so, whom he hath redeemed from the hand of the enemy. Ye have not only been mourning in the bondage of Egypt, but have wandered in a wilderness, in a solitary way, hungry and thirsty, until Jesus appeared and led you forth by the right way to a city of habitation, where you found that rest that remains for the people of God.

. . . O let your hearts melt with love, your souls glow with gratitude, and your minds soar away in shouts of praise of his goodness and his wonderful works to the children of men. Surely you have cause to love much, for you are blest in basket and in store, in time and eternity; for although you may be called through some trying scenes, and sometimes afflicted with losses, crosses and disappointments of this temporal world, yet it is all but to advance your spiritual welfare, and prevent greater miseries; for all things will surely terminate for your good. O you are a people highly favoured of God indeed! Yea, and even you that know not God, how vastly are you indulged? how innumerable are the mercies you enjoy that many cannot? Ah could I but a moment lend you an omniscient eye or discover to your view a map of the disordered world, what peals of death, what marks of misery and tokens of despair would you behold even of temporal calamities? thousands soliciting the cold hand of charity, pinched with hunger, thirst and nakedness; thousands chained to the galley, and others chain of slavery, to endure all the hardship and misery that cruelty can inflict; thousands in prisons, dungeons and places of confinement already destined to the gallows, gibbet, rack, or torture; when every pulse counts the fleeting moments that crowd them with reluctance to their dreadful exit; yea, and perhaps the greatest part of those unhappy beings (too shocking for human thought) will but exchange miseries finite and tolerable, to miseries infinite and intolerable; and in a moment will find their die unalterably cast in the regions of increasing horrors and eternal despair. Good Lord, and were these once the inhabitants of the paradise of God! Ah how is the gold changed and the most fine gold become dim! (*r*) whose heart can but break and say with the Prophet, O that my head were waters and mine eyes fountains of tears, that I might weep day and night for the slain of the daughter of my people! (*s*) or how can your hearts my dear hearers but dissolve with love or break forth with thanksgiving to God for the unspeakable privileges that you are indulged with? O arise, arise and put on the Lord Jesus Christ and live to him, for he is the author and giver of all thy privileges, and is now travelling from door to door and knocking from heart to heart, for admission, and all to bring you to the fountain of all good, and the essence of unspeakable joys, yea, and he waits with unwearied patience till his head is filled with the dew and his locks with the drops of the nights. (*t*) O grant him admission, enjoy his love and live forevermore! O he calls, he calls, with arms extended to receive, you & this day (though by stammering tongue) has unvailed his goodness enough to engage your souls to love him if you would but open your hearts for the attracting view. He has not only created you in love, and came wholly in love to redeem you, but has been labouring in love for you through unspeakable miseries; and is still labouring for you, and in infinite love intreating you to partake and forever enjoy his unchangeable goodness.

And now let me in his Name reinforce the intreaties and point out your steps for to praise and adore him, and this by singularizing my hearers as in their different capacities and stations of life. And God forbid that I should point any of you to God without God; or to be christians without Christ; and therefore I am not about to lead you in a formal path of spiritless externals but an immediate application to the Lord Jesus Christ; and there to partake of that spirit and love that will as naturally produce a christian deportment externally as fire will produce light. O therefore away to mount Calvary and drink from that bleeding love and infinite goodness which will immediately engage your souls to walk with the greatest cheerfulness in the ways of God; yea and never expect to breathe a breath to his praise or taste of his love without a saving knowledge

of the Lord Jesus Christ thro' a change wrought in your soul by
the spirit of God.

And if so how unfit are you to live or serve God while in the
gaul of bitterness and bonds of iniquity with your souls in the darkness of your fallen state at enmity against God and all that is good.

And now let me first intreat you who are leading men of the
Town in Civil affairs to make it your first and chief concern to find
room in your hearts for the despised Nazarene, that you who are
Counsellors may be taught of God, and be as Pillars in his house,
and as nursing Fathers to his people; and great, Ah! unspeakable
great will be your present and everlasting reward.

Yea and great is the influence of men in your state; and as injurious as great when your ways are perverse and your examples ungodly.

Ah! what a shocking sight to see the capital men of the Earth
who ought to be a Terror to evil doers, and a praise to them that do
well living in sin, siting in the seats of the scornful and joining with
the ungodly wallowing in vice and debauchery, & walking in luxu-
rious paths! but god forbid that I should have any cause to suspect
this to be the case with any of you present; but if it is (though I would
treat you with all that respect that is due to your station and would
be far from giving any wilful offence) I am under an obligation to
say as Nathan to David, thou art the man; and intreat you in the Name
of the Lord, and in meekness and love to return before you are landed
beyond hope: for there is yet mercy at your door, and a moment more
for repentance. O embrace the unspeakable privilege, and let me intreat you to adorn your station by the grace of God, and live as lights
in the world, and for the Lords sake, your own souls sake, and the
sake of others around you arise up and witness for God, and let all
your deportment espouse the redeemers cause, and the welfare of
souls.

But O! how shocking when men that should be as pillars in the
house of God, and a bulwark around his fe[e]ble Lambs, are enemies
to the gospel, and a wound to the hearts of his children. And ah, how
shocking to see those from whose lips we might expect the dews of
heaven to water and comfort the mourners in Sion, and whose
Tongue should teach the songs of heaven to the rising generations,
debauched with vain and obscene discourse, and belching out blasphemy? [Surely says many if such men may talk and conduct so we

may too.] But on the other hand when they stand speak and labour for the glory of God and good of souls how would saints admire mourners rejoice and sinners Tremble!

Oh that you might be the happy instruments of such benefit to immortal souls! and great, ah unspeakably great, would be your reward; Jesus will stand by lead and support you thro' all the sorrows, labours and Trying scenes of this mortal world, give you strength equal to your day, and then receive you with a WELL DONE THOU GOOD AND FAITHFUL SERVANT ENTER THOU INTO THE JOY OF THY LORD, there to sollace in his love, Crowned with immortal glory, and forever adore him for his goodness, and his wonderful works to the children of men: but ah some of you I suppose think you would be very happy to be so blest and hope that you shall but as yet your obligations to the important affairs of your publick stations and your affinity with the carnal world, and polite age, is such, that you should greatly expose your earthly esteem and welfare for to practice or discourse much about religion. True my dear hearers you would so but let me tell you it is equally as True that unless you forsake all, you can never be his disciple, and those who are ashamed of him before men he will be ashamed of before his Father and the high angels. (*u*) therefore you may never expect to enter those bright abodes of the everlasting day unless you are willing in this life to have your Names cast out as evil, and bear his reproach without the Camp; yea and did you see things as they really are you would account it the greatest honour that could be conferred upon you to be despised for the Name of Jesus.

Ah could I a moment unvail your minds and discover to your souls one glimmering ray of the transporting beauties and resulgent glories of the Lord Jesus Christ I should have no more labour to espouse you to him, or to court you from every other love, for you would like Rebekah when courted to an unknown husband, say, I WILL GO: (*w*) Ah! you would with the greatest cheerfulness drop your earthly charms, the applause and grandeur of this vain world, and make choice of this Jesus for your present and everlasting portion, and say with the spouse, this is my beloved, and this is my friend O daughters of Jerusalem! (*x*) And then would you with gladness of heart come out and stand as a mark for the ungodly, and turn every stone, and concert every method to advance his glorious cause in the land, and to me (the few moments I am among you) would be as fellow helpers in the gospel, and with me share in the everlasting reward. O then let me again and again solicit your return from all your sinful ways and paths of vanity, and join with heart and voice to praise God for his goodness and his wonderful works to the children of men! and let the world know that you belong to Jesus. And now with God I leave you, hoping you will make the happy choice; for life and death has been set before you.

And now to every head of a family let me say, as the Lord to Zaccheus, make hast and come down for to day I must abide at thy house; (*y*) Jesus is passing by and offering to come in and make his residence with you and your families: Ah! and had you a sense of the infinite privilege of receiving the glorious visitant, you would, like the forementioned Zaccheus, come down and receive him joyfully; and say, with Joshua, as for me and my house, we will serve the Lord. (*z*) And surely my dear friends you have cause to love and adore him for his goodness to the sons of men, and to you in particular. Ah! think but a moment what miseries you have been extricated from, what dangers you have escaped, what kindnesses received, what favours enjoyed, and beyond what thousands could have expected, and beyond what thousands have enjoyed; yea if I mention no other instance but your being called away from the approaching storm that was hanging over your native land, and sheltered here from the calamities of the sweeping deluge, while many under the disolations are saying, *I am the man that have seen affliction by the rod of his wrath (a) for he breaketh in upon me with breach upon breach. (b) I am crushed as a moth, under the devastations of this inhuman war; while, saith some mourning widow in the depths of calamity, not only the partner of my life torn from my bosom, but death ravaging still, my only son, the last of all my stay, the comfort of my widowhood, is wallowing in his gore! and thus I am left nakedly exposed to all that misery and cruelty can prey, & am left to wear out the remains of a miserable life in distress of body, & anguish of soul!* And while many an aged Parent is lingering to the grave with grey hairs and sorrow, under the late news of their last son; slain in such battle, many a helpless infant is thrown an o[r]phan into the wide world by the fatal lead designed to the Fathers breast, while you my dear hearers (altho' you have often murmered that ever you come to those inhospitable wiles, and was ready to say with the murmering Jews *has God brought us here to slay us?)* Have been hedged about with the kind providence of God, and screened from the impending storm in this peacable corner of the earth.

Yea and above all when they are thus wading thro' the terrible storm, and we have been expecting soon to share the bitter cup, we have been blest with the greatest of all blesings, cultivated with the word and spirit of divine grace, many brought to feast at the marriage supper of the Lamb, and to drink of the wells of Salvation. O the goodness, the unspeakable goodness of God to such a people, surely I may term you LITTLE GOSHEN and yet O how barren and unfruitfull are many of you still! Yea I have reason to fear that instead of prayer and praise, or your houses being as worship Temples many of you are keepers of the devils Shops, and your houses as a den of thieves, and ten hours spent in carnal mirth and sinfull pleasures to one in prayer praise or any thoughts on God and his infinite goodness; and thus your children are hurried by, and with, you the slipperly steep to eternal perdition. O the dreadfull thought! O the lamentable scene, Parents and Children all enemies to God, dispisers of Christ, murderers of souls, servants of the Devil, and bo[u]nd to the regions of eternal despair! O let me ask such Parents how can you rest? How can you linger? Or how can you be Masters of such cruelty? Or how can your hearts endure a thought of your approaching doom?

What if at your return this evening from the Sermon to your family you should find one of those children (you have led in sinfull ways) on the confines of the grave and hear them in agonies of despair saying *cursed be the womb that bear me and the paps that gave me suck and cursed be my Parents whose ungodly walk has been the means of my eternal ruin, for I am now plunging in the bottomless gulf, O that I had heard as many prayers in my Fathers family as I have Oaths but Ah, I am lost my day is gone!* I say how would the shocking scene rend your despairing soul, and almost cause you to wish that you had never had a being? O then why will you any longer run the risk? Or why will thus abuse all the goodness of an indulgent God? Are you determined still to persist in your pernicious courses? And are those, all the returns that you will make for such infinite goodness endearing love and long suffering, as has this day been discovered to you?

O that I could prevail with you to return before your fatal dye is cast! Yea methinks I would creep on my knees to intreat your return if

I could thereby in any degree prevail with you only to admit a serio[u]s thought and begin to bethink yourselves. O why why will you lye down in eternal sorrow? I know you will think that I Judge hard and am censorious, but if your conscience, nor the word of God, doth not condemn you neither will I; but if I have it is wholly for your own good, and God knows I speak in love with an impatient thirst for to serve you, and be a means of your everlasting happiness, that you might forever enjoy that infinite goodness, and adore God therefor.

And now to those happy Parents who under a sense of these things are returning, or have returned, and are determined by the grace of God they and their families (as far as their influence may extend) to cast themselves upon the Lord Jesus, forsake every sin, destroy every evil, and concert every meathod for the advancing the vitals of religion, and honour of God, and to exalt the Name of Jesus for his goodness and wonderfull works to the children of men; to these let me say GO ON AND THE LORD OF HOSTS WILL BE YOUR STRENGTH.

Ah it is with cheerfullness of heart I would take you by the hand and lead you on to meet and enjoy your kind Father, your helping Saviour, bleeding friend, and waiting reward. O hasten for the Lord Jehovah is inviting you with extended arms to the bosom of his everlasting love; and I know will give you strength equal to your day; and therefore altho' all earth and hell would obstruct your return yet you shall e'er long come off conquerer, yea more than conquerer thro' him that has loved you and given himself for you. O how I long to endear you to the glorious match! and methinks you will be perswaded to embrace the unspeakable prize.

Yea I am ready to say that the very thought of going hand in hand with your children to the bright abodes of everlasting day would awake in your souls an invincible resolution to arise with all your powers, fight the good fight of faith & lay hold on eternal life: say some thought full Parent some lover of Jesus can you not declare with a christian woman who (in my travails) told me that she would not care if her children were all beggars from door to door in this world if they were but walking with Christ, and she might see them at last at his right hand in glory? yea and would it not rejoice your souls to think that you should one day hear them bless God that ever they were commited to such faithfull stewards who was the means of their Salvation?

O then arise my dear Parents from your remains of sin and sloth and redouble your resolutions and prosecutions for the advancing of the redeemers kingdom in your families and let your own harmonious strains arise to Jesus for his goodness and his wonderfull works to the children of men, remembering that your unspeakable reward is present and everlasting. And now to your offspring let me say, unto you O men I call, and my voice is to the sons of men, (*d*) remember O remember your creator while in the bloom of life before your evil days come & the years draw nigh when you shall say ye have no pleasure in them (*e*) as a Servant and friend to your souls I intreat you while Heaven invites you, and Jesus himself is at your door knocking perswading and promising, riches and honour saith he is with me yea durable riches and righteousn[e]ss, and those that seek me early shall find me and those that find me shall find life; yea everlasting life my dear youth, with joys unspeakable and full of glory. O be intreated to leave the dangerous amusements of this vain world, turn off your eyes from beholding vanity and go in the way of understanding.

O remember what heart aching hours, scenes of sorrow misery, and death, the bleeding Jesus has been wading thro' to save you from eternal perdition and bring you to his Fathers bosom, and can you still persist in pursuit of you Idols wallowing in your sins to the dispising of his grace, crowning him with th[or]ns, piersing his side refreshing his wounds, and plunge your own souls into eternal perdition and despair?

O be intreated to be wise in time and happy to all eternity; turn from every sin, and fly to the waiting arms of the lovely Jesus; for my part I can tell you that I was in all my earthly amusements and carnal pleasures a stranger to peace, and ignorant of a moments rest or Joy, untill I found it in this Christ that I now recommend to you; and ah I can without reluctance or shame declare myself to be one of his dispised, tho' very unworthy, followers, and recommend him to you in the presence of this auditory as a kind Master, a faithfull & loving companion, and constant helper yea altogether lovely the fairest among ten thousands, and all in all.

And by his grace I am more and more in love with him, and resolve to renew my choice of him as my only happiness and portion from this time forward and forever; yea witness God, Angels and men, witness ye Sons and Daughters of Adam present, the posts of the doors and pulpet from whence I now sound forth his Name, that by his grace assisting, I reject and abandon every lover and joy but what I may enjoy in him, and to be for him and him only, and in his Name and presence recommend to you the same choice, and declare that saints and Angels will rejoice at your return, and God himself receive you with delight. And O the unspeakable happiness you will find in him in life, and privilege in death and let me ask how would it gladen the hearts of your surviving christian Parents if they were to see you rejoicing on the confines of the grave entering the gloomy mansions of death without reluctance saying that your redeemer lived that you had known his love enjoyed his grace was now under a feeling sense of his presence, biding an everlasting adieu to all your sorrows and take your Joyfull flight to the mansion of love in your Saviours bosom!

Say some thinking Parent would you not rejoice and be ready to say that you had more Joy in the death of your child than in its birth? O be intreated then my dear young friends to bethink your-selves, fly from the Jaws of eternal perdition, and receive a crown of immortal glory, since God, angels and saints, and your own eter-nal welfare solicits your speedy return.

And I (of all men the most unworthy) expecting thro' boundless grace a mansion in the kingdom, long for your company to bear a part in immortal notes of praise to God for his goodness and his won-derfull works to the children of men.

And now altho' I hope each one of my hearers have been so wise as to make an application of every part of my discourse (which I thus divided to be the more striking, yet seeing a number of my fellow mortals that are in the Military establishment present I shall use the freedom to address myself to them in a few words seperately.)

I am happy my dear fellow men to find those men under whose command you reside influenced to collect you to the hearing of the everlasting gospel this day, may God bless their endeavours in so doing and pour an everlasting reward into their bosom!

And I likewise hope your attendance is accompaniest with your own cheerfullness, and thirst for the knowledge of Christ, if so under the lest conviction of your need of the blessings of heaven O with what gladness of heart would I serve you in my Masters name, hold out to you the offers of eternal life, inviting your souls to embrace and enjoy the same; Yea altho it would not become my office to say much concerning your stations and capacity of life, yet as my fellow mortals I would as willingly serve you as my nearest and dearest friends, or the capital men of the earth; yea and as highly esteem you when your life conduct and conversation corresponds with the Gospel and principles of christianity: and would be so far from treating you with disrespect or disdain that I would at any time rejoice in that christian freedom of giving you the best advice I was capable for the good of your souls either in publick or private.

I know my dear fellow men that your souls are equally precious with my own, equally miserable by your fall, equally needy of salvation, and equally as near and dear to my blessed Master as the king, on the throne; and that you will likewise e'er long be judged by the same God, at the same impartial Bar.

O let me therefore in love to your precious and immortal souls intreat you to adhear to the offers of salvation while it is offered, embrace the Lord Jesus Christ, and live to his glory, that you may die in peace and share with the happy followers of the Lamb in the wonders of immortal Glory. You are notionally convinced that you are born to die and exposed every breath you draw to exchange worlds, and O should death overtake you unprepared you are undone to all eternity! and then what is the world and millions of worlds to you when you must lye down in the regions of eternal darkness and despair?

Yea how many have you seen (some of you) wallowing in their blood that have fell on your right hand and your left, plunged in a moment to a world of spirits (perhaps without time to ask for mercy & doubtless many of them unprepared, and you was spared?) And O did you ever recollect a moment in your own breasts where you would have landed had the fatal lead have passed them and been destined to you?

Or whether you ever allow yourselves any thought of those things or not, whatever you may flatter yourselves of being saved because God is a God of Mercy, or because you expire in the cause of such and such lawful constitutions as you imagine, yet let me tell you that if you die in your sins you will eternally perish in your sins; and unless you are born again, that is your hearts changed by the spirit of God you must as certainly be undone as you have a soul to save or loose. And altho I am so far from charging you with outward acts of vice and debauchery that I must acknowledge my satisfaction in scarcely hearing of a profane Oath among you as I have walked the Streets since I have been in the place, yet you are all sensible it is too commonly practised in such Corporations; yea and altho' you may any of you be guilty of that or any other vice secreted from the world which may exclude you from outward disgrace or corporeal punishment, yet the crime is as heinous in the sight of that all searching eye that is about all your private paths, yea and will be not only as injurious but more so to your own souls: Because your escaping of disgrace and punishment among Men may harden you on to the commission of greater crimes to your eternal ruin: when perhaps an admonition in time might prove the means of reclaiming you and therefore my dear friends never think it any benefit to conceal your sins from men, if they are commited in the sight of God: but fly from every sin, and make it your chief concern to attain a knowledge of Christ and a life beyond the grave.

O think how shocking it is for breath that is given for repentance, and the service of God, to be spent in blasphemy, and in the service of the devil! how shocking to hear a man who is already condemned to everlasting misery, and ought to improve every breath for redemption, and to the glory of God, calling on God to damn their Bodies and souls!

O the heaven daring and soul destroying practice; God forbid that any of you should be guilty of the crime: but if there is O let me tell you in Love and pity great is their danger and e'er long unspeakable will be their misery; but if they will yet return Jesus has mercy in store for the worst of sinners; and if there is any as I hope there is among you that are seeking and enquiring after redemption, O let me take them by the hand and incourage them; Ah the Lord who has bowels of pity, and arms of love waiting to receive you will, surely give you of his holy spirit to lead you on to eternal life, if you will cast your souls on him. O fly fly my dear friends from the wrath to come and make sure an everlasting portion while there is hope. I am sensible you have never found a moment peace, rest nor sollid Joy in things of this vain world: but O in Jesus I can tell you, you will find Joys unspeakable and full of glory, O that you would be intreated to be happy for time and eternity! yea how can you refuse? I dare say if you only had the offer or any prospect of any preferment, or a commission of honour in your establishments, you would spare no pains, but break thro' every opposition, concert every method, by making all the interest that was possible to attain it. Why O why then my dear fellow men will you reject the greatest treasures and grandeur that ever was confered on any created being? Ah, could you but know the rest joy and satisfaction that is to be enjoyed in Christ even while in this world you would esteem a share in his love and a humble place near his feet, far more than the crown of England! And Ah how much greater will be the joys of eternal glory where wars and rumours of wars shall be no more! and O think my dear dear friends the Son of God has bled and dyed to open to your souls those bright mansions of eternal felicity, and is now yea even this day, intreating you to enter in and forever partake of the Joys of immortal light life love and Glory.

How can you forbear opening your hearts to such love and adoring him for such infinite goodness? O that I could prevail with you to carry these truths in your mind to your Barracks, and ponder them in your Sentinel hours! And I know that Jesus would be with and help you to give your hearts to him and then how happy ah unspeakably, happy would your moments glide away!

And when a few more days and nights have run their rounds, Jesus will call you from all your labours and sorrows to the Joys of an eternal day, which God knows is the sincere desire of my soul, that I might see you there with all Tears wiped from your eyes, and bear a part with you, and the countless adorers in everlasting praise to God for his goodness and his wonderfull works to the children of men.

And now with a few words to the auditory I conclude.

I am happy to have an opportunity a few days my dear hearers in this part of the Vinyard to serve you, and as I speak for God with souls immortal at stake, I must without the least fear, favour or selfish ends, deliver my message, and clear my garments of the blood of souls; and altho you may many of you look on me as your enemy because I tell you the truth yet God knows it is out of love to your souls. Yea what else can you imagine would excite me to undergo the fatigues that I do both in body and mind and expose myself to all the rage of the world?

If you imagine it is for a Temporal living surely being in the prime of life I could attain what little I should need with far less Trouble; or if you imagine it is for the applause of mortals surely you may be convinced to the contrary about your own doors; for altho I have some thousands in the province that esteem me far better than I am worthy of yet you will know that I have become a song for the drunkard, & a mark for the reproaches of the ungodly world.

But O let me tell you I think both my trials and reproaches so small that the one I will hang upon my garments as ornaments to be wiped off at the glorious return of my Master, and as for the other methinks I would cheerfully undergo them again and again to see any means of bringing some of your souls to the enjoyment and everlasting, honour of the Lord Jesus Christ.

Ah, I would far rather have some surviving christian passing by my tomb when I am cold in death say *here lyes the stammering tongue that taught my soul the Name of Jesus* than that they could say *here lyes the greatest earthly Monarch that ever existed.* O then let me be but a humble faithfull and successfull servant to Christ and my fellow mortals, and I have all I need; and all I desire; yea I esteem it more than millions and millions of worlds and O my dear hearers let me not be in vain to your souls but receive the message of peace the Lord hath sent by me, adore him to all eternity for his goodness to the sons of men; and I intreat you to labour with me the few moments I am in the Town for the promotion of religion, the advancing of Christs kingdom, as far as the influence of your several stations and capacities in life may extend; and may this day be not only kept as thanksgiving: but an everlasting thanksgiving kept therefore, O therefore resolve from this moment to arise from sin and sloth, and put the Lord Jesus in all your ways, love him, tell of him, walk with him, enjoy and adore him from this time forward and for ever, for his goodness and his wonderfull works to the children of men: which God of his infinite mercy grant and to his Name be the praise, AMEN. [pp. 20–39]

Notes

    (r) Lam 4:1.
    (s) Jer 9:1.
    (t) Song of Solomon 5:2.
    (u) Mk 8:38.
    (w) Gn 24:58.
    (x) Cant 5:16.
    (y) Lk 9:5.
    (z) Josph 24:15.

(a) Lam 3:1.
(b) Jb 16:14.
(d) Prv 8:4.
(e) Rv 13:1.

A GOSPEL CALL TO SINNERS!

A
SERMON
PREACHED BY
HENRY ALLINE

[NEWBURYPORT
PRINTED BY BLUNT & MARCH 1795

Originally published as
A Sermon Preached on the 19th of February 1783
at Fort-Midway
(Halifax, 1783).]

Preface

SINCE the happy moment (never to be forgotten) that Jesus deigned to pluck me from the jaws of hell, and manifest his everlasting love to my soul by his spirit, I have not only vowed (and still renew my choice) to be for him only: but am (by his grace) more and more delighted in his truths, in love with his perfections, confirmed in his gospel, and determined to walk in his ways, and make his name my theme for time and eternity.

Let the mercenary courters of popularity indefatigably pursue the empty sound of applause, the licentious waste all their fires, and stake their whole inheritance in a sensual paradise; let the obscene coquette, and self-adoring fop, paint, powder, decorate, and (hours at their glass) twist, screw, turn and metamorphosis their noisious lumps of clay to strole about as vassals in quest of eyes; let sanguine heroes depopulate kingdoms and wade thro' seas of blood to wear a scar of honour, and the lank-sided miser wear out life, starve body,

and damn soul, to fill a bottomless bag: Be it my whole portion and
labour (during my short race cross this little world) to bear that grand
commission once given from the throne of Heaven to Mary Mag-
dalene (divested of seven devils) *Go quickly and tell that Jesus* (the
despised Nazarene) *is risen*[1] *yea and lives for ever more!* so that it
is with delight I lend my stammering tongue, and unpolished pen, at
every opportunity to labour in, and exhibit the glorious theme.

And therefore when requested by my friends who were present
(almost every person in the place) when this Sermon was delivered,
I hand it to the press (with some small, but useful alterations) for their
further benefit, and the good of others; and may God bless the glorious truths, hand them O Jesus by thy Spirit to the heart of thousands, to their joy and thine eternal praise, AMEN.

SERMON

I Seek My Brethren. Gen xxxvii.   16.

O WHAT stones have been turned! What mountains moved! What
methods concerted! What labour and miseries endured by Jehovah
himself to seek and save a lost world! How doth he travel, call,
knock, wait, woo, and beseech, with unwearied patience, to save
mankind from misery and despair, and bring them to joy and unspeakable glory! Oh, the infinite love of that despised Jesus, which
you have heard me so often since I have been with you, (and will
again) recommend to you my poor, guilty, starving, perishing and
undone fellow mortals!

How hath he stooped from his realms of immortal glory, waded
thro' the disorders of your miserable world in the agonies of death
and miseries of hell, with his vesture dipped in blood, travelling from
kingdom to kingdom, from town to town, from village to village, for
to seek his brethren; knocking from heart to heart with bleeding
hands, and an aching heart, till his head is filled with the dew, and
his locks with the drops of the night! yea, and this night (tho' by a
stammering tongue) is come to your doors calling on sinners, and

---

1. Mt 27:7.

saying in the words of our text, *I seek my Brethren,* which by his assistance is to be my subject and employ in his name this evening, by endeavouring to exhibit a glorious, clear and effecting type of Christ, and shall much insist on Christ's seeking his brethren: But before I proceed to follow the chain of typical histories, I would first speak a few words to guard the minds of sinners from any injury from my using with them the word brethren, a term which I shall often make use of, being the language of our text, for altho' Christ declares his disciples not to be servants, but brethren, which may likewise be applied to the unregenerate: But not in that sense as to his children; sinners or the unregenerate part of the world are so far related to Christ as to be held up by him in flesh and blood by his becoming flesh, and thereby likewise they stand in a possibility of becoming his inseparable brethren, which he is labouring for: Yet while in an unregenerate state they are not his brethren as his children are; yea are so far from it that altho' he calls them branches, yet they are exposed every moment to be cut off and cast into the fire;[2] their standing thus in flesh and blood are so near related to Christ, that by his incarnate spirit they are restrained from that immediate destruction which they would plunge themselves in, if left to act themselves: But they can never bring forth any fruit unto God until they have given up the heart, for the will to act with Christ; and therefore you that are strangers to conversion may be so far from flattering yourselves with the name of christians or Christ's brethren, that you have cause to tremble at the thoughts of remaining so long at enmity against him, and the infinite danger of your being cut off in a moment from all relation to him, or benefit by him, and be consigned over to the miserable state of his most inveterate foes. O, therefore, let me intreat you, as you love your own souls, if Christ (as he really is) is now seeking after you to adhere to his calls, be found of him, and for ever enjoy him; and be his brethren and companions to all eternity.

And now to convince you of his willingness to save you I shall endeavour to discover his love, goodness, free grace, labour, and longsuffering, and willingness to save you, in the life and conduct of Joseph, who in my opinion is the most clear, glorious and effecting type of Christ, that all divine Revelation affords us. First, he was

---

2. Jn 15:2.

his Father's beloved Son, the darling of his bosom: and nothing less, O my hearers, than God's only begotten Son, the darling of his bosom, and beloved of all Heaven, was the seeker and Saviour of a lost world; nor could all the armies of Heaven, if engaged on the important errand, have got one soul home to immortal glory: Because nothing could effect the work, but that wrought in them, which none, but God would possibly effect.

Think, O! Ye sons and daughters of Adam, what a stoop of Jehovah for you and me! and was it for us? And are you the people that he came to seek! Yet, saith our text, and the whole gospel, to every soul present, this evening *I seek my Brethren!* O let him not seek in vain. Again Joseph was hated of his brethren, and set as a mark for all their rage, malice and cruelty: And, O! by woeful experience, I know that the carnal mind is at enmity against the Lord Jesus Christ, not subject to his laws, neither indeed can be. Ah! and by woeful experience he knew what it was to stand as a mark for all the malice of earth and hell! and when he came to his own, his own received him not. Neither imagine my dear hearers, that those ungodly men only, who had their hands engaged in his corporeal punishment and temporal death, were the only hands in his misery, or men enraged against him: for your sins not only pierced his soul then, but likewise are still at enmity against him now; and while you do not find room for him in your heart, and yield your whole soul into his hand, you are among his enemies, and are declaring, that you will not have this man, to reign over you. O sinners awake, and for your souls sake, look about you before your loss is irreparable! Again, Joseph incurred the malice and displeasure of his brethren in a greater degree, because he foretold them what would come to pass: So the Jews and all the wicked are the more enraged against Christ, because he foretells them, what will come to pass: for he came to bear witness to the truth, which he maintained in the very agonies of death; throw down, O! sinners, your weapons of rebellion, and love him, for *he is the way, the truth and the life.* And when Joseph's brethren were keeping their flocks in the field his father called upon him to go and look after them; *go, saith Jacob, and see what is become of thy brethren,* if it be well with them; so when we were *wallowing in our blood, cast out in the open field to the loathing of our persons,* or as the man fallen amongst thieves, *stripped, wounded, and left half dead* without any help from the law or its executors, the Father of all mercies calls upon his only Son to look after us; go, saith God, my Son, my only Son, my delight, my joy, my life, my all, and seek thy brethren; look after thy creatures, the wretched, miserable and lost family of Adam. And O! Shall I tell you my hearers, he cheerfully obeys! Ah! it *was a time of love* indeed! Hark! and you will hear him say, *Lo, I come in the volume of thy Book of Life to do thy will O God;*[3] *I will cast my Skirt over them and say unto them, Live.*[4] And this night, O sinners, he is come to seek you and wraps you in the mantle of his free grace: O believe and live for ever; for Jesus is come to enquire after you, or will you like Joseph's brethren, say, *here comes that dreamer!* Will you reject his calls, despise his offer, abuse his love, and destroy yourselves to all eternity? I imagine you will blame Joseph's brethren, and think they were divested of all the movings of conscience, and abandoned to all the dictates of humanity, for to conspire against him, when they saw him coming; and yet you will be guilty of conspiring against the innocent Lamb of God, thy soul's best friend and only helper, when coming for your good: Joseph perhaps was likewise loaded with some refreshment or temporal good things to nourish them from his father, which he gladly carried to support and comfort his brethren, yet they could say, *here comes that dreamer; let us now lay hands on him and destroy him, and see what will become of his dreams:* and so when the sinners friend was come, and (if I may say in our common language) with his arms full of bread, and loaded with good cheer for his starving, miserable, and perishing brethren, the Jews and all the ungodly can cry out *this is the heir, let us fall on him and kill him; this is he that hath pretended to be king, we'll destroy him, and see what will become of his kingdom; this is he who saith he can build the temple in three days, and that he is the Son of God; if he is, let him come down now from the cross; or if Elias be his friend let us see if Elias will come and help him.*

And will you, O! my hearers, persist in such cruelty, and perpetrate the horrid murder? O! be wise, be wise, have mercy upon yourselves, embrace the despised Nazarene, escape eternal perdition, and be everlastingly happy; for Jesus is come, knocks at your

---

3. Heb 10:7.
4. Ez 16:6.

door, and cries with a loud voice, *I seek my brethren,* and take heed to yourselves my dear hearers, that you do not hug unbelief, that murderer, and reject him while I am speaking. But to return to our type of the Messiah, they cast him into a pit until they saw a company of Ishmaelites travelling from Mount Gilead, and then they took him out and sold him for twenty pieces of silver. And O! must it be told, that the eternal Jehovah was sold for but ten more! O! tremble ye Judas like lovers of money! And bethink yourselves of your danger, lest you sell your souls and an interest in the eternal kingdom of grace and glory for a few ounces of dust.

O leave, leave your bewitching gods before they have bewildered your poor deluded souls to the howling regions of blackness and despair. Why will you run the risk of loosing a soul immortal for that which can neither abide with you, nor make you happy while yo[u] possess it? You may think perhaps you are not guilty of that lust for gold as to sell Christ and loose your soul for it: But let not the devil deceive you my dear hearers; for if the most simple pleasures, inoffensive enjoyments, or lawful concerns (as you call them) of this life, engages your attention, and amuses your mind so as to keep you from giving up your whole soul to God and making the Lord Jesus Christ your chief good, you are as guilty of idolatry as Micah, as guilty of selling Christ, as Judas, and therefore without repentance will soon be as miserable; for the soul-rending moment approaches when all these your amusements will be eternally swept away, and consequently you must immediately be in keen despair; for like Micah you will say, ye have taken away my Gods, and what have I more? O! Be intreated to open your doors this night for the waiting Jesus, and you will have God that will live and stand by you for ever.

But again, to return, Joseph was soon for his purity and chastity (for I must omit many passages of his life) a prisoner between the butler and baker; so was the spotless Son of God for his holiness, purity and truth, a prisoner between two thieves, who were justly condemned, but he unjustly, and as one of Josph's fellow prisoners suffered death, so one of the thieves blasphemed the God that made him and sunk in eternal death; while as Joseph told the butler he should be brought to the king's table to serve with the cup of wine, the other thief cries, *Lord remember me when thou comest into thy kingdom,* and Jesus told him that he should

that same day be with him in paradise;[5] Ah, where he rejoices at
the king's table, and drinks of living wine for ever! O, be incouraged then ye condemned souls, who like the expiring thief are
just biding this mortal world an everlasting adieu, there is yet
hope; Jesus is yet alive; Ah, and as near you as he was to the
dying criminal, and as boundless in his mercy: But, O, remember
the other thief went to hell with a Christ as nigh. O! what a dreadful thought to go down to everlasting perdition so nigh the gates
of Heaven, and sink to hell with salvation at the door! But I must
return, and likewise entreat your most engaged attention with me
to the type reflecting therefrom to the glorious antitype, Joseph is
soon exalted to the second person in the kingdom, and in a time
of famine has the care and command of all the grain in Egypt, so
that if any came for bread, Pharaoh told them to *go to Joseph:*
And O! I can tell you, you that find like the prodigal son a famine
in the land, and begin to be in want, that Jesus, my blessed master, whom you have sold to the Ishmaelites, is become, yea, and
always was, God over all, blessed for ever more, and turns (if I
may use such language) the key of all the heavenly granary; let
me therefore say to you as the Patriarch to his starving sons, *why
sit ye here looking sad one upon the other? behold I hear there
is corn in Egypt, get ye down and buy for us, that we may live
and not die.*[6]

Why sit ye here, O ye starving sons and daughters of Adam,
perishing for lack of bread, when Jesus is yet alive and in your brother's house, there is bread enough and to spare?

O arise! arise, and go down to Egypt, and buy without money
and without price! *but why,* saith one, *or how in Egypt, when I
thought that Egypt, in a spiritual sense, signified a state of death,
darkness and bondage? Or the unconverted state?* True, my dear
hearers it does, and yet ye must go down to Egypt nevertheless for
to get bread for your starving souls; that is, see yourselves thus in
Egypt; and not only so, but the corn is really in Egypt, as soon as
ever the sinner finds himself there; and therefore ye need not say,
who shall ascend up to Heaven to bring you down the bread of life,

---

5. Lk 23:43.
6. Gn 13:2.

nor into the deep, for the bread of life is nigh you, even in your hearts, so that if you will but believe, ye shall eat and live, yea and rejoice for evermore.

And now to a further review of our typical subject, we find the sons of Jacob going down with their money to Egypt for to get corn; and let it never be forgotten, my hearers, that not one farthing of their money was taken: but all returned; each one with his loaded sack and his money in the sack's mouth.

Ah! a glorious truth for the poor! Learn hence, that although, Pharisee like, we may labour hard to wash our hands before we eat, and thereby carry our imagined cleaness, good duties, and strict performance to recommend ourselves to God; or speaking vulgarly to buy bread: yet after all we have done, whoever attains one crumb of the bread of life will receive it as a gift with their money all returned. And blessed be God, he has told us it will not defile a man to come to the gospel feast and eat with unwashen hands![7] O! Come then ye starving (or rather proud) sinners, just as you are, and cease from that custom, which was among the Pharisees, and is still; yea, spread over almost all Christendom, and practised in the heart of almost all professors, to wash before they eat, or prepare themselves to come to Christ; cease, I say, from the God-dishonouring and soul-destroying practice, and come to Jesus as you are; with all your sins, and in all your vileness; Ah! without money and without price; for Jesus, who cannot be benefitted by any of your mercenary services, invites you to a full table. Hark, hear the glad news! *Go ye and learn,* saith he, *what that meaneth, I will have mercy and not sacrifice;* and therefore *eat O friends, drink, yea drink abundantly, O beloved, for the Son of Man came not to be ministered unto, but to minister, and to give his life a ransom for sinners, and when we were without strength, in due time Christ died for the ungodly;* observe the words, my dear hearers, not for the Godly, but *for the ungodly:* And therefore, for your soul's sake, do not bar yourselves out of Heaven with your faithless prayers, spiritless duties, and Christless christianity: But go, like Mephibosheth, lame in both feet to the King's table.

But, saith one, would you not have us pray before we come to Christ? yea, my dear hearer, if there is any danger of getting to Christ

---

7. Mt 15:20.

too soon. But saith one again, must we not pray to get to Christ? I answer yes, if you can pray without Christ, or get to Heaven without Christ, or by your prayers recommend yourself to Christ.

But let me tell you, that, think what you will of your prayers, if ever you come to Christ, they will be all taken away, and you will come to him without one prayer, form or duty, to recommend you; yea, if you have already prayed seven years, and should live to add seven years more of such prayers, you may never expect to receive Christ until you have left them all, and come to Christ without one of them. And now what think you, my dear hearers, of making a ladder of your prayers, or of staying away from Christ until you have prayed more? Christ must be a whole Saviour at last if ever you receive him, and therefore why not receive him as a whole Saviour now? you may think perhaps that I am oversetting all religion by speaking so much against your prayers; but let me tell you, that you will never know or enjoy one spark of true religion, until all those recommending prayers are overset. For although you may excuse yourself that you do not depend on your prayers, nor in the least degree expect to recommend yourself to God by all your duties, or all that ever you can do; yet you are so far deceived that I can prove you are so far depending on them (I mean you that are awakened and seem to be seeking after salvation) as to keep yourselves from Christ thereby; yea, and it is the bar that keeps you this moment from casting yourselves on him; for was you stripped of those false supporters, you would immediately cast yourselves wholly on the mercy of God, and would soon be rejoicing in Jesus Christ, the God of your salvation; which to convince you of, let me only ask you a few questions.

Some of you I am sensible by the private discourse I have had with you, begin to be convinced of your lost and undone condition, and have been forsaking your sins, evil practices, and carnal amusements, and are daily, yea, some hourly, seeking after Christ by your prayers, and labouring to have your souls converted; well, and let me ask you further, have you not been determining of late to be more engaged and faithful in the means of grace, or in pursuit of conversion, than ever you have been? Yea, are you not this very moment, while I am speaking, concluding and resolving in your minds, that you intend to begin your lives anew, and if you live ever to get home, or till the ensuing day, or week, you will be more engaged than ever you have been, and pray more, and pray oftener than you have done? And pray, what is all that determination of amendment of life, new resolutions, engagedness of seeking, more earnestness of prayer, and more repeated cries for? Is it not all to attain conversion with, and thus to recommend you to Christ? for if you did not think you would get nigher to him, and more prepared for his grace, or more likely to attain conversion thereby, you would not do it. And thus, I dare say, you have some of you got a week's work to compleat in your mind to bring you to Christ, or to do before you expect to find him, yea, and some of you a month's or a year's work, that you intend to do before you expect to find him. And now, my dear hearers, if this be the truth of the case with any of you, which I dare say it is, how can you say you have got no self-righteousness, or any thing that you depend on, or expect to recommend you to God, when you have not only got what you have done, laid up in your mind, but intend to get much more before you are converted, or before you will come to Christ? do you expect that God will be more merciful some weeks or months hence, than he is now? Or do you expect, that by doing all that you have designed, you will prevail with him to give consent that you should be saved? or (as I would put the most favourable constructions that I can on your designs) finding a hard heart and stubborn will, do you expect thereby to soften the heart, and bow the will? if not, if none of these are your designs and expectations, then, why would you pursue such steps, or why are you not willing to receive the mercy of God now? if you must at last come to Christ with a hard heart, and all your sins, why are you not willing to cast yourselves on him now? And why are you not convinced now my dear reader, by these arguments, that you are endeavouring to buy salvation, and that you are not willing to receive Christ on his own terms, or his grace as a free gift; although he is now come to seek you. But saith one again, what would the man have us do? Would he have us neglect praying, and all our duties? I answer, my dear hearers, if you have accepted of Christ, you have neither prayed nor discharged one duty, either to the glory of God, or the good of your own souls; and therefore, I am so far from advising you to cease from duties and prayers, that I intreat you to perform them immediately, and that by taking Christ with you; for without him I have proved, that you never have, nor ever can, either pray or perform the least duty acceptable to God, or to the good of your own souls, and therefore if your days should be lengthened out to the age of Methuselah and all wore out in performing those duties and prayers, which you have prescribed, or resolved upon in your own mind, you would not be one step nearer to Christ, or any more prepared for conversion, than you are now; and therefore what think you now of staying away from Christ any longer, to be prepared to come, or of praying and performing duties with Christ? But saith one, what would the man have us do, we cannot convert ourselves, nor think that God will convert us now, or bring us to rejoice in Christ this evening? to which I reply, you may convert yourselves (if I may use such language) as well now as the next year, or ten years hence; and if you cannot convert yourselves neither now nor then, but God must do it for you; is not God as able and willing to do it now, as he will be to-morrow, next year, or the year after, or any time to come? yea, and let me tell you, that, although you have often been taught, and often said, you would and must wait God's time (which is the very language of the devil) and so put it off for some future period! Yet God declares, that his time is now; *now is the acceptable time and to day is the day of salvation;* yea, let me tell such people, that God has been long waiting your time, and waited in vain, and if you should put him off so a few days more, your day will be over, your time at a period, your soul gone, and your loss irrecoverable; and then it may be said by God, *I called and ye refused, I stretched out my arm and ye regarded not, I therefore will laugh at your calamities, and mock when your fear cometh.*

O! therefore, as you love your own souls, put off a waiting Saviour no longer, lest you loose your soul to all eternity. You say you cannot think that God will convert or bring your soul into liberty this evening, and yet, I dare say you expect he will some other time, and this is the very thing still that keeps you from him: For he never can, nor never will be your Saviour until you, not only believe he is able and willing, but so far believe it the present moment, that you will cast yourself on him without any expectation of a future opportunity; yea, you must and will be reduced to such extremity, that you can no longer be put off, or any way pacified with or resting upon, what may, or will be done at some other time, or hereafter, but will in immediate extremity, cry like sinking Peter for help now, *Lord I cannot live any longer without thee, save me, yea save me immediately, or I sink forever.* And then, my dear hearers, and never till then, will you receive the waiting Saviour; so that by this time, methinks you must be convinced, that you have been (under a pretended reverence and humility) putting off the Lord, like Felix, for a more convenient season; and thereby baring yourself from salvation, and thus saying, that you cannot come yet, and cannot believe yet: but you hope you shall by and by, or some other time; which is the strongest terms saying, that you will not believe yet, nor you will not come yet, but by and by, or some other time when you have got some better frame, you will come; but let me tell you my dear hearers, wait and try what you will, and as long as you will for a better heart, a softer heart, a loving heart, a humble heart, or a broken heart, and a better frame, you will be after all, but like the woman who was twelve years trying many physicians for a cure till she spent all her living and instead of growing better grew worse, and was obliged at last to press through the crowd with all her disorders, and touch the hem of Christ's garment, or never be made whole; yea, and if ever you are healed, you must like her, not only despair of all other helps and physicians, but be reduced to that perishing extremity, that you will press through the crowd of every temptation and disagreeable Frame to Jesus the last resource, and complete Saviour.

O believe that you are as fit, and as worthy to come to Christ now as you will be if you labour and mourn and pray all your days, and that the Lord Jesus Christ is now waiting to receive you! O believe that the great Jehovah offers you salvation this moment as a free gift. *But saith one again, must I come to him just as I am now, with a hard heart, dark mind, and polluted soul?* I answer, yes; nor will it ever be any better until you do. You may court the terrors of the law, and the awful apprehensions of death and the grave, together with a dismal discovery of the pains of hell, and the dispairing horrors of the damned, which indeed may alarm some careless sinner that has never been roused scarcely to a thought of his miserable condition before: But those who have been long awakened by the spirit of God, and under a sense of their danger, there is nothing will affect them, but to cast themselves on God, and feel his love and goodness. And therefore instead of your going to Mount Sinai to soften the heart after you have seen your lost undone condition, I would point you to that infinite love, and goodness that so freely bled beneath your sins, and threw open the gates of eternal glory for the vilest of the vile; and therefore ye need not go any longer *to the Mount which burneth with blackness and darkness and tempest, and to such thun-derings and lightnings that made even Moses and all the Hebrew camp to tremble; which Mount, if so much as a beast touch was thrust through with a dart:* but ye may and ought to *come to Mount Sion, the city of the living God, the heavenly Jerusalem, and to an innumerable company of angels, to the general assembly and church of the first born which are written in Heaven, and to God the Judge of all, and to the spirits of just men made perfect;* And O shall I tell you! *to Jesus the Mediator of the new covenant.* Ah, *and to the blood of sprinkling,* my dear hearers, *that speaks better things,* yea, far bet-ter, *than the blood of Abel;* and all this a free gift, to whoever will, may enter and enjoy the glorious privileges for ever: but these bless-ings you can never attain, but by venturing on Christ. And now think a moment (ye that mourn a hard heart) that all this was the price of blood for you, Ah! for you in particular; yea, and the same friend that has done all this, will do and grant all that you need; yea, so willing to make you everlastingly happy, that he not only offers it to you, but his heaviest complaint and greatest grief is, that even after all he has done for you, ye will not believe him, nor enjoy it; and he mourns because of your danger still, or mourns shall I say, because his labour is all to you like to be lost, and you, after all the pains he has endured, for ever abandoned to all that is good, banished from his presence, and lay down, in the regions of eternal darkness and despair: but if you cannot believe this, step with me a moment to the gates of that bloody city where you will see him weeping over a peo-ple, that by rejecting his grace have chained themselves to irrecov-erable ruin and despair, even when thus gone, and that against all that he had done, or could do, yet he feels their misery, and condoles their state with a bleeding heart, and in words that might cause any hardness, but that of sin or final Impenitence to melt; *he beheld* saith God, *the city and wept over it,* Ah, wept over it indeed! *saying, if thou hadst,* or, O that thou hadst! *known at least in this thy day the things that belonged to thy peace, but,* Ah, by rejecting now, *they are* to my almost insupportable grief, *hid,* for ever hid *from thine eyes!*

Yea, so great was his pity, that, if it had been possible, he would yet have brought them to repentance, if his labouring years longer would have done it: laboured years longer, did I say? Ah, I am so far from charging God, as many do, with designing the misery of them that are lost, or consenting to their ruin, that is, permit them to be ruined, when he could have prevented it; neglecting to save them when he could—I say, instead of believing so, I as firmly believe, as I believe there is a God, that his love is so great, his goodness so uncontainable, that if any more of the fallen race could be redeemed by his suffering more for them, he would with as much freedom as he once gave his life, when no man took it away,[8] enter again in the flesh, and undergo all the unspeakable miseries again, even to death; for such is the nature of the Divine Being, as can never be roiled, incensed, or stirred up to thirst for revenge, though a truth which I have been condemned for declaring, yet a truth that I am more and more willing to vindicate by the infallible word; yea, and a truth that I trust I shall believe and rejoice to all eternity. But saith one of my hearers, *I thought God was nothing else but vengeance against the ungodly, and angry with the wicked every day.* True, my dear friends, he is as vengeance to the finally impenitent, because of sin: But you must not imagine this vengeance or anger, so called, to be any thing that is so in God, or awoke in God since the sin was committed, or any thing that is wrath or vengeance in itself; but so to the wicked by reason of the infinite contrariety of their guilt and sin; and thus it is, that he is angry with sin from the consequence of his nature, that is and forever was so opposite to sin, that they can no more abide together than light and darkness, heat and cold; but when light scatters darkness, would you imagine therefrom, that the light was possessed of malice, spite or revenge against the darkness? or when fire dissolves the ice, will you say that the fire was incensed by the ice, or mad with the ice? Why then will you imagine, that God is roiled, incensed, or got a wrath and spirit of revenge stirred up in himself against sin, because he hates and abhors sin? Or why would you say, that he was possessed of wrath and vengeance against the sinner, because his nature is so to them while in their sins, when at the same time his nature in itself is all love and goodness? but some may say again, if God is never roiled nor incensed, why does he cast sinners to hell at all? I answer, my dear hearers, he never does; for they by sin make their own hell, and go to their own place.

But perhaps you will say again, I know they so far make and go

---

8. Jn 10:18.

to their own hell, that they justly deserve it, and therefore God's throne is clear of their blood: but yet I think he could still save them if he would: but as they have so often and willfully rejected, he swears they *shall not enter into his rest*. And now, as that is the conception of many, who are called Christians, I shall speak a few words more in answer, whereby I shall discover the horrible consequences of that principle, first, if that was the truth, then God is changeable, for when he first calls the sinner, he is not got that wrath and vengeance against him: but by the sinner's rejecting the calls, he stirs up a wrath and incenses a justice which never can be appeased or satisfied. Secondly, he is not only less merciful now than he was before the sinner rejected his mercy; but likewise possessed of something incensed, or some wrath & anger, as long as the sinner lies in hell, which God never would have felt or been possessed of, if the creature had not sinned; so that consequently not only the creature, but God too is injured by sin to all eternity; which you see must be the case (let people twist and turn as much as they will, to cover their dark and unscriptural sentiments). And now what think you, my dear hearers, of such blasphemous conceptions of the Deity as many have and hold forth as the truths of the everlasting gospel? Yea, and will level all their artillery against any one who presumes to believe in any better God, or who discovers the nature of their principles: But, blessed be God, I feel more and more delighted with, confirmed in, and impatient to proclaim that glorious truth with the beloved disciple, *God is love,* yea, *he is light,* saith the same John, *and in him is no darkness at all.* O my hearers, fall in love with such a God! A God whose nature is so good as to exclude him from any possibility of feeling or doing any thing but good; yea, a God that will labour to do good as long as the creature is in a capacity of receiving; nor will ever give the creature up to misery, until he is gone beyond recovery; stepping in himself, and saying *what could have been done more, that I have not done?*

But saith one, doth not this doctrine of God, being all love and goodness, open a door to licentiousness, and tend to harden men to go in sin, and put off their repentance? I answer, it is so far from having that tendency, that it is the most invincible bulwark against it; as I will convince you in a few words. For if the creature's salvation could be effected by an arbitrary act of God at any time, and their damnation turned upon his being awoke to anger and resentment and revenge; then God can and may send them to hell whenever he please, if they labour ever so much to attain his favour; and on the other hand, he may save them whenever he please, if they live in sin ever so long, yea may force them into Heaven, even if they live and die in their sins and rebellion; and therefore, if the salvation and damnation of the creatures turn thus, what need have they to put their hearts to the work, or trouble their minds about salvation at all? but when you declare to them (as the truth really is) that although God is nothing but love and goodness, yet if they do not improve their day of probation immediately, they may the next moment (and certainly will soon) be so sealed up in final impenitence within themselves, as to be beyond the reach of an Omnipotent arm; and then that love and goodness will be so far from doing them any good, that it will be their greatest torment; for the love, goodness and purity of God will be to their hellish nature, as oil to the fire, increasing the flame—yea, and when thus gone, are not gone, because God was angry, and rose up against them in revenge, but are become in themselves such as God cannot help no more than he can change; yea and have become such as the nature of God was forever opposite to, and forever will be; and therefore as his nature will forever augment their misery, they must forever endure unspeakable torments thereby; for he can neither change nor cease; and as long as he exists, his presence and nature will be to them an unspeakable addition to torment and misery. And thus, my dear hearers, I have discovered to you the reason why sinners may be eternally lost and miserable, although God is (without change) all love and goodness; a God of love and goodness indeed.—Ah, and so far from being stirred up to seek revenge, that, although like Joseph's brethren, ye have been guilty of murdering your innocent and best friend, yet his bleeding heart is open still to receive you. Ah, see him through all the agonies of a miserable life, labouring for the good of his inveterate enemies! yea, and in the last agonies of life, while so crushed with the infinite weight of their rebellion, that his soul was racked with the acute tortures, and groaning under the insupportable burden, he was so far from being roiled, incensed, or stirred up to resentment, or revenge, by all their insults and cruelty, that his last groan was *Father forgive them:* but O! what was that he said? Think, O my soul! and let me repeat the words, *Father forgive them,* he says: Hear, O sinners, and feel, the affecting prayer; the last groans of thy best friend—and O he dies! Ah he dies! and for whom? Why for you and me. Dies, did I say? Yes, he dies: and yet he lives, and lives forevermore; and where's a God so good? This night, O sinners, under our roof, and near thy heart; yea, blessed be his name, methinks I have some feeling sense, I will not say as is commonly said, his awful presence; no, but his all-glorious, sweet and soul-ravishing presence; but so rapid has the divine truths flowed into my soul, that perhaps I am tedious; I therefore return, and come now to the most affecting passage of our typical scene. Joseph's brethren being found with the King's cup! and brought back therefor as thieves and traitors, refreshes in their memory the horrid crime once committed against their innocent brother, which now stares them in the face, and causes every groan and feature to betray the horrors of a guilty conscience, and the anguish of an almost despairing soul.

O! say they, one to the other, "all this has befallen us on account of our cruelty to our brother; and vengeance hath thus pursued and overtaken us, because that we thus slew him, and refused to pity.

"Ah! now we remember the anguish of his soul, the beating of his bleeding heart, and the groans of his distressed breast, when our hands were abandoned to all the dictates of humanity, our souls divested of compassion, and our hearts obdurate against the melting intreaties of his wounded soul! And what now shall we do? For our iniquities have overtaken us, and by the cruelty of our hands we are hedged upon every side! Oh! wretched men that we are! For the day of our calamity is come! And we are excluded from every helper, and cut off from every prospect of hope! We are destined to misery by every aggravating circumstance, for every thing conspires our ruin, and augments our miseries! We have not only left our aged parents under the distresses of a cruel famine, but to lash on their speedy declines of life, and crush their exhausted frames with the agonies of all that loss can prey.

"Ah! well may they say, when they hear of our hard fate, Joseph is dead! Benjamin is not! and the rest where, are they? And thus in the bitterness of soul and anguish of heart, we shall indeed bring their grey hairs with sorrow to the grave!"

But Joseph, who understands their language, without an interpreter, can forbear no longer—O! saith he within himself, "How can I endure any longer to hear the groans of their sinking spirits, or stand against the humble acknowledgments of their cruelty to me! O! I feel the sighs and groans of their bleeding hearts, and almost despairing souls; my breast throbs, my bosom burns, my heart achs, and my whole soul is dissolved with melting love, and uncontainable compassion for my poor distressed and broken-hearted brethren! and so pregnant is my bowels with compassion, that my labouring soul was vent for the sympathy I feel! O! hand me to my bed-chamber, that I may give vent to the convulsions of my sympathizing bosom!'' Alone he weeps; and Ah, did his brethren know how would it mitigate their sorrows, expel their fears, and ease their desponding souls of their almost insupportable burdens! Well, soon they'll know.— But let me leave them a moment, and view the trembling sinner, when apprehended, if I may so say, and found with the King's cup— How do they shrink when under the thunders of Mount Sinai! they begin to discover the folly, the rebellion, the cruelty, theft and murder, that they have been guilty of Ah! says the convicted soul, with a trembling conscience, ''I have rebelled against Heaven, I have deserted from God, stole, carried away and converted like Belshazzer, the vessels of the house of the Lord to an evil use—I have not only, like Esau, in some degree been selling my birth-right for the deceitful morsal of this world's meat, but like Judas, in some degree, been guilty of selling the Lord of Glory for the polluted joy, and perishing treasures of this sinful world, and have murdered my own soul, and crucified the Lord of Glory! O! what have I done! what have I done! And now my sins have overtaken me, my crimes have prevailed, and, as Job saith of his disease, my guilt and mine iniquities bindeth me about as the collar of my coat; vengeance hath pursued me, and all this is come upon me for my folly, and God is about to destroy me for my sins!'' But, ah! little does the poor soul know that God is now labouring for their good! they imagine that all their happiness and pleasures are now gone forever; they imagine that God is now angry with them, and is going to send them to destruction—when it is quite the reverse: for God who feels a pity for them in labouring to bring them to partake of joys unspeakable, to drink of the rivers of pleasure for ever more; yea, God is so far from desiring or seeking to be revenged upon them for their sins, or sending them to destruction, that he is now come to save them from destruction, pluck them from their own hell; and like Joseph, who understands their language, though they cannot understand his, he feels their distress and condoles their misery. Yea, and if I may use the expression, his bosom so burns with love, and his bowels so yearns over them with compassion, that he seeks a place to weep; that is, his pity and bowels of compassion that is undiscovered to the sinner, is infinitely beyond what they could imagine, or what can be expressed to them. Yea, as little do sinners know of Christ's pity for them, as Joseph's brethren did of his compassion, when he was weeping in private, and they thought he was going to punish them; for no sinner can see, feel or enjoy any love in Christ, until they feel him theirs. And although the poor sinners come trembling like a criminal to the place of execution, and thinks that God is angry with them, and is going to destroy them—yet he has that pity for them that is unspeakable, and is now more willing to receive the returning sinner than the sinner is to return; and thus the Father sees the returning Prodigal, his bowels yearn over him with compassion, and not only meets him, but runs to meet him, while yet a great way off.

O! be incouraged then to return ye mourning, trembling sinners, starving for want of bread, for God has sworn by himself, that he has no pleasure in your death, but that you turn and live.

Ah, saith the disconsolate soul, *if I could see or believe that God had any thoughts of mercy for me, I should be encouraged, but I cannot see any thing, but blackness, darkness and an angry God, and all things seem to conspire for my immediate ruin.* Well, my dear hearers, did not all things appear as desperate to Joseph's brethren, but a few moments before he made himself known to them, wiped all tears from their eyes, fed them from his own table, and caused them to rejoice in his favour?

Ah! And Jesus, who is present this very moment seeking his brethren, yearns over you with bowels of pity, is ten thousand times more willing to receive you, feed you, and manifest his love to you, than Joseph was to his brethren. *Ah but* saith one, *I have sold him, and crucified him, and how can he forgive me?* So had they sold their brother, and been guilty of the most inhuman acts of cruelty, and yet he could freely forgive them; surely you will not presume to say, or imagine, that he was more merciful than the infinite Jehovah, whose goodness, love and compassion is as boundless as himself: O then, venture out against all those discouragements, and cast yourselves on the sinner's friend, and he will deliver you! Ah, so free is his love, and so great his pity toward you, that there is nothing keeps the manifestations of his love from your soul, this moment, while I speak, but your bars of unbelief! O, believe, believe, and all things are possible! Yea, if ye had faith only, as a grain of mustard seed, that mountain of sin would be removed from your soul, and your dead soul raised to life! O, that this might be the happy moment that you would now cast yourselves at the feet of king Jesus, receive his grace, enjoy his love, and adore his name for ever, for he is now come to seek his brethren. But to return to the typical narrative, O, how surprising, how joyful, how affecting, and heart-melting was the manifestation of Joseph to his brethren! not a word or censuring or condemning them for their abuse to him: but with his bowels yearning, and heart melting, salutes them with a *come near I pray you, for I am your brother, whom ye sold into Egypt, now therefore be ye not grieved,*[9] O, what love is now expressed in every groan, sob, sigh and tear, when their hearts are too full to be expressed, and bursts forth in every act of the affecting scene, like an overflowing fountain, that has long been repulsed, but can no longer be contained; their breast through their bosom burn, and their hearts dissolving in love, unite as one, while their souls swoon (as it were) away with the raptures of joy at the happy meeting, and knowledge of each other. O, the affecting scene! And think my hearers, how great, how joyful and unspeakable the change! yea, so great, and so obvious, that was I to assert that all this was imperceptable, and that Joseph's brethren had no knowledge of their being forgiven, nor any manifestations of Joseph's love to them, I should be stared at as one almost bereaved of all reason, repugnant to divine revelation, and in the face of the most glaring demonstrations: And yet how many in this land of light will presume to declare, yea hold it as an article in their creed, that a soul may be converted and not know it! O, the midnight darkness of such minds, and the ignorance of such people, who pretend that so great, yea so unparalleled a change can be wrought imperceptable to the creature, on whom alone the work is wrought! yea, so shocking is such a principle, that was I to give you my mind, it would be, that *it was contrived in hell, and is vindicated* by none but the *advocates for their dark regions,* for it strikes at the very nature, design and consequences of the kingdom of Christ among men; for if there is no knowledge, but only a guess-work, and

---

9. Gn 45:45.

all a matter of uncertainty, who are the children of God, and who are
the sons of Belial, or whether a man is converted or not, then the
Pharisees, the Antinomians, Hypocrites, and the true christians are
all lumped together in one promiscuous crowd, and there is no knowing how they will fare at the last, or which will fare the best; for a
child of God, who is an heir of everlasting glory, does not know (according to that) after all his pretensions to religion, and love to God,
and knowledge of Christ, but he may be the next moment lifting up
his eyes in hell, and blaspheming the God that made him; and on the
other hand, the open profane, who lives and dies without any knowledge of a change, who are dying in the gall of bitterness and bonds
of iniquity, who have been making a mock (as many do in these days)
of all pretensions to conversion, or the knowledge of the gift of the
holy ghost, has as much cause to die in peace, and expect to be
slipped into heaven, and made happy, as any of the followers of the
Lamb, which to me is so shocking and unreasonable, that if I could
believe it, I would this moment close my bible, and speak no more
in that name, nor ever more should you hear my stammering tongue
exhorting souls to repentance, and the service of God; for if they
were to seek, serve, and love and fear him ever so faithful, it would
at last (according to that Hypothsies) be but an uncertain matter.

O! why, why will men love darkness, choose their bondage,
and labour so hard against all true reason, and divine Revelation, to
reject the truth, keep themselves in blindness, and bind themselves
down to perdition? who out of pretended reverence, and (I was about
to say bastard) humility will reply, ''why God is a Sovereign, and
therefore has a sovereign right to dispose of us as he please, without
giving us any account whether he designs us for happiness or misery,
and we ought not to be too anxious to know it he intends to save us
or not, lest we are guilty of presumption: but do the best we can, go
trembling all our days with a hope that he will not finally cast us off,
and if he does after we have cast ourselves on his mercy, he will be
just, and we shall have no cause to complain.''

And thus with all their pretended love, reverence and humility
they have brought forth a brat, that if examined has been an advocate
for the powers of darkness, and a supported antichrist for many centuries, has made God a liar, charged him with cruelty and injustice,
and sent many thousands of souls to hell: For God has declared, that
he so loved the world that he gave his only begotten Son, that who-

soever believeth in him should not perish, but have everlasting life:
But some will say (who believe in an arbitrary partial God) *that is
the elected part of the world;* I wish they would let God speak for
himself; who not only says for the world, but likewise goes on to tell
the reason, why, *that whosoever,* saith he, *believeth on him, should
not perish, but have everlasting life,*[10] and then declares, that he
would have all men to be saved and come unto the knowledge of the
truth;[11] and then, lest we should not yet believe him, or should charge
him with neglect, injustice, cruelty and partiality, he swears as he
lives (and commands his servants in the same verse to proclaim that
oath) that he has no pleasure in the death of the wicked (not the righteous, but the wicked, he saith) but that (repeating over again, who
he means) the wicked turn from his way, and live, and then goes on
with a repeated call, turn ye, turn ye, concluding with an expostu-
lation, for saith he, why will ye die?[12] And now dare they say, after
all he has declared, that we do not know whether he is willing to save
us or not, or call it presumption to claim, an assurance through his
word and grace, until we leave this life, and with regard to knowing
our particular interest in this truth, he declares in positive terms, *ye
shall know the truth, and the truth shall make you free;*[13] and declares
that, he will manifest himself to his children;[14] and pray, what is a
manifestation, but making a thing known? Yea, even your common
reason will teach you, that if things are not made known they are not
made manifest.

Yea, what happiness, what salvation, what joy, what life, can
it be, that a man can have and not know it? How can Christ be a
man's friend, companion, and comforter, joy and strength, and the
man not know that he has any Christ, friend, joy, life, strength or
comforter? But saith John on this point, *hereby know we, that we
dwell in him, and he in us, because he hath given us of his Spirit.*[15]
And we know that we are of God,[16] *and he that believeth on the Son*

---

10. Jn 3:16.
11. 1 Tm 2:3.
12. Ez 33:11.
13. Jn 32.
14. Jn 14:21.
15. 1 Jn 4:13.
16. Jn 5:19.

of God hath the witness in himself.[17] And Job doth not say, I guess, but *I know that my Redeemer liveth;* and Paul doth not say, it may be when we leave this world, God will bring us to Heaven, but *we know that if this our earthly house of this tabernacle were dissolved, we have a building of God an house not made with hands eternal in the Heavens;* and David not only saith, that God hath made with him an everlasting covenant, but offers to tell how he was brought to the knowledge of it by his conversion: *come* saith he, *all ye that fear God, and I will declare what he hath done for my soul;* and saith the spouse, *my beloved is mine, and I am his.* Yea, and so full is the oracles of life of this truth, that if it was necessary, I might continue for an hour, repeating such positive demonstrations from him, that cannot lie; and yet against it all, how many will labour to spread the cause of antichrist, and say *we cannot know, that we are converted in this life,* and look upon it as I before observed, that they are doing God honour, when they are saying, they must leave that with God, must walk trembling all their days, and not presume to intrude into the secrets of God, to be so positive, whether or not he intends to save them. Although the true christian's Saviour, saith to his children, *let not your hearts be troubled, for I will not leave you comfortless;* and saith the Apostle, when speaking in his master's name to his fellow saints, *rejoice, and again I say rejoice;* and if you will but examine, you will find no sin that Christ ever reproved his disciples for so much as for unbelief; even calls them fools, and expostulates with them, why, and how long they would thus harden their hearts by unbelief? and yet now think they are doing God and their own souls service by nourishing and preaching up the necessity of unbelief? Though they will not allow it is unbelief they are pleading for; because they will cover it with some more plausible terms: but the Lord knows they have no cause to plead so much for the necessity of slavish fear doubts and unbelief, if it has been as cruel to their souls as it was to mine; and as for those who argue, that people may be born again and not know it, if I should be asked my mind to give the reason, why they argue so unreasonable and inconsistent, I should reply, *why from the cause, that a blind man thinks it strange, when you tell him black is not white.* But too long has my attention

---

17. 1 Jn 5:10.

be stolen away from our subject to refute inconsistences, and therefore I return: and O, what joy of soul, what melting of heart, does attend the manifestation of Jesus to his brethren, or to the returning prodigal! long has the poor sinner been labouring hard to humble his soul, and soften his hard heart, to hate sin, love holiness, to get some good frames, and find some evidences of grace, but all was in vain: but now a discovery and felt sense of the love and compassion of Christ has done it in a moment; for he looks on his sins (and himself for his sins and folly) with detestation; not because of its condemnation so much as its appearing horribly evil in its nature; and wonders that he could hug the monster in his bosom so long.

Now he sees that beauty and amiableness in God and his ways that his soul falls in love therewith; not so much for a shelter from hell and misery, but for his life, his joy, and his portion; not for the life to come only, or to be sure of some happy place after death, but for his life, joy and portion in this life, and wonders that he has not fallen in love with it long before.

And now, although he before like Joseph's brethren expected immediate destruction, and thought that there was an angry God coming out in vengeance against him, yet he finds that God is love, and has forgiven his sins with freedom; yea, he sees that he was so far from having any desire or design to destroy him, that he has not only forgiven him, but would have forgiven him before if he had believed and cast himself upon him; and his very heart breaks as it were more for his rejecting and abusing such love, than for destroying his own soul; and yet seeing, yea feeling that God has so long been waiting, wooing and beseeching, and now after all his innumerable offences, has freely forgiven him, smiled upon him, shed abroad his love in his soul, and loves him with an everlasting love, and all this through the sufferings, bleeding wounds, and dying groans of his best friend, whom he has long despised, rejected and crucified by his sins, and now while all this he sees, feels, knows and enjoys through the same meek and lowly Jesus that is now present with him, and communing with his soul, causes him, like our type, his soul as it were to swoon away with a rapture of inexpressible joy, and his heart to dissolve with love that is stronger than death; and thus in love, joy, gratitude and humility, he swoons, if I may say, on the neck of his loving, forgiving, and long-suffering, brother Joseph, while he on the neck of the returned prodigal, their souls, if I may say, mingle and become one. O what love, what relenting, what gratitude, what humility do they feel, crying out within themselves, as the Patriarch at the news of his son, it is enough, Joseph is yet alive! and O, saith the soul, he is my friend, my brother; Ah, he is my Saviour, my God, my king, my father, my husband, my helper, my companion, my comforter, my life, my light, my leader, my strength, my joy, my portion, and everlasting reward! but O, these are joys that the stranger intermedleth not with; a white stone and new name which no man knows but him that receiveth it; and therefore I cannot possibly describe them to you that are yet unconverted: But God knows I long to have you all participate in those unspeakable joys of the Redeemer's love; yea, and it is with the greatest delight that I stand to speak to you in his name, to attract your minds to the glorious scene, and O that he might this night while I am speaking (like Joseph to his brethren) manifest his love to your souls! soon would you forget your sorrows, triumph over your fears and foes, rejoice in God your Saviour, and say as the queen of Sheba concerning the fame of Solomon, it was true report that I heard of the wisdom, love, beauty, goodness and glory of king Jesus, but the one half was never told me; O then be intreated to hear the calls of Jesus, who is come this night to seek his brethren, nor will you ever enjoy a happy moment from this time forward forever, until you are brought to a saving knowledge of this meek and lovely Jesus; O therefore be intreated my dear hearers, to adhere to his calls, banishing the world with all its amusing charms, and find place in your hearts for this waiting friend, this heavenly visitant, everlasting comforter, portion and reward. O, could I expel the interposing clouds between you and this Jesus, or unvail your dark minds but one moment, you would be so attracted with his beauties and so ravished with his love, you would not only choose him for your present and everlasting all, but would cry out against all other glories, beauties, joys and delight, *O infamy, misery, and deformity!* But by reason of your blindness, darkness, ignorance and insensibility you are so miserably infatuated, as to pursue and expect happiness in the poor perishing amusements of this deceitful world, where happiness never was, or ever will be found, while in Jesus you see no form or comeliness of beauty that you should desire him; and yet flatter yourselves with the vain hope of going to heaven by and by; pray what heaven would you find, where you did not love the person who was all the glory and joy of heaven? Or what happiness would it have administered to Joseph's brethren at the time they were conspiring his death with their breasts burning with rage and envy, to have been confined to his embraces with their heads on his breast? But when the love of Joseph had melted their hearts, slain their enmity, and expelled their prejudice, why then they accounted it both honours and joys unspeakable to fall in his embraces and enjoy his love.

And therefore never more let the devil make such fools of you as to expect ever to find or enjoy any Heaven until you love Jesus, for he will be a hell to you, and his love increase your torment far more than the wrath, malice and rage of devils, unless your natures are changed and made like him; so that although the greatest part of Christendom vainly imagines, that it will be with the greatest reluctance to the wicked, that they are forced or driven out of Heaven, and imagine they would think it an unspeakable privilege to be admitted to be with God and his angels; yet it will be so much to the contrary, that they will think it the greatest addition to their torment to be so near to God, angels and saints as they are; and instead of praying for, or desiring to go to Heaven, if they could have their request answered, it would immediately be, to be at the most infinite distance from God, and all that was like him; for God himself has declared, that his presence will be of such torment to them, that they will call for rocks and mountains to hide them therefrom—and therefore never marvel any more at Christ's declaring, that ye must be born again; but make it your chief concern to get out of your own hell into the heavenly Jesus, and then you will find a Heaven wherever you may be, even if among devils: But if you live and die in your sins, you will forever be of that natural enmity against God, that although your miseries and tortures are ever so unsupportable, yet you will be so far from any desire to be forgiven of God, helped by God, or happy in God, that you will with the greatest rage abhor, despise and reject him to all eternity: O therefore! let me again drop a word of friendly warning, and say as Lot to his sons-in-law, *up get ye out of this place,* and cast yourselves on Jesus, who alone can change your nature. But now I must return to a few more remarks on our subject.—The Egyptians, observe, were neither in the room, when Joseph made himself known to his brethren, nor when they ate did they eat at the same table; for they thought it an abomination to eat with the Hebrews. So let me tell you, that the children of this world are not only (though bodily in the same room) ignorant of the manifestations of Christ to his brethren; but likewise account it an abomination to eat with them of the same food.

But saith some of my hearers, who never yet saw their own hearts, the man is mistaken now, for God knows I would rejoice to sit down with the disciples of Christ, to eat the same bread and drink the same water. To which I reply, I doubt not but some of you are sensible, by the awakening spirit of God, of your miserable starved condition, that you find the want of something, but do not yet want Christ, nor the bread of life; though you may think, that you would come on any terms; but the truth is, you, like the prodigal, when he began to be in want, instead of going home to his father for bread, he rather chose first to go and join himself with a citizen of that foreign land, and therefore was not only as far from his father's house as before, but likewise still starving and with the swine, with nothing but husks, until he could live no longer there: and then he went home to his father—and I would to God, that you who are in some degree awakened, and begin to be in want of something, was likewise so starved out, that you could no longer stay with the citizen of that country, and then you would come home and eat bread with me in my father's house.

But ah! the language of your souls are, with all your good frames, sincere desires for to receive Christ, and be for him only, like those who would take hold of one man, and say, we will eat our own bread, and wear our own apparel, only let us be called by thy name;[18] and so it is at last, although you may think I judge you too hard, all is but your own bread that you want to eat: for that moment you want Christ you will have him. But O I hope you will now be persuaded to come with all your souls, without money and without price, and receive Christ as he is, and you will soon set around my master's tables, and feast on the wonders of redeeming love, for the Lord is come, by a stammering tongue, to seek you. And although you find yourselves unworthy and unfit, with a hard heart, a stubborn will, and a stupid mind, feeling yourselves barren without any thing

---

18. Is 4:1.

or good frames to recommend you to God, yet come as you are, and you shall not go empty away. God will not reject you because you are poor and miserable, without any thing to help or recommend you; and therefore, why O ye of little faith, *why reason ye any longer because ye have brought no bread?* Do not come to bring bread or good frames, but come and receive bread, and thereby attain a soft heart, and a humble soul. Yea, and you may depend on it, that stay away as long as you will, to attain good frames and evidences of grace, if ever you come to Christ you will come at last as dry and as barren as ever you felt yourself. O try the experiment this night, cast your souls, and see if it doth not remove the mountain of sin, and melt the heart with love. But saith one, would you have me presume to come just as I am now? No, my dear reader, if you can ever get any better by staying away: but if not, I would have you come this evening, and just as you are with all your wants, sins and disorders. And let me ask you, if you wanted to melt a body of ice, would you move it to or from the fire? I dare say you will reply, why to the fire, for nothing else will melt it: so let me say if you want your hard heart melted, your soul humbled, and your barren mind made fruitful, fly with all the disorders to the warm beams of that Sun of Righteousness, and the mountains will flow down at his presence. What would you have thought of the serpent-stung Hebrew, who for a cure had run from the brazen-serpent, and instead of looking to it, would look from it? Look, O then, ye sin-stung souls, look away to the glorious Anti-Type, and you will find an immediate and infallible cure for all your disorders; and this night he is exhibited before you on the pole of the everlasting Gospel. Believe, O ye sons and daughters of Adam, and live forever.

But our subject being so large, and breaking forth into my mind with such rapidity, that I am more at a loss to know what to leave unsaid, than I be what to say; but lest by being tedious I should become unfruitful, I shall hasten to a few more remarks, and conclude.

Joseph, observe, gave his brethren change of raiment, and so does Christ; for every new-born soul doth so far partake of the spirit and nature of God, that it not only cleanses them in a degree from sin and vanity within, but likewise from without; it is the natural consequences or fruits of that immortal principle of love, Christ formed in them the hope of glory to detest and forsake sin and vanity, and love and pursue purity and holiness; yea, and often times they are so impatient for an immediate and complete sanctification, that they are crying out with Peter, *Lord not my feet only, but my hands and my head;* and blessed be God, the time is coming that will deliver them from all their foes, extricate their weary minds out of all their disorders, and thereby bring a happy period to all their sorrows: But O, I could wish, that even the followers of the Lamb kept that divine spark, immortal principle, or heaven-born mind so stirred up, and active, as would produce a more visible change of raiment to the world; for it is the life, and fire of Heaven within, that will make them shine without, and cause them to appear as cities on hills.

And as for you that never know the divine love, I do not wonder that it is so hard for you to break off from this sin, and that sin, and the other vain practice, and to keep on an external appearance of christianity, for it is all but dry forms, and a hard task without any divine love, or heavenly life to produce it.

O why, why will you try any longer to cover your nakedness with fig-leaves, or seek the living among the dead? Ye are dead, and nothing can do you good but that which gives you life: O fly then to Christ! in him is life, and he is come to give life unto the world.

Get your souls alive to God, burning with a principle of love to Jesus, and then it will be your delight to run the christian race, forsake every sin, and walk in the ways of God. O hear the calls of Jesus! for in his name I seek my brethren. O that I might be the means, in the hands of God, of persuading one of this society to throw down all their expectations of ever being any more prepared to come to Christ, and take hold of the offered Saviour! Ah, I should think myself well rewarded for all my labour! yea, and how would your own souls rejoice in the glorious liberty of the sons of God? And will you not be persuaded, will not the glooms of death, nor joys of immortal life awake and engage your hearts to say with Rebecah, *I will go!*

Come my dear hearers, halt no longer between two opinions, life and death has this night been set before you, and if God, be God, serve him, or if Baal serve him. Nay, is it possible for you any longer to treat these things as matters of no importance? Can you return to your former sloth and danger, and close your eyes this night unconcerned? has the Lord sent me here only to amuse your minds and please your ears with a fine story? O do you think that all that God requires is just to comply with the custom of attending with your poor miserable bodies, and when you return, say with thousands "*Well, I think we have been entertained with a very good discourse.*" And if they can say so much as that, they think they have done very well, and may go home and lay down in peace; I say will that suffice you to go and lay down with ease? If it is, the Lord have mercy upon you, for great, yea unspeakably great is your danger. Well, but saith one, should I not judge if the discourse be good? Yes, my dear hearer, but let me tell you, that there is no discourse can be good to you, but that, that tends to get you to Christ. And God did not send me here to ask sinners whether or not the gospel is true, or its doctrines good; but to beseech them in the name of the Lord to accept of the gospel proposals, and be reconciled unto God, that they may be eternally happy in the enjoyment of that which now they are strangers to. O then let me prevail with you my dear fellow mortals to make the grand enquiry, what blessing, what knowledge of yourselves, and of Christ you have attained; and for your soul's sake do not go as stupid, and as far from Christ as you came.

Your everlasting salvation is at stake, your life is as a bubble on the water, soon broke and gone; time is ever on the wing, and some of you on the declines of life, just drawing your mortal days to a period; and perhaps this night gone for ever.

O what a lamentable scene is your capacity without a Christ! God knows my heart condoles your standing, and longs to be instrumental for your good; and this night in the name of Jesus I seek my brethren. Oh, arise in the name of the Lord, for ye are yet prisoners of hope; and you that feel the least movings of his spirit, hear the glad tidings spoken to you, *even to day,* saith he that is now knocking at your doors, *after so long a time, if ye will hear my voice, and harden not your hearts, ye shall find rest to your souls.* O that I could encourage you to open the door that he might come in and sup with you, and you with him: yea this is my errand in the name of him that cannot lie, and died for the world, to declare his boundless love and free grace to sinners; and to invite you that are in the broad ways, and hedges, and ditches, to the marriage supper of the Lamb.

O come in, come in, ye poor, ye blind, ye sick, ye sore, ye lame and miserable; for all things are ready, and the God of the armies of Israel has sent out for you and waits to receive you; ah venture upon his grace, and all the joys of heaven are yours for ever.

Stand amazed O my soul, while I feel and contemplate the importance of what I deliver! What immortal crowns, eternal life cryed through the streets among condemned and perishing rebels as a useless drug! Yea, and Jehovah himself the travelling messenger; or shall I say the sinner's servant? Labouring for the eternal salvation; good Lord, and must I say the greatest part of the world labours in vain!

O! is it possible for sinners to be so cruel to their own souls! or can there be any here this night, that can neglect so great salvation? Will any of you, turn your backs on the Lord Jesus Christ, who is come in the power of his gospel to seek you? O hear, hear, ye sons and daughters of Adam, for the eternal God has stooped to labour for your good, and is now calling you from the depths of misery and despair to immortal glory, and will you not hear? Will you reject his calls, abuse his love and sink your souls in eternal perdition?

Methinks I feel for your souls, and can but again and again intreat you not to suffer this evening to be eternally lost to your souls. O think that your everlasting salvation is now at stake; and should you neglect a few more hours, your dye is cast, your state fixed, and you gone for ever: But if you will hear the voice of God, give up soul and body into his hand, and receive his love in your heart, be made one with the Lord Jesus Christ, and live in glory for ever; and conclude therefore, my dear hearers, this evening whether or not you will receive the glorious offer, for the Lord Jesus is now come to seek his brethren.

But lest I weary my hearers, I return to the last remark that I shall make on our subject, and conclude—and that is, Joseph sending for his father, and settling of his brethren in Goshen, that he might have them under his care, to be as a father to them, to feed them and supply all their wants.

And O! let me tell you, as Joseph sent his waggons to fetch his father, and all that belong to his brethren, so the Lord Jesus hath sent the chariot of the gospel to bring you down, you and your little ones, and all that you have into Goshen, a place of rest and peace, where you shall be under the protection of the God of the armies of Israel, and fed from the King's table, even of the banquet of Heaven.

And now, O sinners! O what can I say more? Will you leave your bondage, your misery, and your famine, and go to a land of rest, of peace, liberty and plenty? O that you would say as old Jacob said when the message came for him, "it is enough Joseph is yet alive, I will go and see him before I die.'' And O let me tell you, that if you will go and see him, and eat of his living bread, which he will freely give you—you shall never want. Come, my dear hearers, methinks some of you will be persuaded to embrace the offer, and be eternally happy, for I am sure you have never found one moment of peace or happiness in all your fatigues; no, nor you never will, for there is a famine in the land.

And being so happy as to find a number of young people giving their attention this evening, who are in the prime of life, and who I dare say are seeking and expecting of happiness in this world. I can but speak to them in a few words singular, though I hope they have apply'd the whole that has been said already. O I can tell you that I know by experience, that all your expectations will fail you; you may contrive your frolicks and balls, and rush into company and revellings, but they will all deceive you and leave you at last a starving, and perishing soul in guilt, blackness, death, and exposed to eternal despair, for such paths are paths of death, and such steps takes hold on hell. But O turn to my Jesus, my all, and my master, who hath sent me this night to seek and call you, and you shall find food for your souls, peace for your conscience, joy for your hearts, and an everlasting friend and portion, when this vain world is no more.

O can you, can you reject such an offer, and abuse such love, and ruin yourselves for ever? Will you choose hell before heaven, misery before joy, death before life, and the company of devils before the company of angels? Good Lord is it possible? And can mankind be so infatuated? Bleed O my heart, and burst my eyes over the unhappy beings.

But O let me hope, yea I can but hope, that there is some among this society that begin to feel their need of redemption and groan for help; yea I am convinced there is some. And O! let me intreat of you then, to exclude every amusing charm, and give your whole attention to the only thing for which you have your being; and especially you, my young friends, that are in the bloom of life, if you feel the least moving or call by the spirit of God—O nourish it as the welfare of your precious and immortal souls; for if you stifle it, or cast it out, it may harden your hearts beyond all recovery, and you mourn at the last, and say, *how have I hated instruction, and my heart despised reproof!*

I remember once discoursing with a poor sinner on his dying

bed, who told me in some of his lamentable discourse, "*Ah saith he the time was I had a time when the Spirit of God was striving with me; but now I fear the day is over; for,* said he, *when I was about fourteen years of age, I was awakened under the preaching of George Whitefield—I felt the power of the Spirit of God; and for a while I forsook my vain company and amusements, and gave my attention to the means of grace; But O I turned away, and never experienced a saving change! But from that time I grew more careless, and never had much convictions or concern for my soul since, and now,* saith he, *I am fifty years old, and upon a dying bed, without a saviour; being a stranger to the new birth.*

O take warning, take warning, my dear young friends, and now, while your breasts are full of milk, and your bones are moistened with marrow, make sure to flee from the wrath to come, and marry the Lord Jesus Christ—marry the Lord Jesus Christ did I say? What may such wretches as we be espoused to the glorious Prince of Peace! O yes, yes, it is a truth declared by him that cannot lie; and this night, O sinners, he is come to make you the proposal: Nor does he seek his own benefit as the earthly suitors, for they are fond of seeking after beauty and fortune: But O let me tell you, that he will marry you without beauty or fortune; for you are not only miserable and starving, but are in debt ten thousand talents, and have nothing to pay, and by your sins are deformed and as black as the lower regions; yet he will receive you in his bosom, and make you happy forever; for the offer is now made you—yea, if I never see your faces more, and this should be the last time you should ever hear my stammering tongue, I charge you to embrace the offer, remembering where you were, that such an evening you heard the Lord declaring, by his servant, I SEEK MY BRETHREN. My message is delivered. AMEN.

ALLINE'S THEOLOGICAL WRITING

Alline wrote two theological books, *Two Mites, on some of the most important and much disputed Points of Divinity*, originally published in Halifax early in 1781, and *The Anti-Traditionist*, first published in Halifax, probably in 1783. *Two Mites* was reprinted in 1804 in New Hampshire by the Free Will Baptists and *The Anti-Traditionist* in 1797. This latter work, only sixty-four pages of text, highlighted the major themes to be found in the much larger *Two Mites* but did so in a "far more rhetorical and extravagant"[1] fashion and in a style that obviously had far more popular appeal. According to Maurice Armstrong, "At times" the "eloquence" of *The Anti-Traditionist* "reaches the heights of ecstasy and enthusiasm":

> Sometimes the author soars through a whole page in one sustained sentence. Every chapter ends with an outburst of passionate pleading whose rhythmic cadence helps one to understand the tremendous effect of Alline's preaching.[2]

Though sometimes complex and opaque, Alline's theological writing was not so esoteric as to make it "almost totally incomprehensible to most of his audience."[3] Rather, as has recently been argued, most of what he wrote in his two theological treatises was

---

1. Maurice Armstrong, *The Great Awakening in Nova Scotia*, p. 92.
2. Ibid.
3. Jack Bumsted, *Henry Alline*, p. 81.

"straight-forward and easy to understand."[4] He has been called "Canada's first metaphysical and mystical philosopher"[5] and a literary genius who permitted "the interplay of mystic, revivalist, and reformer in his pages."[6] John Wesley would not have agreed with any of these positive assessments of Alline's theology. For the Methodist leader, the Falmouth evangelist and writer "is very far from being a man of sound understanding; but he has been dabbling in Mystical writers in matters which are too high for him, far above his comprehension. I dare not waste my time upon such miserable jargon."[7] Jonathan Scott would agree with Wesley's devastating critique. For Scott, Alline's two books were

> interspersed with Poetry calculated to excite and raise the Passions of the Readers, especially the young, ignorant and inconsistent, who are influenced more by the Sound and Gingle of the words, than by solid Sentences and rational and scriptural Ideas of divine and eternal Things; and hereby are prepared to take in, and embrace all the destructive and Religion-destroying and Soul-destroying Sentiments contained therein.[8]

A careful examination of Alline's theological writing underscores the fact that he was very dependent on the four English writers William Law, John Fletcher, Edward Young, and John Milton. Even though there may have been some similarities between Alline's ideas and those of Jacob Boehme, there is no available implicit or explicit evidence to suggest that the Nova Scotian ever read anything written by the German mystic. "All that can be confidently stated," it has been persuasively argued, "is that Boehme greatly influenced William Law who in turn influenced Henry Alline."[9]

---

4. James Beverley and Barry Moody, eds., *The Journal of Henry Alline*, p. 231.

5. Bumsted, *Henry Alline* (see the publisher's jacket).

6. Armstrong, *The Great Awakening in Nova Scotia*, p. 93.

7. John Wesley to William Black, July 13, 1783, in John Telford, ed., *The Letters of Rev. John Wesley* VIII:182.

8. Jonathan Scott, *A Brief View*, p. 168.

9. Beverley and Moody, eds., *The Journal of Henry Alline*, p. 21.

Some scholars see in *Two Mites* and *The Anti-Traditionist* a "genuine mystical vision" and a preoccupation with "the resurrection and the day of judgement."[10] Others see "a touch of genius . . . and enough of substance to realize that it is lamentable that Alline had no formal theological and religious training."[11] And despite his heterodoxy, it has been suggested that Alline's theological "roots are inbedded in Protestant soil."[12] He was a Trinitarian; he believed in a loving God, in Free Grace, in the New Birth and the Bible as the Word of God; he expected the imminent return of Christ and was certain of the ecstasy of heaven and what he called "an eternity of exquisite torment" for those who refused to accept salvation by grace. Alline often felt so close to God—"so wrapped up in God"—that he felt that he was a God on earth—the "ONE ETERNAL NOW."[13]

TWO MITES

ON

Some of the MOST IMPORTANT and
much disputed POINTS of

DIVINITY

Cast into the TREASURY for the Welfare
of the Poor and Needy, and committed
to the Perusal of the unprejudiced and
impartial Reader

BY

HENRY ALLINE,

Servant of the Lord to his
Churches

[Halifax: Printed by A. Henry
MDCCLXXXI]
[pp. 120–138; 192–199; 264–301; 320–331]

And now my DEAR READER, if you would receive any Light on

---

10. See Armstrong, *The Great Awakening in Nova Scotia*, pp. 93–104.
11. Beverley and Moody, eds., *The Journal of Henry Alline*, p. 17.
12. Ibid., p. 18.
13. Henry Alline, *The Anti-Traditionist*, p. 62.

this Point, you must know, that it is not the Greatness of a Man's Sin, that will keep him from thus being redeemed; neither is any one redeemed, because his Sins are less in Number; but it is according as he forsakes or retains this World, or himself into which he has fallen. For as the Death of Man was caused by his falling from GOD in Love with this World; so he can never be restored to Life, but by returning back from this World to GOD again, neither is there any other Redemption: therefore it is, that the great Redeemer would so often inculcate the absolute Necessity of forsaking all to follow him [Mark 8: 34, 35.] and declares that his Kingdom is not of this World [John 18: 36.]: He doth not say, that one Man may be redeemed, because his Sins are small, and another cannot, because his Sins are great: We hear nothing of all this in all his preaching, but we may repeatedly hear him positively declare the Impossibility of Redemption, while attached to this World, & that no one can ever be redeemed until all is forsaken [Luke 14: 27, 33.]. For as long as Man is seeking or expecting of Happiness in this fallen World, his Mind, is chained down to his fallen State, and cannot be restored. Therefore the great Work of the Spirit of GOD is as before observed, first to bring the Man to a Sense of his fallen Condition, and the Impossibility of Happiness or Redemption, while in Love with the Enjoyments of this fallen World: Neither can he be restored, until he is thus convinced. Therefore altho' the Work of Conversion is instantaneously, yet the Work of Conviction may be gradual; for Conversion is a Union of the inner Man to CHRIST, or the turning of the inmost Soul, after GOD; but the Work of Conviction is only the bringing the Sinner to a Sense of its fallen, helpless and deplorable Condition: And when thus convinced, if a Surrender is made of Soul and Body, and all his Concerns into the Hand of the great Redeemer a Union takes Place between CHRIST and the Soul, and the rapid Will is turned after GOD nor can the Soul be in a safe State till then.

WELL, but I am surprized, saith one, at this, that there is no true Religion, but by a vital Union to CHRIST; for I was in hopes, that what I had done outwardly, would have been of some Service to my Soul. You will be more surprised perhaps, if I should tell you, that many have thought the same, that are now in Hell: But you may take it for a Truth of no less Importance, than the everlasting Concern of your precious and immortal Soul, that without this vital Union to CHRIST, and the Turn of your inmost Soul after GOD, all your external Matters will prove abortive, and your Hope is but the Hope of the Hypocrite, and will unavoidably prove your eternal Ruin.

BUT as I have made something of a Digression from the Matter now in hand, I shall return to enlarge. And as we have thus seen Man in a State of Probation, standing with REDEEMING LOVE at his Door, yea and as far in as it can get in without his Consent, we may be the better informed of the Nature of his Recovery, by attending to what is said by the Great REDEEMER himself. "Behold, saith he, I stand at the Door and knock; if any Man hear my Voice, and will open the Door, I will come in and sup with him, and he with me" [Rev. 3: 20.]. As if he had said, I am now about to deliver a Matter of no less Importance, than that which immediately concerns your eternal Happiness; therefore be intreated to attend, take Notice, or observe, what I am about to express. "That I the great Restorer of Mankind stand waiting, Day after Day, at the Door of Conscience my Viceregent, and knock to quicken, alarm and convince you of your fallen and deplorable Condition": therefore if any Man, Jew or Gentile, bond or Free, Male or Female, old or young, rich or poor, none excepted [Gal. 3: 2, 8.] will hear my Voice, adhere to the Dictates of Conscience, and the moving of my Spirit, and will open the Door, only consent to give up all without any reserve, or Expectation of Help from any other Quarter, and will receive me for his GOD, his Prophet, his Priest, and his King; his present and everlasting Portion; I will come in: Nothing shall hinder; neither the Greatness of his Sins, nor the Strength of his Enemies; for my Delight is with the Sons of Men [Prov. 8: 31.]. Therefore only consent, and the Work shall be done. I will take Possession of the inner Man, unite you to myself, will sup with you, and you with me; will give you the communications of that DIVINE LIGHT & LOVE, which you have lost by your Fall. And now to be more plain in this important Point still (as I would be understood by every Reader), I will endeavour to speak of the Operations of the Spirit of God, in redeeming this lost Soul from its fallen State, as it may appear to them while under the Work; which is first to convince of Sin, that is, sets them in Order before him, both Actual and Original; and this with such Power, that the Sinner not only hears of his being a Sinner, but feels it in his own Soul: He is convinced of his lost and undone Condition in his own Conscience, without having any Claim to GOD'S MERCY or the least Favour from his Hand. He is so convinced of his helpless Condition, that he finds his utter Inability, either to obtain Relief for his perishing and immortal Soul, or to extricate himself out of that deplorable State of Sin and Misery, which he is now convinced that he has plunged himself into. He has long been trying perhaps to recommend himself to CHRIST by Repentance and Humility; he has been labouring with Prayers and Tears to love God & Holiness, to hate his evil Ways, and be sorry for his Sins: But the Spirit of GOD has now wrought so powerfully on his Heart, that he appears worse than ever: He finds his Heart is hard, and his Will stubborn: His Nature is at Enmity against GOD, and all that is good, and perhaps filled with blasphemous Thoughts against GOD and his Ways: He has long had a secret Hope, that he should be yet more prepared to receive CHRIST, but now all these Hopes fail; and he appears more unfit than ever: He has sometimes, under some agreeable Frames, thought himself almost through, and so would rest on them; but now; he appears so vile, that Conversion seems at a greater Distance than ever. He is like a Man lost in a Wilderness, who has been trying every Path he could find in Hopes to find the way out; which instead of leading him out, has got him more lost & entangled than ever. He has tried every possible Way, to flee from the Wrath to come, & to recommend himself to CHRIST, or to prepare to be converted, but now all appears in Vain, and he finds no way to step another Step, and all his Supporters are now gone. He sees that to fly from his Guilt and Misery is impracticable; and to reform or make Satisfaction, as much impossible, and therefore like the four Lepers at the Gates of SAMARIA [2. Kings 7: 3, 4.] he is determined to try the last Remedy; for to stay where he is, is certain Death, and to return back unto his former State of Security, will be Death, and therefore, altho' he cannot see, that CHRIST has any Love for him, or Pity towards him; neither doth he see, whether He intends to have Mercy on him or not; yet, he is determined, to cast himself at his Feet, and trust wholly to his Mercy, and Free Grace for Salvation; and cries out with the trembling Leper. *Lord if thou wilt* [Mark 1: 10]. And when he is thus brought to a Sense of his Condition, and is willing to be redeemed out of his fallen State, on the Gospel Terms, viz. to forsake all, with the Bent of his Mind turned after GOD, panting after Redemption from his fallen State, and depends wholly on the Mercy of GOD thro' JESUS CHRIST; then the REDEEMING LOVE enters into his Soul; CHRIST the Hope of Glory takes Possession of the inner Man; and altho' some, by Reason of Fears and strong

Temptations, may not be so sensible of their Conversion the very same instant, Hour or Day of their Union to CHRIST; yet they will soon receive an Evidence of their Redemption from Death to Life, by the sealing Evidences of the Spirit: [Rom. 8: 16., I John 5: 10., Rev. 3: 20., John 7: 38, 39. John 16: 14.] They will find the Burden of their Sin gone, with their Affections taken off of this World, and set on Things above, with their Hearts oftentimes drawn out after CHRIST, under a feeling Sense of the Worth of his REDEEMING LOVE; at the same Time, with a Sense of their own Vileness, and the Vanity of all Things here below, together with the Worth and Sweetness of heavenly Things, and the Amiableness of the DIVINE BEING, they find an encreasing Thirst after more Liberty from Sin and Darkness, and a continual panting after the Enjoyment of GOD, and a Likeness to the meek and lowly SAVIOUR; for their Hearts, which before were set on Things below, are now set on Thing above.

Now, Dear Reader, be assured, that there is not one Spark of true Religion in all the Externals, that ever were performed by Man, without this vital Union to the Lord JESUS CHRIST; Therefore how groundless and dangerous, as well as unscriptural, is the Dependance on any Externals for Salvation; since all Religion is a Work of the Holy Spirit on the inner Man. Neither need we say much to prove, that a true Principle of DIVINE LOVE will produce an external Conformity to the Ways of GOD; For it is as certain that this internal Work of the Spirit of GOD will reflect a chearful Conformity to the Externals of Religion, as a Fire will reflect Light. Therefore, saith the Apostle, "IF any Man be in CHRIST, he is a new Creature. Old Things are done away, and all Things are become new." [2. Cor. 5: 19.] That is, they are so far redeemed out of this World, as to have their Hearts and Affections set on Things above; and therefore altho' they may remain in this World a few Years, bearing about a Body of Sin and Death: By which Means, they are sanctified but in Part, and exposed to many Snares; yet they have not their Life and Enjoyment in the Things of this World: For their Lives are hid with CHRIST, [Col. 3: 3.] and therefore they have here no continuing City, but are as Pilgrims and Strangers seeking a better Country which hath Foundations, whose Builder and Maker is GOD [Heb. 11: 10.] "Foxes have Holes, and the Birds of the Air have Nests (saith the great REDEEMER) but the Son of Man hath not where to lay his Head." [Matt. 2: 20.] Not only that Particular Body of CHRIST, that was on Earth

Seventeen Hundred Years ago, but likewise the Spirit of the Son of Man in the Souls of all his Children hath no Place of Rest, or Abode in this World: For CHRIST did not come down to this World, to make his People happy in their fallen State, or to mend & patch up their Disordered World, but to redeem them out of it; and declares himself, "that his Kingdom is not of the World," [John 18: 36.] and therefore, whoever presumes to name the Name of CHRIST, and call themselves Christians: (altho' they may pretend to be born again) if their Hearts and Affections are not redeemed, but are still going on in the Pleasures and Enjoyments of this fallen World, will unavoidably find themselves fatally deceived, and eternally ruined. I do not mean, dear Reader, only those, who are going on in carnal Security, Vice and Debauchery, without any Constraint or Reluctance; or those greedy Worldlings, like the unsatisfied Miser, which perhaps you may not be guilty of, and so flatter yourself, with a groundless Imagination, that you are a Christian, and that your State is good: But I mean those, who have their Conversation, Life and Enjoyment in this Word; who find the Enjoyment of the Thing of Time and Sense to be their highest Good: For the new-born Soul is redeemed out of this World, and therefore the Food, and the Life and Enjoyment of their Souls are not in this World, but in Heaven, and on heavenly Things; their Conversation and Desires are set on things above. "For where a Man's Treasure is, there will his Heart be also" [Luke 12: 34.] and "out of the Abundance of the Heart the Mouth speaketh" [Matt. 12: 34.] Therefore be not deceived, dear Reader, respecting the State of your precious and immortal Soul: you are now acting for a whole Eternity; and if you should unhappily build the Hopes of your everlasting Happiness on the Sand, great would be your Fall, and irrecoverable your Loss. You may practise many Externals of Religion, have some Convictions of Sin, be sometimes much affected under the Means of Grace, refrain from many Vices, and have your animal Spirits lifted up, and something transported with an expectation of an Escape from Misery to everlasting Joy; yea, you may pass through many Visions and strange Dreams, and yet never have your perishing Soul redeemed. Let me ask you the following Question. Where do you get your greatest Happiness, and enjoy the sweetest Moments, not only at some particular Time and Place, but Days and Hours, Weeks and Years; or ever since you professed to be a Christian? Is it in your Husbands, your Wives, your children, your Friends, your Food, your Raiment, your Houses, your Lands, with any of the Pleasures of this World, and the Things of Time and Sense, which you have, or expect to have: or is it in the Enjoyment of CHRIST, the Vitals of Religion, and a feeling sense of DIVINE THINGS between GOD and your own Soul? Pray do your precious and immortal Soul Justice, and do not give your Conscience the Lie; and if upon a diligent and sincere Search, you find it in and after the former; then for the Lord's Sake, and your own Soul's Sake, do not flatter yourself with the Name of a Christian; for that is all you have: and therefore you may never expect to see GOD's Face in Love, until a Miracle of Grace is wrought upon your Heart: For the true Redemption by Christ doth not consist in all the Eternals, Promises, Resolutions, Fancies, Dreams, or Visions, that ever was seen or known by all the Men on Earth; but it is a Redemption of the Soul from its fallen State to GOD, raising the Desires and Life of the inner Man out of this miserable, sinful and bestial World, and turning it to GOD, from whence it is fallen: And therefore, every newborn Soul is daily hungering and thirsting after its original Source, viz, spiritual and Divine Food; panting after Light and Love, from which it has been so long a miserable Deserter, and to which it is now returning; and these new born Souls, being united inseparably to the Lord JESUS CHRIST, become Members of his Body. Therefore how inconsistant, GOD dishonouring, and unscriptural [Rom. 8: 38, 39., Heb. 6: 18, 19., John 6: 39., Luke 10: 42.] is that Soul destroying Doctrine, that denies the final Perseverance of the Saints, and sends Men to the Covenant of Works for to confirm their Salvation.

And thus, dear Reader, I have endeavoured to show you how the fallen Man is redeemed from his fallen State, and restored to GOD; which if you believe, you will not look on every one to be a Christian, that is called so. And as I have considered the man thus far redeemed, I shall now proceed to show the Nature of Sanctification; about which many have been so ignorant as to expose themselves to great Errors: Some holding it to be something dropped into the Soul which they call Grace, that may be lost; because it is cast into so much filth and Polution: others holding that a Man born again is wholly a perfect Man, and without Sin. Now it is evident that these are both as far from the Truth, as the East from the West: Others there be that seem to be something free from those unscriptural Conceptions, imagine that a Man at the hour of Conversion has his Soul partly cleansed, or sanctified; and that God continues to cleanse the Soul by Degrees, until the Soul is wholly sanctified. Now if this were the Case then GOD would not only stand united to a Spirit that was part Devil; but another Inconsistancy likewise must appear, and that is, if sudden Death should arrest the Man, his Soul would be torn asunder, and Part Lost; for no unclean thing can possibly enter into the Kingdom of Heaven. And if the Man, at Conversion was perfect; or could some imagine arrive to perfection in this world, they could no more be contained here than ENOCH and ELIJAH: Perfection being nothing less than a compleat Sanctification, and as for their falling from GOD after Conversion; CHRIST has declared they can not more be seperated from him than he from his Father. [John 14: 19 and 17: 21.] Yea, the very Nature of the Thing renders it impossible: For what is the Conversion but CHRIST changing, and taking Possession of the inmost Soul; which is at the Time of the Change compleatly sanctified. And now to shew the Reason why the Man thus converted is not wholly sanctified, or without Sin, I will proceed, Man in his fallen State as has already been observed, consists of Body, Soul, and Spirit. viz. an animal, or Elemental Body, a spiritual and im-mortal Body, and an immortal Mind, and at the Hour of Conversion, the Son of GOD takes possession of the inmost Soul, or immortal mind, but leaveth the fallen immortal Body in its fallen State still: [Heb. 4: 12.] And now when you see this Division, you may not only understand how that, that is born of GOD cannot sin; [I. John 3: 9] but likewise what is said by the inspired Apostle to the ROMANS; I have a Law, saith he, in my Members waring against the Law of Mind. [Rom. 7: 23.] Not a Law in his Mind; against the Law of the Mind; But of the Members against the Mind; for the Mind cannot Sin; because it is born of GOD, and he delights in the Law of God (saith he) after the inward Man. [Rom. 7: 22.] Viz the immortal Mind that is redeemed; and then he goes on to complain of this fallen Body of Death, which he is burdened with; [Rom. 7: 24.] which re-mains yet fallen, and when speaking of the same Body again, saith, he waits for its Redemption. [Rom. 8: 23.] And thus you may see wherein consists that Warfare so often spoken of between the old and new, or carnal & spiritual Man. And now what remains while mortal Life endures, is the Mortification of the old Man which is commonly called Sanctification; and this Mortification we may clearly see is carried on by the Growth of the inmost Soul, or immortal Mind, by which Means it becomes more than a Match for the unsanctified Part; and thereby mortifies, or keeps under the Powers of Corruption that remains in that Body of Sin and Death; and this Growth of the inmost Soul consists in what is commonly called the continual Acts of Faith: But to speak more closely on the Nature of this Work, it is the quickening, stretching or growing of the inmost Soul; which our LORD himself declares to be as a Well of living Waters, springing up unto everlasting Life, [John 4: 14.] Yea, as the very Nature of an intelligent and immortal Spirit, is a Power of Growth, or Seed of Generation: (not of Numbers, but of Capacity) therefore it wants nothing but Room to act itself, (when possessed of the Spirit of the Son of GOD) For to get the Victory over all its Foes. O therefore, let me now drop one Word or two, to those happy Followers of the LAMB, who are thirsting for Holiness, and the Victory over Sin. O remember the Kingdom of GOD is within you, and will work its own Release, and gain its own Conquest: if it is not chained and led into Captivity by the old Man, and every Leap it gets, is so much Growth for Eternity, & every hour it is led captive, or imprisoned by giving the old Man Liberty, is an everlasting Loss. O therefore as you love your own Soul, keep under your Body. Yea, suffer me to say, starve the old Man to Death; for every Thing that feeds or nourishes that, starves and imprisons the Kingdom of GOD within you; that is, obstructs the Growth of the inmost Soul. But how shall I know, saith one, when I am feeding the one and starving the other? I answer infallibly, when you are nourishing a Spirit of self, and enjoying the Creature, (in ever so small a Degree) you are fighting for the old Man; but when you are after the Spirit of the LAMB, and Enjoyment of the Creator, you are fighting for the new and spiritual Man. Therefore saith your LORD and MASTER, if your right Eye, or right Arm offend you, pluck them off; tho' ever so dear to you, and occupy till I come. Now I suppose the Question will arise, which has partly been debated in one of the foregoing Chapters: Who, or how many out of this fallen Race, are to be redeemed, or how many that GOD elected? To which I answer again, GOD doth elect and will save all that can possibly be redeemed. For you may remember, that it has been sufficiently proved already, that the very Nature of GOD, and his high Decree among all his Creatures, is a Freedom of Choice, and therefore GOD cannot redeem those, that will not be redeemed, or save them without their Consent . . .

And now I have a few Words to those happy, those Heaven-born Messengers of the Lord JESUS CHRIST, that have experimentally known the fore-mentioned Truths, who have not only known a Work of Divine Grace upon their Hearts; but have likewise received a Commission from the KING of Heaven to go forth with a Dispensation of the Gospel of Peace, to proclaim to their Fellow Mortals the joyful News of REDEEMING LOVE. Fear not O ye Heralds of the Gospel tho' Earth and Hell are engaged against you; as they always were, and always will be against the faithful AMBASSADORS of the LORD, and altho' you meet with many Tryals in your way (as I presume to say you do) both from without and from within: Yet fear none of those things, which you may suffer, but be faithful unto Death, and you shall receive a Crown of Life [Rev. 2: 10.] O! remember those Soul-Transporting Words, which are as firm as the everlasting Hills "Lo I am with you," and if CHRIST be with you, what need you more? You are called to an arduous Work, your Strength is Weakness and your Light Darkness, but mighty and faithful is He that has called you, who promised to send his Spirit to lead you into all Truth. [John 16: 13.] Therefore in Him you can do all Things; for in the Lord JEHOVAH is everlasting Strength. [Isa. 26: 4.] And altho' I am of all Men the most unworthy to bear his Name to the Gentile World, and have Reason to lye in the Dust under a deep Sense of my Nothing-ness, and acknowledge myself the least of all the Labourers in CHRIST'S Vineyard; yet I can do no less than drop a few Words to you by Way of Advice, and that, I trust with the greatest Tenderness, in the Bowels of our LORD and MASTER.

I know that your Work is great, and that your Day is short. You have nothing less than the Welfare of precious and immortal Souls (in some Degree) committed to your Charge. O! therefore let me in-treat you to be up and doing, to do the Works of Him that sent you, while it is called Day before the Night cometh, in which no Man can work. [John 9: 5. John 12: 35.] And as you love your own Souls & the Souls of others, shake off the Frowns & the Flatteries of this en-snaring World. Many of the Servants of the LORD have brought Death upon their own Souls, and fallen into a legal State of Formality by fearing the Cross, and by shunning to declare the whole Counsel of GOD, for Fear of offending some of their principal Hearers, and the great Men of the World, by their thirsting for the Applause of Mortals, by joining Affinity with the world & the Ministers of Antichrist and by carrying about some of the Babylonian Stuff. Neither be too anxious for a great Share of this vain World. You have already got a far better Portion than this World can possibly afford you; and GOD, who has undertaken for you, will never leave you to want or suffer beyond what may be for your Good. The Dust of PERU and the Hearts of all that live are in the Hand of your Master, who can give or withhold, as He sees may be for your Good. And I think you had better be fed by Ravens, than by Rates and Fines; yea a few Penny-Worths of Bread will support your Bodies thro' the Short Period of your Pilgrimage. Let me likewise intreat you to endure Hardships, as a faithful Soldier of CHRIST JESUS; Regard no small Tryals in your Way; for you may certainly expect many, not only outward but inward; for unless you experience you cannot Preach. And as for my own Part I account it no Privilege to go to Heaven upon a Bed of Sloth, but would rather go thro' a Storm than a Calm, if I am but indulged with strength equal to the Day. Neither imagine that the Greatness of your Work consists in your public Administrations every Sabbath, for that is but the smallest Part of your Labours, if you are determined to live and die in the Cause of CHRIST. O! therefore labour Night and Day with Tears to spread the Cause of your blessed Master, and to warn the wicked to flee from the Wrath to come, and spare no Pains to win Souls to CHRIST. The Foundation stands sure, and the LORD knows them that are His. [2. Tim. 2: 19.] Neither shall your Reward fail, therefore be determined, by the Grace of GOD, to spend and be spent to the Glory of GOD and the Good of precious and immortal Souls. For the Work of the Ministry is and ought to be your chief employ till your dying Day. Neither have I much Charity for those, who make it a Work by the by, or for to get a good Living, and so, when that either falls short, or over flows, their Labour ceases. Let me likewise intreat you to divest yourselves as much as possible of the strong Ties of Tradition. By no means embrace or retain any Practice or Principles as Right or Scriptural, only because it was a precedent set up by your Predecessors. All Men are fallible, and the best of Christians are liable to Mistakes; but the Word of GOD can never fail: And I believe that many Men would increase much in spiritual Wealth, if they would give themselves the Trouble of digging for it; but they too often neglect to do it, because they imagine, that their good old Fathers have dug deep enough. But as the Word of GOD is yet an unexhaustible Fund, make that your chief Study, the Man of

your Counsel, and the Rule of your Life, and let the World around
you know by your Life and Conversation, that you have been with
JESUS. For Example is more forcible than Precept. And O! be rejoiced and encouraged under all your Labours. Remembering that
your Sorrows are short, and your Hours of Tribulation will soon be
at a Period; when you shall rest from your Labours, and your Works
follow you. [Revel. 14: 13.] Be faithful to stand the Storm a few
Hours more, and you shall reach your desired Haven. Preach the
Word, be instant in Season and out of Season; reprove, rebuke, exhort with all long Suffering and Doctrine [2 Tim. 4: 2.] and as the
Lord has told you, that without him ye can do nothing, [John 15: 5.]
be sure to keep near to him, watching and praying, as those that must
give an Account of the Blood of Souls, and the Lord who has promised to be with you unto the End of the World, will never leave nor
forsake you, but will give you stength equal to your Day. I am a
Witness for GOD, that He is faithful to his Promise, and kind to his
Servants; altho' I have been unfaithful to him, and his Cause. He has
promised you, that those that Water, shall be also watered [Prov. 11:
25.]. He will strengthen your Hands and encourage your Hearts with
the Consolations of his Holy Spirit; which, blessed be GOD, I have
known to be more sweet, more encouraging, and more supporting
(yea far more) than all the Riches and Enjoyments of Time and
Sense. You are in a glorious Cause, you serve a glorious Master; and
glorious, yea inexpressibly glorious will be your everlasting Reward.
Rise therefore, arise my dear Fellow-Labourers (if I may presume to
claim the Title) arise, and exert every Faculty of Body and Mind to
spread the Mysteries of the Cross, and proclaim the Wonders of RE-
DEEMING LOVE,

> Go forth, go forth ye Heralds of the LORD,
> Girded with all the Armours of the Word.
> Go spread REDEEMING LOVE from Shore to Shore,
> And bid the guilty World to weep no more.
> Triumphant ride o'er all the Powers of Hell,
> And spread the Light where Men in Darkness
>   dwell.
> Go warn the hard'ned from Mount SINA's Flame,
> And heal the wounded with the SAVIOUR's Name.
> Go shew the Guilty the attoning Blood,

And feed the Hungry with immortal Food.
Go out with Joy, a frowning World to face,
With the transporting News of Gospel Grace.
Turn not aside to court the World's Applause.
But spend your Breath in the REDEEMER's Cause.
Withstand the Storm of a few hard Moments more,
And you shall safely reach the peacefull Shore.
Far from the Regions of eternal Night,
There you shall reign in everlasting Light.
Your Names are there in the bright World above
And there's your Portion in unbounded Love. . . .

Oh, the Midnight Darkness that now overspreads the World! Darkness covers the land and gross Darkness the People, setting at nought the most alarming Dispensations of God's Providence, and rejecting the most endearing Expressions of Love and Bowels of Compassion, Calls despised, Mercies abused, Warnings neglected, Judgements defyed, Consciences feared, Minds stuped, Souls condemned, the Day of Grace over, and the World undone. Hark! Hark. The Cry is made, the Midnight Cry. Behold the Bridegroom cometh. Go ye Virgins, go all ye Sons of Men to meet your Judge. [Math. 25: 6]. MICHAEL appears; MICHAEL the great Archangel now bestrides both Earth and Sea, and thereby denotes his Power to alarm the just and the unjust, the watery Tombs and the most profound Caverns of the Earth; with lifted Arm to Heaven, not only claiming the Attendance of all the Heavenly Hosts, but likewise a Demonstration of his God-like Power with his dread Commission from the eternal Throne; and this calling Heaven, Earth and Sea to attend, he lifts his Hand and swears (by what) by HIM, who gave Being to all that do exist, and whose Commands Heaven, Earth and Sea obey; Armies in Heaven, Legions in Hell, and Millions on Earth are all by HIM preserved, and now all feel his solemn Awe; by him the Great I AM, who lives unmoved, eternal and uncontrouled for ever and for ever reigns; by Him I swear (swear what) that Time shall be no longer. [Rev. 10: 5, 6.]

Cease, cease ye flying Moments, cease to roll,
And cease, ye rolling Orbs from Pole to Pole.
Times Actors with enormous Crimes loud call,

For threat'ning Vengeance on their guilty Ball.
Swift and impetuous hear the last Trumpet roar,
Her bellowing Thunders reach from Shore to Shore,
Arise ye Dead, ye slumbering quick appear;
Start from your Couch and the last Sentence hear.
Your Judge descends, your final Doom is nigh
The pompous Morning rends the melting Sky.

See, see a threatening Deluge now awakes; sulphurous Worlds burst forth their Magazines of Fire & instantaneous start up Ten Thousands formidable Sons of Thunder, the Heavens shake with the approaching Scenes; the blazing Sun is extinguished as a Taper; the Moon and Stars all convulsed refuse a Gleam of Light to the Poor Guilty, distracted and dissolving World; [Matt. 24: 29.] and fallen Nature feels her approaching Doom.

> *Methinks I hear her, conscious of her Fate,*
> *With fearful Groans and hideous Cries*
> *Fill the presaging Skies*
> *Unable to support the Weight*
> *Of the present or approaching Miseries*
> *Methinks I hear her summon all*
> *Her guilty Offspring, raving with Despair*
> *And trembling cry aloud, prepare.*

POMPHRET

The Seas roar, the Rocks melt, the Earth trembles, the Thunders rattle, Lightnings play; Earthquakes rend; Inundations overflow; Houses burn; Pyramids reel; Villages, Towns and Kingdoms sink; while burning Hills exceed Mount Aetna's or Vesuvius's Flames; the Graves open; the Dead arise; the quick are changed; and first the Saints appear; Heaven's Love is so great for the Followers of the LAMB, that Men and Devils shall behold his peculiar Regard for them; for the Lord himself shall descend from Heaven with a Shout, with the Voice of the Archangel, and with the Trump of GOD, and the Dead in CHRIST shall rise first: [I. Thes. 4: 16.] And blessed and happy are they that have Part in the first Resurrection; on such the second Death hath no Power. [Rev. 20: 6.] The King of Kings is now making up his Jewels, and will first serve his chosen Sons from the rude Mass of Sinners.

> *See how the joyful Angels fly*
> *From ev'ry quarter of the Sky*
> *To gather and to convoy all*
> *To one capacious Place*
> *Above the Confines of this flaming Ball,*
> *See with what Tenderness and Love they*
> *   bear*
> *The Righteous Souls thro' the tumultuous Air*
> *While the ungodly stand below*
> *Raging with Shame, Confusion and Despair*
> *Amidst this flaming Overthrow*
> *Expecting fiercer Torments and acuter Woe*
> *Round them infernal Spirits fly*
> *O Horror! Curses, Tortures, Chains they cry*
> *And roar aloud with execrable Blasphemy.*

POMPHRET

What awful Throws! What Heart-rending Groans and chearful Shouts are now heard thro' the promiscuous and innumerable Throngs! Above Angels shouting, Seraphs praising, and Saints triumphing; beneath Devils blaspheming, and Sinners roaring. Good God! And where am I?

> All sensual Ties dissolved, and off all Mortal Thrown
> No more shall Time, or Weight of space be known.

For it would not be possible for Mortals to hear, see, or receive the approaching Scenes, which are spiritual and immortal. Now all Mortal puts on Immortality and prepares to meet the immortal King, to hear and receive their everlasting Doom. The Mask is now thrown off; the Prison-walls are down; and nothing more to interpose between Man and Scenes unknown to mortal Eyes. Now the Bodies arise, but not the Elemental Bodies, for they are to be burnt up and dissolved [2. Peter 3. 10, 12.] but that spiritual Body which Man was made with at first, and which fell from GOD at his Rebellion, and which every Man has tho' fallen, is now to be raised and restored to its primitive Rectitude and Purity. [I. Cor. 15. 38. 44. 45. 46. & 47.] The Dust or scattered Particles of Ten Thousand Saints now starting from their long Slumbers, which have been scattered by Fish, by Flame, by Rack; in the Sea or on the Land, all rise and claim a kindred to each distant Mote, all purged, all pure, all harmonious, all bright, all Angelic, and all immortal.

And now their Friend appears.

> The happy Morn awakes. O blessed Day!
> That wipes their Tears, and all their grief away
> Now all the Saints have reach'd the peaceful Shore
> Where Darkness, Sin, and Death shall reign no more.

THE GREAT ANCIENT OF DAYS now owns all his despised Followers. Long have they been accounted as the Filth and Offscouring of the Earth, and trampled in the Dust by the Feet of the Ungodly. Long were they loaded with Reproaches, and esteemed as Madmen and Enthusiasts; but now they are exalted: While the wicked World shall for ever wail, and call in vain for Rocks & Mountains to hide them from Him, that sits upon the Throne, and from the Face of the Lamb [Rev 6:16]. And now he that loved them with an everlasting Love, shall receive them in his kind Embraces, while Angels and Archangels acclamate their safe Arrival to the celestial World. Now breaks forth the bright and Morning Star; now the Arms of everlasting Love, encircles them, divine Beauty sparkling in every Eye, and sacred Love flushes in each Angelic Face. Is this the LAMB, cry out Ten Thousand Saints, is this the LAMB that was Slain? Ah slain, the sinking World to save. Is this the Man of Sorrows, that bore our Sins up Mount CALVARY, and groaned beneath our Guilt? Is this the great Physician of Souls that appeared for our Redemption, when all Help failed from every quarter; when Death and Hell conspired our Ruin; when Destruction yawned, Vengeance threatened, and Misery pursued. Then, O then, in that distressing Moment appeared the Sinner's Friend, the Comforter of Mourners with Balm from GILEAD, to the wounded Conscience.

Great was the Love and strong the Arm of Grace
That brought Salvation to the fallen Race
Let Angels love and every Saint adore
The slaughtered LAMB, who did the World Restore.

Now all the Followers of the LAMB have left their guilty World,
and found that Rest, which GOD in infinite Love has provided for his
People; where all is Peace, and uninterrupted Joy. No longer shall
they complain under a Body of Sin and Death, no longer shall they feel
the Temptations of the grand Adversary, nor be insnared with the Allurements of a deceitful World. No longer shall their Breasts throb
with Grief, nor their Eyes flow with briny Tears, nor even mourn the
Absence of their Souls chief Delight. Now are they landed beyond all
the Storms and Tempests, beyond all Sin and Sorrow: for these are
they that are come out of much Tribulation, whose Robes are washed
and made white in the Blood of the LAMB; [Rev. 7. 14.] and these are
they that died in the Lord, and rest in their Father's Bosom. O what
unspeakable Scenes of Joy now appears, when they awake in his Likeness and are satisfied; [Ps. 17. 15.] and those that have turned many
to Righteousness shall shine as the Stars for ever and ever; [Dan. 12.
3.] while Thousands by them called home to the Lord are as Stars in
their Crown, crying out with Shouts of Praise. Blessed be GOD for the
Feet of those, that brought Glad Tidings to our Souls, that published
good Things in Sion, [Isa. 52. 7.] by whom we received the Messages
of Peace: these are the Flames of Fire [Psalm 104. 4.] that warned us
with Tears to flee from the Wrath to come. Blessed be thy Name, almighty Parent, say those brought to the Knowledge of his Love thro'
the Instrumentality of Godly Parents, that ever I was committed to the
Care of such faithful Stewards. Blessed be GOD, for their Prayers,
Counsels, and Admonitions; but above all for the accompanying Influences of his Grace and Spirit, that attended them; and Blessed be
GOD, that ever I was stationed in a Land of Light, where the Feet of
the Gospel Herald have trodden; and here, say the Parents, O thou
great Desire of Nations, we are with those that thou has given us.

Here, blessed Prince, we are for ever thine,
To sound thy Praise, and to thy glory shine.
Thy sons, thy Daughters, dear bought Children are
The Price of Blood, REDEEMING LOVE to share.

All Hail, all Hail, say the Messengers of the Lord, thou great immortal Prince of Peace, that ever the Gospel of Reconciliation was committed to earthen Vessels, and we of all Men the most unworthy, sent forth to proclaim the glad Tidings of Salvation to our Fellow-mortals. Our Tryals were few, and our Sorrows short. Lacked we any Thing during our Mortal State? Altho' Earth and Hell were against us, and Glory to GOD the Storm is over.

> Safe, safe our Feet have trod the Desart thro'
> And reach'd the Shore, where Sorrows must adieu.

Here all the Prophets, Patriarchs, Apostles and Teachers, Jew and gentiles, bond and free, Male and Female, old and young, rich and poor that have known the joyful Sound, rest from their Labours, and their Works follow them. Here all the poor Disciples of CHRIST, that have been long wandering up and down in the World in Sheepskins, in Goatskins, in Desarts, in Dens and Caves of the Earth [Heb. 11. 37.] sit down in everlasting Joy, with all Tears wiped from their Eyes. Long have they mourned under the Disorders of their fallen World; but now they have exchanged Sins and Sorrows for immortal Glory, Corruptible puts on incorruptible, and Death is swallowed up in Victory; and now they sing the triumphant Song, where Clouds and Darkness shall never more interpose between GOD and their Souls. Ah happy, happy Souls, it is well for them, that ever they had a Being;

> Their Joys are now begun; their Sun arose
> Their Day eternal broke, no more to close.

With what unspeakable Joy and Delight do they now reflect back from the Chrystal Battlements of Heaven their native Purity to their fallen World, remembering their deplorable State, and the innumberable Disorders from which they are now redeemed. Now they remember that Gulph of Misery, into which they had plunged themselves, and see from whence they are redeemed. All Souls are now awake from their Sleep, and released from their imprisoned State. The Clogs of their fallen State and the Mask of Mortality are now thrown off, and clearly they remember their first Rebellion in the Garden of Eden; which rought Destruction with all her Furies thro' the new-made World. Now they remember the bloody Mount, where the bleeding Saviour bore their Sins, and opened a State of immortal Glory to the guilty World. Ah, He it was, that took away their Sins, and now they behold Him Face to Face; the GOD of all Glory and Consolation; the Brightness of his Father's Glory, and the express Image of his Person. And now all the Glorious of the Godhead appear in the Face of the blessed IMMANUEL; the least Glimpse of whose visage outshines Ten Thousand Suns. Every Soul is now ravished with his divine Beauty; Gratitude fills every Heart and Love sparkles in every Eye; while the Soul-ravishing Look and Voice of the Redeemer kindle in every Breast, Flames of immortal Love. Blessed, forever blessed, saith the King of Kings are ye that are the Purchase of my Blood and the Fruit of my Bowels. Ye are the Fruit of my Hands, and Trophies of my Victory, the Favourites of Heaven and the objects of my everlasting Love. Welcome, welcome now to immortal Glory; welcome to the Seats of Rest prepared for you by the Sufferings of the King of Heaven. Welcome to the Society of Seraphs, to the Band of Angels and Archangels. Welcome to the Glory of Heaven and all the Joys of the celestial World. Welcome to the Fields of Divine Beauty and unbounded Ocean of Delight. Welcome to the eternal Ages of Felicity, and all the Sweets of REDEEMING LOVE. And welcome to your Father's Bosom. Never more shall a Cloud vail your Saviour's Face, nor Darkness interpose between you and your God. Behold with Joy and Triumph the impassable Gulf between you and the Regions of eternal Darkness; and remember the deplorable State from which I have redeemed you. It was I that beheld you in all your Blood, cast out in the open Fields to the loathing of your Person, and then was the Time of Love; my Bowels yearned over you with Pity, I cast my skirt over you and said unto you, live. [Ezek. 15. 5. 6.] I was the good SAMARITAN, and saw you fallen among Thieves, stripped, wounded and left dead in Trespasses, and Sins, when the Law and its Executors offered you no Relief; then poured I in the Oyl and Wine of my Grace, and bound up your Wounds, and sealed you on the Heart of everlasting Love. [Luke 10. 33.] I followed you with tenderness and Love thro' all the Dangers of your Pilgrimage State, and have now brought you to your desired Home and everlasting Rest; and now live and reign with me for ever: As I live, ye shall live also. Never, never, saith the Bride of the LAMB, shall we forget the Day of Espousals, and the Time of thy

Love. O thou, by what Name shall we call thee? The mighty God, the everlasting Father, the Prince of Peace, thou great, thou all wise Father of all Spirits, Author of all Beings, GOD of all Grace, origin of all Existence, Source of all Happiness, Light of Lights, the Angels Joy, and the Seraphs Triumph, or greater Wonder still, the Sinner's Friend, the Rebels Advocate, the Traitors Plea. Reign, O reign thou King of Kings, whose love was stronger than Death, and who gave thy life a Ransom for many. O thou, whose Body was torn and mangled for our Redemption.

Reign, reign, thou great eternal Saviour, reign
O'er all the Host of the Angelic Train;
Let Angels bend, Seraphic Armies bow;
And the REDEEMER's ransom'd Virgin glow,
With Love Divine to thy incarnate Name,
And Worlds unnumbered speak thy lasting Fame.

This, this is He, say Angels and Archangels, that gave being to all our heavenly Hosts; and this is He, that preserved our mutual Feet, when Thousands of our angelic Armies rebelled. Once the Morning-stars sung together, and all the Sons of GOD shouted for Joy. Happy we stood, when they unhappily fell, and by his unbounded Love, we are confirmed. [Eph. I. 10. Col. 1. 20.] This is He, whose Divine Light and Smile of unchangeable Love kindle in our Breasts a Flame of sacred and immortal Fire. Welcome ye Saints, to your blest Abode, while we rejoice at your safe Arrival to the Arms of everlasting Love. Come now and taste, what we have ever since our Creation enjoyed: And blessed be GOD for your Company. It is an Addition to our vital Flame, and an Honour to our angelic Band to be vitally related to the Bride of the LAMB, But little have ye enjoyed the Sweets of REDEEMING LOVE, While Inhabitants of yon fallen Region; but come now and feel that sacred Flame, that inspires all the Armies of Heaven and unites our Songs of Adoration to the Lofty Throne; and look back ye happy Heirs of everlasting Love with Wonder and Amazement on the Love and Tenderness of your compassionate Saviour, whose all searching Eye followed you with Care thro' all the unspeakable Dangers of your mortal State. Often have we attended you with Chearfulness, when commissioned as ministering Spirits, invisible to mortal Eye but above all remember that Day which filled all the heavenly Armies with a joyful Surprise and Wonder, when the Creator of the Universe hung on CALVARY's Hill, and groaned under the Weight of human Guilt; that Day, when Millions of Angels, invisible to mortal Eyes, covered all the bloody Mount, where your Redeemer was extended: When, if our immortal State would have admitted of Sorrows, all Heaven would have been drest in Mourning. But new Themes of Joy were soon opened in Heaven, when his expiring Groans declared the grand Work of Man's Salvation was finished, and triumphant Songs awoke at his mighty Conquest over Death and Hell; and this, ye Souls for ever blessed, shall be your everlasting Song.

> Welcome arriv'd ye Saints forever blest
> To Angel's Glory and eternal Rest,
> Let Gratitude your Heav'n-born Souls inspire
> While bending round the Throne of sacred Fire
> Burning with Love unite seraphic Lyre.

The Saints are now gathered from the four Winds of Heaven, freed from all the Insults of Earth and Hell, all safely environed by the Arms of Omnipotence. And now more shocking Scenes appear; The Righteous are severed from the wicked; the Wheat from the Tares; and now the Ungodly must awake and appear before the awful Tribunal.

> O! must the guilty Spirits trembling come
> To meet their Judge, and everlasting Doom.

Well would it be for them now, if some dark Cavern or incumbent Shade might shelter them from the approaching Judge. O could they cease to exist! But no, they must exist Strangers to Annihilation, and endure the approaching Shock. O intolerable! And must they meet him once a Man of Sorrows, but now a GOD in Glory; And now they behold Him in all his Grandeur, with all his Saints and Ten Thousands of his Angels, all winged with Light and Glory, to attend him in the last Assize.

> Say, O my Soul, is this the Man that once
> On CALV'RY's Mount sustain'd the Sinner's Weight?

Whose Glories vail'd within a mortal Frame,
With Sorrows press'd, and groan'd upon the Tree
To save a guilty World, and to restore
Poor rebel Man to everlasting Love.

Ah this is He, once a Babe at BETHLEHEM, but now Archangel's King; once crowned with Thorns, but now with Omnipotence and Light unapproachable. He, that was once arraigned at PILATE's Bar, now calls Kings, Princes, and Monarchs before him: Whole Kingdoms bow; yea and Worlds submit to his Imperial Sway. Millions on Earth and Myriads in Hell constrained from their dark Abodes to attend his awful Court. See, see the unnumbered Throng; Belial with all the reprobate Sons of ADAM, who have sealed themselves down to eternal Perdition must crowd the solemn Bar.

Nor Man alone; the Foe of God and Man
From his dark Den, blaspheming drags his
    Chain,
And rears his brazen Front with Thunder scarr'd
Receives his Sentence, and begins his Hell.

YOUNG'S NIGHT-THOUGHTS

These, the first Rebels in Heaven, must stand the awful Day, and view their black Rebellion. O with what Reluctance will they meet Him! He that was once their Father and their Friend and did all that was necessary for their everlasting Happiness. What Tortures will rack them at the Remembrance of the cruel Hand, that without any Temptation or Provocation, was lifted in Heaven, and bid Defiance to the GOD of all Goodness, and struck the fatal Blow to their own eternal State. Once they were Spirits of Light solacing themselves in everlasting Love, and shouting forth the Praises of the King of Heaven: but now they are Spirits of Darkness, racked with Guilt and Despair, raging with Malice and blaspheming the GOD that made them.

How will they meet the great offended GOD
And bear the Weight of their infernal Load?
Chains of their own will drag them down to dwell
In the dark Caverns of abysmal Hell.

And how, O how will the ungodly Sons of ADAM appear! Murderers, Whoremongers and Adulterers; Thieves, Drunkards, Lyars and profane Swearers; the unjust Worldling with the profligate Man of Pleasure; the Pharisee, the Hypocrite, the Careless and most Supine and the worst of all Wretches, the enlightened Apostate; all Despisers of Grace and Rejectors of the Gospel; all have crucified their approaching Judge, and imbrued their Hands in his Blood. And now all awake in keen Despair, no Cloak for Crimes, no Shelter for Guilt, no Friend, no Intercessor. Rocks forsake them, and Mountains deny them any Shelter. He that hath long been about their private Paths, now sets all their Sins in Order before them. No Bribe, nor City of Refuge for the Murderer; while the injured Ghost, that by his cruel Hand was hurried to an unknown World, stares him in the Face, and reads condemnation thro' all his guilty and Despairing Soul. O how he trembles at the awful Sight. The poor Drunkard now remembers his Taverns, and intoxicate hours, but has no Wine, nor Bowls of Pleasure now, to lull his Conscience to sleep; (as he has often done) or to drown the Sorrows of his tortured Soul. Every Faculty now awake in exquisite Horror. The Sensualists can no longer find a Thirst for his former Pleasures; his Powers of Lust has failed, and he finds a gnawing Detestation against his obscene Delights; now he beholds with Regret his Accomplices in Debauchery, and curses the Day that he ever saw them; all their Sins, publick and private, and now exposed to their Shame and everlasting Confusion. The blasphemous Wretches, that have so often profaned the Name of the GOD of Heaven, must now appear to meet their Judge, and behold their black infernal Score. Ah how often have they profaned that worthy Name, which Angels and Archangels reverence; & from whom they themselves have received every Breath they drew! O what a shocking Truth! Is this Breath given for Repentance turned over to Blasphemy? Now they feel that Damnation, which they did often carelessly or maliciously imprecate on themselves and others. But, O too late, they now see and feel the Weight of their Sin and Folly.

> Ah now he roars among the guilty Throng,
> Nor can he find for his Blasphemous Tongue,
> One cooling Drop to mitigate the Flame.

He curses now that dreadful GOD he fears,
Feels his own Hell, while raging Conscience tears
Him thro' the Regions of eternal Shame.

Now the poor Worldling and cruel Oppressor must bid all their Riches and Possessions an everlasting Adieu. Often have they turn'd away the hungry Poor pinched with Cold and Distress; and now they are themselves turned out of House and Home, with neither Friend nor Plea, Food nor Rayment: And now the Judge of all the Earth makes Inquisition for the Mammon of Unrighteousness, and they with nothing to return.

Where O where will they now flea for Shelter? They have not only crucified the Lord of Glory, despised his Love, and rejected his Grace, but have likewise squandered away all the temporal Favours of their indulgent Preserver. O how much Goodness have they abused!

The Hypocrite and Pharisee can no longer deceive the World with their Cloak of Religion; they have nothing now to hide the Shame and Pollution of their guilty and despairing Souls; neither dare they any longer mock the Searcher of all Hearts with their Lip-service, or plead their close Conformity to the Externals of Religion. O unhappy Spirits! All their Wickedness and Hypocrisy is now unmasked, and they exposed to stand the Test of Divine Security, and rue their Folly in everlasting Confusion. (Adapted to the capacity of our day, and to be the more striking; I speak of the Judgement as successive; yet I would not be understood any such Thing as a successive Trial, or pleading, there, for that Moment the mortal Mask is dissolved, and the spiritual Body united to the immortal Soul, they are immediately in the Presence of an all searching Eye, and every Man with a Tribunal in his own Brest.) And where now is the careless, and supine Mortal, that could sit Day after Day under both Law and Gospel, without any Concern or Regard to the Truth. How often have they been warned from Mount Sinai by the Sons of Thunder, and how long have they been sleeping under the most endearing Charms of the Gospel, and treated all with Disregard or Contempt; while every debauched Lover, or vain Amusement of Time and Sense was earnestly pursued and embraced! Ah, what would they give now to recall those glorious Privileges and precious Moments, which they have so carelessly slept under, and squandered away in

Sin and Vanity! But now their Day is over, the Means of Grace are gone, and their Sun is set never more to rise: Neither can they sleep anymore, but must for ever wake in a surprise of Misery. And O how cutting must the Sight of the Judge be to the enlightened Apostate that was awakened by the indulgent Saviour, who had been so long at their Doors, and so often intreated them to forsake all and to follow him; while his Head was filled with the Dew, and his Locks with the Drops of the Night. How often has he intreated them not to reject his Calls, nor despite his Grace, telling them, that his Spirit would not always strive with Man! How often has his Bowels yearned over them with Pity, entreating them to be wise in Time; but they would not have him to reign over them; and these are they that sinned against the Light of their own Conscience, and against the most endearing Expressions of Love. These are they, who for one Morsel of Meat sold their Birthright; and now they find no Place for Repentance, altho' they groan with everlasting Horrors. These are they, that for the Love of the World, or some earthly Enjoyment, or Fear of the Cross, turned away and walked no more with him. [John 6. 66.] These are they that tasted of the good Word of GOD, and the Powers of the World to come, who crucified to themselves the Son of GOD afresh, and put to him open Shame. [Heb. 6. 4. 5. 6. 7.] How often did he tell them, if any Man drew back, his Soul had no Pleasure in them, but all was in vain. And how will they now bear to meet him, whose Love they have so much abused? How often were they warned with Tears, to have Pity on their own Souls, while there was Hope, by the faithful Servants of the Lord; who will now arise to their Condemnation. Ah how often have they intreated them to hear the Lord's Message and accept of Life and Salvation; but they esteemed them as Enemies, because they told them the Truth. But now the Gospel Trumpet is blown no more; the Ambassadors of the Lord are all called home; and the Day of Grace is now over; the mediatorial Hour is gone, and all the unbelieving World is now arraigned at the Bar. All guilty and all undone, all have rejected the Gospel of CHRIST, despised his Grace, and trampled his Blood under their Feet. How often has He wept over them with Tears of Pity, because they would not know nor improve the Day of their Visitation. [Luke 19. 42. 43. 44.] How often has he tendered his precious Blood for the cleansing of their guilty and polluted Souls, and woed them to accept of his Grace, and flee from eternal Perdition, and take up their everlasting

Abode in his kind Embraces! But now He, that made them, has no mercy on them, and He that formed them, shews them no favour. And where now are those Soul-destroying Wretches; those blind Leaders of the Blind, who preached up a few Morals and Externals of Religion sufficient for Salvation; and for some temporal Gain or sinister Views have not only destroyed themselves, but led many other precious and immortal Souls blindfolded down to Perdition; who will now curse them for their Neglect and false Instruction. They have spent all their Days deceiving the World, and are gone down to the Grave with a Lie in their right Hand; pretending to the blinded World a Dispensation of the Gospel was committed to them; when at the same time they were both Strangers and Enemies to both CHRIST and his Gospel. And now they must forever rue their Folly under the Weight of their Sins, cast out in utter Darkness under the keen Reflections of those unhappy Souls, which they have deceived, and the gnawings of a guilty Conscience.

And where are now the ungodly Parents, who, instead of a godly Instruction, have ensnared and corrupted their Children with their GOD-dishonoring and Soul-destroying Practices? O how will they now give an Account of their Stewardship! These, say their un-happy Children, are the ungodly Wretches, into whose Hands our Souls were committed; who instead of praying with and for us, sac-rificed our Souls to Moloch by their evil and ungodly Instructions and Examples. Often, saith one, have I heard cursing and swearing by my Parents, but seldom a Prayer in the Family: They were fond of supporting and decorating my Body, but wholly neglected the Welfare of my precious and immortal Soul. O that ever I was com-mitted to the Care of such ungodly Wretches, who, instead of en-couraging me to the House of GOD, and where the Waters were troubled, would encourage me, or indulge me to Balls, Frolicks, and Houses of carnal Mirth and sinful Recreation. O cruel Parents, cursed Murderers of your Children! I acknowledge, saith another, that I have often sinned against Lights and the Dictates of my own Conscience, and therefore am justly condemned; yet ye were the cursed Instruments of my everlasting Destruction; and now I must be your company forever among the miserable Blasphemers in Hell. O that ever I was born to live and die in such a Family. We were an ungodly Family on Earth, but we shall be a far worse Crew in Hell, where we must take up our everlasting Abode. Cursed be the Womb that bore me and the Paps that gave me suck, and cursed be the unfaithful Ministers, those blind Guides, that have neglected my precious and immortal Soul. O must I lie down with Ministers, Parents, Brothers and Sisters in the Regions of everlasting Sorrow, with Devils and damned Spirits, and what is far worse, with the gnawings of a guilty Conscience. The Time was, when I had the offers of Salvation sounding in my Ears, but I rejected them: And now the Day is over, and I am gone forever. But ah! what an unhappy Being is now the Scoffers of Religion, who have so often made a Derision of the Children of GOD, and the Truths of the everlasting Gospel. I once thought, saith he, that the true Christians, and the faithful Servants of the Lord, who were so zealous, to be censorious Men, and Enemies to my peace; but now I believe it was really in Pity to my Soul & a sincere Desire for my everlasting Happiness. I have often scoffed at them as Madmen and Enthusiasts, and told them out of Derision to spare themselves and not to be righteous over much; yea and sometimes even against the Lashes and Dictates of my own Conscience. But O my proud Heart, infatuated by the Devil, who was then seeking my everlasting Ruin, would not suffer me to acknowledge my Folly, and turn to the Truth; and often for fear of the Cross, or to please the vain Company I was in, would join in making a Mock of Religion, or of those People I pretended were deluded; and my Conscience would afterwards reprove me, which instead of adhering to, I would by some Means or other lull to sleep. But O such Means have now failed me for ever; my Conscience is now awake, and will sleep no more, but will forever gnaw and torture my guilty and despairing Soul. Ah! was it for a Million or Millions of Years, there would be a Hope to mitigate my Torment; but no my Misery is begun and will never end. O had I been a Stock or a Stone, or any Thing but a never dying Soul! The Judge approaches, and my unhappy Doom draws nigh. How can I bear that shocking Sentence, depart. O Eternity, Eternity! And must I for ever tread the gloomy Regions of eternal Darkness! Must I wonder and howl with banished CAIN, and traiterous Judas, and Myriads of Blasphemous Wretches, tormented with reflecting Men and Devils, and scorched with a guilty Conscience, without one Drop of Water to cool my tormented Tongue. But ah! too late I am convinced of my Folly, and nothing but Loss, irrecoverable Loss, sounds through every Faculty of my Despairing Soul. I now remember, how little I regarded the repeated

Calls of a bleeding Saviour, and now I shall be as little regarded, when I cry, Lord, Lord, open unto me. For I am now forever banished from the Gates of Hope, and have nothing to expect, but increasing Horrors thro' the revolving Rounds of a miserable Eternity; and all Things past, present and to come conspiring to make me miserable. I am glutted with inexpressible Torment from every Quarter. Ah! had I Ten Thousand Tongues, I could not express my Horrors, and yet I must endure them for ever. O how intolerable are my Pains, how exquisite my Horrors, how eternal their Duration, and how unalterable my State! Hark the shrill Outcries of those guilty Wretches.

> *Lively bright, Horror, and amazing Anguish,*
> *Stare thro' their Eyelids, while the living Worm*
>   *Lies*
> *Gnawing within them.*

DR. WATTS

TEN Thousands Thunders now awe the Attention of all the guilty Throng to the dread Tribunal; and now that all searching Eye pierces thro' the hidden Recesses of every Soul, and points out all their Sins. The Sins most private and long forgotten are now all refreshed in their Memory, and all their Shame exposed. How heavy the Load, how black the Score, how Heaven-daring the Crime, and how cutting the Lashes of a guilty Conscience, which now heaves the final Bar, and reads their own Condemnation; each one standing as separate before the Omnipotent Judge, and as individually judged, as if he was the only Soul in being. The Judge and he alone to stand the naked Test, how can their Hearts endure, or their Hands be strong, when the Judge of all the Earth undertakes to deal with them; [Ezek. 24. 14.] whose very Nature is a Hell to them. For as the Fire dissolves the Ice by Reason of the Contrariety of their Natures, so the approaching Judge increases their Torment by Reason of the two Natures; his Divine Light, Love and Goodness being so opposite to their Malice, Fire and Darkness, that their Misery and Hell is increased and inflamed thereby. It is Divine Love and Goodness that they hate, and therefore beholding such Love and Goodness in him is like Fuel to their Souls increasing their infernal Rage. But behold, He comes, and see Him they must in all his Glory, Light and Purity, and hear Him in Justice and Equity set all their blackest Crimes together with the Love and Condescension, which they have so much abused, all in Order before them. In infinite Love and Pity to the fallen World, saith He, I left my Father's Bosom, and came down to suffer and die for your Redemption; and in Pity to your perishing and immortal Souls, I have long waited at your Doors, beseeching you to flee from the Wrath to come: But all was rejected and despised. Days and Hours have my Servants laboured for you and warned you with Tears to escape from Misery, to embrace the Gospel Call and enjoy the Privileges of my incarnate Love. And long has my Spirit been waiting upon you, and been striving with your Consciences to restore you from your fallen State; but all was still in Vain. Ye trampled my blood under foot and despised my Grave. Ye have rejected my Gospel and grieved my Holy Spirit, Ye have abused my Mercy, and wounded my Cause. Ye have reproached my Children and derided my Ministers. Therefore I will laugh at your Calamities, and mock now your Fear is come: [Prov. 1. 26.] Ye have chosen Destruction, and ruined your own Souls against all that I have done or could do for your everlasting Happiness. Therefore go now accursed Spirits, and learn the infinite Evil of Sin; go learn the Folly of rejecting my Grace; go rue the Loss of all my Light and Love; go ye Despisers of my Grace and inhabit your own Regions of Wrath and Darkness, where Hope and Pity can never come; go feel the Weight of your own Guilt, go endure the Hell which your own Hands have made, and the Wrath, which you have treasured up to yourselves against the Day of Wrath. Remember how my Bowels have yearned over you; and fain would I have gathered you in my Arms of REDEEMING LOVE as a Hen gathereth her Brood under her Wings, and ye would not. [Luke 13. 34.] What therefore could I have done more than I have done, to make you happy? And yet you have made yourselves miserable to all Eternity. Depart therefore ye cursed, into everlasting Fire prepared for the Devil and his Angels. O what mortal Tongue can express, or what Heart conceive the unspeakable Horrors, into which they have plunged themselves! How intolerable is the Anguish of the guilty Conscience, and how exquisite the Tortures of the despairing Souls! All friends forsake them, and Foes exasperate them; Conscience gnaws them, and Saints reject them; Angels despise them, and GOD the Author of all good abhorrs them and banishes them for ever; and all help fails from every Quarter; no Mercy, no Sleep, nor Mitigation of Misery.

Hopeless Immortals. How they scream and shiver,
While Devils push them to the Pit wide yawing
Hideous and gloomy to receive them. Headlong
     down to the Centre.

                                              DR. WATTS.

O! Unhappy Beings! How will they endure an Eternity of increasing Horror, burning with infernal Rage; tortured with keen Reflections, and blaspheming the GOD that made them! Their Die is cast, and their Doom is now settled for ever; the Righteous are severed from the Wicked; and all the Race of ADAM gone to their own Places as they are made by accepting or rejecting REDEEMING LOVE. The Wheat is gathered into the Garner, and the Tares cast into everlasting Burning. [Matt. 13. 24. 43.] The Spirits of Light to the Realms of Light, and the Spirits of Darkness to the Regions of Darkness. The great Work of Man's Redemption is now finished, and the second ADAM has restored the Ruins of the First. The Globe that fell by Man's Rebellion, is not annihilated, but purified, and immortal like unto a glassy sea, mingled with fire, where those that are redeemed by the Blood of the Lamb are to reign for ever; [Rev. 15. 2.] while the nature of the Wicked makes an impassable Gulf between them and the Righteous. And now while all the dark Caverns of eternal Darkness are shook with dying Groans, hideous Yells, and blaspheming Cries, the glorious Arches of Heaven are ringing with Doxologies of eternal Praise; and all the innumerable Throng of Saints, Seraphs, Angels, and Archangels crying out Hallelujah! For the Lord GOD Omnipotent reigneth. Amen and Amen.

          Methinks I hear the vast unnumber'd Throng
          Unite their Voice in one Eternal Song.
          Shouting they cry, All Hail Incarnate Name
          Let Love immortal all our Hosts inflame,
          To sound abroad, thine everlasting Fame.
          While Rage infernal Storms of Vengeance blow
          Thro' the dark Caverns of the Worlds below
          Let rebel Angels feel their tort'ring Chains
          In the black gulf, where Guilt and Darkness reigns
          And the curs'ed Race of ADAMS offspring too
          In their own Hell their Guilt and Folly rue.

Let Angels shout, Seraphic Armies sing
Songs of immortal praise to God their King
While the pure Bride from yon dark World restor'd
Strain lofty Notes to the incarnate Board.
All Hail, all Hail, ye heav'nly Armies join
To laud that precious Name with Songs Divine
Let thankful Shouts thro' all the Realm resound
And glide harmonious one revolving round.
Let sacred Love inspire the lofty Strains
That echo Praise thro' all the Heav'nly Plains
To God. Amen, our GOD for ever reigns.

Be intreated, my poor unhappy Fellow mortal, O be intreated
to consider the Danger of your Way, before it is too late, and take
heed that you are not found fighting against the meek and lovely SA-
VIOUR, and destroying your own Soul, and take heed you do not call
a Work of Grace a Delusion, because it is not agreeable to your carnal Inclinations, Forms, and Traditions: For you see, that all the
High-priests, Scribes and Pharisees, who opposed the Work of GOD,
and crucified the LORD of GLORY, had the same Pretences, and made
the same Excuses, as you do; they would not acknowledge, that they
were crucifying the LORD of GLORY, or opposing the Work of GOD,
but said, they were only bearing a Testimony against Impostors, and
deluded Men, to obstruct Errors; and Enthusiasm creeping in to the
House of GOD &c. you say, this is not right, and that is not right;
such a Man is not properly authorized, and another preaches without
License; one is deluded, and another led away by a blind Zeal, and
such a Man hath no Right to exhort, and these private Conferences,
repeated Lectures and Night-meetings you do not like; for, you say,
it breaks up Families, keeps People from their Work, causing Servants and Children to be disobedient, &c. And was this not the Language of all the Enemies of CHRIST before you, even from the
Beginning of the World, and had they not the same Reasons for opposing all the Servants of GOD, when sent among them? [Luke 61.
23.] This was not right, and that was not right, and CHRIST himself
was not right; [Matt. 23. 34.] and his Disciples were all wrong;
sometimes they were drunk with much Wine; [Acts 2. 13.] and
sometimes much Learning had made them mad. [Acts 26. 24.] And
is it not plain to be seen, that to such People as them and you, all the

Work of GOD is wrong; because it is against your carnal Reasoning and not according to your old Traditions. Do not think that I am your Enemy, because I have discovered your evil Conduct, and intreat you to desist, before it is too late. GOD knows, I wish your Souls well; and would rejoice to be instrumental in bringing you to a Sense of Danger, and shew you, that you are on the Enemies ground; that you might make your Escape from everlasting Misery, unto eternal Joy. O be intreated to consider, that the infallible Word of GOD has declared, that unless you have been born again of the Spirit of GOD, you are an utter stranger to the Truths of the Gospel; and the Things that be of GOD are foolishness to you; [I. Cor. 19. 18. 23.] and therefore you may be so blinded in Sin, so bribed by carnal Reason, and so chained down by the Prejudice of Education and Tradition, as to take Light for Darkness, and Darkness for Light, and if your Light should be Darkness, how great is that Darkness; [Matt. 6. 23.] nay you may be so infatuated by the Devil, and led astray by a deceitful Heart, as to oppose the Work of GOD, and persecute the Followers of CHRIST; and at the same time vainly imagine, that you are doing GOD Service. [Acts. 16. 9.] You may pretend, that you are earnestly contending for the Faith once delivered to the Saints, when at the same time you are a stranger to any Faith in Christ, and are only fighting for a poor dry Form of Godliness, without the Power. [2. Tim. 3. 5.] You may likewise pretend that you are labouring to support the Cause of CHRIST, and of the Word of GOD when at the same time you are enemies to Christ, and making the Word of GOD of none Effect through your Traditions. [Matt. 15. 3.] And if this should be the Case, that you are so unhappily deceiving yourself, how can you stand out in Opposition any longer, or if you are contented to live with a dry Form, without the Power, why will you oppose the power among others? Why will you not let them enjoy a Liberty of Conscience; or if they are deluded, as perhaps you may say, why do you make a Scoff at them? Surely if that was the Case, they are not to be laughed at, but ought to be pitied and prayed for. But pray remember, there is a Possibility of what you call a Delusion, and Enthusiasm, being the true Work of the living GOD. Therefore mock not, lest you make your Bands strong; [Isa. 28. 22.] for it would be better for you, that a Mill-stone were hanged about your Neck, and you cast into the Sea, than to offend one of CHRIST's little Ones. Perhaps you will not believe it to be of GOD, because you cannot understand it;

but if you have not experimentally known a Work of Divine Grace in your own Soul; if you have not been born again by the Spirit of GOD; if you are not become a new Creature in CHRIST JESUS, then it is certain, that you are so far from being a Judge; whether it is of GOD or not, that if it be of GOD, it will appear to you Foolishness. [I. Cor. 2. 14.] O therefore be intreated to hear that Solemn Word from Him, before whom you must shortly stand. Behold ye Despisers, and wonder and perish: For I work a Work in this your Day, that ye shall in no wise Believe, tho' a Man declare it unto you [Acts. 13. 41.] O consider what an awful account you must one Day give before GOD's impartial Bar, if you should be found fighting against GOD; for you are not only ruining your own Soul, but you are likewise instrumental in the Destruction of the Souls of others, by casting Reproaches on the Work of GOD, and labouring with poor Souls that are around you, to keep them from attending where the Waters are troubled. So unto you, saith the LORD, for ye will neither enter the Kingdom yourselves, nor suffer ye them that are entering to go in [Matt. 23. 13.] Why will you bring the Blood of Souls upon you, and willfully plunge yourselves into eternal Perdition; or if you will ruin yourselves, why will you destroy others? Pray let them enjoy the Privileges of the Gospel, for as they must one Day be judged for themselves, why may they not have the Liberty of seeking for themselves, now while they are Probationers for Eternity.

But I suppose some will say, we are not against their enjoying a Liberty of Conscience, or seeking for themselves, but they are forsaking the good old Way, turning away from their Ministers, separating from Churches, encouraging separate Meetings, and the like. To which I answer, that by no Means I would advise a Separation in a Church of CHRIST. Neither is such a Thing common: But perhaps it is you, that have left the good old Way, by sinking into the Form of Godliness, without the Power; and they are now returning back to the Liberty of the Gospel, and separating from the Seats of Antichrist: And, if so, it is no more than what GOD himself has strictly commanded them. [2 Cor. 6. 17., Rev. 18. 4.] And I presume to say, that in such a Case, if you saw the Difference between Light and Darkness, you would be so far from labouring to keep them in Bondage; that you would thirst for Liberty yourselves. For what Fellowship hath Righteousness with Unrighteousness? What Communion hath Light with Darkness? What Concord hath CHRIST with Belial?

Or what Part hath he that believeth with an Infidel? And what Agreement hath the Temple of GOD with Idols! Therefore how is it possible for them to travel together? For what the Heaven-born Soul loveth, the Moralists cannot bear; they may seem to go together in Peace, in a Time of Darkness, but when GOD is showering down the Bread of Life, the one eats and rejoices, while the other rejects and is offended: Which I have not only been an Eye-witness to, in the short Compass of my Work in the Vineyard, but have likewise proved it by the infallible Word of GOD. Therefore let not the Devil persuade you, that this is only a Fancy, or blind Zeal of mine; for unless you are convinced, my dear Reader, of these Things, before your Day of Grace is over, you will unavoidably be convinced of them to your everlasting Sorrow. Neither count me your Enemy, because I tell you the Truth. There is yet a Time for Repentance, and who can tell, but you may yet escape everlasting Misery, and for ever rejoice in what you are now despising; as ST. PAUL doth now in that Saviour, whom he once persecuted. [Acts. 22. 4.] And for your Encouragement I can testify, that in the short Compass of my Travels I have known many, who have been opposing the Work of GOD as a Delusion, and making a Scoff at those, that are called Newlights and Schemers, who are now Advocates for the Cause of CHRIST, and rejoicing in that, which they once called a Delusion and Enthusiasm. O therefore let me entreat you in the Bowels of the Lord JESUS CHRIST, if ever you expect to see GOD's Face in Love, to consider these Things, let them be impressed on your Mind, when you lie down, and when you arise; when you go out, and when you come, in Search your own Foundation, consider your Conduct, examine, whether or not, you was ever slain by the Law, and made alive by the Gospel; whether you have experimentally known a vital Union to the Lord JESUS CHRIST; whether you have ever received the Seals of GOD's Love to your own Soul, and enjoyed the Communications of Divine Grace: And if you have not, why will you risk your precious and immortal Soul on such a Pinnacle of Danger? Why will you say, that such a Man is not right, and such a People are all led astray; when the Word of GOD has declared, that (let them be as they will) you are so far from being right, that you are justly condemned, and wholly exposed to be cast into Hell every Breath you draw. Why therefore will you pretend to dispute so much about Religion, when you have no Religion? First make sure to get a Religion in your own Soul, that will stand you instead, if GOD should this Night call you before his dread Tribunal: For why will you spend so much time disputing about the Chaff, when you are not sure, that you will ever taste of the Wheat? First get the Beam out of thine own Eye, and then thou canst see clearer, to pull the Mote out of thy Brother's Eye: First get the Love of the Blessed JESUS shed abroad in your own Soul, and then you will be a better Judge between Truth and Error; and will likewise be sure to rejoice, when all Discords and different Forms of Religion shall cease. O consider how inconsistent you are conducting to be so zealous for some external Observations, and at the same time wholly neglecting of that most important one Thing needful, on which hangs your present and everlasting Happiness! Who that has any Bowels of Pity, can forbear grieving to see the Cruelty, that mankind exercise upon themselves? I suppose, if I were to tell many of my Readers, that it was no Matter, whether or not they were baptized with the HOLY GHOST and with Fire, they would not be much disturbed; but if I were to tell them, it was no Matter, whether they were baptized with Water or not, they would cry out with the greatest Zeal, away with such a Man, away with such a Man, for the Church is in Danger. Well might GOD pronounce a Woe against such People. [Matt. 23. 23.] O take heed therefore, my dear Reader, that you are not found among those, against whom such Woes are pronounced; and if, upon diligent search into your own State and Condition, you find it to be your unhappy Case; then let me intreat you for the Lord's Sake, and for your own Soul's Sake to Look around you, and let every Faculty of your Soul be wholly attentive to that most important, and friendly Advice of the KING OF HEAVEN. Labour not, saith He, for that Meat which perisheth, but for that Meat which endureth to everlasting Life. [John 6. 27.] Thus hoping and praying that these few Lines may not be wholly in vain to your Souls I shall conclude with the earnest Groans and most imphatic Language of ELIEZER. O Lord GOD of my Master ABRAHAM, I pray thee send me good Speed this Day. [Gen. 24. 12.] Send O thou compassionate Saviour, for thy Name sake, and in Pity to perishing and immortal Souls, the accompanying Influences of thy Holy Spirit, with the weak Desires, and unfaithfull Labours of thine unworthy Servants. Send, O blessed GOD, a Word of Power, and Peace, to the Hearts of those, into whose Hand thou mayest see fit to cast out these Lines; that some precious and immortal Soul may have cause to raise an immortal Note to thy Name for these TWO MITES.

THE

ANTI-TRADITIONIST.

THE AUTHOR

HENRY ALLINE

(Halifax, 1783)
[pp. 8–70.]

Think, O Think my dear Reader, how unspeakably wretched, cruel, insensible, and miserable is the condition of fallen men! And if you are one still sleeping and amusing in your fallen and undone state a Stranger to the Messiah, O let me say to you, as the Shipmaster to Jonah "ARISE SLEEPER AND CALL UPON THY GOD," Ah awake, before you awake in keen Despair, where Conscience will slumber no longer.

What! Shall Heaven, Earth and Sea, Sun, Moon, and Stars, Fire, Air, Earth and Water, Angels and Worms, yea the very Dust under your Feet labour in vain to marry you to the Author of your Life? Shall all nature indifatigeably serve you, and you utterly reject thy God, thy Creator, Preserver and benefactor, and eternally renounce all Submission to his Sway, and swear thyself his inveterate Foe?

O for Godsake, and in pity to thy Soul, awake, and bethink thyself before thou art in Hell: for one step or Breath more, and perhaps thou art gone forever.

And O ye thoughtfull Souls, that have thought on your Ways and turned to God, the Author of your Existence, and have felt the Sweetness of his immortal Favour, drop, O drop (by a friendly Warning) a Tear of Condolence over thy unhappy fellow Men, that are sleeping in Sin on the Borders of eternal Despair; O tell them, tell them, there is a God!

And bleed, O my Heart over the effecting Scene,

How wretchedly miserable, how unspeakably exposed, and yet

almost unmoveably careless are countless millions, untill they drop
the fatal and irrecoverable Dye!

> See how they croud the downward Road,
> Both Strangers to themselves and God,
> While rapid Time drives on their speedy Race,
> They labour hard to lash the horrid Chace,
> Till all confus'd despairing left their Eyes,
> Their Race is out, they've lost the expected Prize.
> And rue their loss where gnaving never dies!

O what, what shall, or can be done, for a guilty, perishing and
sinking World! Will nothing awake them out of their Danger and Insensibility! O for Mercies or Judgments, or any Thing that may prove
effectual to alarm the poor Sons and Daughters of Adam to escape
the Gulf before their Day is over and they irrecoverably gone! O that
I could tread from Land to Land to tell the Gentile world that the hour
was come and now is, that the Dead shall hear the Voice of the Son
of God, and they that hear shall live! *(a)* Send me, send me, O thou
Life-Giving Father, as the Angel to Lot, that I may take my fellow
Men by the Hand with an "ESCAPE, ESCAPE, O YE SONS OF MEN TO
THE MOUNT, AND LINGER NOT ON ALL THE PLAIN, LEST YE BE CON-
SUMED!" *(b)* FOR THE PLACE YOU ARE IN WILL SOON BE DESTROYED.

> But are they still involv'd in Sin and Death,
> And chain'd of Choice to everlasting Pain,
> Still hurry'd on the Fatal dye to cast
> Till lost (O thought!) In everlasting Woe!

> Think mighty God upon the abandon'd throng
> Redeem from Death and loose the stamm'ring Tongue
> To make thy Name their everlasting Song.

*   *   *

THOUGHT THE SECOND

On the DEITY; *the great and first Cause of all Things.*

O For that sacred Hand that from the deep
Of Midnight Darkness first expell'd the Gloom,
And broke to Man heav'ns bright immortal Day,
To 'nspire my Soul with his own sacred Pen,
To point the Gospel from the Arts of Men,
And lead my reader in the Paths divine!

But let not my reader imagine, that I am about to fathom the unfathomable Ocean; that is attempt to comprehend the DEITY: for blessed be his Name (to the Joy of all that love him) he is, ever was, and forever will be incomprehensible! Yea was it possible there would be an immediate period to all happiness; I shall therefore (with Joy) forever cease from either Expectation or desire to find out God to Perfection: Yet for the glory of his great Name, the incouragement of his Children, the alarming of Sinners, and the vindicating of the Gospel Truths against the Enemies, of the Redeemer's Kingdom, I shall endeavour to discover something of the Certainty, consistency, and Nature of an infinite, unbeginning, everlasting, self-existent and supreme Being.

It hath been sufficiently proved, that no being or system could ever have been brought into existence from nothing or of chance; and therefore when we have proved any Thing in being, either spiritual or corporeal, we have discovered the Certainty of some first Cause; and if any first cause, it must be uncreated, and without beginning; otherwise we are involved in the same Inconsistencies and Impossibilities as before; because this first cause, if so called could no more come into Existence out of nothing, or by chance than the smallest Dust or most abject Being that exists: So that only a proof that any thing is in being discovers not only some first Cause, but likewise that this first Cause is self-existant; existing in and of himself without any beginning.

And therefore, it must be consistent that the Existence and happiness of this being arises wholly from what he is in himself; consequently he must in himself be possessed of an infinite unbeginning self-necessary Source of Life, which in itself is a self-existent Fountain, of Wisdom and Glory; which Life, Wisdom and Glory, called in divine Revelation the Father, Word, and Spirit *(c)* being in themselves so attractingly glorious are ravished one with the other (using such terms for want of better), are naturely attracted centering themselves in love one with the other, which thus now discovers to us a self-existent, self-necessary, self happy and TRIUNE-BEING; so that existing thus in himself, married to himself in love with himself, makes him eternally unchangably happy in, & of himself; wholly independent, & excluded from any possibility of change, sorrow or loss: because thus existing of centering in, married to, and ravished with himself.

O WHAT A GOD IS THIS! AWAKE, MY SOUL! AWAKE, GAZE ON, FALL IN LOVE WITH, AND FOREVER ADORE SUCH A BEING!

But saith one, who so fond of Slavery, chooses their ear bored to the Door Post *(d)* the Man is intruding into things that doth not belong to us, and I dare not follow him. Let me tell such an one that if they love Darkness and choose their Bondage, and think it enough, just to get to heaven if they can but squeeze in, (if I may say) behind the Door, I am not so: But love Freedom, and was commanded to covet earnestly the best Gifts, *(e)* and dig for those Truths as hid Treasure; and if I have a Father and Friend, it is my Duty to know, who and what he is: Neither is there any Thing that so engages my Soul to love and serve him, as to behold his Grandeur. And as for those Things being not for our Enquiry is far from the Truth: Because God himself hath revealed it.

First, Hath he not declared not only that in him was such an infinite Fountain of Life *(a)* But likewise swore with his lifted hand, that it was so forever? *(f)*

2dly Hath he not declared, that he was forever delighted with his Wisdom, and declares, that it was brought up with him? *(g)* And

3rdly, That the eternal Glory (called the Spirit and Comforter) was with him and proceeding from or of himself *(g)* and then declares, that these three bear his eternal Record in heaven, *(h)* The Life declaring that Wisdom was not only his unchangeable Delight, but beloved, and in whom he was ever well pleased *(i)* and then this eternal Wisdom declaring that he was not only the Bread of God *(j)* but that he and his Father was one *(k)* and that they were forever glorify'd in and with each other *(l)* And now, what think you of my intruding into Things that doth not belong to Man, and especially when it is the foundation of all Religion.

And this my dear Reader, I have endeavour'd to discover not only the Certainty, but something of the Nature and Consistency of a Glorious Triune, first Cause of all things: And that even by the simple Hypothesis of admitting, that there is any thing in being.

And to those that are like the wise Scribe bringing out of the Treasury Things new and old *(h)* I commit these few Thoughts for your help; and to such I am ready to say, you will rejoice to see (like Moses) *(i)* the hinder Parts a glimmering Ray of the Life, Wisdom and Glory of your Father, Friend, Saviour and everlasting Portion, in which you have a Discover of that immutable Foundation and Cause of all Joys both for Time and Eternity.

And O what a Soul ravishing Thought or Discovery must it be to your Souls, who have cheerfully sealed your devose from every other Lover, and all created good, and made Choice of such a Being for your Life, your Joy, your Comforter, your Friend, your King, your God, your Present and everlasting Joy! O gaze, gaze a Moment on the infinite Grandeur, unlimitted Power, unfathomable Wisdom, unbounded Goodness, and Soul ravishing Beauty of your eternal, unchangable and invaluable Prize! And by gazing, I am sure you will naturely renew your Choice; for this and this only, will be the everlasting Joy, and Confirmation of all the Armies of Heaven, both Saints and Angels for the more they see, the more they will admire and renew their Choice and Strength for the same Choice to all Eternity; O what Glories, what Goodness, what power, wisdom and love will you e'er long behold, when you throw off the Fetters of Mortality and awake from the Ten Thousand Disorders of your fallen State, disentangled from all the Death and Darkness of Sin, breaking forth in the Transporting Realms of uncreated Day, and see this grand Jehovah in his Meridian Brightness! Yea you will then be ready to say (if asked) that I fell so far short from an adequate Discover of his infinite Glories, that I almost marred the Truths, perluted his Name, and cast a vail over the unspeakable Glories of this grand Omnipotent.

Or break forth with the Queen of Sheba (at the Sight of the famous King *(k)*) it was a true Report that I heard in my own Land: But O the one half or Thousandith Part was never told me!

Well lift up your Eyes, ye Lovers of God, ye Followers of the dispised Jesus, for the happy Hour (the Day of your Redemption) draws nigh when like the ancient Prophet, you will drop your Mantle *(l)* and mount the flaiming Car to enter the bright Mansions of eternal Felicity, and sail with Angels the boundless Sea, that Ocean of perfect Bliss, the transporting Perfections of the Deity; O my Soul and shall I be there! Good Lord is it possible! Can the Grace be so free; Yea how can it be otherwise from Love so great and Goodness so unbounded?

> Ah like itself breaks forth unbounded Love
> To fill the void of ev'ry hungry Mind
> That pants to drink from that o'er flowing Sea;
> Nor can that ancient Fountain be contain'd.
> O Love Divine transform me like Thyself
> That when the fleeting Scenes of Mortal Climes
> (And Sin, thou Foe!) all in Oblivion sunk
> To gaze on thee all ravish'd with the View
> (Ah humble Sear) I'll sound while Thought is known
> Thy worthy Fame in one begining Song
> (My God!) that grand immortal Note! Amen.

But O my Soul can I view the ravishing Scene, glide the attracting Stream, feast on the living bread, and drink the essence of Angellic Cordials, without a friendly Warning, and an endearing Call to that wandering Soul, starving Stranger, benighted Mind, unfeeling Reader, wandering Jew, that never tasted of the clusters of Eshcol? O no I must (while you read) knock at your Door, and point you to the fragrant Fields of celestial Canaan, and tell you Jehovah reigns, and you (tho' Earth and Hell against you) are fully able, and may yet go in and possess, ah eternally possess, those glorious Mansions of eternal Delight. I mean, for I know, nor can tell, of nothing more, nor wish no greater than to know and Enjoy a God like this.

How long, O ye earthly Courters, will ye be voluntary Slaves to Sin, and destign yourselves to continual Sorrow, when Liberty is proposed, and Joy with its gladening Streams so sweetly gliding by your Doors and courting your Attention?

How long will ye tread the barren Mountains of Vanity, and indefatigably pursue an empty sound wasting Life and Soul to grasp a Vapour, when the Showers of immortal Glory, and the Seas of unspeakable Felicity surrounds you continually? How long will you murder yourselves, when Life eternal intreats you to have pity on yourself, and be forever happy? How long will you sport the slippery Descent, and lash your speedy Race down the black Paths to eternal Perdition? O desist, desist! Yea be intreated to desist from the cruel Murder! For there is yet a God whose Bowels condole your Misery, and with Arms extended invites you to his Bosom of everlasting Love; O be intreated to make a happy Choice, leave your Idols, forsake your Misery, believe in a God by Profession and practice, extoll his Grace, adore his Name, and enjoy his Love to all Eternity. Reflect a Moment and review the expensive Prosecutions of your innumerable Schemes for happiness, together with your unspeakable trials and hard Labours, and say what have you gained? What dangers have you escaped? What Disorders have you removed, What Miseries have you fled from! What Prizes have you attained, consolations enjoyed, fortune made or Portion secured in all the indefatigable Engagements of your past Life? Yea must you not say, that your Expence has been infinite, your Attempts continual, and yet your Disappointments innumerable, your Trials unspeakable, your Sorrows insupportable, and still your Danger increasing, your Miseries Augmented, and you a remaining Stranger to Peace, abandon'd to Joy, and yet ignorant of any Possibility of a Moments sollidness or lasting Treasures?

O then, why my fellow Mortal, will you longer persist the dangerous Expensive and cruel Siege? Return from your Desertion, cease from your Rebellion, lay down your Arms, and hear to the charming Dictates of all things about you, that are courting you to their Father; and no longer live ignorant of, deserting from, in Rebellion against, or a stranger to such a Being. O serve him for he is thy Father; love him for he is thy Friend; trust him for he is thy Preserver; adore him for he is thy King; follow him for he is thy Leader, and choose him for thy Portion, and he will be thy everlasting Joy. And if you would find him only, think a Moment on the beating of thy Pulse, or moving of thy finger, or a Dust of Sand beneath thy Feet, and there behold a self-evident Demonstration of this mighty Fiot; yea there is a grand and alarming Proclamation this instant in thy Room, yea at the Center of thy Life, of a present God, a mercifull Father, an Omnipotent King, in only the Breath thou art now drawing; O believe him, rejoice in him, breathe Angellic Life, and live forever!

*   *   *

THOUGHT THE THIRD

On the Design and Nature of Creation.

HAVING proved the great Jehovah to be self-existent independant, and beyond any possibility or receiving either Injury or Benefit
from any of the Works of Creation, and infinitely good and happy
in himself, we are obliged to conclude, that all his Works, and every
Operation of his Hand must not only be a natural Production: but
likewise all good and glorious; and all not to add to his Happiness or
Glory: But to manifest his Glory, Goodness, Happiness: For he is,
as he is eternally self-existent, unchangable, independant, and nec-
essarily happy in and of himself; with or without Creation; and therefore the first, and whole moving Cause of his breaking forth in the
creaturely Systems was the infinite Love and Goodness, that was in
himself, breaking forth like itself; and that not for to add in the least
Degree to his Happiness or Glory; but for the Display or manifesting
of that Happiness and Glory which he himself was possessed of unchangeably.

Neither was the Design of Creation the Satisfaction or Pleasure,
that their Angellic Magnificence, humble Acknowledgements or
harmonious Strains of Adoration would discover or administer to
him: For if it was in the lest Degree then by Creation he received an
Addition of Pleasure and Satisfaction, and therefore more happy than
before: But all his Happiness and Delight arises in himself, and therefore was he to cast his Eye on Millions of angellic Systems, that were
blazing in all their Grandeur, adoring in all their Strains, it could not
awake a new pleasing Thought in the Breast of their Creator; Because
not only that Grandeur was all in himself, and came from himself,
not to add to his Glory, but to display his Glory, but likewise that
his Pleasure and Happiness, arises wholly from the View and Enjoyment of himself: & therefore we must conclude, that a Millions
of Worlds made cannot awake a new pleasing Thought, nor a Million
fallen a distressing Thought; And then consequently all Creation
must be brought forth as the natural Productions of such Goodness,
Glory for the displaying and manifesting of itself.

Not that Creation when brought forth should please or make happy the Creator, but Creation pleased and made everlastingly happy and glorious in the Creator; that is in the Knowledge and Enjoyment of that Goodness, that ever was in the Creator before Creation; and therefore O how shocking, how hellish, cruel, and blasphamous, is that God dishonouring thought or inconsistent Principle, that has been exhibited by many dark Zealots from both Pulpet, and press that Millions of immortal Spirits have been destined to the Racks of eternal Despair by this good God; and many more, who will not come out to discover their Nakedness so bare, who will say, that he did not design them for Misery but for his own Glory left them to be eternally miserable, when he might have prevented it and likewise, that they must be punished to all eternity, to satisfy and appease something that sin has stired up in him! and suffer me to say, that the latter bares, when examined, a far more wretched complex, than the former, for they not only act the hypocrite themselves, but charge God with it too, saying, that he offers Mankind Salvation when he has none for them and will forever consign them over to the Tortures of eternal Punishment for not accepting of that, which was not for them, and which he did not give them Power to embrace; so that they charge this good God, with Hypocrisy, Deceit, Injustice and unparellel Cruelty.

And therefore as it evident he doth, & must act like himself, wholly according to his own nature, without receiving either Injury or Benefit from all that he doth, what an ill, cruel, tormenting Nature must he be possessed of? Or what Sort of a God must they worship? How can they say he is possessed of glorious Perfection, when he can take Delight in such Dispensations of Vengeance & Cruelty, without ever relenting, or withholding his Sword of Revenge, when he receives no benefit thereby? And as for his being gracious & mercifull, how can that be, when but for the smallest Number of his Creatures have mercy or Grace from him, but what will, & is to add to them Misery? yea since the greatest Part of his Creatures are made miserable and but the smallest part happy, since more of his Family receives Vengeance then Mercy, may he not with more Propriety be called a cruel God, than a merciful God, for even, that small Number that are the Subjects of his Mercy have no cause to love him for what he is in himself; but only for the singular Act of his Kindness to them, because his acting like himself had admitted of more and far greater

Displays of Cruelty and Dispensations of Misery, than of Kindness and Mercy.

And therefore tell him what they will of their Love for him, the Truth amounts no higher than this, *We cannot love thee as a free Cause of good, or a natural Benefactor: For if the Display of thy Goodness, or thy Benedictions were natural in thee, and like thyself, thy Mercy and Goodness would have extended certainly to the greatest Part of thy Family, but it has not, to but for the smallest part; and we love or rather are there we love, or rather are glad with thee, that when so many (as worthy of Mercy as we) are made marks for thy Vengeance and Monuments of thy Displeasure, we were distinguished as Favourites by a singular Act of sovereign Kindness, and therefore are glad, that we are out of the Misery we deserved, and feel ourselves happy, which we must forever attribute to a singular act of thy Kindness.* And let me ask any rational Christian (let others twist and turn to serve themselves out as much as they will) whether I have not raised them to the towering Summit of all their Love and Adoration? But if we return to that self-evident Hypothesis A NATURAL SELF NECESSARY GOOD GOD, we shall naturally produce every necessary Argument, or Assistant, to harmonize in raising a self reasonable uninterrupted, immutable, unchangeable, magnificent Structor, eternally standing, self supported against every Invasion, for if the Fountain be sweet the streams are sweet, and if the Root be good the branches must consequently be the same; in deciding of which INVARIABLE TRUTH, steps in and saith A GOOD TREE CANNOT BRING FORTH EVIL FRUIT *(m)* and if we wait on invariable Truth we shall hear him declaring again, that GOD IS LIGHT, AND IN HIM IS NO DARKNESS AT ALL, and then concludes GOD IS LOVE, from which it is not only reasonable and scriptural, but self evident, that every Opperation of Dispensation of his must be a voluntary Display of that Fountain; yea and as much inconsistent and impossible to be otherwise, as for Light to bring Darkness, or Darkness produce Light; or falling Lead to go of itself with the utmost Rapidity, repugnant to the Attraction.

And therefore the Truth is, yea cannot be otherwise, that this God in acting like himself, doth every thing that he does in Love & Goodness, with a Design to display his Goodness, and make his Creatures happy therein: Nor can possibly either design, consent to, or take Pleasure in the Misery of any of his Creatures; and in Demonstration of which he arises (in Manner and Expression almost unknown in his revealed Mind) and gives me the following possitive Command SAY UNTO THEM AS I LIVE *(as True as I Live)* SAITH THE LORD I HAVE NO PLEASURE IN THE DEATH OF *(even)* THE WICKED; and therefore consequently must do all that can possibly be done, like (or consistent with) himself, to make happy, and prevent Misery; yea as he can neither receive Benefit or Injury from Creatures miserable, or Creatures happy, it must be the most horrid Reflections on the divine Being, that Hell itself could invent to say, that he either designs his Creatures for Misery, or even consents to their being Miserable, when he could prevent it, so that I need say no more to prove that the Works of Creation, Preservation and Redemption are all moved by infinite Love and Goodness, and wholly designed for the Display of the same; and every Operation of his Hand to manifest the Goodness of himself, and make his Creatures happy therein: Without any Design to add to the Happiness or Glory of the Creator.

And now, what thinks my candid Reader of that cloud of Darkness, that has been spread over the World interposing between a good mercifull God, and a cruel and miserable Race of Adam, by such a Number of arbitary bigots, who tell you, *Its true God is a God of Mercy, and you ought to seek whether he has any for you or not; but still he has not only a secret Prerogative to dispence his singular Favours or Rewards and Punishments at his Pleasure: but likewise he is possess'd of something in himself of Vengeance, wrath or Justice, that may be stired up, roiled, or insenced, which (when so roiled or displeased) takes Pleasure in inflicting Punishment on the Offender, and will be pleased with seeing them under the Torments of his Vengeance, wrath and hot displeasure to all Eternity?*

Or is it possible for you, either to reject, or stand aloof from this Soul-ravishing God-exalting Truth, a GOD NATURALLY SELF-NECESSARILY, ETERNALLY INDEPENDANTLY AND UNCHANGEABLY GOOD, and this God forever acting in and like himself in infinite Love and Goodness to all his Creatures? Yea methinks if you do not labour hard exclude yourself from Conviction, and choose your Bondage, your whole soul must be so attracted with the ravishing Truth as to seal your Devose from every other Lover, and stake your present and everlasting Inheritance in the Heart of that Goodness and Essence of that eternal Spring of self-existent unchangeable, yea uncontainable Love!

And O let me tell you, that this infallible Truth is the spring of uncreated Happiness, the Joy of the FATHER-SON-SPIRIT-GOD; this is all the Joy of Angels and Arch-Angels, Saints, and Seraphic Armies.

Yea, and let me tell you, that whatever gross and inconsistent Conceptions you, or any others, may imbibe of this great and good God, while in this State of Death, Darkness, and Disorders: yet if ever you are so happy as to be disentangled from all the Disorders of your miserable fallen State, awake in his Likeness, see him as he is, and join the countless Band of immortal Adorers, you will find my Hypothesis so true and ravishing, that you will not only view it as the Essence of all the Glories and Joys of every created Clime: but likewise find their Notes of Praise and joyfull Acknowledgments so diverse from the Language of the fore mentioned Song, that you will scarcely find Room in Heaven for that inferior Note or I love thee for thy Goodness to me but hear the countless Millions all harmonizing in this one eternal and uninterrupted Theme.

Thou and thou alone art worthy! and therefore we love thee as such, we adore thee (not so much for thy gifts or Favours,) for what we behold in thee, and for what thou art in thy self; yea so glorious Art thou, and so worthy of all our Love and Songs of Adoration, that if it were possible that we had received no Favour from, were under no Obligations to thee, had never been created, preserved or re-deemed by thee or could be forever happy without thee yet thy Beauty, thy love, thy wisdom, thy glory, thy goodness, and all thy perfections are in themselves so love worthy, praise worthy, so glorious, and attracting, that we could but be ravished with thee, and call up every power of our souls to love and adore thee; yea and the longer we gaze the more we admire and are carried away with the View in the Torrent of the Rapturous Attraction; and therefore O thou great Jehovah, thou mighty Fiot, thou spring of Life, thou Source of Hapiness, thou never failing, thou over flowing Fountain of unspeakable Joy, and ravishing Delight, we not only love thee, but shall forever begin to love and increase out beging Songs of Adoration to thy Name, and this our Song, thou Joy of Joys, Life of Lives, Love of Loves and Glory of Glories.

Yea we love thee with love too great to be expressed for thou art so good, that nothing has been left undone by thee that could dispence thy grace and display thy goodness; & therefore we cheer-fully join in Heaven's composed Song, Salvation unto our God which

sitteth upon the Throne and unto the Lamb, amen. Blessing and
Glory and Wisdom and Thanksgiving and Honour and Power and
Might be unto our God forever, and ever
   Amen.

   Having thus viewed and discovered the Cause and Design of the
creaturely Systems, I shall now pass on to examine and discover the
Nature of this glorious Production, or Work of Creation, (so called
in the Language of Men) the first moving Cause or Author of which,
we have found to be infinite, immense, self existant, uncreated and
unchangeable, and the sole Cause and Author of all Beings: So that
consequently he is not only the author, but Father of all, and therefore, altho' it is the vain Opinion of many that he made all Things
out of nothing, yet it is in itself inconsistent and impossible, with our
infallible Hypothesis: For if God be thus infinite and immense, there
cannot be any empty void, or room, where God is not, for he must
be every where, and therefore it is impossible for any thing to be
made out of nothing. Yea the Existence of an infinite immense
Being, and therefore those who confess an infinite Jehovah, and yet
say, he made things out of nothing contradict themselves; and might
with as much Propriety say, that he is infinite and not infinite, all and
not all: so that the Term nothing in a strict Sense is inconsistant, for
there is no such empty place as nothing; or any empty void where
God is not; and therefore altho' many think it impeaching the character of God to say, that he doth not make Things and are doing him
Honour by saying that he made the Worlds and all Things out of
nothing, yet if they did but examine the Consequences of what they
say, they would find they were denying the very Essense of self-Existence and declaring there was once a period, when God did not fill
immensity, or that he was finite and limited, and is more great and
glorious now then he once was, because he doth now rule and possess so many Worlds, which are all made out of nothing; and if he
should still continue in the Works of Creation, he would increase in
Grandeur still by the same rule he may make Thousands and Millions
more out of nothing. And not only so but another Inconsistency will
appear and that is, if God made them out of nothing, they may all
return to nothing again: for it is self evident, that whatever comes
from nothing may by the same Rule return to nothing, for it can have
no uncreated Essence for its Maintainance.

   But if my reader will only consider and examine the natural

Consequences of the acknowledging God to be an INFINITE, IMMENSE UNLIMITED BEING, I shall have no cause to labour for the Proof of Things being not made out of nothing, and therefore I proceed to discover the Truth. God being the only Life and Cause of all Things, and being a God that was every where, it is self evident that every thing came from him; and therefore when Adam was made he declares, that he was his Son, & now if he was made out of nothing or from some Matterials, that was not from God; how could he be his Son, surely he cannot be said to be his Son, because he only formed him into that shape, for if that would make him his Son, then the Ark that Noah made out of Gopher wood was the Son of Noah. And God expressly calls Adam his, for saith the Word of Adam which was the Son of God *(n)* yea and again God declares, that not only Adam, but all the Sons of Men are the Offspring of the divine Being *(o)* and what is the Offspring of any Being, but a being coming into a seperate Existence, realy from the Father? And therefore Adam was realy from God and was God's Son, but as some will enquire, why it is then said, that man was made out of the Dust of the Earth, I answer, that all the Account that God has given to the World about the Creation was given from Mount Horeb to Moses after Mankind had been two Thousand Years involved in the Darkness, Death and Disorders of their fallen State, and had so lost all Knowledge of their primitive State, or a spiritual World, that had God have spoken to them of such Things, as they where in a strict sense; they could not, possibly have understood the Relation, and therefore you have cause forever to adore him for his Condescension, but saith one again, why the Man signifies, that God did not speak of Things as they realy are; True my Reader, not as they were in themselves, but as they appeared to them to whom they were spoken; and if you would cast the Fault of this Manner of speaking on any one, you must cast it on God; for he hath often declared, that he could not change nor repent *(p)* and yet in the very Narative given of the Creation, and fall of the World, he declares, that after they had fallen and he had seen the Greatness of their Sins and Disorders, (as tho' he did not know it before) it so grieved him at the heart, that he repented he had made them *(q)* and therefore what think you now, my dear reader, of my taking the Liberty of diviating from the strict Sense of the Letter and shewing the spiritual Correspondence, when, if I did not I must charge God with speaking false? And now after intreating you to banish all Thoughts of any Contradictions in the uninterrupted Chain of divine Revelation, and at the same time adore God for his unparallel Stoop in his manner of Expression, that when we could not understand his Language or the Nature of a spiritual System he stoops, to converse with us in our Language according to the nature of a Temporal World and replies himself, that if we cannot understand him now how much less should we understand him if he spake in the Language of a spiritual World? *(r)* And now I shall return to my intended subject.

When God brought forth his Son, his immortal Power of thought was from the Life of God, and his immortal Cloathing or Outbirth from Gods eternal Outbirth, but as there will be some enquiry in this Matter, I shall a little enlarge.

And now after reflecting back on the Nature of the Triune God, as has already been discovered, you must observe, that thro' the whole chain of Revelation you hear of God's being in Heaven, and of the Kingdom of Heaven; which is the Kingdom of God, some times called his Pavilion, and some times the everlasting Hills; all holding forth his Residence, or everlasting Out-birth, but let not my Reader, imagine these created, or corporeal Heavens or any Place made for his Residence, but what he was from Eternity possessed of, in and of himself; and therefore from this eternal Kingdom, Pavilion or Out-birth, Adam and all angelic Beings derive their Clothing or Out-birth, or paradisical Kingdom.

But to offer more Light still, let us observe, what is said by God, when about to make Man, *Let us make Man in our Image,* and when made, declares, that he was in the Likeness of his Father. *(s)* And therefore when we see the Offsprings brought forth, and hear his Father declare, that he is in his Father's Likeness, we thereby learn something of the Father; or discover what the Father is: Neither can it be otherwise than for the Offspring to be like his Father, for he must partake of his Nature and all his Perfections;

And it is evident, that this Son stands forth in the Likeness of his Father, and as he now stands forth, he is an immortal intelligent Power of thought, clothed with a spiritual, immortal, paradisical Outbirth; and all this paradisical, Clothing, as much, yea more, under the command of the inward Creature or Power of Life and Thought as the Feet and Fingers of a Man is now: for as the whole Frame is now ruled and moved by the Power of Thought, much more the whole clothing was ruled and moved by the Power of Thought, before any Disorders had taken Place.

Yea and his Father told him, that while he stood in that State of Perfection he would have the Command of all the outward Creature. *(t)*

But we must no more imagine, that outbirth or outward Creature to be something seperate from the inward Creature, and then put under his Command, then we must imagine, that the hands and feet of a Child doth not belong to the Child but only something given or added to the Child: for as the Child is brought forth with the Hands and Feet, & the hands & feet are part of the Child, so this Creature is brought forth both inward & outward Creature; & this outward Creature or all this paradisical Clothing as much belonging to the Creature & Part of the Creature as the Hands & Feet of the Child is Part of the Child, yea let me further say, that without this outward Creature he could no more be complete, than a Child without his Feet and Hands. And thus you have seen this Offspring of the divine Being perfect, in beauty clothed (saith God) in Stones of Fire, and thus before sin, walking up and down in the paradise of God *(u)*.

But as further Evidence to demonstrate this grand Truth (tho' new to many), let me observe, that when Christ came into the World for Man's Redemption, he did not come to create another Set or Number of Beings, but to redeem those that were made and fallen; and therefore, as the second Adam restores the ruins of the First, when Man is restored he will, as he would have been, if he had never fallen. Yea and God when giving us a Description of the redeemed World when restored *(w)* it is the same as is described to be before it fell *(x)* when speaking of their Paradise or Stones of Fire calls them by the same Names; and not only so but God likewise declares, that those who are redeemed shall again be stationed in that Paradise, and again eat of that Tree of Life, which they turned from and lost *(y)* and therefore I think that any national Christian that will adhear to Reason, and read the Word of God as a Spiritual Chain, can no more imagine that that Paradise was corporeal, or that Adam eat of corporeal Food, than that we must believe in Transubstantiation, because Christ declares, that we cannot be saved unless we eat his Flesh and Drink his Blood: for the one is as possitive as the other, and as plainly signifies Corporeal.

And therefore, I trust by this Time, my reader is convinced that a Spiritual Father did not bring forth a corporeal Son: but that this new System was Angellic, Spiritual and immortal.

And as for this man, so called, you must not imagine him as a single Man, or as a Father with Power to make more: But an innumerable Throng of angellic Beings, brought forth in his glorious System; and therefore altho' many have been much puzzled to be satisfied how Adam's Family would have spread, if they had not fallen, yet it is evidently they would never wanted to spread if they had fallen no more than the Saints in Heaven when made once again by Christ will wish to be seperated. For there is no Bulk in Spirits to be obliged to seperate for to make Room, and it was their Breaking off from God that seperated the Male and Female Powers of the Creature, for Adam himself was a Male and Female, being when he was as he came from God *(y)* And therefore it is evident they were all once and would have so remained if they had not sinned (to be discovered more clearly) yea and all that is restored will be as much one again as they were before they fell, which Christ declares in positive Terms, for who would presume to say there was any Seperation between the Father and the Son? And he declares, that those that are redeemed, shall be as much one as the Father and Son are one *(z)* And now you have a more clear Discovery of the Glory of this angellic systems and innumerable Crowd of Adorers standing as one in divine Union and Glory a paradisical System to bask in the boundless Ocean of their Father's Love and Perfections, and altho' this may seem strange, that there was so many brought forth and stood together, yet God himself hath declared it, for he hath not only called Adam male and female, but likewise no less than three Times called him, them before the Woman was taken from him *(a)* and therefore thus stood the whole Family, as one, yea not only this world, or what we call the Family of Adam, but likewise all this innumerable Crowd of Worlds that now stands in a corporeal Relation brought forth at the same time, and in the same Manner as this; and in as near Relation with this as the two Polls or friged Zones of this is now; and nearer, for now there is Seperations, Wars and disorders, and then there was none: but one uninterrupted Relation harmonizing thro' the whole; and all Angellic and immortal.

But saith my Reader this is more strange still, that all these Worlds or Systems of Worlds, were all once spiritual Worlds, brought forth with this. True my Dear Reader, it may be strange, as many other Scripture Truths are, by being so carelessly strided over: But as new and as strange as it is, it is the very first Thing, that God has revealed in the Oracles of Life.

IN THE BEGINNING GOD CREATED THE HEAVEN *(b)* and I trust, my Reader will not presume to say it was God's eternal Kingdom of Heaven (or Out birth) for that was uncreated, and therefore, when we find ourselves (this corporeal World) in such Relation as we do with the whole corporeal System, and hear Jehovah declare in the same Sentence, that he created the Heaven and the Earth in the beginning, how can we be any more at a loss, than that this World was then created, when the Relation is given at the same time, in the same Manner, and same Sentence, unless we choose Darkness rather than light?

And now my dear Reader, you have not only a greater Discover of the Glory of this new System, but likewise see more of the infinite Goodness of God in bringing forth this glorious System in such Grandeur as it thus evidently appears in its primitive State; all brought forth in his own Likeness, all Paradisical, all Immortal, and all in a fit Capacity to sollace in the boundless Ocean of his unchangeable Love and Glory. Ah! think, think, my dear Reader, what a glorious Display of Love, and Manifestation of infinite Goodness, is here broke forth from the overflowing uncontainable Fountain! Countless Millions of empty Vessels forever to drink large Draughts of the celestial Stream.

And all this not a strained Favour, or singular Act of God's kindness: but the natural Manifestations of his own Nature; or the natural Productions of his own Perfections. O THE GRANDEUR OF SUCH A BEING! WHO CAN BUT LOVE AND ADORE HIM? Ah so transporting is this Truth that was it not for the Death and Darkness of the fallen Race, all Nations and People, would immediately choose their Devose from every other Lover, and chain the Choice and Attention of every Power of their Souls with ravishing Delight on this once only GOOD GOD, for Time and Eternity. And O how longs my Soul while I write to alarm my poor, starving, perishing fellow Mortals, to seek, find, know, feel, and forever enjoy, the Soul transporting Truth! Rouse, Rouse, O ye sleepy Supine Inhabitants of a dead miserable unfeeling World! Awake, love, and forever adore this unspeakably good God.

How can you starve my dear Reader, with bread so nigh? Or why will ye die, while floating in the Fountain of Life? O be intreated to arise and look about you! O listen a Moment to the wispering calls of Ten Thousand Charms, that are courting you to the Bosom of unbounded Goodness, and heart of eternal Love! I can but call you, yea I must invite you, to the Embraces of Heaven, and everlasting Enjoyment of my Father. My Father did I say, good Lord, and am I one of thy Sons I ask, I need, nor can I have, any more. And O ye redeemed Souls, ye Lovers of good, ye Warriors for Heaven, ye Heirs of eternal Bliss, in such a Case whose God is the Lord! Awake your Hearts, alarm your Souls, loosen your Tongues and arise with Joy to spread to tell and shout forth the Wonders of his infinite love; and let his Name be known, and his Goodness proclaimed, wherever the Sons of Men reside. Ah! with cheerfull Delight wear out your mortal Stay in the glorious Theme, THERE IS A GOOD GOD: LOVE HIM O YE SONS OF MEN! And O fear not ye Sons of Wisdom, ye Lovers of Truth, but rejoice and sing out your christian Race! For Altho' you may yet labour under the remaining Contrariety of your fallen Nature, yet the Conquest is yours, the Field is won, the Crown is safe, and e'er long you shall divide the Spoil, and share the Prize, and enjoy the Palm to all Eternity. And O for your Joy and supporter under all the Trials of your way, remember, THERE IS A GOD, A GOOD GOD, A PRESENT AND UNCHANGEABLE GOD; he is your FATHER, your PRESERVER, your LIGHT, your LIFE, your BOSOM FRIEND, your ALL-CONQUERING KING, your JOY, LEADER, STRENGTH, AND EVERLASTING REWARD. O then fix your Eyes on the Prize of your unlimited Treasure, and go on Rejoicing! Ah rejoice ye DISPISED OF THE WORLD, ye SPECTACLE TO MEN AND DEVILS, ye WORLD'S FOOLS, ye CHRISTIAN MARTYRERS, ye PRISONERS OF HOPE, ye HEAVENLY WARRIORS, ye HEIRS of BLISS, ye COMPANIONS of ANGELS, and SONS OF UNCREATED LIFE AND LOVE, harnished with the invincible Armour of the everlasting Gospel, and shine as celestial Stars, while you cross this benighted World, until you drop your Mantle, and in mortal Climes are known no more.

And O ye disintangled SONS OF IMMORTAL LIGHT, ye HAPPY INHABITATS OF UNCREATED REALMS that behold his unvail'd glories and bask in the Meridian Blaze of that eternal Sun, the glimering Rays of which I pant to enjoy and labour to discover; shout, Ah shout the Wonders of that Love, which with you I hope forever to enjoy and adore: Yea methinks your immortal Strains eternal Anthems and harmonious Doxologies, might so ring your blazing Realms, and celestial Arches, as to echo and resound thro' the interposing Glooms, read the Dark world: Inhabit, and alarm my almost impenitable Soul from its dark Cavern of Insensibility, to feel the sacred Ardour, and cement the glorious Harmony: but O! no, no, nothing but Jehovah's touch! touch O thou bleeding Hand of God my obdurate Soul, and melt my Adamant. With one Spark of thine immortal flame, and then, (O shall I say I thine and thou mine forever!)

*   *   *

THOUGHT THE FOURTH

The Cause and Effects of the Fall of this glorious System.

AFTER having seen something of the original State, and primitive Grandeur of this new System, let us now turn and take a lamentable View of its miserable Fall, and immediate ruin. And O who, that hath been in the lest Degree restored back by the bleeding Hand to enjoy but a glimmering Ray of their primitive Glory, can forbear to grieve, when they behold so sudden, so unspeakable, so miserable a Change, has hath taken place in the New System.

Ah how is the Gold changed, and the most fine Gold become dim! And happy would it be, if but one Ray of divine Light might so far discover the Wound to the fallen Race, as to excite a Thirst for Help.

> And thou, O thou, who did the stripling Arm
> And point the stone from the unpollish'd sling,
> To drop the daring Champion of the Camp.
> Direct my Arrow with as blest Effect!

And now as I would fain serve my Fellow Men in the Gospel, let me intreat my dear Reader to reflect back a Moment, and review what once you were even an angellic being with the vast throng united with and sollacing in the perfections of God thy Father and he had only possible Good, and therefore thy everlasting Happiness, and Welfare wholly Depending in retaining that union, with him, and being confirmed therein; and the inward Creature, the ruling Power of all the whole System; as that turns so turns the whole, all standing as one together. And this innumerable Crowd or angellic System standing between the Means of Confirmations and Apostacy called two Trees the one of Life and the other of Death; the knowledge of Evil *(c)* but not as many vainly imagine them corporeal Trees for I cannot as yet be so imposed upon as to believe, that this Son of God stood in continual Need of Sweet and Sower Apples and other corporeal fruit together with Turnops, Cabbages and Potates, &c.

No for altho' I shall expose Myself to the Censures of almost all our Expositors, and be accounted ever so ignorant and wild, and stand as a mark for all their Arrows: Yet God forbid, that ever I should imagine that those Sons of God stood in need of any such beastly Good, being taught the Contrary, not only by the Word of God, but likewise, by my own Experience: for when thro' boundless Grace I was restored so far back as to taste but one glimering Ray, or small Gluster of the Fruits of that paradise, which Adam was in the full Fruition of, it was so infinitly Superior to all created Good, that had it been possible for me to have stood out my mortal Watch without the Enjoyments of Earth, I would never have divided the Spoil any more with the Beasts; now if but one Glimpse of that eternal Love, when under so many Disorders, wafts the Creature so far beyond all Thirst for earthly Enjoyments, how can any rational Being, that has ever tasted the Difference, imagine, that those Offspring of God swiming in the Boundless Ocean of his uncreated Good, could possibly stand in need of thirst for, or bear to partake, any corporeal, created or sensual Pleasures and Enjoyments?

But to return, it is evident, that there was no other Way to come to the Knowledge of Evil but by thirsting after and falling in Love with created Enjoyments and therefore it was called not the Tree of Knowledge: but as plain as can be expressed the Tree of the Knowledge of Good and Evil, *(d)* Good they already knew, and would have known nothing else, if they had not thus have turned from good and their Father told them, that if they began to thirst after and taste of that Tree they would come to the Knowledge of evil, and therefore know Good and Evil too.

And as for the Tree of Life, how is it possible for a christian to be at a Loss about what Tree that is, when they have been eating of it themselves? *(e)* besides it is evident, that there is Life in none, but

God, and in him is Life; yea he hath Life in himself *(f)* and this Fountain or Spring of Life in God that which gives Life to the World. *(g)* and therefore when God had brought forth his Offspring the first thing, that he warned him of, was the Danger of turning from this Tree of Life, and the Danger and Evil Consequences of turning his Affections after any Thing else, for God knows as his inward Creature turned that is the Power of Choice so would turn the Whole; and as he turned and acted choice, the Rapidity of that Choice would increase: for that acting of Choice is the Growth of the Will; and the Growth of the Will is the confirming the Creature, and engaging of them in the same Act and Choice again; and therefore the Consequence, if this ruling Power of Choice has sentered to that Fountain of Life, the Will would have immediately began its Confirmation, as it began its Growth, therefore increasing in Choice and Strength, and Will and Desire to Act the same Choice, must have been confirmed beyond all Possibility of falling or appostacy; and so likewise increases the Will and Choice in the Act of Appostacy; and therefore when he began to have a Thirst for any Good or Enjoyment, but the Tree of Life, the Choice acted with the will in pursuit of it; and by this Action the will increasing in Strength, and thirst for to Act the same Choice still, and therefore when the Choice was acted from the Tree of Life, the Will was turned, and likewise increased in Strength and consequently in the rapid, miserable Course of Appostacy; and therefore gone beyond all Possibility (in itself) of returning or even a Desire for to return.

But now the question will arise, what could cause this pure Spirit the Offspring (and in Likeness) of God to thirst after any thing else but God, or to turn from God to his own Ruin? and as I am fond of being a Servant (in these Truths) to my fellow Men, I shall pass on to a further Discovery. You remember my dear Reader, we have already seen the Nature of Confirmation and Appostacy by the Act and Growth of the Will and choice; you have likewise seen this new born Offspring between the two means, and now the next thing we have to observe is, that as the Growth of the Will and Capacity wholly consists in the Action of Choice, there is therefore a natural Cause, why all created Beings must come forth in a State of Trial, neither consigned to misery, nor forced to Happiness; altho' so many have cut, and mangled the Truth so much about Man's free Agency,

Why they was suffered to fall or not confirmed by God beyond a Possibility of falling.

And upon the whole, after all their Labour and Travel, they have brought forth this Monster, *God as an arbitrary Sovereign hath made a Law, and set Man between Life, and Death, Heaven and Hell, to Try his Obedience to that Law. And will punish the Violators of that Law with his hot Dispeasure, vindictive Wrath and insenced Justice.* When at the same time (according to their Hypothesis) he might prevent their Fall if he would.

But I need not say much to refute such vain conceptions for the Truth is very obvious, as hath been proved, that they could not be brought forth any other way, but in the image of God, or in Likeness of their Father, who is an uncontroulable free Agent; and therefore they could neither be confirmed in Life; or distined to Death, until they begin to Act their Choice, and improve the Will: For there was, no other means, that can effect, it but the action of choice, which is the Growth of the Will; and therefore you see this Angellic Being in a State of Infancy, nor could be otherwise, until the Will and Choice begins to Act: for as nothing could confirm them to Life or destine them to Death without the acting of their Will and Choice, they be capable of Action! before they could fall or be confirmed to Life, and now the next thing you are to understand is, that this Creature being brought forth in the Likeness of his Father could not know or conceive of any thing but what was holy, pure and happy like itself, and therefore, consequently an utter Stranger not only to Death and Misery, but likewise to fear (for where there is Fear, there is Misery and Torment already *(g)*) and therefore altho' warned by his kind Father of the Danger of Sin, Death and Misery (which warning he ought to adhere to) yet he could not fear any such Thing, nor have any Conception, what was meant by evil Death and Misery, they were all to him wholly unintelligible: For he was happy, holy, pure, and alive; and therefore could have no more Dread or Fear, of evil Misery and Death, that if he had been warned of the Danger of Life, Joy, and Happiness: for this is an infalible Hypothesis, that he could not know of any thing, but that which was like himself; and therefore his Nature wholly excluded him from any Possibility of fearing Misery until he felt it. So that if warned a Thousand Times of the Danger of loosing his happy and exalted State, he could not have the least

Concern, or fear: for he could have no Conception of Loss; and therefore might be as much terrified if warned of the Danger of gaining
Life and happiness, as loosing of it; and as for this point, viz. his
Ignorance of every Thing, but what he was, if disputed by any, we
will hear, what is said by the Father, of his offspring himself, why
saith he, UNTO THE PURE ALL THINGS ARE PURE *(h)* and therefore can
conceive of nothing else. And now after you have taken a small View
of one Truth more, viz. the Happiness and Grandeur of his State, you
will not be at a Loss about the cause of his turning; for he was as
before observed, brought forth in a state of unspeakable Happiness,
and Grandeur, (tho' but an Infant) and as much in Possession (and
command) of himself, both inward and outward Creature (the glorious Paradise) as a man now has of his Hands, Fingers and Feet.
And therefore when he found himself awake (as it were) into such a
State of Happiness and Grandeur, all (as it felt to him) his own, and
at his own Disposal, he begins to view all the Beauty and Grandeur
of his outward Creature: which pleasing Thought of his own Grandeur began to draw his Attention, and cause him to fall in Love with
his paradisical Clothing; so that of Consequence the inward Creature
or Power of Choice, turned from the only Spring of Life into his own
Clothing, and therefore his will not only turned, but began to increase that way; nor could he, when viewing of his Beauty and Grandeur, have any Fear of loosing it, no more than of adding to it, and
thus looking on himself of Choice he immediately, not only centered
the will, but increased its Strength and Desire for the same Choice;
so that the Action of the Choice must of consequence grow stronger
and stronger in the same Act, and therefore sink the Creature beyond
all Recovery (in himself) because like falling Lead (when feeling the
Attraction) the Rapidity increases continually.

But if any of my Readers, should still be so chained down by
Darkness and Tradition, as not yet to be convinced, or believe, that
my Conceptions are scriptural, we will hear what is said by God himself in the very first Account of his Fall, he declares, that he saw the
Fruit pleasant to the Eyes, and a Tree to be desired, and took thereof
which is as plain as can be expressed, that they saw and fell in Love
with the outward Creature to his immediate Ruin; and again when he
is giving us a Narrative of the Fall, he first discovers the primitive
State, saith in these express Terms, THOU SEALEST UP THE SUM FULL
OF WISDOM, AND PERFECT IN BEAUTY; THOU HAST BEEN IN EDEN, THE

GARDEN OF GOD, EVERY PRECIOUS STONE WAS THY COVERING, comparing the Glory of his paradisical Clothing to every precious Stone, Yea saith God, WAS PREPARED IN THE DAY THAT THOU WAST CREATED; and saith again THOU ART THE ANOINTED CHERUB, THAT COVERETH; AND I HAVE SET THEE SO: yea saith he again, THOU WAST UPON THE HOLY MOUNTAIN OF GOD and then speaking of his exalted and grand State and Thought, saith, THOU HAST WALKED UP AND DOWN IN THE MIDST OF THE STONES OF FIRE; yea saith he, THOU WAST PERFECT IN THY WAYS, even, FROM THE DAY THAT THOU WAST CREATED, TILL (the unhappy Moment) THAT INIQUITY WAS FOUND IN THEE; (or Awoke in thy Breast,) and then after declaring what was his miserable Doom by Reason of this destructive Thought, he goes on to give the Cause of this Evil, and thought of Iniquity, THINE HEART, says he, was LIFTED UP BECAUSE OF THY BEAUTY.

Would my Reader, have any thing more plain? Or could it be more clearly expressed, that his beholding his Beauty and Grandeur lifted up his Heart with Pride? And again saith God, THOU HAST CORRUPTED THY WISDOM BY REASON OF THY BRIGHTNESS, *(i)* God thy Brightness, Glory, Beauty and magnificence, which ought to have been a Means of painting thee to its Author, and engaging thy whole Soul to love and adore him, thou hast made so vile a use of, as to lift up thy Soul to Idolatry, turning from the Root and Fountain, to love and worship the Stream and Branches; and instead of centering thy whole Soul to the Author of thy Beauty and Grandeur thou hast fallen in love with it, and gone a whoring after it as thy God and chief Good, seperate from, and exclusive of the Fountain. And thereby corrupted thy Wisdom, defiled thy beauty and destroyed thyself, and art now sinking in thine own Misery.

And thus I have discovered to my reader, the Cause and Means of this Fall, in such a clear light, that you may no longer be at a loss about his primitive State, and miserable Rebellion; nor will have any cause to charge God any more with designing his Fall, or with the Neglect of preventing it.

And as you have seen the fall of this World or Family so you have discovered the Fall and Ruin of the whole of this new System, for as they was all brought forth at the same Time, and in the same Manner, and stood not as many, but one, so they must of Consequence act and fare as one; or if any should ask, why some part of the System (altho' brought forth at the same Time) might not stand even if some part fell, I answer (from a consequence of your own faith) by the same rule, and for the same Reason, as that one Part of Adam's Family could not stand, and the other fall. But as one fell so they all fell, for before they fell, as hath been proved, they was not two but one; and therefore must act as one; and by the same rule as the People, that are now in Africa, was once in the Rebellion with the People, that are now in Asia, so were those, now, distant Parts of the System once one with this: And therefore if the Disorders of Sin could thus separate these, that are now no more in Relation than two Stars, surely by the same rule it might seperate the larger Parts of the System.

And O that you would now think a Moment on the woefull effects of that fatal Blow, that plunged all in ruin and nor only fear that vile, that Soul murdering (yea World destroying) Monster of Thought from God: but return from its destructive Course and forever love and adore that infinite Love and Goodness that interposed before the Whole was irrecoverably gone, even beyond the Mercy and Power of Omnipotence! Ah how can you but love and adore that Good God, that bleeding Saviour, that meek and lovely Jesus, that has interposed, and there dies, for your redemption. But O let me turn one thought more after the miserable sinking System, and O I see not only Millions of Souls, but worlds with their countless Millions of empty desparing, raging and self-tormenting Creatures, sinking in all the Racks and increasing Miseries of fallen Nature, and each one continuing the same unhappy and destructive course in the most increasing Rapidity! O my Soul, and must they, and will they sink, will they never flinch, retract nor return; no if once they pass the Redeemer's Hand for the wicked in Hell, tho' in Racks of Misery and keen Despair, will with the utmost Resolution of Soul renew their Rage, repeat, their Crimes, and choose their sinking Rapidity from God, and all that is good, and choose to blaspheme the God, that made them, and remain in Opposition to his love, in a growing Capacity to all Eternity.

> O dreadful Scene, what Heart of Stone but bleed
> To see those countless Millions plunge, Ah plunge,
> In Death and Loss, whatever could be lost?
> Down; down they sink, with rapid Force to the
> Unfathomable Gulf of Pain and Woe,

Where all the Racks of fallen Nature crowd,
But O! as yet there is, a Who can tell
Tho' none but God hath Power to interpose!
Hark, Hark glad news, Jehovah looks with Love,
Assumes their Guilt, bears their innormous Load,
And bleeds and dies to lift a dying World.
While love doth graft them on the Tree of Life,
O! Jesus ride victoriously to spread
Thy love thro' all these mortal Regions now,
Bring countless Millions from the Jaws of Hell,
To thy dear Heart with me among the Crowd.

* * *

THOUGHT THE FIFTH

Fallen nature interposed by the Incarnation of the Deity.

FROM what Discoveries hath been made of the Creation, and fall of this angellic System, I shall now pass on to the view the Cause and Design of its present standing: For it is neither as it was when first brought forth, nor yet in the State of fallen Nature; for as it was originally Spiritual, so it would likewise have remained Spiritual tho' fallen, if not interposed: For the falling of an angellic System would not change it to corporeal, for if it would, then the Devils would have been corporeal; and if Man was fallen, he was fallen; and therefore if nothing done for him he must become the same as the Devils; so that only the Existance of a corporeal World is an evident Demonstration, that it is neither in the State it was made in, nor yet in the State of fallen nature; and therefore it's evident likewise by its being now corporeal, that it is fallen Nature interposed; which Interposition could never be effected but by God himself, and thus we are brought to see, that God hath stopped the fallen System, which stopage was God's Incarnation. That is God himself by coming into fallen Nature stoped its Course, holding it under such Suppression as to keep it from acting itself; which Suppression caused it to stand forth as it now is corporeal.

But to help my Reader further still to the Cause and Nature of this System standing forth thus corporeal by god's incarnation, let it be observed that the Creature tho' fallen was not passive, but still an active being, and now acting and raging in Contrariety to God; which Action (as hath been proved) was its Fall and Ruin; and therefore of Consequence nothing could help or do him good, but what stoped and redeemed from that acting in Contrariety to God; so that if God undertakes for his Redemption he must stop him from acting that Course, and therefore this was God's Incarnation so to enter in the fallen Creature, as to hold his active and raging Powers from Action, and as God was not a passive but active Spirit, therefore of Course they were acting in Opposition one to the other; and when God thus holds this contrary Spirit under such Suppression as to be kept from Action, it must consequently stand forth corporeal; so that neither God nor the Creature are in themselves corporeal: but made or become so by the meeting Contrarieties of their two Natures. And thus my Dear reader, may see, that wherever there is any thing corporeal, there is fallen Nature interposed, so that Sun, Moon and Stars; Rocks, Hills and Stones; Fire, Air, Earth and Water, and every Thing that you see or feel corporeal, proclaims God incarnate, and that you are stoped a Moment from the Course of fallen Nature to be redeem'd, O, my Soul, and what could God do more! but has he stooped so low? Yea he has, for the eternal Word has become Flesh and dwells among us. Yea not only dwells among us as a Helper, but realy in us as a supporter from eternal Perdition; for there is nothing but this interposing Hand or suppressing and restraining Spirit that keeps the Race of Adam from the same Pain and Misery, that the fallen Angels endure, yea and that Moment, that this restraint is broke thro' the Creature awakes in keen Despair; but God being thus in them by his Incarnation they are held in a Possibility of Redemption; and thus, God himself entered into all the Sin, Misery, and Contrariety of the fallen Creature; O can it can it, be? Is it possible?

> What God the great the good first Cause self-mov'd
> Steps in the sinfull Region (Dark Abode!)
> Assumes our Guilt and wades thro' all our Shame
> With Pains exquisit and expiring Groans,

By Loss of Life, and Streams of blood Divine,
Treads out the Torters of the Rebells Hell,
To turn their Choice, regain their sinking Will,
Restore them back to his immortal Charms;
And reinstate them in consummate Bless,
Makes them again Sons of the Deity!
And yet, O must I say, the World asleep!
Ah sleeping o'er the wretched gulf of Hell,
Expos'd to plunge where hope is known no more,
Persuing Shades as if they toil'd for Life,
While rapid Times hurls off the mortal Stage.
Till instantaneous sunk in Endless Night!

Be astonished, O my Reader, fall in Love with and forever adore that God, that stooped so low; and sleep no longer, lest ye sleep the Sleep of Death, and then awake where sleep is known no more.

O it is God, that holds you out of Despair, and at the Expence of suffering and Death, spreads his Love around you, and courts you to himself! O can you forbear to love him? O, how can you any longer persue your sinfull Amusements, and risk your Souls on such a Pinacle of infinite Danger! O turn in at Wisdom's Call, and adhear to the endearing Voice of the heavenly Charmer.

But I must return in Persuit of my intended Subject to discover something more of the Nature and Effects of this Incarnation of the Deity, it hath been sufficiently proved, that nothing can help, or do good to the fallen Creature, but that which restore it back, and that nothing can effect that, but they regain the Choice, and thereby turning the Will, for which and the Creature must be held under a Suppression that is kept from acting itself and therefore when this innumerable Throng had broke off from the Triune Father, they thereby broke up and made a Division among themselves, and in their own Male and Femal Powers, not only at Enmity against God; and at War one with another, but each one having that Triune Life broke up at War with and a Torment to himself.

And therefore when God became incarnate and began the work for their Redemption, he first lays a suppression on their raging Powers, and then brings them who was already devided spiritually into a seperate State corporeally, that each one might have all the Advantage of his Incarnation, and that those, which would be brought back might not be obstructed by the sinking will and Choice of them that would not;

But as I imagine, my reader will start and say, that we have no Account of any Sin untill after the Woman was taken from the Man, I must endeavour to ease their Minds, and that I shall be enabled to do without much Trouble, for it is evident, that altho' the native of their eating the Fruit is not given untill after the Woman was taken out, yet it is evident, that there was a Disorder and they were falling and wanted immediate help for he had not only declared, that all was good but very good, and now he declares it is not good for him to remain as he was, *(k)* and thus it is evident, that they were falling and would have been soon sunk beyond all Possibility, if God had not steped in with the Seed of the Woman to bruise the Serpent's Head, and God now takes him in Hand, and works an important Work upon him before he took out the Woman, that is, lays them under such Suppression as to hold (as I before observed,) their raging, destructive within such a State of Inactivity as to stop the acting of their Choice and Will, for he declares, that he not only laid them in a Sleep, but a deep Sleep *(l)* and therefore when he was thus restrained, as to have his Choice and Will kept from any further Action; the Woman's Seed begins the work by bringing them (who were already divided) into a separate corporeal State, that each one might have all Means or Benefit of his Incarnation without any Obstruction from those who would still continue their fallen Course, and yet how many hold forth that unreasonable inconsistant and God dishonouring principle, that Christ did not die for some Thousands of the fallen Race, when each one is individually brought forth into this corporeal state, and thereby wraped up in God's Incarnation, and then Christ himself declaring, that he tasted Death for every Man.*(m)*

And thus God began his Work and has been carrying on the Redemption ever since the fall of the system, by holding the Family called in deep Sleep while he Brings them out individually into a corporeal State that each one might have their Trial and will continue the same until every one has come thus into Visibility, and had all that could be done upon them by this Incarnation, and those that reject and break thro' all this restraint and Work of God continuing their falling Course will soon get their Will increased in Strength and Rapidity beyond all restraint or help, and then naturally go their own way the irrecoverable Course of fallen nature: while those that are redeemed (more or less) are brought back to be one with God partaking again of that Triune Life, which they had lost, which restores the Union of the Male, and Female Powers of the inward Creature, and likewise reunites all that are redeemed, by which they stand again as one in the same Union Male and Female as before they fell, and thus the second Adam restores the Ruins of the First and declares that when thus restored, they shall be as much and undividedly one as he and his Father *(n)* and that they shall be reinstated in Paradise and eat of the Tree of Life *(o)* and yet how many are so chained down by Tradition, and so ignorant of a spiritual System, that they imagined that Paradise to be corporeal, and Adams food and Enjoyment corporeal, but I trust I have said enough to convince them, that are in any Degree open to Conviction, that he was altogether spiritual untill he was fallen and interposed: (and then indeed he might eat for he stood in need of corporeal Food) nor can they ever be completely happy untill wholly restored back to a spiritual paradise, and to spiritual enjoyments again and the outward creature is but as a prison (with the restraining incarnation) for to keep the inward creature from action untill their time of trial for the inward Creature being held by the Spirit of God in the outward Creature is so far held from acting like itself, that it is something amused in the outward Creature, and her it is held for to have so far a Discovery of itself as to cause it to flinch from itself, that the Will might thereby be regained; and therefore saith God, this spirit shall convince the Creature of his Sin *(p)* that is open his Eyes to look into himself and see his miserable State, for altho' the Creature when thus awaken is ready to think, that God is angry with them, and about to destroy them, yet all the Anger and Destruction is in themselves, which God is now discovering to the Creature, to cause the Creature to flinch from his own Gulf, that God might thereby regain the Will and Choice.

For the natural Course of his Will is to ruin himself and run from God still, for he's in himself a Choice to the Creature still, but nothing in him that can make Choice of God out of any desire to enjoy God or any Love for God. And if the Inquiry is made, why the Creature can not make Choice of God out of Love, and thereby return from his sinking State, I answer for the same Reason as I gave before, every Nature Acts like itself; and every thing appears in its own Likeness, and God himself desides this for *unto them, that are defiled and unbelieving it is nothing pure, but even their Mind and Con-*

science is defiled and therefore all Things, even God himself, appears to the Creature Darkness, Malice and Revenge by Reason of the Creatures Hellish Nature, for *with the forward* saith David, *thou wilt shew thyself forward* and therefore it is not possible for them to have any Love for God, or desire to enjoy him (altho' often they vainly Imagine they do) and therefore you may see something of the unspeakable Condescension of God to the Creature, who knowing the Nature of the Creature was such as could not see any thing lovely or desirable in God takes this Method to bring him home, viz. thus far shews the Creature himself, or (if I may say) opens his own Bottomless Gulf to his Sight, (a Truth known by Experience to every Christian) so that the Creature cannot see nor conceive of any Thing worse than to sink where he sees himself now going; and therefore tho' he sees no Beauty in God, nor has any Love for God, yet he is convinced, let God be what he will, or do with him whatever he will, he cannot be worse, nor in a more miserable Condition, than to go in and with himself the Course he is now sinking; and therefore like the four Lepers at the Gates of Samaria *(q)* they are brought to see and conclude if they remain, or return, there is nothing but Death, and Misery: But if they go to God, and cast themselves on his Mercy, they may possibly be made happy; or if not they can but die, and therefore will be no worse, nor loose any thing by the Trial. And now in this Capacity, when shoke over their own Hell, and see what they are, and must be, unless this last Resource should help them, they do with all the Soul choose God for their Helper. Ah let him do what he will with them, they are willing to enter! Yea eve'y other Help, Hope or Expectation fails them; and they abandoned all Thoughts of ever being bettered or helped any other way; and if this fails they know they are utterly and eternally gone; yea and altho' they see nothing in God, that is lovely, neither do they know whether he will help them or not, yet by such a dreadful Discovery of themselves, they are reduced to such Extremity they choose, (altho' they see their everlasting Concerns are at stake) to cast their Dye in this last Resource, sink or swim, live or die; but still with strong Hopes and longing Desires, yea impatient cries for Help, and thus speaks the Will and Choice. LORD HELP ME, AND DO WITH ME AS THOU PLEASE, FOR I CANNOT BE WORSE THAN TO REMAIN IN MY OWN GULF. And O when thus bought (tho' they could not see it before) the Remedy is infalible, and the Prize is sure! which soon they find to their Joyful surprise and unspeakable Satisfaction; not only because they find themselves happily escaped the Jaws of that Yawing Pit, where they so much feared to be: But for that Love they now enjoy, that beauty they behold, and that glory they admire in one glimering Ray of the Perfections of God; for that Moment the Will and choice was turned after God they acted with God, and therefore partake of God; and thus again brought to enjoy the Tree of Life, which they had lost; and are reinstated in that Paradise that they fell out of. And therefore TO HIM THAT THUS OVERCOMETH, saith God, I WILL GIVE TO EAT OF THE TREE OF LIFE, WHICH IS IN THE MIDST OF THE PARADISE OF GOD, *(r)* so that I may say agin, that unless my Reader chooses to be in Bondage and loves Darkness rather than Light they will understand what that Paradise was, which once they possessed, but by Sin lost, and by Christ are restored to. And O how can you but admire the stoop Wisdom and Love of God in this glorious Work of the second Adam? Yea can you forbear the following at his Feet with ravishing Delight and Songs of Gratitude? Methinks your Hearts must break for Sin, and melt with Joy, when this love but wispers to your Souls: or can you still bind your obdurate Souls with Chains of Adamant, and say *we will not have this Man to Reign over us and therefore away with this Man, and release unto us Barnabas?* can it be, can it be that you can so abuse such Love, and exercise such Cruelty to yourself? O that I could thus far prevail with my Reader, as to open the Doors of your Soul as to receive but one Word from that waiting Jesus, who with Bowels of Pity, and Heart of Love is knocking with his bleeding Hands for Admission of your Hearts, until his Head is filled with dew, and his Locks with the Drops of the Night.

And O let me tell you, you can never entertain a more Glorious visitant: for he is all and in all; he will be to thee a Servant to wash thy Feet, a Physician to heal thy Wounds, a King to conquer thy Foes, a Pillow to rest thy Head, a Friend to bear thy Burdens, a Comforter to cheer thy Heart, a leader to conduct thy steps, and an everlasting Reward to ravish thy Soul, when the Joy of Earth, Grandeur of Crowns Favour of Kings, and Friendship of Mortals, shall be sunk in everlasting Oblivion. And O let me tell you that you need not ascend up to Heaven to fetch him down, nor descend into the deep to bring him up from the Dead for he is nigh thee even in thy Heart *(s)* only believe and he will arise. Yea hear him speak while you dead, BEHOLD saith he, I STAND AT THE DOOR AND KNOCK IF YE WILL HEAR

MY VOICE, AND OPEN THE DOOR I WILL COME IN AND SUP WITH YOU, AND YOU WITH ME. *(t)* for the Kingdom of God cometh not with Observations; neither shall they say lo here, or lo there; for the Kingdom of God is within you. *(u)* But if ye turn a deaf Ear to his Calls, reject the Offers, and stifle the Spirit of God, that is labouring for your Redemption, you will soon sink yourself within yourself beyond all Possibility of Recovery: which I will endeavour for easing of your Mind from many Difficulties (concerning God's designing of leaving the World to be lost; or not preventing their ruin) now to discover, we have already proved, that the Action of the choice is the growth of the Will, and thereby strengthened for and in the same Action; and therefore of Consequences the Continuance of this Act and Choice from God is the Cause of final Appostacy, and if not stoped from acting in its infancy will soon get beyond all Recovery as hath been proved.

And now when God's Incarnation begins to do its Office, viz. shew the Creature thus far himself as to cause him to shrink back for help, at this Time the will is in some Degree at Liberty for Action (for it must be thus far, as in a Capacity of acting a Choice to return) and therefore when thus called upon by the Spirit if it Acts still against, and from God, must of course soon so increase in Strength as to be beyond all Possibility of Help; which Act of the Creature is the whole cause of their reprobation.

And as it was the falling in Love with the outward Creature was the ruining Choice, so it is still; for all Mankind is by nature still in Love with the Beauty, Pleasures, and Enjoyments of the outward Creature; Altho' it is now corporeal; and the whole Word of God declares, that until devose therefrom, or while in Love with any created Good, they are still sinking, and cannot be redeemed; yea this was the Doctrine continually preached and enforced in the strongest Terms by Christ during the whole of his Ministry while visible in the Flesh.

TURN FROM ALL: DENY ALL: LEAVE ALL; FORSAKE ALL; YEA HATE ALL; EVEN THE NEAREST AND DEAREST LOVERS IDOLS, AND ENJOYMENTS; NOT ONLY HIS HOUSES, LANDS AND HONORS; BUT PARENTS, WIVES AND CHILDREN; YEA AND HIS OWN LIFE ALSO. So that nothing can be more clear and evident that this, that there is nothing, but the being in Love with the outward Creature, and making choice of it from God, that will keep the fallen Creature from Redemption; fly therefore O my dear Reader! Fly from that Whore of the Nations, that destroyer of Kingdoms, that Crucifier of Christ, that Murderer of Souls and Sinker of Worlds: For she is a deep Ditch, and Millions have fallen therein; yea many mighty have been slain thereby and fallen a prey to her infernal Wiles.

I do not mean the outward and criminal Acts of Idolatry and Debauchery only: but any and every Thing in the Creature, that in the least Degree amuses the Mind or leads the Choice from God. For even the most simple Enjoyments and Pleasures of Life, will keep the Choice in Action, and therefore the Creatures amused from God, and consequently sinking deeper and deeper in its fallen and irrecoverable State. Nor will you ever return or be redeemed until every Idol, Joy, Hope, or Amusement, so fails that you are wholly starved out, and there is not only a Famine, but a mighty Famine in all created Good. *(w)* Ananias and Sapphira were both destroyed for the Love of a little Money; *(x)* Essau was lost to all Eternity for but a morsal of Pottage; *(y)* and the young Man turned away from Redemption because he loved his great Proffession. *(z)*

O therefore as you love your immortal Soul, and wish to escape the Despairing Regions of fallen Nature, and see the bright Abodes of everlasting Day let every Idol and Enjoyment go for the Sake of Christ, and turn a deaf Ear to every Temptation and earthly Charm, and Amusement, while the Spirit of God is striving with you, and adhear to the Dictates of that glorious Helper, that is labouring to reclaim thy Choice, and regain thy Will, and Redeem thy Soul.

For altho' you may have been taught, that God can force you to heaven by an arbitrary Power, when he please: yet you may take it for a Truth, that immediately concerns your everlasting State that there is no Possibility of your being redeemed without your Choice, yea it is all the Work of Redemption to regain the Choice and therefore it is as inconsistant to say that the Choice can be forced as to say, that the negative is the affemative, or that a Man can choose to do a thing, and at the same time choose not to do it.

And as long as you choose any Happiness, Joy or Amusement seperate from God, you are choosing to act in Contrariety to God; and therefore sinking further and further from Redemption into an irrecoverable State; and this is the reason why those who have been enlightened, or wrought upon by the Spirit of God, when willfully turned away, can never be redeemed; it is not because that God's

Mercy is lessened, contracted, or witheld more than before: but because they have acted their Choice in the Means of Appostacy until their Will is got strengthened in its destructive Cause beyond all Possibility of Help. And therefore the Creature hath done that for himself that never can be undone by God.

But now my Reader starts and says, that with God all Things are possible: not my dear Reader, it is not possible for God to lye, *(a)* and therefore altho' you may think it impeaching the Character of the Deity to say, that he cannot save Mankind against their Will, or force their Choice, yet you will find it not only impossible, but the greatest Reflection that you can cast upon him to say, that he can do any thing contrary to his own Nature, and altho' it has been so evidently proved, that it is Repugnant to the Nature of God to force the Will and Choice of a Creature, yet as it is a Matter of so vast Importance I shall further discover the Reason why he cannot.

First, the very Nature of God's Self-existence, and that excluded him from any Possibility of being injured, vexed, roil'd or insenced, is the Humility of all his divine Perfections; for there is nothing that is excluded from a roiled Resentment, or being vexed when insulted, but Humility; yea even the smallest Degree of real Humility when insulted is so far from being wounded, roil'd or awoke to resentment when insulted, that it awakes still a greater Pity for the Offender: Witness the praying Stephen, when under the Pains of his Murderers inflicted Rage. *(b)* And as the Divine Being is wholly possessed of this invincible Humility, it must therefore be utterly against his Nature, to act in Rigour, or with an arbitrary Hand; yea it is impossibte for him to do any Thing, but what can be done by the Spirit of Meekness and Humility; and therefore every vessel that cannot be brought in a Capacity of receiving the Displays of this Meekness and Humility, must lay eternally under the torments of their own Pride. Again you must remember, that we have already proved God to be an uncontroulable free Agent, that doth all Things in all his Opperations freely and of Choice, and all intelligent Beings, being his Offspring must likewise be thus like him all free Agents; and therefore as inconsistent, and as impossible, for them to be forced as to be annihilated; yea it would be Annihilation, and thus you may see the Impossibility of his forcing the Creature's Choice; and therefore it is no more limiting the Power of God to say that he canot force the will of his Creatures, than to say, he hath not Power to Sin; for they are both contrary to his Nature one as the other, and therefore both Impossible. And yet O how many Thousands risk the Salvation of their Souls upon a groundless Expectation, that some time or another, God will come and force them into the Kingdom of Grace, until their Day of Grace is over, and they sunk in irrecoverable Ruin, and Despair! they will often say *they are waiting God's Time:* When god who has been long waiting their Time, declares *now is the acceptable Time, and to Day is the Day of Salvation* without any Account of Promise of another Time or future Opportunity, yea, long, long has he waited, my dear Reader, (if I may say) with a bleeding Heart, and impartient Desires at thy Door for your consent, saying in these Intreaties, and Expostulations WILT THOU NOT BE MADE CLEAN? WHEN SHALL IT ONCE BE? *(c)* Surely if he could have forced Mankind to Redemption he would never have gone thro' such Heart-aking Agonies and insupportable Grief, on Account of their not embracing his Offer, for he would force them to accept. Did you ever hear him express the Grief of his Soul (my dear Readers) in these Words, O JERUSALEM, JERUSALEM THOU THAT KILLEST THE PROPHETS AND STONEST THEM THAT ARE SENT UNTO THEE, HOW OFTEN (not only once but often) WOULD I HAVE GATHERED THEE AS A HEN GATHERETH HER BROOD UNDER HER WINGS, AND YE WOULD NOT? *(d)* And again with Tears of Condolence falling from his lamenting Eyes, IF THOU HADST KNOWN, EVEN THOU AT LEAST IN THIS THY DAY, THE THINGS WHICH BELONGS TO THY PEACE? *(e)* or will you charge him with desembling, and when he says, that he could not do many mighty Works in Nazareth because of their unbelief, will you tell him that he could if he would, for he had power to force them to believe, and when he tells you, that he had done all that could be done, and even demands of you what he could do more, that he has not done *(f)* will you reply, that he could do much more, than all that he has done if he would: for he hath saved but for the smallest part of the world, when it was in his power to have forced them all to salvation? By making them believe. But O methinks I am censuring my reader, and charging him with invincible Ignorance and impenitrable Darkness, if I say any more to prove, that God is love, and has done all that could have been done to redeem the fallen Race, and make a Display of his (I was about to say) uncontainable Goodness! O therefore let me turn and join with my Reader, who I hope is not only convinced, but so ravished with the glorious Truth as to be breaking out in a Surprise of Joy with Shouts of Wonder and Praise, *'O thou great, thou good, 'thou overflowing Fountain of all goodness! Ah thou art good! thou 'delightest in Goodness! and thy tender Mercies are over all thy Works! 'And thou openeth thy bountiful Hand, and satisfieth the Desire of every 'living Thing.*

But observe my dear Reader, (for I am delighted with thy Expressions) the extent of thine Acknowledgments, and the import of thy Notes of Praise. Ye not only say HE SATISFIETH THE DESIRE OF EVERY LIVING THING but HIS MERCIES ARE OVER ALL HIS WORKS. Ah! over all his Works indeed; then let me believe that his Mercy has not only reached you and me (as many who pay Homage to themselves imagine) but likewise to all the Race of Adam. Adam did I say? Ah! and all the innumerable systems that were brought forth, and fell with Adam or with this small Part of Creation; and therefore of Consequence the whole fallen System will share in redeeming Love. Yea and God forbid, that I cast such Reflections on him or so contract his unbounded Goodness and Dishonour his Name as to imagine, that any Part of needy Systems should be excluded from his Thoughts of Mercy, and divine Benedictions! but saith one, this appear's more strange and groundless still, to Imagine, that the innumerable Worlds around us, are in a state of Probation by the Lord Jesus Christ; I answer that by reason of your light Attention to the Word of God it may be strange: but I shall by no means allow any Thing to be Groundless, that I see with my own Eyes and God himself has declared. For first, we have already proved, that as God was a Spirit, his Works must be Spiritual, and that nothing could produce any Part of them corporeal, but the interposing of that which was falling, and therefore when you see these corporeal Worlds around you (which could not be discovered to corporeal Eyes, if spiritual) and likewise find them standing in such corporeal Relation with your world, that you can no more do without them, than you could do with a body without head, you have not cause to be at any Loss concerning the Nature and Cause of their present Standing: for they could not more stand corporeal than this without the same Interposition. Or if this be not a sufficient Demonstration for you, surely a Declaration from him, that cannot lye, will decide the Matter: for saith he, *'That in the 'Dispensation of the fullness of Times he might gather together in one 'all Things in Christ, both which are in Heaven and which are on the 'Earth, even* (saith he again) *in him. (h)*

Well saith my Reader, I believe that all Things are gathered together in him in Heaven; that is bow to him and own him as Lord of all; but that is no Proof of their being fallen and redeemed. Well my dear Reader, if this be the point you are in the dark about, viz. Whether, that gathering signifies redeeming or not, the Matter will soon be decided by God himself, in plain Words. First, observe, that when God is speaking of redeeming this Fallen World, he uses this Expression, GOD WAS IN CHRIST RECONCILING THE WORLD TO HIMSELF *(g)* surely you will allow this reconciling to signify redeeming, and bringing back a fallen Creature from a state of Contrariety, and does not God when speaking of his gathering the before mentioned Heavens not only say, MAKING OF PEACE (which could not be if there was not first an Enmity) but likewise RECONCILE ALL THINGS UNTO HIMSELF; BY HIM I SAY (saith he, repeating the Declaration) WHETHER THEY BE THINGS IN EARTH OR THINGS IN HEAVEN? *(i)*

And now therefore unless you labour hard to wrest the plain Word, you must not only be convinced without a remaining Doubt, but break forth with a joyful Thankfulness and Shouts of Praise to the adorable and good God, and be ravished with the meek and lovely Jesus, O! to think of that love that infinite, overflowing, and uncontainable Goodness; that has (at the Expence of blood divine) made such a Display of Love and unbounded Grace, not only unto us, but unto all the innumerable Crowd of our miserable, Rebellious and sinking Brethren.

For altho' many of our arbitrary Predestinarians have such a high Esteem of themselves, that they think, they have a greater cause to love God for picking them out only, than if he had extended his Goodness and Mercy to more of their Poor Fellow men, yet Blessed be God, I am as far from their Conceptions as the East from the West, that is to Praise him for Partiality, or love him more for his leaving the greatest Part of my poor Fellow Men to perish, than if he had saved them, when he had it in his Power. For Methinks (if I am so happy as to awake in his Likness) my highest Notes of Thankfulness and Praise will arise from this, that God's Nature was such, as must make a display of his grace to all that can possibly receive it, and that his Perfections were such, as would not admit of neglecting to do good, wherever it was possible to be done; and instead of having my Eye evil, because his is good, or think him an austere Man, reaping where he has not sowed and gathering where he has not strowed;

I would believe in the Song my Reader was lately singing HIS MER-
CIES ARE OVER ALL (even all) HIS WORKS. Yea and both myself and
Reader are commanded in the strongest terms to understand and believe and embrace that glorious Truth I have so long been labouring
to introduce as one of the essencial Articles of your Faith; GO YE,
saith God, AND LEARN WHAT THAT MEANETH I WILL HAVE MERCY AND
NOT SACRIFICE. *(k)*

O therefore receive his Mercy, enjoy O his Love, extol his
Grace, adore his Name, and be for ever ravished with the Perfections
of such a God, and now having discovered so far the Nature and Office of God's Incarnation while invisible, I shall pass on to shew the
cause and nature of his Sufferings, and the Design and Effects of his
assuming a body of Flesh and Blood, and the Manner of his Death.
First, with regard to his suffering it was not to satisfy or appease any
Thing inscenced or stired up in God, for he was God himself; and
therefore if we admit it possible (as is imagined by many) we shall
meet with those two Inconsistencies in our way, which proves it impossible. First, that he was wounded and injured by Sin even to the
insencing of himself, and awaking up a Wrath which must cause him
to be in Torment, for where there is Wrath stired up or any Thing
insence, there is a thirst for Revenge, and likewise a Spirit of Resentment; and therefore if God was insenced, or had any Wrath stired
up in him he would be in Misery, and the next Inconsistency will be,
that God punished himself to satisfy, for Christ was really the very
God: But if you would now know and understand the Cause, and the
whole cause, of his sufferings, you must again view him really in,
and under the Weight and Torment of all that Contrariety of the fallen
Race; and consequently thereby under all the Racks of Misery, that
hellish Contrariety, could inflict. Yea God himself declares, that for
Sin he condemned Sin in the Flesh *(l)* and likewise that he so suffered
this Contrariety of the Sinner's Nature even to the sheding of Blood.
(m) Yea and this his Agony of Soul was thereby so great even when
under no Corporeal Punishment, that it crushed his Frame even to
the sheding of Blood, that is the Weight of his Sin and Contrariety
was so insupportable that his Body could not endure the Weight but
shrunk beneath it. And thus after he assumed a body of Flesh and
Blood, the Sufferings and Labour of his Spirit began to appear; for
the Spirit that was before in the World under all the Contrariety of
the fallen System had now assumed this Body, so that all the Suf-

ferings of his Soul were centering to that Body, and thereby began to break forth in visible Marks of exquisit Pain and agony; and therefore this Body was all his days sinking and expiring under the Weight of that Hellish Contrariety, which his Spirit laboured in; yea to that degree, that if the Jews had never laid Hands on him, nor inflicted any corporeal Punishment on him, his Body would have expired under the insupportable Agonies of his spiritual Conflict; for altho' the Jews were really guilty of Murder, yet far be it from me to believe, that the great Work of my Salvation was any way depending on their murdering of him; or that the Work would not have been as soon, and as effectually completed, if they had let him entirely alone, and never inflicted no corporeal Punishment on him; nor yet was his Death caused by the Punishment inflicted on him, but wholly by the distress and anguish of his Spirit under this hellish Contrariety: for he declares that they did not take his Life away, but be laid it down himself. *(n)* And as he was thus labouring with his incarnate Spirit all the same time, thro' all the fallen Race and Agonies of that Spirit or Soul, which was made an offering, for Sin was so racking and insupportable, that at that instant he was extended on the Cross nor could they get him there before the time come that he was to expire in the conflict, *(o)* he would have expired and completed the grand Work, if no Hands had been laid on him, nor any corporeal Punishment inflicted; and therefore my dear Reader, you will have no cause to imagine, that Christ died to appease or satisfy any thing, that was insenced or stired up in himself; nor yet to attribute any Part of your Redemption to that Murder committed by those blood thirsty Jews; for it was the Creature that was wounded by Sin and not God, and therefore the Creature wants healing and not God: and as for suffering and misery, surely, it was enough to crush and destroy his Body, for his Soul, to bear all the Weight of that Contrariety of the whole fallen System; yea if the sins of one Soul, when felt in but part will cause a Christian to groan under the Burden, how insupportable must be the Weight of all the contrariety of innumerable Worlds upon his Soul, which was intirely spotless. For altho' he was without sin, yet he had taken the Sins of all the fallen System unto such near Relation with himself, as for to be as near his Soul as the Christian's own Sin, is to him; and therefore since you have thus seen his spotless incarnate Spirit, agonizing under all this Contrariety, as near to him, as if it was his own Sin to regain the course of fallen, and reclaim those raging tormenting Spirits, you will not be at a loss about the cause of his Sufferings and death; nor wonder to hear him crying out, while pressed in the agonizing conflict as a cart is pressed with sheaves, O MY FATHER IF IT IS possible that THIS CUP MAY PASS AWAY FROM ME, BUT NEVERTHELESS not my Will but thy Will be done.

So bitter was the Cup, that if there had been any possibility for Man's Redemption without it, he would have had it passed by: But since there was no, and Man must forever perish or he endure the Agonies, he would drink it as bitter as it was.

O my Soul, and was it possible! was there Love in God so great? Ah there was; O wonder, of Wonders! nor was it a strained Expression of his Love, or a scanty Act of Kindness: But a cheerfull Step, and an Act that was the natural Product of his divine Perfections.

O Lord my God, and yet the World asleep!
Will nothing pass the impenitrable Shrow'd
Or call them to the Scene unparellel?
O send an Arrow by my willing Pen,
A Message to my fellow Men in Chains,
To Loose with Joy their twice Ten Thousand Bands;
Lead them to see, what made Arch-Angels gaze,
And woke surprise in all the Realms of Bliss,
When from eternal Grandeur stoop'd a God.
Ah stoop'd the Great, I am to fallen Earth,
Enters the Manger cloth'd in mortal Flesh!
O thought! with Beasts the Visitant first seen!
Ah worse than Beasts, our vilest selves we see,
Before our Hearts will find this Infant room!
But O is God, a Bethlehem's Babe in Clay!
Witness ye Brutes that gave your Manger up,
And ancient Sages, that beheld the Star,
Say was Jehovah there? But small your Gifts:
Yet O enough since ye pour'd out your all.
Say O ye countless Millions that unseen
To mortal Eyes thick round the Manger flew,
How burn'd your Breasts and strain'd your Eyes
    when on

The scene ye gaz'd? Strange Scene to all your
  Hosts!
But O and say, is this your God! Ah this
O Adamant, my Heart! not melted still.
Here lies thy Friend; nor passive long remains:
How soon he's called to walk the Fields of Blood,
And wast his Life to gain the Prize for me,
Witness ye Stars, that Fourty Nights beheld
This Jesus wandering thro' the desert Wiles
With but thy sable Canopy, or the
Cold Mists to screene the innocent Divine;
Or while beneath the bending shrubs he lay;
Witness ye howling Monsters of the Wood
Have you not roaming cross'd his lav'ring Paths,
Or seen your exile Maker pass your Ken
Without the common Good, his Hand so oft,
When you were howling throw'd around your Den?
While hell loose augmenting still his Grief,
With Rage and Lyes deride him with a Stone,
And court him with the Shadows of the World
To prostrate Heaven in Homage to their Gulf,
O Heaven stand amaz'd! Rouse Earth, and self
Such Love! what Pains, sustain, O wretched Men
What Pangs of Woe, and all for you and me!
And now emerging in the raging World
A Mark for all the Arrows of the vile;
Yet all his Life one constant lib'ral Act
A heart exhausted; inexhausted Fund.
But O how fast the Floods of sorrow Pour
Like rapid Torrents on his spotless Soul!
Witness that night (Angels can ne'er forget)
When Peter and his Mate so dead with Sleep
Left him to sink in Agonies and Death!
O Gethsemane how couldst thou bear the Shock!
And witness ev'ry Garland to Perfumes
More rich (tho' all in Blood) than all your Banks?
Nor was you wet with dews Divine till now.
Oh, had those Tears (too rich for you) but reach'd
(One dropt) the Barren garden of my heart,

Nor Tears alone your Greens are ting'd with Blood,
(Keep near my Reader) see his Vester stain'd
From ev'ry Pore of his dissolving Heart.
(Mingled with Tears) my Soul! O what a Garb!
With Bended Knees and lifted Eyes behold
His Gesture all an interceeding Look!
Hark my Soul! THE BITTER CUP he says,
For who? For me! Ah me, O break my Heart!
But who are those? Methinks I hear a Mob,
Yes, see the wretched Band as black as Hell!
Ah! Lanterns! Torches! but you'll need e'er long,
A light Divine unlike your hellish Lamp:
Or midnight Roam and never find the Man.
Is Judas there? O my Soul deceit!
Drag'd without Pity to the Bar unjust,
With Verdicts brought from all the Courts of Hell,
And he consign'd to all they can inflict;
Mangled with Thorns; O the reproachfull Crown
And yet he Crowns poor Sinners with his Love
At the Expence of his Own vital Flood.
But see their Rage! O how the scourging Thongs
Plow deep their Furrows thro' his mangled Back!
O agonizing Scenes, and Pains accute!
My Bones, saith he ALL THRO' MY SKIN I TELL
Now on he goes crush'd with the massy Wood,
(Gauling it Grates) and all his bleeding Soul
(Press'd like a Cart) with more enormous Weight;
Thus up to Calvary (Place of a Scull) he wades
Without the Camp indeed; Reproach and Pain.
O Peter! Why desert? Fear not; step up:
Thy Saviour's weary steps are mark'd with Blood.
Think on that Hour "I sink"! well the same hand
Is night (tho' Bleeds) can save from sinking still!
But O I'm lost! Is this the Lord of all?
Gaze O my Reader, stand amaz'd and say
Why this? For what? O how! for me! Ah my
Desertion, Guilt and Woe hath crush'd him thus.
Now on the Cross the helpless Victim stretch'd
(Tho' Power to call Twelve Legions to assist)

His Limbs, extended to the last Extent,
Then thro' his Nerves, O how the Irons grate!
Till Pains accute rack all his torter'd Frame.
What! Where! O! yes! good Lord how can I write!
Feel, Feel my Soul! O break my Heart with Love
While Floods I weep with Sorrow and with Joy.
Nor Wonder that I weep: greater Wonder
My writing not immense in Tears of Blood,
While I record the Scene unparallal.
But O! Impress ah! Thou whose Name I speak
The Record on my Heart with Marks Divine,
To stand and shine when other Suns shall cease,
And Tower and Monuments of Praise to thee.
Once more with Wonder on the bloody Scene;
Raised with the Cross they give the sudden Plung.
To rack his Frame sag on the ragged Nails,
O how! Good God, how canst thou yet survive!
And why my Soul, why all this Rack of Woe?
Is it for me the God of nature Growns?
How can I write? or dare forbear? I gaze!
I'm lost! believe, then doubt; the Scene so strange
My faith is staggerd by the stoop so great;
And yet again I feel, and must believe;
It must be true; its like the God I own.
And near your Hearts, O reader waits the same,
Knocking with his endearing Charms of Love.
O hear, receive, and feel the sacred Truths!
Give him thy Sins, receive his Grace then shall
This Christ, the Conquest, and the Crown, be thine
And then eternal Ages speak his Worth.
But Hark! Methinks I hear him cry what's that,
"ELI ELI LAMA SABACTHANI?"
Has he a God? why then without a Friend?
Ah that he might befriend th' abandon'd World.
But O what poor Relief! Ah oft I heard
"THE TENDER MERCIES OF THE WICKED'S CRUEL."
See the vile Wretch with Vinegar and Spunge
Reproach and gaul for an expiring Prince!
Ah deep he Drinks in more malignant Gaul

While Pains accute, like Daggers thro' his Heart,
His tortured Soul is sorrowfull to Death.
Ah see the Sun! well may he vail his Face
While the great Sun in Midnight Darkness clad.
And Rocks of flint can feel his dying Groans
While O this heart an Adament remains!
O when dear Lord shall it dissolve with love,
And all my soul feel him that bleed for me?
But O he hangs yet on the bloody Cross
And Groans methinks, I hear but Groans for who?
For you and me, O reader, see him Dye,
And in his Death make sure eternal Life;
And from his Groans immortal Songs of Joy.
And O my Jesus thou inspire my soul,
And point my pen to reach the readers heart,
To teach them more than Angels can express.
But hark "I YEILD" methinks I hear him say
"INTO THY HAND O GOD MY BLEEDING SOUL"
"AND DYING PRAY MY GOD THEIR SINS FORGIVE;"
"O PITY THEM THAT PITY NOT THEMSELVES,"
"AND SHEW THEM MERCY THO' FOR ME THEY'VE
     NONE."
But am I not deceiv'd? and does he pray?
What pray for those who brue their hands in Blood?
Yes 'tis the Truth; it is I hear him pray;
Listen O heavens! and hear ye Sons of Men.
"FATHER FORGIVE THEM" Cries the dying Lamb;
The Bleeding Victim in the pangs of Death.
Say O my reader dost thou hear the Cry?
Or canst thou stand against such melting Love?
And O he dies! but no my Saviour lives.
Ah lives for me, and lives to die no more.
Rejoice ye dying Sons of men, he lives,
And Crowed with all your sins, ye Mourners
     Crowd,
Ye sinking Millions to his Courts of grace;
His grace is free, and all is done for you;
Ye've seen him wade thro' all your guilt and woe
In seas of Blood thro' all his Life, or Death,

A ling'ring Death thro' all his servile walk
From the course Manger to the Bloody Cross:
There won the Field in Death, then tower'd aloft
With Scars of honour to the realms of Light,
To spread for you the Gates of endless Day,
And court you to the Mansions of Delight.
O what displays of everlasting love!
Free grace the News; free grace the lasting Song,
Free grace to Jews and to the Gentile throng;
Free grace shall be the everlasting theme;
Jehovahs product, and Jehovahs fame;
Goodness his nature, boundless love his Name.

* * *

THOUGHT THE SIXTH

Christ's Intercession. The certainty and nature of the Resurrection

RESURRECTION a doctrine of Truth, and much contended for, yet I shall be as far from the common opinion of the World as the Northern from the Southern Pole.

We have viewed the incarnation of God and found it to be wholly for the good of the fallen System; and therefore how inconsistant to imagine that God doth now and will forever wear a Body of corporeal Flesh and Blood! can any rational Christian admit of a belief that the infinite Jehovah would come down to this fallen Earth to get an Elemental Body for his own benefit, or to carry to Heaven?

But you will say he did come and take an Elemental Body. True my dear Reader but for what? was it for any thing else but to carry on man's Redemption? you would not imagine that God would ever have taken that Body if Man had not fallen; but when Man was fallen if he undertook for their Redemption he must certainly step into that Capacity and assume such means as would qualify him for that office; and therefore it was that he assumed such a Character, and took on him such a Body.

But it is as inconsistant to imagine that he will keep that corporeal Body when the work is done, as that he should continue for ever in the Agonies of a soul Sorrowful even unto Death: for that was more essential for Mans Redemption than the other. And now after you have paused a while I may venture to tell you that if man had not fallen God would not have become incarnate: but when Man fell he in infinite mercy undertake to bring Man back again; for which he steped into the fallen Creature the moment of his revolt, and was in Flesh from that time carrying on the grand Work; (tho' not visible in a particular Body.) Yea and had carried some Thousands of the fallen Race to glory who were now safe in the confirmation of Eternal Life; and undoubtedly would never have returned even if Christ had stoped his work, and never assumed the particular Body of Flesh and Blood: but as it was his good will and design to do all the good to the fallen Race that could be done he not only Labours GOD-MAN internally, but in a time that the World was in a Capacity to hear it, assumes an Elemental Body; appears Visible among Mortals, and for their Conviction and a Demonstration of his invisible Spiritual kingdom does every thing, suffers every Trial, and works every mirracle, externally, that must be wrought, and was essentially necessary to be wrought, internally, in every creature that is redeemed.

And now in this Body he labours and Wades visibly to mortal Eye in the work and Sufferings of Redemption which work and Sufferings he had been wading thro' Spiritually even since the Fall, *(a)* tho' invisible to Mortals. Yea and so great were the Sufferings of his Spirit that his Body when he had assumed it could not long endure a relation thereto: But was soon crushed, as has been proved, & expired under the infinite weight, but when thus expired you must not imagine that he has done his Work, or left the fallen System from his say *'It is Finished'*, (which was his getting greater possession of his Kingdom among Men, and the end of all his Corporeal Sufferings) for God has declared that altho' all things are put under his Subjection, yet as yet all Things are not put under him. *(b)* And again he repeats the same seeming Contradiction, first saying that all Things are put under his Feet, and then says when all Things shall be put under him, *(c)* so that there is nothing more evident than this that his Mediatorial Office, or Saviours work is not yet concluded, or Finished; for he goes on to say again, then cometh the End, when he shall have delivered up the Kingdom to God even the Father; when he shall have put down all Rule, and all Authority, and Power: which if his Work was done he would have put Down all Rule, Power and Authority, already or if I admit that the remaining part of his Work consists in his intercession: For it is generally held that Christ after he Rose from the Dead he went to some distant World or Place which they call Heaven, and there interceeds with the Father to prevail with him to have Mercy on Sinners.

But saith one do you deny Christ's intercession: no my Dear Reader by no means, yet such intercession as that I must deny in the strongest Terms or else I must deny his Being God, and likewise hold him and the Father to be two, and that he is more Mercifull than his Father: for if he was the very God and thus pleading with God to be merciful to Sinners, he is talking like a Child to himself; or if he is not pleading with himself but with God as another person, then he and his Father is two: tho' he said they were but one; *(d)* and not only so but if he is thus pleading with his Father we shall meet more difficulties in our way still.

First according to that Hypothesis his Father is not so merciful as he is: for he is willing to save the Sinners without his Father's making a continual intercession with him: but he is obliged as long as the world stands to be continually praying, or interceeding with the Father to spare the Sinners; or to give consent that they should be saved. And the next difficulty that will arise from this confused notion of Christ, is that the Father is changeable: For by the intercession of the Son he is pacified and prevailed with to save the Sinner, or permit him to Heaven.

Now think my Dear Reader what an inconsistant, confused, unreasonable, unscriptural, and God-dishonouring Principles is collected by the Dark minds of Men, and then held out to the poor blind world as the truths of God.

Yea and I expect to be set up as a mark for the powers of darkness and shot at from the pulpit and press for uncovering their Nakedness, but trusting it is love for God and my fellow Men, that I thus venter out against their darkness, I doubt not but their Javelins will pass by me, and as for contending with them, by the grace of God I will not attempt, but only hold up the light & abide the consequences, yea and count it an honour to be reproached for the gospel.

And now as for Christ's intercession it is a truth I must both acknowledge and experience, or forever fall short of the benefits of his death. And first this intercession must be here, for I am the creature that is wounded and Christ who is God himself is here, and his kingdom of grace is here.

Secondly he had told me that the kingdom of God comes not by observations, neither shall they say lo here or lo there, for saith he the kingdom of God is within you. *(e)*

And when I make any enquiry after him, the eternal work of life, he says, I need not ascend up to Heaven to bring him down, or descend into the deep to fetch him up: for the word is nigh me, even in the Heart. *(f)*

And then tells me, that he makes intercession in the Heart of the fallen creature with Groans, that cannot be uttered, nor can we pray, says he, without it. *(g)*

And therefore I am obliged to believe that Christ is exalted at the Right hand of Power, interceeding for the lost World, and that intercession by the Spirit of his incarnation among the Fallen Race.

Nor can any thing redeem us out of our laborinth of woe and Misery, but this interceeding Spirit. For there is none that can ascend into Heaven but the Spirit of Christ which is in Heaven; even while on the Earth *(h)* and thus he interceeds for the poor Fallen Creature by no means to pacify, Turn, Prevail with, or alter God: but to Awaken, turn; draw and redeem, the Creature, and bring the Creature in a Capacity of receiving what God, FATHER-SON-SPIRIT waits to give.

But saith some dark mind who lives far from the warm beams of the Sun, *if God so freely Displays his Divine Rays that there needs no intercessions to get him willing to have mercy, then what need have we of Prayer?*

I answer my Dear Reader, I should be sorry that any one in a land where ever those words had been sounded. *Bring ye all the tithes 'into the Store-House and prove me now therewith saith the Lord of Hosts, 'if I will not open you the Windows of Heaven and pass you out a 'Blessing that there shall not be room enough to receive it. (i)* Should ever imagine that poor Sinners had any cause to Pray for to turn, or to pacify God, or prevail with him to give Mercy: but I would to God that you would believe that you could not be redeemed until you choose it, and was so convinced of your Miserable sinking Condition, as to begin to Groan for help and thirst for Re-

demption, for so great is your need of Prayer and a Spirit of intercession, that you can never be Redeemed without it: But when I speak
of Prayer, I do not mean such poor dry insignificant wind as your
Lip service and spiritless forms: but the hungrings, thirstings, groan-
ings, and insatiate longings of the inmost Soul; for which end God
has given every poor Sinner this Spirit; *(j)* and that for to awake the
mind, unlock the Heart, and bring the perishing Soul in a Capacity
of receiving the displays of divine Goodness that is continually Shin-
ning around and upon him, as the Meridian Sun upon a Blind Man;
and therefore you have no more cause to wish or pray that God would
bring down his Grace, or look upon you with Pity than that a blind
Man has to wish or pray that the Sun would shine: but O I must tell
you, you are in perishing need of crying with all your Soul like your
Neighbour Bartimous, LORD THAT I MIGHT RECEIVE MY SIGHT *(k)* neither must expect your Prayers ever to be of any more benefit to you
than they do by that Spirit of God prove the means of stirring up,
engaging, and Redeeming your Soul; nor yet the prayers of the Saints
help you any other way, or any more, than as by the Spirit of Christ
(which is but one Spirit and spread over the whole World) reaching,
alarming, lifting, engaging, Redeeming, or drawing your poor Soul
to God, and therefore it is that they are a Kingdom of Priests, *(l)* for
they (tho' dispised by the ungodly as the offscouring of all things)
are God's Royal Priesthood. *(m)* And are in God's hand by his Spirit
pleading for, labouring with, and Redeeming of the miserable unconverted part of the World, and therefore they are workers together
in Redemption with God; *(n)* and many are Redeemed thro' their
word. *(o)* And having thus discovered to you how and wherein consists the intercession of Christ, I have now two important requests to
make. First, as you love your own Soul and ever expect your portion
among the Saints in the Realms of Glory, be tender of them here; and
take heed you do not Drink in prejudice, and enmity against them:
for if you reject the Spirit they are of you reject the only spirit of that
can ever do your souls good; for it is the spirit of that Christ that Died
for you and knocks at your Door, and if you dispise them you are
thereby at the same time dispising of Christ. *(p)* And therefore he
tells you it were better for you that a milstone were hanged about
your Neck and you cast into the Sea, than to be guilty of offending
one of them. *(q)* And Ah, if you knew the wrestling Groans, cutting
Pangs, longing desires, and Heart-aking Hours they have for you,

Methinks you would esteem them as the Apple of your Eye, and bless God that there was such a People among you. (I mean when I speak of Christians those only who have the spirit of Christ.) And O let me inform you that like Lot they will soon be hurried out of Soddom, will bid you an everlasting Adieu, and there will be (by the contrariety of the two Natures) and unpassable Gulf between them and you, when they shall reign where the wicked cease from Troubling, and where the weary are forever at rest.

Secondly, let me intreat you (Ah on the knees of my Soul) that whenever you feel the least moving of that intercession of Christ in your heart, the least conviction of Sin, sense of your miserable condition, or desire for Redemption, O adhear to it, Nourish and Cherish it as the very Essence of your everlasting Welfare or the leading Hand to the realms of eternal felicity. And O remember, that whenever you have the least moving of this Spirit on your Soul, that the waiting, the wooing, and bleeding Saviour is at your Door, crying, BEHOLD I STAND AT YOUR DOOR AND KNOCK IF YE WILL HEAR MY VOICE, AND OPEN THE DOOR I WILL COME IN AND SUP WITH YOU, AND YOU WITH ME. *(r)* And you may take if for a Truth of the greatest Concern, that your everlasting happiness or misery turns on your adhearing to, or rejecting of that Spirit; therefore saith God. *'if ye will be willing and obedient ye shall eat the 'good of the Land: But if ye rebel and refuse, ye shall be devoured 'with the Sword for the Mouth of the Lord hath spoken it. (s)* O think, that an Eternity is at Stake, Life and Death is before you, and while the Spirit of God is striving with you, is your choosing time; O let Jesus in, and he will be your Bosom Friend to all Eternity. Having thus discovered where Christ is, how he interceeds, and carries on his Work, and what he works for, I shall now discover with far less Trouble his Resurrection, and the Resurrection of his People

First, as he was in Heaven when he was here on the Earth clothed in Clay, *(t)* surely he had no cause to go any distance to get to Heaven, when he arose from the Dead, or ceased to be visible among Mortals: for he was still in Heaven; for altho' many put such a Construction on his Saying, that he was not ascended, as to imagine that he was not in Heaven, yet, it is very evident, that he was, for declared to the Thief that he should be with him in Heaven the same Day, that he was Crucified. *(u)* So that it is evident, that his Resurrection did not consist in his going up above the Stars some where to find Heaven: but was his Triumphing over Sin, and Death, and his completing his Work and getting the Victory thus far, and as for that Body of Clay I need not say much to convince a rational Christian, that it must of consequence naturally cease to be corporeal: For if it had remained corporeal it must have remained as, and where it was; for its going to Heaven or a spiritual World did not consist in Change of Place, but nature; and therefore whatever Christ carried with him must be spiritual.

And as for the Plea's that are made by some for their maintaining, that it was corporeal after his Resurrection from his telling THOMAS to handle and feel him, *For a Spirit hath not Flesh and Bones as ye see me have* is entirely groundless: for if it was thus corporeal, that he was to feel it would have been wholly in vain: for faith does not come by feeling with Corporeal Hands: but by hearing *(w)* besides the same THOMAS had heard him declare, that he must likewise eat his Flesh *(x)* and had as much Reason to believe that the one was meant corporeal as the other; God declares we are Members of not only his flesh, but likewise of his Bones *(y)* and now if my Reader would understand the Truth, you must know, that THOMAS, & you too, must feel him, or never enjoy him; and when Christ gave him the command (not to feel with his corporeal Hands) he immediately obeyed, and so felt him, that he was constrained to break out in a divine Rapture MY LORD AND MY GOD! which many thousands have heard obeyed and felt in these Days.

Besides it is evident that Christ appeared wholly spiritual, for he not only came in while the Door was shut: but appeared in the same Manner, Shape and Dress as when he was with them, (for you would not imagine he appeared as a Man naked) and his Dress, which he appeared to have could not to be corporeal; for the Soldiers had got his Cloathing, *(y)* and therefore it is evident that he appeared in a Spiritual Representation, & might have appeared the same in Ten Thousands rooms at the same Time. And the infalible Word declares, that he will never be seen or known in corporeal Flesh any more. *(z)* but was raised altogether spiritual and will so remain forever; and so likewise the Saints who will really rise, will rise altogether spiritual, *(a)* and all these Bodies which are of the Eliments be dissolved: *(b)* and God declares. (After giving a large Account of the Resurrection) that Flesh and Blood cannot inherit the Kingdom of God. *(c)* besides it has already been proved, that all the Corporeals commenced at the Interposition of fallen Nature; and therefore when this interposition ceases, and ever thing acts like itself, and goes to its own Place, it is self evident, there can be nothing corporeal. And thus my dear Reader, I have proved (and still attest to) the Resurrection in the strongest terms, but by no means a corporeal Resurrection.

And as for time of this Resurrection if you are determined to believe, that there is any Succession of Age, or passing away of time, or any such Thing as future and past Periods in Eternity, I cannot force you to the contrary; neither do I believe that conception only (altho' so inconsistant) will bar you from Salvation: But if ever you are so happy as to awake in that boundless Ocean of delight, or even if you are lost and awake in eternal despair, you will be convinced, that any Successions, future or past Periods are known no more there, than a Change in the Deity: for the Truth is this.

The unbeginning, never-ending Existence of Jehovah is one ETERNAL NOW; and altho' I have been condemned by some for so saying, I still repeat it that God knows no beginning to himself, nor to his Decrees: for there was no Beginning: yea I should it no less than blasphemous denying of his Self Existence, unchangableness and Immutability to presume a thought to the contrary; and expecially since he declares in possitive Terms, that his GOINGS FORTH HAVE BEEN FROM OF OLD, (even) FROM EVERLASTING. *(d)*

And if God inhabits ONE ETERNAL NOW, surely his Offspring must inhabit the same: but do not understand, that they comprehend this ETERNAL NOW as he doth: no by no Means: but they must inhabit the same and be strangers to time, for their Father hath no Time to put them in, while they retain their primitive State, or exist in the Perfection he designed them for; and therefore it is evident that Time, and Space, and successive Periods, was never known untill corporeals commenced; viz. by the interposing of fallen nature thro' God's Incarnation. And therefore had Adam remained as he was brought forth all one, and one with his Father, he would have remained in that ETERNAL NOW, and indeed when he fell he would never have known or inhabited Time, if he had not been stopped, but as God in infinite Mercy interposed, (as before observed,) and stopped him, he thereby became thus corporeal, and an Inhabitant of Time; & therefore when the Creature awakes in Eternity they have broke all Relation corporeal, and with Time, and act like themselves Inhabitants of this ETERNAL NOW, and can have no more Conception of Weight, Space or Succession than you, while corporeal have of an Eternity and Spirit.

And therefore it is as inconsistent to imagine that those who have awoke in Eternity are waiting for, or expecting any future Periods as to imagine, that they are waiting for or expecting an End.

So, that you may see how inconsistent it is to suppose the Saints now in immortal Glory are waiting for some future Period, when they shall return to this Globe of Earth to receive a corporeal Body! when in the first Place if a spirit was to go in search for an Thing corporeal, they could not find it, for corporeal to them is no more hard or matterial than a void; or more properly speaking corporeal to them is no other than incorporeal.

For (speaking in our gross Language and Comparison) if a Spirit was in the Heart of a Flint, or mass of Iron they would not Know the flint or Iron was there, any more than you know, see or feel the Spirits that are now about you while you read; the Truth of which you may knew by this Moments Experiment: for this you must allow, that as much as Spirit can relate with Matter, matter can with Spirit, and therefore just as much as you now find any Knowledge of, or Relation with the departed Spirits, the Spirits may with you, so that I need say no more to prove this Point.

And therefore it is evident, that to those who have thrown off the Canopy of Matter and Time, all Things must be both spiritual and NOW, but saith one, I thought, that the Resurrection of Abraham, Isaac and Jacob, and others, that are gone were yet to come.

Well my Dear Reader, if you are not yet convinced, that with those in Eternity there is no such Things, as Times and Periods to come, we will adhear to what God himself declares about this Resurrection, and that when speaking of the Resurrection of the very Men you mentioned.

Observe, he saith, that God is the God of Abraham, Isaac and Jacob, and then declares that GOD IS NOT THE GOD OF THE DEAD BUT OF THE LIVING *(e)* when if those Men had dead Bodies in the Grave he must be the God of the Dead: for Abraham, Isaac & Jacob are but part alive, and the other part Dead, besides could you ever conceive of a possibility of any being either immortal or mortal from the most exalted Angel to the meanest Worm or insect to be devided in two, and both Parts exist and come together again in Life? and then what can be more inconsistent than for an Offspring of God to be divided and exist in two Parts? Besides doth not Christ declare at the same Time when speaking of the Resurrection, that they are like the Angels? And therefore do not charge me with denial of that glorious and important doctrine of the Resurrection, because I refuse to hold in such a Manner as would be impossible to be True; or if any should say again *this appears as if they rose some before the others,* let me again repeat it, that under this Canopy of Time in this mortal and corporeal State, there appears a Succession: but there is no such Thing as before or after and therefore they cannot rise one before the other: for altho' you may think it strange, yet let me tell you, that if Stephen, who was martyred four Thousand Years (to us in this World) after Able had have asked (as soon as he awoke in Eternity) the First Martyr how long he had been in Heaven he would 'have replyed *no length of Time at all: for I have just this instant 'left my imprisoned State and Awoke in Eternity.* Yea and let me further inform you, dear Reader, that to the Joy of those in Glory, it will be so forever AL-WAYS NOW; ALWAYS NOW. *(f)* so that you may still believe, and the more rejoice in the glorious Doctrine of the Resurrection, but saith my reader, if this be the case what must I understand by God's so often speaking of the day of Judgment, and that we should not sorrow for those that sleep in Jesus &c.? I answer, first that God stoops to converse with the Inhabitants of Time according to their Conceptions of Things, as I have proved already, which indeed is clearly manifested by the very Words, that you expressed: for he there declares, that they are asleep *(g)* not the Bodies only, but the whole Creature for he says, then; and therefore if that is spoken of them as it really is with them, then they are both Body and Soul in a State of Sleep and Insensibility: for he doth not say that their Dust only is asleep: but they are asleep; so that nothing can be more plain, that as it is spoken to us, to us it appears; for surely you can but know, that so great is our Ignorance of a spiritual World, that when Thousands and Tens of Thousands exchange Worlds before your Eyes they are to you not only as fallen into a Sleep, but seemingly out of Existence; yea and Ignorance of them even now so sinks us and staggers our faith, that we are ready to shrink from the Precipice, altho' God in infinite Love to us, and Pity for our Ignorance has declared, that we have no cause to sor-

row for them, or shrink from the Grave as those that have no Hope
of Immortality, for we shall see them again, and appear with them
in Glory.

And with Regard to the Day of Judgement, I need not say
much to ease your Mind about that: for what is the Judgment but
the Creature with open Conscience being brought before the Judge
of all the Earth? And surely you will believe, that this is the Case
with the Creature the Moment he awakes in Eternity; for God is
every where; and therefore you cannot imagine them to be put into
some Prison from the Presence of God, from which they are
brought out and judged, and then put back again from his Presence:
for they are always in his Presence, & therefore always standing
at the impartial Bar & are forever in the Agonies of Despair to get
away from that Bar, but cannot, *(h)* & therefore I not only attest
to a Day of Judgment, but to an eternal Judgment: nor can it possibly be otherwise, since the Creature is unmasked, & God's Presence is every where, so that by this Time you will bear to hear me
conclude, that IN ETERNITY YOU ONCE, WAS, AND KNEW IT; IN ETER-
NITY YOU ARE NOW, BUT KNOW IT NOT (by Reason of your being
wraped up in Corporeals under a Canopy of Time) AND SOON YOU
WILL BE IN ETERNITY AND KNOW IT, and therefore O think, my dear
Reader on the Position that you are in and above all learn, that the
whole Design of your present standing is for the inward Creature
to be redeemed, which if redeemed will carry back all the outward
Creature to be all again spiritual, immortal, and altogether unspeakably glorious; and if not redeemed will awake both inward
and outward Creature in all the Contrariety, Torment, & Despair,
of fallen nature, under the Weight of an eternal Judgment, by Reason of your miserable Contrariety to the Nature of that God, whose
Presence you can not flee; and therefore, let me intreat you in the
Name of the Lord Jesus Christ, for your Soul sake, no longer
ground the Hope of your Salvation on a bare Expectation that God
(who is so infinitely good,) will by and by, when you come to
leave this World, bring your Soul to any happy Place and save you
from Hell: for there is no way that God can bring you to Heaven,
but by making you heavenly, and if that Work has not been done
by the Incarnation of God, you have now the Nature of Hell, and
when God interposes no more, or you have broke thro' that Restraint, you will awake like yourself, act your own Nature, go your

own Course, feel your own Hell, and endure the Torments of your own Nature to all eternity: but if you are redeemed to God, receive the nature of God, related with God, and are brought to the Enjoyment of God, while in Time, you will awake with God, in God, and like God, with all your Nature pure, holy, happy, Angellic, glorious, and immortal in Possession of all your glorious Paradise & glassy Sea, *(i)* when to you all things, that you can see, feel or know will be spiritual, paradisical and immortal, & to them that are lost, all that they see, feel or know, is hell and misery, like themselves: For to the Conception of the Creature every Thing is like its own Nature, *(k)* And thus my dear Reader, you are really in, like, and surrounded with, all the Nature and Miseries of Hell: altho' you don't feel it now, or else, you are in, and surrounded with all Purity, Joys and Glory of Heaven: tho' by Reason of the Remains of Sin you do not yet fully know and enjoy it. And can you now after all you have seen and heard, my dear Reader, be so unspeakably cruel to yourself, as to slumber any longer in your carnal state, without examining, which of those two infinite Extreams your inmost Soul is now in? and where you will soon awake? Are you so married to the little Amusements of your mortal Stage, that you cannot find Time to ask or think, where you will plunge the next Moment if you should (as perhaps you may) step your last step of mortal Life? Can you close your eyes this night over the Bottomless Gulf without Fear: or desire to escape? or can you tread the Ground beneath your Feet without asking whose Shoulders it is on? Can you see, Sun, Moon and Stars hurrying on their Rotation without thinking that their Event will produce to you; Can you see Millions and Millions drop out of all Relation with you, and tread on their Heels with Laughter, while you crowd the downward road, or glide the slippery Steep? Or if your Hearts are impenetrable to Fear, and can stand invincible against the Threats of eternal Misery; yet will not all the Glories of eternal Felicity, the ravishing Perfections of thy Creator, the innumerable Favours of thy indulgent Preserver, the bleeding Love and endearing Compassion of thy dying Saviour, find a Crack or Crevice thro' the impenetrable Shroud to thine adamantine Heart or Obdurate Soul?

Must God suffer, Heaven bleed, Angels wait, Creatures Labour, Nature groan, Grace bleed, mercy offer, Love court, and misery threaten for thy poor Soul, and all in vain, the infinite Expence abortive, and thou wilfully rush on to the Regions of eternal Darkness.

> Fly wretched Mortal from the Gulf of Hell,
> Forever in the Heart of Glory dwell,
> And share in Joys beyond what Tongue can tell!

O that I could a Moment expell the interposing cloud, that holds you ignorant of thy Creator's Love, and point you to the bleeding Wounds of that compassionate Saviour, that now stands at thy Door! Ah how would you in a Moment bid adieu to all other Lovers, tread Earthly Crowns and Kingdoms, as Dust beneath thy Feet, while every Power of your ravished Soul would cry out, *'Stay me with 'Flagons, comfort me with Apples, for I am sick of Love! for as the 'Apple Tree, among the Trees of the Wood, and the Lilly among the Thorns, 'so is my beloved among the Daughters! and this is my beloved, and this 'is my Friend, O Daughters of Jerusalem!*

But O must I believe, or can I bear, that the greatest Part of my poor rebellious, starving, sinking, perishing, fellow Men will disdain these Glories, abhor this Love, and turn a deaf Ear to all its Charms, while they indifatiguably wear out their Days in persuit of a shaddow until they awake, where hope can never come, and the place that now knows them shall know them no more!

Why, why, O ye Sons and Daughters of Adam, will you perish with Life eternal at your Door? Why will ye dispair when Jesus pleads? Why will ye sink when Jesus rises? why will you die when Jesus lives? why will you wander in the Dark surrounded with the Sun in its Meridian Brightness? Why will you famish with Thirst so near the wells of Salvation, and Rivers of eternal Pleasure? Why will you starve in a Land of plenty, and rush to Hell so nigh the Gates of Heaven?

> O turn immortals! Turn ye Sons of Men!
> Heav'n's Gates are spread and Crowns invite you in
> There Love immortal courts you to his breast;
> There Seas of Pleasure, Seats of Joy and Rest;
> Rivers of Consolation glide along,
> And Flaiming Love the everlasting Song;
> There Joy, unmingled, are forever new,

And Millions Reign tho' once as vile as you,
And you may share in all their Glories too.
Or ask you *'How so may Pleasures there.'*

THERE JESUS DWELLS: and what can there be more?

And now to a People near my Heart (I trust) with ties divine, I drop a few words more and conclude.

Seeing in the short Compass of my Travels, and in some Degree knowing by Experience the Misery of Man's fallen State, the injury of Tradition, the Prejudice of Education, the Distress and Torment of the Slavery thereby, together with some small Experience of Redemption the worth of Liberty, the Sweetness of divine Life, the Joys of immortal Love, and attracting Views of the Nature and Perfections of the Deity, my Obligations have been pressing to venture out for the Glory of God, and good of Souls in these few Lines against the rage of Hell, the frowns of the Profane World, the Censures of the Pharisee, and inveterate Arrows of the unconverted Clergy; hoping and trusting that God will bless them to the unspeakable Benefit of Saints and Sinners.

And O how unspeakable should I think myself rewarded, if one poor Soul might be by them brought to raise an eternal Song of Praise to my blessed Master!

And altho' some of these Truths may seem strange even to some of you, that are already savingly acquainted with the Lord Jesus Christ, yet if you have been as much Embarrassed with the Inconsistencies of your Traditional Sentiments, as I have, you will not exclude these Truths from your Scrutiny; yea and so highly I esteem them, that I am constrained not only to propose them, but solicit your Attention, O fear not to dig deep for Jewels of so unspeakable Worth! Yea I am so far from believing it possible for a Christian to sit down satisfied with Knowledge attained, that I am ready to say, if you have tasted the Sweetness of Wisdom, you will be like the Miser sparing no Pains for to increase your Treasure.

And O let me intreat you to Remember, that even if you could get into Heaven on a Bed of Sloth, yet by such Negligence you would loose much Groath of the immortal Mind, and thereby sustain an everlasting Loss; your Vessel not being so large to drink from the Rivers of everlasting Joy, that Fountain of uncreated Love.

Besides methinks, you can but feel an Emulation in the Strains with most exalted Angels, that Tower their lofty Notes! for if ever you saw but a sparkling Ray of the bright and morning Star, or felt the warm Beams of that immortal Sun it has awoke an insatiate Ardour in thy burning Breast, and stole the Affections of thy soaring Mind. And O if you have felt the prolifick Ray, your Hearts are pregnant with an unextinguishable Zeal for the Glory of thy Husband, and Welfare of thy fellow Men. And O for the invigorating of that immortal Flame, gaze on the blazing Sun, and thereby you will be constrained to proclaim a crucified Saviour to the gentile World untill the latest Period of your mortal Stay.

And Ah, while you feel but the glimmering Rays of that melting Love, let others say, what they will, of a revengefull God or insenced Deity, you will be constrained to cry out with John GOD IS LOVE.

And for my own part let others imagine, or say what they will, of their being Love and Mercy in Heaven for to give to his Children and Vengeance and Wrath to pour on the Wicked in Hell, yet I not only believe, that to these in their Contrariety sinking in their own Hell in the despairing Regions of fallen Nature, will find the infinite Goodness, Love and Purity God far more tormenting, than if he was Wrath and Vengeance like themselves: but likewise that if I am so unspeakable blest as to be wholly extricated out of the Hell and Miseries of my own hellish Nature, I shall never see, nor feel, any other Hell, and if Jesus will transform me to his Likeness, I never expect nor do I fear to find any Vengeance, Wrath, or Hell in him. But O shall I ever find a Mansion in his Heart! Yes if he finds a Mansion in Mine in Time, but not else.

And therefore, let others depend on some thing done for them in some future Period after death; or built the Hope of their Salvation on what they will, I never expect to love & enjoy God in Eternity, unless I Love and enjoy him in Time for I know the Contrariety of my Nature to be such, that instead of falling in Loveing, in love with God I shall forever hate him, unless I am made like him, so that God's being all Love and Goodness will be so far from any Benefit to them that die in their Sins, that it will infinitely more augment their Misery, and increase their Rage, than if he was possessed of Wrath, Malice and Rage; for it is Love and Goodness that they are diamatrically in Opposition to, and therefore consequently infinitely tormented with, and herein is the infinite Love and Goodness of God made manifest in coming down into our Hell, to endure our Misery, change our Nature and bring us to Glory.

Ah what love indeed, Think my fellow Heirs of everlasting Felicity, how unbounded, uncontainable, and unchangeable that Goodness, that first moved for our Redemption!

O does not your Hearts burn with Love, and your raptured Souls tower aloft to reach Angellic Day, when you cast an eye to Calvaries Hill, and gaze on the Blazing Star, or behold the bleeding Fountains gushing out immortal Love? O gaze on him still, till your Heart is ravished, and your mind disentangled from all the Snares, Clouds, Clogs, and Impediments of this disordered State! For a little while longer, and your mortal Watch is out; your Trials at a Period, the Storm blown over, and you awake in the Meredian of Heavens pure Day; where thro' the boundless grace of him that has loved us, and given himself for us, I hope e'er long to share my Part with the countless Throng; thereto sollace in the Life, Love, and Glory, Wisdom and Joy, of that infinitely good God: for ever adoring him for creating Goodness, for preserving Mercy, and redeeming Grace; for O above all for what he is in himself; for the ravishing Goodness, and Perfections, we shall behold in the infinite and blazing Sun. And O forever join in one harmonious Strains, Holy, Holy, Holy Lord God Omnipotent and worthy, worthy, worthy, forever, worthy, unspeakably worthy, is the LAMB, AMEN!

FINIS.

Notes

(a) Jn 5:26.
(b) Gn 19:17.
(c) 1 Jn 5:7.
(d) Ex 21:6.
(e) 1 Cor 12:31.
(a) Jn 1:4, 5, 26.
(f) Dt 32:40; Prv 8:30.
(g) Jn 15:26.
(h) 1 Jn 5:7.
(i) Mt 3:17.
(j) Jn 6:33.
(k) Jn 10:30.

(l) Jn 17:1, 2, 3, 4, 5.
(h) Mt 13:52.
(i) Ex 34:23.
(k) Kgs .
(l) 2 Kgs 2:13.
(m) Mt 7:18.
(n) Lk 3:38.
(o) Acts 17:29.
(p) Nm 23:19.
(q) Gn 6:6.
(r) Jn 3:12.
(s) Gn 1:26.
(t) Gn 1:28.
(u) Ez 28:14.
(w) Rv 21:1, 19, 10.
(x) Ez 28:13.
(y) Rv 2:7.
(y) Gn 1:27.
(z) Jn 17:22.
(a) Gn 1:27, 28.
(b) Gn 1:1.
(c) Gn 2:17.
(d) Gn 2:17.
(d) Rv 2:7.
(f) Jn 1:4.
(g) Jn 6:33.
(g) 1 Jn 4:18.
(h) Ti 1:15.
(i) Ez 28:12, 13, 14, 15, 16, 17.
(k) Gn 2:18.
(i) Gn 2:21.
(m) Heb 2:9.
(n) Jn 17:22.
(o) Rv 2:7.
(p) Jn 16:8.
(q) 2 Kgs 7:4.
(r) Rv 2:7.
(s) Rom 10:8.
(t) Rv 3:20.
(u) Lk 17:21.
(w) Lk 15:14.
(x) Acts 5:10.

(y) Heb 12:16.
(z) Mt 19:22.
(z) Mt 19:22.
(a) Heb 6:18.
(b) Acts 7:60.
(c) Jer 13:27.
(d) Mt 23:37.
(e) Lk 19:22.
(f) Is 5:4.
(h) Eph 1:10.
(g) 2 Cor 5:19.
(i) Col 1:20.
(k) Mt 9:13.
(l) Rom 8:3.
(m) Heb 12:3.
(n) Jn 10:18.
(o) Jn 8:20.
(a) Rv 13:8.
(b) Heb 2:9.
(c) 1 Cor 15:27, 28.
(d) Jn 10:30.
(e) Lk 17:21.
(f) Rom 10:21.
(g) Rom 8:26, 21.
(h) Jn 3:13.
(o) Mal 3:10.
(j) Jn 1:9; 1 Cor 12:7.
(k) Mk 10:51.
(l) Ex 9:6.
(m) 1 Pt 2:9.
(n) 2 Cor 6:1.
(o) Jn 17:20.
(p) Lk 10:16.
(q) Lk 17:2.
(r) Rv 3:20.
(s) Is 1:19, 20.
(t) Jn 3:13.
(u) Lk 23:43.
(w) Rom 10:17.
(x) Jn 6:53.
(y) Eph 5:20.
(z) 2 Cor 5:16.

(a) 1 Cor 15:44.
(b) 2 Pet 3:10.
(c) 1 Cor 15:50.
(d) Mi 5:2.
(e) Mt 22:32.
(f) Rv 5:9.
(g) 1 Thes 4:15.
(h) Rv 6:16.
(i) Rv 2:7, 22:14, 15:2.
(k) Ti 1:15.

HYMNS AND SPIRITUAL SONGS

Two volumes of Alline's *Hymns and Spiritual Songs* were eventually published. A slim 22-page volume consisting of twenty-two hymns was published in Halifax in 1781, and reprinted in Windsor, Vermont, in 1796 under the title *Hymns and Spiritual Songs*. The same title would be used for Alline's major work, his 381-page volume, first published in Boston in 1786. Nine years later, in 1795, a new edition was produced by the Free Will Baptists and two years later it was yet again reprinted, this time with a new hymn included, "A Call to Sinners" written by Benjamin Randel, as well as some of the Reverend McClure's description of Alline's last days on earth. A fourth and final edition was published in 1802. Thirty-eight of Alline's hymns were reprinted in Smith and James's widely used *Hymns Original and Selected* and for a time the Falmouth preacher's hymns were almost as popular in New England as those written by Isaac Watts. But of Alline's more than 500 hymns, only one has survived in modern collections—"Amazing Sight the Saviour Stands."

It has been perceptively observed that the "appearance of two editions of Alline's *Hymns* within two years is evidence of the popularity of their sentiments among the Free Baptists."[1] His hymns were obviously very widely known and popular in the New England–Nova Scotia–New Brunswick area, especially during the three or four decades following the Revolution.[2] These hymns and spiritual

---

1. Maurice Armstrong, *The Great Awakening in Nova Scotia*, p. 89.
2. See George Rawlyk, ed., *New Light Letters and Songs*, pp. 68–71.

songs, sung to lively popular tunes, appeared at precisely the moment the "Revival of Singing" was sweeping New England and the Maritimers,[3] and there is evidence to suggest that Alline's *Hymns and Spiritual Songs* played a key role in channelling popular religion into New England's Second Great Awakening.

Thus not only was Alline a charismatic preacher and controversial essayist but he was also an unusually gifted hymn writer. His hymns and spiritual songs contained the simplified essence of what has been described as his "Radical Evangelical" and New Light message. As with his preaching, he made superb use of "sensuous imagery and subjectivism, and Biblical paraphrase"[4] in his hymns to communicate deep religious truths. His hymns and spiritual songs articulated language ordinary folk could understand and could resonate with for they "represented the common denominator of plainfolk religious belief"[5] and captured the simple essence of their faith. Repetition, the use of striking phrases, the creative linking of lyrics to popular folk tunes, must have drilled into the inner consciousness of those who sang Alline's hymns and spiritual songs unforgettable experiences as well as New Light beliefs.

The core of Alline's New Light theology is to be found in his *Hymns and Spiritual Songs*. On the whole, these are powerful and evocative hymns, and it is not surprising that for many of the inhabitants of Nova Scotia and New England during and after the Revolutionary War years they contained the essential truths of the Christian gospel in graphic language that, according to Alline, "alarmed" the heart and stirred it "up to action, by local objects or vocal sounds." "Although persons may sing, such subjects as they have not experienced without mockery," Alline observed "by acknowledging their ignorance of, and groaning after the things they express; yet as I think it far more likely to stir up and engage the heart

---

3. Armstrong, *The Great Awakening in Nova Scotia*, p. 90. See also Margaret Filshie, " 'Redeeming Love Shall be Our Song': Hymns of the First Great Awakening in Nova Scotia" (M.A. thesis, Queen's University, 1983); and A. Beauchner, "Yankee Singing Schools and the Golden Age of Choral Music in New England, 1760–1800" (Ph.D. diss., Harvard University, 1960).

4. Stephen Marini, "New England Folk Religions," p. 479.

5. D. D. Bruce, Jr., *And They All Sang Hallelujah, Plain-Folk Camp Meeting Religion, 1800–1845* (Knoxville, University of Tennessee Press, 1975), p. 95.

(especially souls enlightened and groaning for liberty) when they express the state, groans, and desires of their own souls.'' And consequently Alline ''endeavoured to be various in my subjects, to be adapted to almost every capacity, station of life, or frame of mind.''[6]

Alline's 381-page *Hymns and Spiritual Songs*—his major work—is divided into five sections or books dealing with ''Man's Fallen State,'' ''Free Salvation,'' ''The New Birth,'' ''Christian Travels,'' and ''Transporting Views and Christian Triumph.'' Taking into account the generally confused state of Nova Scotians in the late 1770s and 1780s it is not surprising that such hymns as the following became unusually popular during and after Alline's lifetime:

> O What a heart, a heart of stone
> And Load of guilt I bear
> Seeking for help, but finding none,
> And bord'ring on despair!
>
> I mourn beneath my heavy load,
> And think I want release
> But something keeps me from my God
> And bars my soul from peace.
>
> It's hard to bear these pangs of death,
> And lug these heavy chains,
> And yet for want of acting faith
> My burden still remains.[7]

But ''guilt'' and ''despair'' were removed by Jesus Christ's sacrifice:

> And dids't thou die for me
> O thou blest Lamb of God?
> And has thou brought me home to thee;
> By thy own precious blood?

---

6. Henry Alline, *Hymns and Spiritual Songs,* pp. i–ii.
7. Ibid., pp. 51–51.

How coulds't thou stoop so low?
O what amazing grace!
He saves me from eternal wo,
And gives me heav'nly peace.[8]

Peace was provided by the New Birth and, as might have been expected, some of Alline's most moving hymns dealt with what he called "the New Birth and the knowledge and joys of that glorious work."

Dark and distressing was the day,
When o'er the dismal gulf I lay,
With trembling knees and stutt'ring breath
I shudder'd on the brink of death.

Destruction yawn'd on ev'ry side,
I saw no refuge where to hide,
Ten thousand foes beset me round,
No friend nor comforter I found.

I groan'd and cry'd, while torn with grief,
But none appear'd for my relief,
'Till Christ the Saviour passing by,
Look'd on me with a pitying eye.

He brought me from the gates of hell,
The wonders of his grace to tell
O may he now inspire my tongue
To make his lovely name my song.[9]

And in a hymn entitled, "A Miracle of Grace," Alline graphically used his own conversion experience to appeal to others:

No mortal tongue can ever tell,
The horrors of that gloomy night,

---

8. Ibid., p. 13.
9. Ibid., pp. 153–54.

When I hung o'er that brink of hell,
Expecting soon my wretched flight!

I felt my burden waste my life,
While guilt did ev'ry hope devour,
Trembling I stretch'd with groans and strife
For to escape the dreadful hour.

But in the midst of all my grief,
The great Messiah spoke in love;
His arm appeared for my relief,
And bid my guilt and sorrow move.

He pluck'd me from the jaws of hell,
With his almighty arm of pow'r
And O! no mortal tongue can tell,
The change of that immortal hour!

Then I enjoy'd a sweet release,
From chains of sin and pow'rs of death,
My soul was fill'd with heav'nly peace,
My groans were turn'd to praising breath.[10]

For Alline, regeneration made—as he put it—"Heaven on
earth" a very real possibility:

Some happy days I find below
When Jesus is with me;
Nor would I any pleasure know
O Jesus but in thee.

When I can taste immortal love,
And find my Jesus near,
My soul is blest where e'er I rove,
I neither mourn nor fear.

---

10. Ibid., p. 162.

Let angels boast their joys above,
I taste the same below,
They drink of the Redeemer's love,
And I have Jesus too.[11]

In an especially moving and memorable hymn entitled "The great love of Christ display'd in his death," Alline captured what he considered to be the essence of his profoundly spiritual conversion experience. Many of his followers must have made Alline's vivid description their own unique experience and used his language to describe their own New Birth.

As near to Calvary I pass
Me thinks I see a bloody cross,
Where a poor victim hangs;
His flesh with ragged irons tore,
His limbs all dress'd with purple gore,
Gasping in dying pangs.

Surpriz'd the spectacle to see,
I ask'd who can this victim be,
In such exquisite pain?
Why thus consign'd to woes I cry'd?
"Tis I, the bleeding God reply'd,
To save a world from sin."

A God for rebel mortals dies!
How can it be, my soul replies!
What! Jesus die for me!
"Yes, saith the suff'ring Son of God,
*I give my life, I spill my blood,
For thee, poor soul, for thee."*

Lord since thy life thou'st freely giv'n,
To bring my wretched soul to heav'n.
And bless me with thy love;
Then to thy feet, O God, I'll fall,

---

11. Ibid., pp. 182–83.

Give thee my life, my soul, my all,
To reign with thee above.

All other lovers I'll adieu,
My dying lover I'll pursue,
And bless the slaughter'd Lamb;
My life, my strength, my voice and days,
I will devote to wisdom's ways,
And sound his bleeding fame.

And when this tott'ring life shall cease,
I'll leave these mortal climes in peace,
And soar to realms of light;
There where my heav'nly lover reigns,
I'll join to raise immortal strains,
All ravish'd with delight.[12]

In possibly the last hymn he ever composed, Alline discussed his own imminent death:

Now to the pilgrims born of God,
In Jesus' name these lines I hand,
To cheer you on your Christian road
And point you to the heav'nly land,

When I am gone and ye survive,
Make the Redeemer's name your theme,
And while these mortal climes ye rove,
The wonders of his love proclaim.

Soon I shall end this rapid race,
And tread your mortal climes no more;
But through Jehovah's boundless grace,
Save shall I reach the Heav'nly shore . . .

I drink, I soar, I gaze, I rove,
O'er the transparent scenes of bliss,

---

12. Ibid., pp. 348–49.

Still lost with wonder in his love,
My soul! and what a God is this!

Ten thousand blazing realms of light
Proclaim their God, and say, Amen!
My soul still soaring in her flight,
My God is all, I drop my pen.[13]

Alline's hymns are still sung in a few Baptist churches in New Brunswick and Nova Scotia. They are not to be found in hymn books but exist in the amazingly retentive memories of scores of worshipers who still regard themselves as disciples of Henry Alline. These hymns are an integral part of an oral culture that still exists in the upper reaches of the St. John River Valley of New Brunswick, and in the Yarmouth region of Nova Scotia. Few in the region may now have any knowledge of Alline's printed sermons or treatises or have seen his *Journal,* but they do remember some of the *Hymns and Spiritual Songs,* perhaps the most lasting legacy of Alline's all too brief sojourn in what his followers frequently referred to as "this vale of tears."[14]

Hymns and Spiritual Songs (1781)

HYMN II. COMMON METRE.

Free Grace: or, The Gospel Call

1
Come, all ye dying sons of men,
Attend the gospel feast;

---

13. Ibid., pp. 380–81.
14. I have attended a Sunday service conducted by Frederick Burnett, near Hartland, New Brunswick, where this oral tradition is still an important feature of religious worship. Burnett, a Free Christian Baptist preacher, has provided me with a great deal of valuable information about the continuing impact of the Allinite tradition on New Brunswick and Nova Scotia.

Come ev'ry soul oppress'd with sin,
And be the Saviour's guest.

2

Redeeming love is at your door,
And offers mercy free;
Come blind, come deaf, come sick, come sore,
Come, helpless as you be.

3

Although your guilt and fears are great,
And you have long delay'd;
Yet come to-day, 'tis not too late:
Come and the match is made.

4

The Saviour dies to make you whole;
See how his bowels move!
He'll ne'er despite the guilty soul—
O come receive his love.

5

For you his precious blood was spilt;
O then forget your grief!
Come to his feet with all your guilt,
And you shall find relief.

6

Sinner, sinner, will you die,
When JESUS bleeds to free.
Come, see him bleed, and hear him cry,
"Sinner, I die for thee."

HYMN IX. LONG METRE.

The Sinner convinced of the necessity of receiving CHRIST *in the Soul*

1

What shall a wretched sinner do,
When press'd with guilt in all my soul,

And hurried to eternal wo,
As fast as fleeting moments roll?

2

I hear the saints of God declare,
There is a Christ whose grace is free;
But if I don't his goodness share,
Pray what is all that grace to me?

3

They say there is a gospel feast,
And every hungry soul may feed;
Yet I may starve and never taste
One crumb of that immortal bread.

4

Jesus, they say, has life divine,
Poor dying sinners to revive;
But if that life is never mine,
How can my soul be made alive?

5

They say his blood was freely spilt,
To cleanse polluted souls from sin;
But that will ne'er remove my guilt,
Unless my soul be wash'd therein.

6

Lord, seal thy glorious truths to me,
Or I shall sink in death and hell:
O take my life and soul to thee,
And in thy nature let me dwell.

HYMN XI. COMMON METRE.

The Sinner's Complaint

1

O HARDENED, harden'd heart of mine,
That loads me with distress;
And doth like iron fetters bind
My soul from happiness.

2

O was there ever wretch on earth
In such a state as I?
Expos'd to everlasting death,
Unwilling yet to fly.

3

Mount Sina's thunder doth not wake
Me from this stupid frame;
Nor doth the love of Jesus break
My heart in to a flame.

4

The greatest grief that I endure,
Or trials that I find,
Is, that I am distress'd no more
With this unfeeling mind.

5

I mourn, because I cannot mourn,
And grieve, because not griev'd,
I think, I long from sin to turn,
Yet fear I am deceiv'd.

6

Good God, receive me as I am,
And let me see thy face;
And all my heart and soul inflame
With thy redeeming grace.

Hymns and Spiritual Songs (1786)
Book I

Chiefly consisting of man's fallen state; together with reproofs to the ungodly, and the language of awakened sinners

HYMN XV.

An aged sinner awakened

I.

O What a wretched state I'm in!
In midnight darkness and in sin;
In chains of death, the devil's slave,
Just stepping in the gaping grave.

II.

O God, look down, look down on me,
Forgive my sins, and set me free;
O soon I'm fix'd, O wretched doom!
Where help nor hope can never come.

III.

I may perhaps, for who can tell?
I may escape the jaws of hell;
Lord here I fall before thy face,
Make me a miracle of grace.

HYMN XIX.

A sinner convinced of his death and blindness

I.

HARD heart of mine! O that the Lord
Would this hard heart subdue!
O come thou blest life-giving word,
And form my soul anew.

II.

I hear the heav'nly pilgrims tell
Their sins are all forgiv'n,

And while on earth their bodies dwell,
Their souls enjoy a heav'n.

III.

While I, poor wretch, in darkness stand,
With guilt a heavy load;
And ev'ry breath expos'd to land
Beyond the grace of GOD.

IV.

The christians sing redeeming love,
And talk of joys divine above
And soon, they say, in realms above
In glory they shall shine.

V.

But ah! it's all an unknown tongue,
I never knew that love;
I cannot sing that heav'nly song,
Nor tell of joys above.

VI.

I want, o GOD, I know not what!
I want what saints enjoy;
O let their portion by my lot,
Their work be my employ.

VII.

Fain would I know that Saviour mine,
And take his bleeding love,
With all the heav'nly pilgrims join,
While I this desert rove.

VIII.

Then O to those transporting realms,
My soul would soar away,
Where all the warriors wear their palms
In everlasting day.

HYMN XLI.

On death

I.

SOON I must hear the solemn call
(Prepar'd or not) to yield my breath;
And this poor mortal frame must fall
A helpless prey to cruel death.

II.

Then look; my soul, look forward now,
And anchor safe beyond the flood;
Now to the Saviour's footstool, bow,
And get a life secure in GOD.

III.

Before these fleeting hours are gone,
I'll bid this mortal world adieu;
And to the Lord I'll now resign
My life, my breath, and spirit too.

IV.

Then welcome death with all its force;
No more I'll fear the gaping grave;
Jesus my God, my last resource,
Will reach his arm my soul to save.

V.

He will not hide his smiling face,
Nor leave me in that trying hour;
I'll trust my soul upon his grace
And chearful leave the mortal shore.

HYMN XLVII.

Man's miserable choice, and condition

I.

HIGH was the crime, great was the fall,
And fatal was the daring blow,

When man with paradise and all,
Plung'd in a labyrinth of wo.

II.

Deep did the damning poison seize,
The num'rous throng of human race;
Beyond all help for their disease,
But by Jehovah's arm of grace.

III.

And when redeeming love comes down,
By the incarnate Son of GOD;
How many disregard the crown,
While others think to spill his blood!

IV.

Where GOD his boundless grace has spread,
Ten thousand souls sink deeper still;
Beneath the curse among the dead,
Against the Saviour's love and will.

V.

While life is sounding in their ears,
And heav'nly floods spread all around;
They turn their backs, and drown their fears;
And thus of choice to hell they're bound.

VI.

How many sinners sit and hear,
The glorious gospel trump in vain;
Sleeping in sin, they rest secure,
Till they awake in endless pain.

VII.

Thousands and tens of thousands more
Pretend to love the gospel sound,
Who hold the form, and hate the pow'r;
Despite the cross, and lose the crown,

VIII.

And thus of all the sinking race,
O shocking thought! there is but few
Who e'er obtain that work of grace
That forms the inmost soul anew.

IX.

O pity, Lord, these heirs of death,
That lay condemn'd to endless night:
Breathe, O immortal spirit, breathe
And make them children of the light.

HYMN L.

*On a storm of thunder; when two trees were struck
with lightning not far from where I sat*

I.

SEE, see what heavy clouds arise,
And veiling the resurgent skies,
They spread a midnight shade!
Like angry bulls with rapid force.
Spread o'er the hills with mutt'ring voice,
Doth all our tents invade.

II.

Impetuous streams their floods disperse
The meads, and vallies soon immerse
In the o'er spreading flood;
Tempetuous blasts their strength engage,
Augmenting the rapacious rage,
Spread awful scenes abroad.

III.

Hark! hark! what thunders rend the sky.
While sheets of liquid nitre fly,
And burn the sulph'rous air!
Beneath me shakes the solid ground;
An awful bell'wing all around,
While clouds in flames appear.

IV.

What threat'ning dangers now resound,
And gaping graves spread all around,
To seize a helpless worm.

What scenes of night, and arms of death,
Pursues me now at ev'ry breath
Amidst this fiery storm!

V.

A blazing blot now rolls with strife,
And points to my unguarded life,
From which I cannot flee:
But heav'ns almighty arm of care
Now bids the threat'ning bolt forbear,
And strike some neighbouring tree.

VI.

The rugged elm now feels the stroke;
A stately trunk in shivers broke,
While I securely stand;
O may the scene effectual prove,
To fill my soul with thanks and love,
To GOD's indulgent hand!

HYMN LXIII.

The awakened sinner inquiring after Christ

I.

TELL a poor soul that I may find;
Where is the Saviour of mankind?
And let me see his smiling face
That I may know, and sing his grace.

II.

Ye foll'wers of the heav'nly Lamb,
Who're bound to spread his bleeding fame,
O, if you can, I pray you tell
Where doth your blessed Jesus dwell?

III.

O let me know that I may flee
To him, and your best friend may see,
Nothing can make my soul rejoice
Until I hear his saving voice.

IV.

O could I find his blessed feet.
There would I choose a humble seat;
There would I choose to spend my days;
Enjoy his love and spread his praise.

V.

O thou that passeth by my door,
To give salvation to the poor,
Since thou doth blessings freely give,
O speak that my poor soul may live.

VI.

I cannot bear to let thee pass,
Without a portion in thy grace;
O let my soul no longer rove,
A stranger to redeeming love.

HYMN LXXXVI.

On death

I.

While the swift wings of time doth fly,
Rouse up my soul, stretch ev'ry thought;
This world with all its joys must die,
And ev'ry mortal scene is short.

II.

Soon must I leave this house of clay,
And instantaneous take my flight
To the bright realms of endless day,
Or down to everlasting night.

III.

O for a blessed Saviour nigh,
To help in that important hour,
To waft my soul above the sky,
By his almighty arm of pow'r!

IV.

But if no Christ how dark the day,
When shudd'ring o'er th'important brink!
Helpless and guilty hurl'd away
In everlasting pain to sink.

V.

Lord help me now to take my flight
From darkness and the charms below;
O seal my life in realms of light.
Before death strikes the fatal blow.

VI.

Then welcome death to call me home,
To heav'nly joys with GOD my friend;
Where storms and sin can never come,
And all my fears shall have an end.

Hymns and Spiritual Songs (1786)
Book II.

*Chiefly consisting of gospel invitations, and a
free salvation.*

HYMN I.

A free salvation by the death of Christ

I.

Ye sons of Adam lift your eyes,
Behold how free the Saviour dies,
To save your souls from hell!
There's your Creator, and your friend;
Believe and soon your fears shall end,
And you in glory dwell.

II.

Doubt not his word; his grace is free,
Believe he died and calls for thee,
And your poor souls shall live:

Can free salvation be deny'd,
When in his dying groans he cry'd,
"Father their sins forgive."
III.
Believe and feel his boundless love;
It soon will bear your souls above,
To peaceful realms on high;
He swears as certain as he lives,
His hand a free salvation gives
"Why sinner will you die?"
IV.
Will you despise the vast renown,
And choose despair before a crown?
O have eternal joy!
Receive a kingdom in your heart,
Of life and joy that ne'er'll depart;
Nor earth or hell destroy.

HYMN XIV.

Christ's love display'd in his death

I.
WHO can, or dares refuse to love,
The bleeding Lamb of God,
That from the glorious realms above,
Displays such grace abroad?
II.
He dies, he dies, and bows his head,
Upon the fatal tree,
To raise poor sinners from the dead,
And let the pris'ners free.
III.
O was there ever love like this
To rebels doom'd to hell!
Or was there ever grief like his!
His pain no tongue can tell.

IV.

'Wake ev'ry soul with sweet surprise,
And bid your fears adieu;
The mighty Saviour freely dies
For you, poor souls, for you.

HYMN XVIII.

A free salvation proclaimed

I.

All hail, all hail, ye souls that dwell
Just on the verge of death and hell,
Behold your mighty Saviour's come!
To day he spreads his arms abroad,
Inviting sinners home to GOD;
Come mourning souls, with Jesus dwell.

II.

Unbounded goodness waits for you,
To heal your wounds, and feed you too;
With life and joys that are divine;
Come every soul, attend the call,
The Lamb of GOD invites you all;
O hear, and Jesus shall be thine.

III.

He's bid his servants all declare
His grace is free, and you may share
In joys beyond what tongue can tell;
No longer hug your unbelief,
Believe in him, and find relief;
He's come to set the pris'ners free.

IV.

Sinners no more reject his call,
He's life, he's peace, he's all in all;
Oh come and snare his boundless love:
If once you knew the glorious theme,

And drank of this delightful stream,
You'd choose your all in realms above.
V.
O hear the heav'nly charmer's voice,
Now is the time to make your choice,
And reign eternal ages blest;
No longer court your earthly bliss;
There is no joy compar'd with this;
O come and have eternal rest.
VI.
Why will you to destruction go?
Say, will you have this Christ, or no?
This day he calls and waits for you,
He'll lead you to the realms above,
And feed you with immortal love,
And give you joys forever new.

HYMN XXIV.

The Prince of Peace riding victoriously

I.
JESUS thy gospel armour gird,
To spread abroad thy gracious fame,
Ride in the chariot of thy word,
And teach the dying world thy name.
II.
Triumph in mercy through our land,
And cause the poor dry bones to move;
Display thy love, make bare thine hand,
And teach immortal souls thy love.
III.
Here's some immers'd in shades of night,
And some involv'd in deep distress;
O send some rays of sacred light,
And ev'ry mourning sinner bless.

IV.

Here's some that's deaf, and some that's blind,
    And some that's wounded with their sins;
They mourn and rove some help to find,
    Yet do but more increase their pains.

V.

Here's some that feels their heavy chain,
    And others senseless of their woe;
Some captive souls where Satan reigns,
    Some lost and knows not where to go.

VI.

Some much in debt, with nought to pay,
    Condemn'd and into prison cast,
And wall'wing in their filth they lay,
    All hopes and helps but thee are lost.

VII.

Here's some that mourns a stupid mind,
    And some that's lame, and some that's dead;
Some sick, and can no comfort find,
    While others beg for crumbs of bread.

PAUSE

VIII.

Come in, thou great physician, come,
    Thou that delight'st to help the poor;
Get to thyself a glorious name,
    At thy expence work ev'ry cure.

IX.

"I come, saith Jesus, lo, I come,
"To help the poor is my delight;
"Love is my nature, love my name;
"My help is free both day and night.

X.

"Bring all your money now to me,
"Your weak, your wounded, bound and poor,
"Rebels and pris'ners I will free,
"The worst of all diseases cure.

XI.

"I'll labour at my own expence,
"Cancel all debts and pay the cost;

"And give my bond for their defence,
"That not one patient shall be lost.
XII.
"I'm bound by my own love to be,
"Physician and a father too;
"A friend to all eternity,
"What more can I propose, or do?"
XIII.
Enough, O Lord, and we adore
Thy wisdom, pity, and thy love,
Thou giv'st thyself, we ask no more
Now we may reign with thee above.
XIV.
Let all the sons of men rejoice,
And join to laud thy precious name;
And ev'ry heart, and ev'ry voice
The wonders of thy love proclaim.
XV.
Let saints and angels join above,
The glories of thy name to sing,
While the sweet wonders of thy love,
Makes all the heav'nly arches ring.
XVI.
Let all creation join as one,
Through endless years thy love proclaim,
While sacred echos, cry Amen,
Amen, all worthy is the Lamb!

HYMN XXVIII.

On the death of Christ

I.
WHAT solemn groans are those I hear,
It's like some bleeding victim near;
From Golgotha methinks they rise;
Ah! tis the Saviour bleeds for me;

For me, for me, for me, for me,
He bows his head and groans and dies.
II.
Angels, behold your maker GOD,
Nail'd to the tree now dress'd in blood,
That he might spread his boundless grace:
Adam with all your sons behold,
Behold, behold, behold, behold,
The Saviour of your guilty race.
III.
All dress'd in purple gore he hangs,
In agonies, and dying pangs;
And praying gasps th' expiring breath
Freely the great Messiah dies,
He dies, he dies, he dies, he dies,
To save immortal souls from death.
IV.
Think, O my soul, how can it be,
The king of glory bleeds for thee!
Behold, behold thy Jesus die!
How great thy goodness, O my GOD!
MY GOD, my GOD, my GOD, my GOD,
To bleed for such a wretch as I!

HYMN XXXVII.

Christ inviting sinners to his grace

I.
AMAZING sight, the Saviour stands,
And knocks at every door;
Ten thousand blessing in his hands,
For to supply the poor.

II.

"Behold, saith he, I bleed and die,
"To bring poor souls to rest;
"Hear, sinners, while I'm passing by,
"And be forever blest.

III.

"Will you despite such bleeding love,
"And choose the way to hell;
"Or in the glorious realms above,
"With me forever dwell?

IV.

"Not to condemn your sinking race,
"Have I in judgement come:
"But to display unbounded grace,
"And bring lost sinners home.

V.

"May I not save your wretched soul,
"From sin, from death, and hell;
"Wounded or sick, I'll make you whole,
"And you with me shall dwell.

VI.

"Say, will you hear my gracious voice,
"And have your sins forgiv'n?
"Or will you make a wretched choice,
"And bar yourselves from heav'n?

VII.

"Will you go down to endless night,
"And bear eternal pain?
"Or dwell in everlasting light,
"Where I in glory reign?

VIII.

"Come answer now before I go,
"While I am passing by;
"Say, will you marry me, or no?
"Say, will you live, or die?"

HYMN XXXVIII.

The mourning soul answered by Christ

I.

WHERE, saith the mourner, is this Christ,
That call the hungry to a feast?
Where is that grace proclaim'd so free?
Say, herald, point the way to me.

II.

If, as you say, he spilt his blood,
To bring immortal souls to GOD;
Then tell me, tell me, where I'll go,
To find if this be true, or no?

III.

"Well, saith the Saviour, hear I be?
"Where is the soul inquiries for me?
"I by my spirit now declare,
"My grace is free, and you may share."

IV.

O saith the soul, I wou'd receive;
Speak, Lord, and help me to believe;
Since thou declar'dst thy grace is free,
O give one precious drop to me.

V.

"I wait, saith Jesus, at your door,
"With love that knows no bound nor shore;
"And far more free I am to give,
"Than you are willing to receive.

VI.

"Freely I die, I mourn, I bleed,
"I weep, I wait, promise and plead;
"Lab'ring for you all dress'd in gore,
"What can I do or offer more?

VII.

"Say, will you now my love abuse,
"And all the joys of heav'n refuse;

"Must I leave you? must I go?
"Will you choose eternal wo?

VIII.

"O be beseech'd to hear my voice,
"And make eternal life your choice;
"Say, will you choose to sink in hell?
"Or else with me in glory dwell?

HYMN XXXIX.

Chosing nothing but Christ

I.

I choose the Lord for all my joy;
His praise I count my best employ;
His name my constant theme shall be;
Lord I would follow none but thee.

II.

Without my Lord I cannot rest;
There's none but he can make me blest;
In him I find a solid peace,
And in him all my joys increase,

III.

O let me never, never part,
From him the pleasure of my heart;
Dear Jesus, keep me always near,
Till I with thee in heav'n appear.

IV.

O may I once at thy right hand,
Rejoice with all the glorious band;
The unveil'd glories then I'll see,
Of him that gave his life for me.

V.

Transporting scenes! ah, glorious sight!
Shall wrap my soul in sweet delight;
And each immortal pow'r of mine,
Shall in exalted praises join.

HYMN XL.

A call to sinners

I.

Sinners arise, the Saviour's come,
And bleeds for wretched souls like you;
His mercy calls the rebels home,
Forgives their sins and loves them too.

II.

Come to the feast without delay,
Before the gospel call is o'er;
Embrace the blessed Lord to day,
Lest he should go, and call no more.

III.

Ten thousand souls have enter'd in,
And found a feast of love divine;
Come then, poor souls, with all your sin,
And the Redeemer will be thine.

IV.

Those happy souls that's gone before,
Were once in sin as vile as you;
O doubt the Saviour's love no more,
But come and taste his goodness too.

HYMN XLIV.

Free grace, the gospel call, and salvation by faith

I.

NATIONS attend, let ev'ry mortal hear,
The gospel trumpet sounds the jubilee year;
The Saviour's death declares unbounded grace
To ev'ry soul of Adam's guilty race;
Sinners behold your friend and Saviour bleeding,
Fly to his arms while he is interceding.

II.

No more attempt to cleanse the guilty soul,
Or work to make your wounded spirits whole;
But hear, and let the waiting Saviour in,
His rising pow'r will cleanse from all your sins;
Fly, mortals, fly, fly ev'ry town and nation.
While the Redeemer stands with free salvation.

III.

"I want not works, saith he, to make you whole,
"I came to save the vile poluted soul;
"My grace is free, I am the mighty GOD,
"My arms of love for you is stretch'd abroad";
Sinners behold the great incarnate Saviour,
And fly for refuge to his lasting favour.

IV.

Behold, behold his wounded hands and side,
And then believe it was for you he died;
He waits in love the sinners to receive,
And will you not his dying groans believe;
He waits and calls, O sinners hear him pleading,
And then believe for you the Lamb is bleeding.

V.

"How long, saith he, will you my love abuse;
"How long will you my boundless grace refuse;
"How long, poor sinners, will you shut the door?
"Or must I leave, and call on you no more?
"Say, wretched mortal, must my love be slighted.
"Or will you come to GOD while your invited.

PAUSE

VI.

"Behold, behold I am the sinners friend;
"Believe my word and all your griefs shall end,
"Or lack you faith, 'tis faith I freely give;
"Look up to me, poor dying soul, and live.
"The great Jehovah offers you a kingdom;
"Come ev'ry soul, come as you are, and welcome.

VII.

"Your heart is hard, my love can melt away
"Both rocks and hills; why will you longer stay?

"Once more I ask, poor soul I'm loath to go,
"Say, dying sinner, will you live, or no?
"Your sins tho' great they shall be all foregiv'n,
"And you shall live and reign with me in heav'n.

VIII.

"With all my countless hosts in realms above,
"Your souls shall share in everlasting love;
"I'll be your father and your portion too,
"And you shall swim in joys forever new;
"Say now, poor souls, why are you unbelieving?
"Or what, say what, doth keep you from receiving?

IX.

"I'll conquer death and hell beneath your feet,
"Behold my great salvation is complete;
"I've drank your bitter cup, and bore your load
"Of sin and death, to bring you home to God.
"I'll change your heart, and take away your blindness;
"How can you now abuse such loving kindness?

X.

"Eternal riches shall to you be giv'n,
"And a blest mansion to the seats of heav'n;
"Unbounded glory I will freely give,
"If thou wilt but consent with me to live;
"Say wretched sinner, will you have a kingdom,
"Now is the time, consent; and come to welcome."

HYMN LVII.

Christ's death declares his grace is free

I.

AWAKE, O guilty world awake,
Behold the earth's foundations shake,
While the Redeemer bleeds for you!
His death proclaims to all your race,
Free grace, free grace, free grace, free grace,
To all the Jews and Gentiles too.

II.

Come, guilty mortals, come and see
The Saviour on the cursed tree,
For you, all dress'd in purple gore;
His weight of wo has veil'd the sun,
'Tis done, 'tis done, 'tis done, 'tis done,
That man might live forevermore.

III.

See how the wounded Lamb of God
Extends his bleeding arms abroad
To save a fallen world from death!
Behold him in his agonies,
He dies, he dies, he dies, he dies,
And yields the last expiring breath.

IV.

He dies and triumphs over death
To give the dead immortal birth,
And spread the wonders of his name,
Shout, mortals, shout, with chearful voice,
Rejoice, rejoice, rejoice, rejoice,
And give the glory to the Lamb.

HYMN LXIII.

Christ's work, and love, and success in the gospel

I.

LORD, in the chariot of thy work,
Ride forth with pow'r thy name to spread;
Give speed unto thy gospel sword,
Through these dark regions of the dead,

II.

"Lo, saith the Saviour, here I am,
"With all my vesture dip'd in blood;
"The FREE PHYSICIAN is my name,
"Seeking to do the needy good.

III.

"I love to feed the hungry poor,
"To heal the sick and raise the dead;
"I love to see them crowd my door,
"That I my boundless love may spread.

IV.

"I love to set those pris'ners free,
"That are in debt and nought to pay;
"No guilty soul that comes to me,
"Shall ever go condemn'd away.

V.

"Now where's your guilty, weak and poor,
"Your sick, your deaf, your dead, your blind,
"Call each by name around my door,
"And they shall all a helper find."

VI.

Lord, saith the poor and trembling soul,
I come with all my wants to thee;
My sins forgive, my wounds make whole,
And from my bondage set me free.

VII.

"Then, saith the Lord, the work is done,
"It was for you I bled and died;
"Cast all thy wants on me alone,
"And all thy wants shall be supply'd."

VIII.

O, saith the soul, my Christ is mine!
I feel thy grace, I love thy name,
And I will be forever thine,
O Lord to sound thy worthy fame.

IX.

Hossana! let the christians join,
A soul is added to our band;
And welcome soul, the prize is thine,
To reign with us at Christ's right hand.

X.

Amen, with joy our souls shall sing,
And let the fame resound abroad;

Amen, all glory to our king,
A soul is born to Christ our GOD.

HYMN LXXI.

The christian surprised at Christ's love

I.

AND didst thou die for me,
O thou blest Lamb of GOD?
And hast thou brought me home to thee,
By thine own precious blood?
II.
How couldst thou stoop so low?
O what amazing grace!
He saves me from eternal wo,
And gives me heav'nly peace.
III.
My soul, how can it be,
That Jesus freely bore
The pangs of death and hell for me,
And yet I love no more!
IV.
O let me now arise
And soar to realms above,
And shouting gaze, with sweet surprise,
On such amazing love!

HYMN LXXVI.

Met for worship

I.

ALL hail thou lovely Lamb of GOD!
This day with us make thine abode,

And cheer our spirits with thy love;
We long to see thy smiling face,
And run with thee the christian race,
To thine eternal realms above.

II.

O heal the sick and raise the dead,
And feed us with immortal bread;
Warm ev'ry heart, loose ev'ry tongue;
O let thy love our souls inflame,
We shall rejoice to feel thy name,
And make redeeming love our song.

III.

We love thy name, and long to feel
More of thy love, and thirsting still,
Our souls for larger draughts would soar;
Nor would we e'er contented be
'Till all our souls are made like thee,
And safely reach'd th' immortal shore.

IV.

We almost long to quit this stage,
That all our pow'rs might once engage
To love and praise without annoy;
Then as immortal stars we'll shine,
In glory, Lord, forever thine,
And solace in unmingled joy.

HYMN XCI.

Heaven begun on earth.

I.

On earth I know immortal love,
And taste of all the joys above;
My soul enjoys the great I AM;
And there's no pleasure but in him.

II.

My light is but a feeble ray,
Yet it is from eternal day;
Nay, joys are by my Jesus giv'n,
And he is all the joys of heav'n.

III.

Though in my self I am but death,
Yet Christ in me the word of faith,
Lifts up my heart to realms above,
And feeds me with immortal love.

IV.

O when shall I be wholly free?
I want no joys, O GOD, but thee;
Thou art my all, my life, my peace,
In thee my joys shall never cease.

HYMN C.

The stupidity of the world, and the goodness of GOD

I.

O the dead state of Adam's race,
Surrounded with redeeming grace,
Wasting their days, their life and
     breath,
For shades that lead to endless death.

II.

While Jesus bleeds and dies for them,
And waits and woos to get them home,
They choose in darkness still to dwell,
And laugh the downward road to hell.

III.

Where e'er they go, what e'er they do,
The Lord doth still in love pursue,
Intreating them to turn and live,
With all the blessing he can give.

IV.
But still for some poor empty sound
They rush on still, to ruin bound,
And risk an everlasting mind
While they pursue their chaff and wind.

V.
Thus millions last their wand'ring
    chase,
'Till they conclude their mortal race,
Then 'wake as wand'ring stars to dwell
In their own blackness, death and hell.

VI.
O sinners leave the enchanted ground,
God's love is still without a bound;
O bid the charms of earth adieu,
The Lord is waiting yet for you.

VI.
O come and taste immortal love,
And ever reign in realms above;
There shine in everlasting fame,
And give the glory to the Lamb.

Hymns and Spiritual Songs
Book III.

Chiefly consisting on the new Birth, and the
knowledge and joys of that glorious work.

HYMN VI.

Sion comforted, or religion reviving

I.
DARK was the day, our fears were great,
And mournful was our captive song,

When wandering our captive state,
And all our threat'ning foes were strong.
II.
Sing us a song of Sion now,
They laughing in derision said;
Our hopes were hung, our hopes were low,
And all our souls a prey was made.
III.
'Twas hard to speak of Sion then,
And hard to think our GOD would fail;
How could we bear that cruel men
Should triumph and at last prevail!
IV.
Then did the pow'rs of hell blaspheme,
Because our broken walls were love,
Saying *"Where is your boasted fame?*
"And where's your mighty Saviour now?"
V.
But in the midst of all our grief,
Our God made known deliv'ring power;
His arm appear'd for our relief,
And brought the long desired hour.
VI.
Soon he expel'd the gloomy shade,
Our hopes, and strength, and joys restor'd;
The lambs which from his fold had stray'd,
He call'd, and fed around his beard.
VII.
'Tis now we'll sing the Victor's song,
And laud our heavenly Captain's name;
Eternal praise to him belongs,
While all our foes are cloth'd with shame.
VIII.
All glory be to Sion's King,
Whose love redeem'd us from our wo!
Let saints above his praises sing,
And we with humbler notes below.

HYMN XIII.

A miracle of grace

I.

NO mortal tongue can ever tell,
The horrors of that gloomy night,
When I hung o'er the brink of hell,
Expecting soon my wretched flight!

II.

I felt my burden waste my life,
While guilt did ev'ry hope devour,
Trembling I stretch'd with groans and strife
For to escape the dreadful hour.

III.

But in the mind of all my grief,
The great Messiah spoke in love;
His arm appear'd for my relief,
And bid my guilt and sorrows move,

IV.

He pluck'd me from the jaws of hell,
With his almighty arm of pow'r;
And O! no mortal tongue can tell,
The change of that immortal hour!

V.

Then I enjoy'd a sweet release,
From chains of sin and pow'rs of death,
My soul was fill'd with heavn'ly peace,
My groans were turn'd to praising breath.

VI.

How did my tongue rejoice to tell
The goodness of the Lord to me!
And O! my soul with him shall dwell
Ere long from all my sorrows free.

VII.

O may I live to spread his name
While mortal life with me remains,

Then will I sound his lasting fame
In glory with immortal strains.

HYMN LV.

Longing to be with Christ

I.

My soul, O GOD, aspires to be
From interposing darkness free,
  And filled with scenes divine;
I need to swim in boundless grace,
And meet my Saviour face to face,
  And know my God is mine.

II.

I long to find my happy seat
Where I might wash my Saviour's feet
  In humble tears of love;
To praise my God with all my heart
And never from his love desert
  Till I awake above.

III.

Millions of years of carnal joy,
With earthly crowns, are empty toy
  Compar'd with Christ my friend;
In him alone I can be blest;
'Tis he that gives me solid rest,
  And makes my sorrows end.

IV.

O shall I, shall I ever be,
Where I this blessed Christ shall see,
  And ev'ry storm blown o'er?
On wings of the celestial dove
I'll soar and drink immortal love,
  And leave my friend no more.

V.

There I shall bask in sacred beams,
And solace in celestial streams
    Of sweet unmingled joy;
There I shall find my long abode
In perfect likeness of my GOD,
    Where nothing can annoy.

VI.

A palm of honour I shall wear;
With all the heav'nly armies share,
    In all their joys divine,
There I shall find eternal peace,
My songs of joy shall never cease,
    And Jesus shall be mine.

HYMN LIX.

In debt to everlasting love

I.

DOWN from the glorious realm above
Descends the Saviour cloth'd with love;
Assumes a body (can it be!)
To bleed and suffer death for me.

II.

Freely he spent his life and breath
To save me from eternal death;
And when no helper I could see
Made known his dying love to me.

III.

He took me from the jaws of hell,
And told my soul that all was well;
His love so great, his grace so free,
He said he spilt his blood for me.

IV.

O love amazing! boundless grace!
To me the worst of mortal race;

How could the Saviour die so free
For such a worthless wretch as me.

V.

What shall I do? what shall I say?
What can my soul to him repay
Who spilt his precious blood so free
For such a guilty wretch as me?

VI.

Lord all I have is double thine;
And I with pleasure will resign
My everlasting all to thee,
Who died for such a wretch as me.

VII.

This name shall dwell upon my tongue;
With joy I'll make his love my song;
I'll laud that name that stoop'd so free
To save a soul so vile as me.

VIII.

Forever in the realms above,
Bound up in everlasting love,
I shall with joy and wonder see
That Christ who gave his life for me.

IX.

I'll sound with all the countless race
The wonders of redeeming grace;
And this shall be my lasting plea,
The highest note belongs to me.

Hymns and Spiritual Songs
Book IV.

Consisting chiefly of christian travels; the joys
and trials of the soul

HYMN IX.

The happy state of christians

I.

BLEST are the souls that know the Lord,
And humbly walk before his face;
They feast upon immortal food,
And sing with joy redeeming grace.

II.

Cheerful they tread this desert through,
Led by the blest Redeemer's hand;
And when they bid the earth adieu,
With joy will reach the heav'nly land.

III.

There from their sorrows they shall rest,
With angels on the peaceful shore,
And with immortal glories blest,
To leave their chief delight no more.

IV.

O might it be my portion too,
To have the blessings they enjoy!
I'd bid all other joys adieu,
And join in their divine employ.

HYMN XXXI.

A prayer for increase of faith

I.

O Give me strength of living faith,
My Lord my GOD I pray,

Then shall I feel what Jesus saith,
And night be turn'd to day.
II.
I fain would soar to realms divine,
But oh, my faith is low;
And if I'm ask'd if thou art mine,
Some time I do not know.
III.
When I have faith then I can move
Mountains of death and sin;
When I have faith I see thy love,
And find a heav'n within.
IV.
But unbelief rejects the grace
That Jesus would bestow,
And veils me from my Father's face
Chain'd down to guilt and woe.
V.
Lord give me faith to set me free
From chains of sin and death,
And let no spirit reign in me,
But thou the word of faith.

HYMN XLII.

*An advice to the new-born souls never to part for
their different opinions about non-essentials*

I.
LET not the sons of Jesus call
That common which the Lord hath cleans'd;
When Christ who is their all in all,
Has lov'd them, and their hearts have chang'd.
II.
They're fav'rites of the Lamb of GOD,
Who freely spilt his blood for them;

If then they're wash'd in his own blood,
Who dares their chosen names condemn.
III.
Jesus has sealed them on his heart,
And loves them as his heavenly seed,
Then why should christians ever part
When in essentials they're agreed?
IV.
O then no more ye heaven-born race,
For modes and forms so warm contend,
You're all redeem'd by the same grace,
And all have Jesus for your friend.
V.
'Tis love that doth fulfil the law,
And meekness spreads the Saviour's name;
But warm debates will never draw
Not one poor soul to Christ the Lamb.
VI.
Proclaim ye saints your Master's love,
In ev'ry hour and ev'ry breath,
And soon you'll land with him above
To join the triumphs of his death.

HYMN L.

On the birth of Christ

I.
SEE Jesus in a manger lies!
Archangels gaze with sweet surprize,
At their Creator's mortal birth;
Hark! hark! the heav'nly arches ring,
When GOD their King, when GOD their King
Appears among the sons of earth.
II.
Angels descend, with joy proclaim
To mortals his incarnate name,

And bids the world forget their fear;
Lift up your eyes, O Adam's race,
An act of grace, an act of grace
By Jesus comes, O sinners hear.

III.

Sinners behold your only friend,
But you his arms doth wide extend,
Tastes death for you, and all mankind;
Fear not, O shepherds, this is he,
Arise and see, arise and see,
The Babe at Bethlehem you'll find.

IV.

Shout, dying mortals, shout his praise,
Let ev'ry tongue his honours raise;
Glad tidings to your world is come;
Go tell the world from shore to shore,
Despond no more, despond no more,
He's come to call the rebels home.

HYMN LXXXV.

Between hope and fear

I.

SHEW me O GOD how stands the case
Between the Saviour and my heart;
If I had known thy saving grace,
How could my soul so far desert?

II.

'Tis true I once thought I believ'd,
And had a crumb of living bread;
But if my soul was not deceiv'd
Why is my hopes and comforts fled?

III.

If Jesus had redeem'd my soul,
And I had known that he was mine,

How could this world so soon have stole
My heart away from joys divine?
IV.
I've seen the time I did rejoice,
And thought I felt a heav'nly flame,
But if that was the Saviour's voice,
How could I get this stupid frame?
V.
If I have the Redeemer known,
O may the truth now set me free,
And if he is my help alone
I cannot rest till him I see.

Hymns and Spiritual Songs
Book V.

Consisting chiefly of infinite wonders, transporting views, and christian triumphs

HYMN XVIII.

Invincible arguments of the reasonableness and necessity of every soul knowing of God, and what their future state will be now

I.
A GOD omnipotent I own,
Eternal things allow;
But what of GOD have I e'er known?
Or how's my standing now?
II.
I say that Christ for sinners died,
And that a truth may be;
But if not to my soul apply'd
'Tis not a truth to me.
III.
I say he gives his people rest,
And gives them life divine;
But if this life I ne'er possess,
How is the blessing mine?

IV.

I talk of everlasting death,
And thousands of despair,
And do not know but the next breath,
I die and enter there.

V.

Saints I believe with GOD will dwell
In everlasting bliss;
But is it mine? or can I tell,
That I am sure of this?

VI.

Or if in time its all unknown,
Where we at death shall go,
Then I may the next breath be gone
To everlasting wo.

VII.

How then can earthly charms allure
My mind while here I dwell,
When ev'ry breath I am not sure
But I'm the next in hell?

VIII.

Why all the toil for sacred things,
Or revelations giv'n,
If all no real knowledge brings,
Nor makes us sure of heav'n?

IX.

Some point me here, and others there,
And some say all is well;
But I dare trust my soul no more
On all they do or tell.

X.

If I am bound to bliss or wo,
And stand for trial here,
Then for myself I ought to know,
Where I shall soon appear.

XI.

If none but GOD can mercy shew,
Nor give me life divine,

Then from this GOD I ought to know,
That life and heav'n is mine.
XII.
Sure he that first my being gave,
Can witness who he is;
And he that dy'd my soul to save,
Can tell me I am his.
XIII.
Then let it be O GOD impress'd,
From thee by pow'rs divine,
On all my soul that I am blest,
And am forever thine.

HYMN XXVII.

The Messiah is come

I.
The Prince of Peace is come,
And cloth'd himself in clay;
Whoever find him room,
He'll take their guilt away,
Ye souls distress
In him believe,
And you shall live
Forever blest.
II.
This is the slaughter'd Lamb,
Who freely spills his blood,
To bear the sinners flame,
And bring them home to GOD;
Unbounded grace
To sinners giv'n,
And soon in heav'n
Immortal bliss.

III.

Sinners receive his love,
And let your souls rejoice,
A crown of life above,
For all that hear his voice.
O flee from hell;
Enjoy his love;
In realms above
Forever dwell.

IV.

O GOD my soul divest
Of ev'ry pow'r but thine,
Thy love shall make my breast
A kingdom all divine.
When time is o'er
O let me be
Wrap'd up in thee
Forevermore.

HYMN XXXIX.

Soaring away with life divine

I.

ONE spark O GOD of heav'nly fire
Awakes my heart with warm desire
To reach the realms above;
Immortal glories round me shine,
I drink the streams of joys divine,
And sing redeeming love.

II.

O could I wing my way in haste
Soon with archangels I would feast,
And join their sweet employ;
I'd glide along the heav'nly stream,
And join their most exalted theme
In everlasting joy.

III.

Too mean this little globe for me,
Nor will I e'er contented be
To feed on things so vain;
Its greatest treasures are but dross,
Its grandeur short, its pleasures curst,
Its joys all mixt with pain.

IV.

But resting in my Saviour's arms,
My soul enjoys transporting charms
And everlasting love;
There's life, there's joy and solid peace;
There's friendship that can never cease;
A rock that cannot move.

V.

Soar then my soul, stretch ev'ry thought,
To reach within the heav'nly court;
Above this mortal orb;
There let me with archangels rise,
And find my seat above the skies,
Where sins no more disturb.

VI.

There with an everlasting band
Of kindred saints at GOD's right hand
My happy lot shall be;
To soar, to shout, to reign, to rest
For ever, and for ever blest,
With thee, O GOD, with thee.

HYMN XLVIII.

On the Deity

I.

WHERE, what, or who, art thou great GOD,
Whom I profess to own?

Thy works, thy self, and thine abode,
Most known, and most unknown.
II.
If worlds unnumber'd as the sand
Are search'd to find thee there,
They're but small traces of some hand
Their Maker to declare.
III.
Ask angels where this GOD doth dwell
(Tho' wrap'd in him) would say,
"Tis not all our climes to tell
"But just some feeble ray."
IV.
Not found by mortal hand or eye;
In empty space not found;
Not time nor yet eternity
Can reach his utmost bound.
V.
Should I attempt to find him out
By philosophic strains,
Still far beyond the reach of thought
Unknown to me he reigns.
VI.
Angelic realms before his eye,
Tho' countless they may be,
So much like nothing all would lie
Too small for him to see.
VII.
Yet nothing doth in being dwell,
Small or conceal'd they lie
In heav'n, or earth, or sea, or hell,
But's naked to his eye.
VIII.
Immense he is, and leaves no void,
All nature's in his hand;
A million worlds made or destroy'd
Are as the smallest sand.

IX.

Good GOD! and yet within thy hand
A guilty mote I rove;
I live, I move, and guarded, stand
Partaker of thy love.

X.

The smallest insects that are made
Notic'd and guarded be;
And hairs of my unworthy head
All number'd Lord by thee.

XI.

O give me then a humble place,
Inspir'd with sacred flame;
A large partaker of thy grace
To sound thy boundless fame.

HYMN LIII.

The birth of Christ

I.

HARK! glad tidings to the shepherds,
Joyful news the angels bring;
God himself in flesh has enter'd,
Jesus is the new born King
Hail all glory, hail all glory,
Let the whole creation sing.

II.

Shepherds start from midnight slumbers,
See the glory shining round;
Gazing on the blaze they wonder,
'Till they're prostrate on the ground;
Hallelujahs, hallelujahs,
By the seraphs doth resound.

III.

"Fear not shepherds saith the angels,
"Banish sorrow from your eyes;

"For in Bethlehem's coarse manger
"God a spotless infant lies,
"See Jehovah, see Jehovah,
"Veil'd in clay below the skies."
IV.
Haste away ye eastern sages,
See the star proclaims your GOD,
Fear not Herod, tho' he rages,
Sending peals of death abroad;
Rachel mourning, Rachel mourning,
For her children he destroy'd.
V.
Sinners roar, and saints rejoices,
At the great Redeemer's birth;
Angels join their cheerful voices,
Good will to men, peace on earth;
Hallelujah, hallelujah,
Glory in the Saviour's birth.
VI.
"Let all people have salvation,"
Saith the heralds from above;
"Sound his name thro' ev'ry nation,
"Teach the world redeeming love.
"Go ye heralds, go ye heralds,
"Spread his name where e'er ye rove."
VII.
Jesus spread thy gospel glory,
Save poor dying souls from hell;
Let all nations bow before thee,
Love thy name and with thee dwell;
Haste ye heralds, haste ye heralds
Your Redeemer's name to tell.

HYMN LIX.

The great love of Christ display'd in his death

I.

As near to Calvary I pass
Methinks I see a bloody cross,
Where a poor victim hangs;
His flesh with ragged irons tore,
His limbs all dress'd with purple gore,
Gasping in dying pangs.

II.

Surpriz'd the spectacle to see,
I ask'd who can this victim be,
In such exquisite pain?
Why thus consign'd to woes I cry'd?
" '*Tis I*," the bleeding GOD reply'd,
"*To save a world from sin.*"

III.

A GOD for rebel mortals dies!
How can it be, my soul replies!
What! Jesus die for me!
"*Yes, saith the suff'ring Son of God,*
"*I give my life, I spill my blood,*
"*For thee, poor soul, for thee.*"

IV.

Lord since thy life thou'st freely giv'n,
To bring my wretched soul to heav'n,
And bless me with thy love;
Then to thy feet, O GOD, I'll fall,
Give thee my life, my soul, my all,
To reign with thee above.

V.

All other lovers I'll adieu,
My dying lover I'll pursue,
And bless the slaughter'd Lamb;
My life, my strength, my voice and days,

I will devote in wisdom's ways,
And sound his bleeding fame.
VI.
And when this tott'ring life shall cease,
I'll leave these mortal climes in peace,
And soar to realms of light;
There where my heav'nly lover reigns,
I'll join to raise immortal strains,
All ravish'd with delight.

HYMN LXII.

The kingdom of God within

I.
LET others their salvation rest
On outward forms, or distant heav'n,
I want GOD's kingdom in my breast,
And there to feel my sins forgiv'n.
II.
Some make their boast of cancel'd sin,
Before the worlds or they were made,
While still they have a hell within,
Imagine GOD their heav'n decreed.
III.
While others think some law fulfil'd
By Jesus when he bled and dy'd,
Who never knew salvation seal'd,
His life or death to them apply'd.
IV.
While many more their souls destroy,
Who wait for death to find a heav'n;
Yet strangers to the heav'nly joy,
Or the new birth, and sins forgiv'n.
V.
But I can trust in no decree,
Or law fulfil'd by Jesus Christ,

But that which works a birth in me,
And brings me to the gospel feast.

VI.

I am by nature dead in sin,
My soul bound down with heavey chains;
Then I must have my Christ within,
Or else in death my soul remains.

VII.

I have a hell within my breast,
For there is all my weight of sin;
Then Christ can give my soul no rest,
Unless he gives a heav'n within.

VIII.

My Christ forbids "*lo here or there,*
"*The secret chamber or desert,*"
And then he doth to me declare
GOD's kingdom is within the heart.

IX.

Then in my heart, O Jesus, reign,
With thy blest kingdom all divine;
Remove my death, break ev'ry chain,
And change my nature pure as thine.

X.

Then shall I be forever blest,
From all my sins and sorrows free,
A peaceful kingdom in my breast,
And I forevermore with thee.

HYMN LXXVI.

The believing Hebrews

I.

SHOUT brethren for the Lord hath broke
The fatal bands of Pharoah's yoke!
Our souls have left the slavish ground,
And now to Canaan's land are bound.

II.

GOD hath destroy'd by his high hand
Both horse and rider in the sand;
And we with Miriam will sing
All glory to the Hebrew's King.

III.

He still will make our foes to fall;
He'll be our Captain, strength and all;
Our Jesus leads us by his hand
For to possess the promis'd land.

IV.

Then let us tread the desert thro',
Bid all our loves and fears adieu;
A fire by night shall lead our way,
And a blest cloud of love by day.

V.

Christ is the stream shall us pursue,
And cheer us all the desert through;
We are surrounded with his love,
And feed on manna from above.

VI.

Let unbelief no more be known,
And ev'ry murm'ring thought be gone,
If we the GOD of truth believe
We shall go in, the crown receive.

VII.

O thou immortal Hebrew's King,
Thy name with joy we gladly sing,
Thou bought thy tribes with blood divine,
And now we are for ever thine.

HYMN XCIII.

The christians singing on their way

I.

SHALL those that tread the road to hell
Go laughing on with merry songs,
And we who'll soon in glory dwell,
With scarce a note upon our tongues?

II.

Awake O all ye heirs of bliss,
And bid your sloth and fears adieu,
Since Christ is yours, and you are his,
You may sing all your journey through.

III.

Who but the sons of light should sing?
Who else can wear a cheerful smile?
They're children of th' eternal King,
All others in the road to hell,

IV.

Lord we would raise our cheerful strains
While through these mortal climes we rove,
Then soar to those immortal plains
To lose ourselves in thy great love.

HYMN XCIV.

A heavenly rapture

I.

METHINKS I feel a warm desire,
Enliven'd with immortal fire,
    In this imprison'd heart of mine;
And longs to wing itself away
To realms of everlasting day.
    To lofty themes and scenes divine.

II.

In records of eternal fame
There is my portion, there my name,
   And there methinks my GOD I see;
Where angels sail with lofty wing,
And seraphs tune th' immortal strings.
   There, there my spirit longs to be.

III.

Those boundless realms of joy divine,
Those saints and angels all are mine,
   Jesus my Saviour makes them so;
And soon he'll call me home to rest
At his right hand for ever blest,
   With all that saints or angels know.

IV.

There I shall tread above the stars,
And laugh at hell's intestine jars,
   The sun and moon beneath my feet;
There I shall tread the blissful shore,
And mourn my distant friend no more,
   Where Jesus reigns there is my seat.

V.

Unbounded love will shine on me,
The mighty Fiat I shall see
   Shine forth in his meridian blaze;
Perfection in transparent light
Shining beyond conception bright,
   Calls ev'ry power aloft to gaze.

VI.

Thus gazing with delight I stand,
Surprising scenes on either hand,
   To suck me in their joyful tide;
The more I see the more I love,
My raptur'd soul still soars above,
   From pole to pole in wonders glide.

VII.

Thus burning in the sacred flame,
Lost to the state from whence I came,
   Nor room to ask how, where, or when;

The present scenes engage my soul,
And every pow'r of thought controul,
I'm lost with joy in GOD, Amen.

HYMN XCV.

The Christian's theme

I.

Let earthly minds feed on a dream,
And make an empty sound their theme,
Jesus shall dwell upon my tongue,
His dying love shall be my song.

II.

His name deserves my heart and voice,
This is the name makes me rejoice,
Nor dare I boast another name,
Therefore this Christ shall be my theme.

III.

Was I to speak of joys above,
This Jesus is their sea of love;
Or if I tell of joys below,
This Christ is all the soul can know.

IV.

Should I of wisdom think to tell,
There's none but what in him doth dwell;
Or speak of beauties here I'm charm'd,
While others all appear deform'd.

V.

If I am ask'd to tell his name,
It's LOVE; his nature is the same;
Goodness he is a boundless sea,
And loves that goodness to display.

VI.

He loves to help the vile and poor;
He spreads his love at ev'ry door;

He takes delight to raise the dead.
And fill the hungry souls with bread.

VII.

This is the Christ I would adore,
Whose love hath neither bound nor
　　shore;
But O his worth I ne'er can tell,
If on the theme I ever dwell.

VIII.

Yet I so much have felt his name,
It shall forever be my theme;
But lost in wonder I shall be,
Long as I sail the boundless sea.

SELECTED BIBLIOGRAPHY

I. VOLUMES WRITTEN BY HENRY ALLINE,
LISTED IN CHRONOLOGICAL ORDER.

Two Mites On Some of the Most Important and much disputed Points Of Divinity. . . . Halifax, 1781.

Hymns and Spiritual Songs. Halifax, 1781.

Sermon Preached to, And At The Request Of A Religious Society of Young Men United and Engaged For The Maintaining And Enjoying Of Religious Worship in Liverpool On The 19th November, 1782. Halifax, 1782.

A Sermon on a Day of Thanksgiving . . . on The 21st of November, 1782. Halifax, 1782.

A Sermon Preached on the 19th of February 1783 at Fort-Midway. Halifax, 1783. Reprinted in 1795 at Newburyport, Massachusetts, under the title *A Gospel Call to Sinners.*

The Anti-Traditionist. Halifax, 1783.

Hymns and Spiritual Songs. Boston, 1786.

The Life and Journal of the Rev. Mr. Henry Alline. Boston, 1806.

II. VOLUMES WRITTEN BY SOME OF ALLINE'S
NOVA SCOTIA CONTEMPORARIES.

Scott, Jonathan. *A Brief View of the Religious Tenets and Sentiments . . . of Mr. Henry Alline.* Halifax, 1784.

Bradley, Mary Coy. *The Life and Christian Experiences of Mrs. Mary Bradley*. Boston, 1849.

Harvey, D. C., and Fergusson, C. B. eds., *The Diary of Simeon Perkins 1780–1789,* Vol. II. Toronto, 1958.

Scott, Henry E. Jr., ed. *The Journal of The Reverend Jonathan Scott*. Boston, 1980.

Stewart, Gordon, ed. *Documents Relating to the Great Awakening in Nova Scotia, 1760–1791*. Toronto, 1982.

III. BOOKS, ARTICLES, AND THESES
DEALING WITH ALLINE.

Armstrong, Maurice. *The Great Awakening in Nova Scotia, 1776–1809*. Hartford, 1948.

———. "Neutrality and Religion in Revolutionary Nova Scotia." *The New England Quarterly* IX (March 1940): 50–62.

Bell, David. "The Death of Henry Alline: Some Contemporary Reactions." *Nova Scotia Historical Review,* 1984, pp. 4, 7–12.

Beverley, James, and Barry Moody, eds. *Life and Journal of the Rev. Mr. Henry Alline*. Hantsport, 1982.

Bumsted, John M. *Henry Alline*. Toronto, 1971.

Filschie, Margaret, " 'Redeeming Love Shall Be Our Song': Hymns of the First Great Awakening in Nova Scotia." M.A. thesis, Queen's University, 1983.

Rawlyk, George A. *Ravished by the Spirit: Religious Revivals, Baptists and Henry Alline*. Montreal, 1984.

Scott, Jamie S. " 'Travels of My Soul': Henry Alline's Autobiography." *Journal of Canadian Studies* XVII (1983): 70–90.

Stewart, Gordon, and George Rawlyk. *A People Highly Favoured of God: The Nova Scotia Yankees and the American Revolution*. Toronto, 1972.

IV. THE GREAT AWAKENING IN NOVA SCOTIA.

Anderson, Louise. "Crowd Activity in Nova Scotia during the American Revolution." M.A. thesis, Queen's University, 1985.

Brebner, John B. *The Neutral Yankees of Nova Scotia: A Marginal Colony during the Revolutionary Years.* New York, 1937.

Clark, S. D. *Church and Sect in Canada.* Toronto, 1948.

Marini, Stephen. *Radical Sects of Revolutionary New England.* Cambridge, 1982.

Rawlyk, George, *Nova Scotia's Massachusetts.* Montreal, 1973.

Stewart, Gordon, "Socio-economic Factors in the Great Awakening," *Acadiensis* III (1973):18–34.

————. "Charisma and Integration: An Eighteenth Century North American Case." *Comparative Studies in Society and History* 16 (1974): 138–49.

V. THE ALLINITE INFLUENCE.

Bell, David, ed. *Newlight Baptist Journals of James Manning and James Innis.* Hantsport, 1984.

Cuthbertson, Brian, ed. *Journal of the Reverand John Payzant (1749–1834).* Hantsport, 1981.

Levy, George, ed. *Diary and Related Writings of the Reverend Joseph Dimock (1768–1846).* Hantsport, 1979.

Rawlyk, George, ed. *New Light Letters and Spiritual Songs, 1778–1793.* Hantsport, 1983.

————. "New Lights, Baptists and Religious Awakenings in Nova Scotia, 1776–1843: A Preliminary Probe." *Journal of the Canadian Church Historical Society* 25 (1983): 43–73.

INDEX TO INTRODUCTION

INDEX TO TEXTS

Other Volumes in This Series